UNDERSTANDING THE OLYMPICS

The Olympic Games is unquestionably the greatest sporting event in the world, with billions of viewers across the globe. How did the Olympics evolve into this multi-national phenomenon? How can the Olympics help us to understand the relationship between sport and society? What will be the impact and legacy of the 2016 Olympics in Rio? Now in a fully revised and updated new edition that places Rio 2016 in the foreground, *Understanding the Olympics* answers all these questions by exploring the social, cultural, political, historical and economic context of the Games.

This book presents the latest research on the Olympics, including new material on legacy, sustainability and corruption, and introduces the reader to all of the key themes of contemporary Olympic Studies including:

■ the history of the Olympics
■ Olympic politics
■ access and equity
■ the Olympics and the media
■ festival and spectacle
■ the Olympic economy
■ urban development
■ Olympic futures.

The most up-to-date and authoritative introduction to the Olympic Games, this book contains a full Olympic history timeline as well as illustrations, information boxes and 'Olympic Stories' in every chapter. *Understanding the Olympics* is essential reading for anybody with an interest in the Olympics or the wider relationship between sport and society.

John Horne is Professor of Sport and Sociology at the University of Central Lancashire, UK.

Garry Whannel is Professor of Media Cultures at the University of Bedfordshire, UK.

Also by the authors

By both authors

Understanding Sport: A Socio-Cultural Analysis, London: Routledge, 2013 (with Alan Tomlinson and Kath Woodward)

Understanding the Olympics, London: Routledge, 2012

Understanding Sport: An Introduction to the Sociological and Cultural Analysis of Sport, London: E&FN Spon, 1999 (with Alan Tomlinson)

By John Horne

Sport and Social Movements From the Local to the Global, London: Bloomsbury Academic, 2014 (with Jean Harvey, Simon Darnell, Parissa Safai and Sebastien Courchesne-O'Neill)

Sport in Consumer Culture, Basingstoke: Palgrave, 2006

Edited by John Horne and Wolfram Manzenreiter

Sports Mega-Events: Social Scientific Analyses of a Global Phenomenon, Oxford: Blackwell, 2006

Football Goes East: The People's Game in China, Japan and Korea, London: Routledge, 2004

Japan, Korea and the 2002 World Cup, London: Routledge, 2002

By Garry Whannel

The Trojan Horse: The Growth of Commercial Sponsorship, London: Bloomsbury Academic, 2013 (with Deborah Philips)

Culture, Politics and Sport: Blowing the Whistle Revisited, London: Routledge, 2008

Media Sport Stars: Masculinities and Moralities, London: Routledge, 2002

Fields in Vision: Television Sport and Cultural Transformation, London: Routledge, 1992

UNDERSTANDING THE OLYMPICS

SECOND EDITION

JOHN HORNE AND GARRY WHANNEL

Routledge
Taylor & Francis Group

LONDON AND NEW YORK

First published 2016
by Routledge
2 Park Square, Milton Park, Abingdon, Oxon OX14 4RN

and by Routledge
711 Third Avenue, New York, NY 10017

Routledge is an imprint of the Taylor & Francis Group, an informa business

British Library Cataloguing in Publication Data
A catalogue record for this book is available from the British Library

Library of Congress Cataloging-in-Publication Data
Names: Horne, John, 1955– author. | Whannel, Garry, author.
Title: Understanding the Olympics / John Horne and Garry Whannel.
Description: Second edition. | Milton Park, Abingdon, Oxon ; New York,
NY : Routledge, 2016. | Includes bibliographical references and index.
Identifiers: LCCN 2015043671| ISBN 9781138890244 (hardback) | ISBN
9781138890251 (pbk.) | ISBN 9781315712529 (ebook)
Subjects: LCSH: Olympics—History. | Olympics—Social aspects.
Classification: LCC GV721.5 .H64 2016 | DDC 796.48—dc23
LC record available at http://lccn.loc.gov/2015043671

ISBN: 978-1-138-89024-4 (hbk)
ISBN: 978-1-138-89025-1 (pbk)
ISBN: 978-1-315-71252-9 (ebk)

Typeset in Sabon
by Keystroke, Station Road, Codsall, Wolverhampton
Printed in Great Britain by Ashford Colour Press Ltd

CONTENTS

CONTENTS

ILLUSTRATIONS

FIGURES

BOXES

TIMELINE

A selective timeline of the modern Summer and Winter Olympic Games: 1896–2024.

Year	Number	Host cities for Summer and Winter (W) Olympics	Continent	Olympic President
1896	I	Athens	Europe	Demetrias Vikelas
1900	II	Paris	Europe	Pierre de Coubertin
1904	III	St. Louis	N. America	Coubertin
1906[1]		Athens	Europe	Coubertin
1908	IV	London	Europe	Coubertin
1912	V	Stockholm	Europe	Coubertin
1916[2]	VI	Berlin	Europe	Coubertin
1920	VII	Antwerp	Europe	Coubertin
1924	VIII	Paris/Chamonix (W)	Europe	Coubertin
1928	IX	Amsterdam/St. Moritz (W)	Europe	Henri de Baillet-Latour
1932	X	Los Angeles/Lake Placid (W)	N. America	Baillet-Latour
1936	XI	Berlin/Garmisch-Partenkirchen (W)	Europe	Baillet-Latour
1940[3]	XII	Tokyo; Helsinki/Sapporo; Garmisch-Partenkirchen (W)	E. Asia Europe	Baillet-Latour
1944	XIII	London/Cortina d'Ampezzo (W)	Europe	J. Sigfrid Edstrom
1948	XIV	London/St. Moritz (W)	Europe	Edstrom
1952	XV	Helsinki/Oslo (W)	Europe	Edstrom
1956	XVI	Melbourne[4]/Cortina d'Ampezzo (W)	Australasia/Europe	Avery Brundage
1960	XVII	Rome/Squaw Valley (W)	Europe/N. America	Brundage
1964	XVIII	Tokyo/Innsbruck (W)	E. Asia/Europe	Brundage
1968	XIX	Mexico City/Grenoble (W)	N. America/Europe	Brundage

Year	Number	Host cities for Summer and Winter (W) Olympics	Continent	Olympic President
1972	XX	Munich/Sapporo (W)	Europe/ E. Asia	Brundage
1976	XXI	Montreal/Denver; Innsbruck (W)[5]	N. America/ Europe	Lord Killanin
1980	XXII	Moscow/Lake Placid (W)	Europe/ N. America	Killanin
1984	XXIII	Los Angeles/Sarajevo (W)	N. America/ Europe	Juan Antonio Samaranch
1988	XXIV	Seoul/Calgary (W)	E. Asia/ N. America	Samaranch
1992	XXV	Barcelona/Albertville (W)	Europe	Samaranch
1994		Lillehammer (W)[6]	Europe	Samaranch
1996	XXVI	Atlanta	N. America	Samaranch
1998		Nagano (W)	E. Asia	Samaranch
2000	XXVII	Sydney	Australasia	Samaranch
2002		Salt Lake City (W)	N. America	Samaranch
2004	XXVIII	Athens	Europe	Jacques Rogge
2006		Torino (W)	Europe	Rogge
2008	XXIX	Beijing	E. Asia	Rogge
2010		Vancouver-Whistler (W)	N. America	Rogge
2012	XXX	London	Europe	Rogge
2014		Sochi (W)	Europe	Thomas Bach
2016	XXXI	Rio de Janeiro	S. America	Bach
2018		Pyeongchang (W)	E. Asia	Bach
2020	XXXII	Tokyo	E. Asia	Bach
2022		Beijing (W)	E Asia	?[7]
2024	XXXIII	Budapest, LA, Paris, or Rome [Decision September 2017, Lima, Peru]	Europe/N. America	?

Sources: adapted from Chappelet and Kubler-Mabbott (2008: 23); Greenberg (1987: 9); Hampton (2008: 20–22); Toohey and Veal (2007: 49, 199); IOC (2010a).

NOTES

1   This event celebrated the tenth anniversary of the first modern Games; while officially intercalated by the IOC, it is not numbered as an Olympic Games.
2   The VI Games (scheduled for Berlin) was not held due to the First World War, but the IOC officially counts it.

3   The XII and XIII Summer Olympic Games (scheduled respectively for Tokyo, then Helsinki before finally being called off in May 1940, and London) were not held due to the Second World War, but are officially counted by the IOC. The Winter Olympics in 1940, scheduled for Sapporo, were relocated to Garmisch-Partenkirchen even after the German invasion of Poland in September 1939, before finally being called off.

4   Because of Australian quarantine laws, the equestrian events were held in Stockholm, Sweden.

5   Awarded to Denver in Colorado, the Winter Olympics were transferred to Innsbruck when Colorado residents rejected the hosting decision.

6   The IOC decided in 1986 to reschedule the Summer and Winter Games, so a new four-year cycle for the Winter Games began in 1994 with the Summer and Winter Olympics staggered two years apart.

7   Elected for two four-year terms, Bach will have to stand down in 2021 unless re-elected for one more term.

PREFACE TO THE SECOND EDITION

Writing three years since the first edition of *Understanding the Olympics* and London 2012, and one year before Rio 2016, this is a good place to take stock of Olympic events as part of an apparently never-ending story. This second edition looks back to London, forward to Rio, and beyond. As we wrote back in 2012, most books on the Olympics will feature accounts of the great moments and stars, repeating oft-told tales of Olympic mythology. Our book offers an understanding of the Olympic movement in its broader social and historical context. It provides ways of understanding the politics, economics and cultures within which the Olympic Games was forged and within which it grew to become the pre-eminent sports mega-event. We hope it will answer most of the questions that someone who wants to understand the Olympic Games in its social and cultural context will ask.

That we are both from London and that the Summer Olympic and Paralympic Games were held there in 2012 is one reason – but not the only one – why we collaborated in writing this book. As social and cultural analysts we have been observing and commenting on sporting cultures for over 30 years, and we wanted to explore the continuing fascination with the Olympic Games – neither as a celebration nor as a condemnation, but as a critical reflection. In particular we wanted to examine aspects of the Games that, we suspect, many other books will neglect.

Writing in 2015 we appear to be entering a new phase of Olympic Games development. In recent years there appears to have been waning public acceptance of the benefits of hosting an Olympic Games or other sports mega-events in certain nations. In the decision over who would be the 2022 Winter Olympics host, four cities withdrew following public referenda, leaving only Beijing and Almaty in the running (eventually decided as Beijing).[1] That these two cities, from societies perceived as autocratic by Western standards and where public opposition is less easy to develop, sustain or articulate, remained to contest which one would be host, has led some commentators to speculate that the likely future of sports mega-events was to be with more autocratic and less democratic societies. In the face of anti-bid activism and social movements protesting the Games, rather than simply anti-Games alliances, the IOC has undertaken a stock-take of possible reforms, referred to as the 'Olympic Agenda 2020', which were agreed at its session in December 2014. That Budapest, Paris, Rome and LA all subsequently submitted Part 1 of their Candidature File in February 2016 (with Hamburg standing down after a public referendum) suggests that the situation is more complex and that the allure and attraction of being an Olympic

Games host city remains strong. If there is a pattern to the next three Summer and Winter Olympic Games after Rio 2016, it is that they will be staged in the neighbouring East Asian states of South Korea, Japan and China. Whether this amounts to a significant 'moving East' of the Olympics, however, will be discussed in more detail elsewhere. Whatever the trends, the IOC will make the decision about 2024 at its session in Lima, Peru, in September 2017; President Bach stated that the IOC would conduct 'confidential polls' to ascertain public support for the Games in each of the bidding cities.

What is not in doubt is that in recent years a burgeoning scholarly literature offering new ways of thematically and conceptually understanding the development of the Olympics and mega-events has emerged. Some have suggested new theories to understand the Olympics and coined concepts such as 'celebration capitalism', and 'festival capitalism' to try to capture the distinctiveness of, and role of, mega-events in contemporary social life (Boykoff 2014a; Giulianotti *et al.* 2015). Our revised book cannot possibly discuss all the available literature, such is its size; for some analysis of the explosion in Olympic-related publications stimulated by London 2012, see Girginov and Collins (2013) and Polley (2014).

Reviewers of the first edition wanted to see inclusion of many more topics than we could comfortably fit into this revised edition. This edition of *Understanding the Olympics* does, however, contain two completely new chapters, two refocused chapters and eight thoroughly revised and updated chapters that we hope go some way to meeting the challenge. Three themes running throughout the book are the hosting of mega-events in the context of massive global social inequities; the role of sport in social development; and debates about mega-events and sustainability. Our discussion of the unfolding politics of Rio 2016 in Chapter 1 reveals some of these debates. Reflections on London 2012 (in Chapter 2) trigger consideration of other debates about legacy and regeneration that also appear elsewhere in the book. The impact of London 2012 on the Paralympics and ideas about disability sport are also taken up in Chapter 11. The relationship between the Olympics and politics, for example contestation over legacies, rights and the work required to deliver the Games, and international reputations, is discussed in Chapters 8 and 9. The fading allure and remaining attraction of hosting the (Winter) Olympic Games and Commonwealth Games is taken up with comparisons to FIFA and other international sports organisations in Chapter 3. Involvement of the 'global South' and East Asian societies, as well as the 'Middle East', in global sport is considered in several other chapters (for example, Chapters 9 and 12). The question of whether this contestation spells the end of the mega-event boom or if the commercial boon for mega-events such as the Olympics from television and sponsorship will continue is taken up in Chapter 4. Despite questions about their sustainability and environmental costs, mega-events are still used to create the conditions for urban development and place promotion or branding (Chapter 5). The book also considers the distinctive origin, history and values of the Olympic Games (Chapters 6, 7 and 8) and the way the Olympics contribute to the ambition to stage spectacles and carnivals of consumption (Chapter 10). Athletes and sports participants in the Olympics and Paralympics remain disproportionately drawn from socially exclusive backgrounds (Chapter 11). The final chapter considers recent developments affecting the organisation of the Olympics and other mega-events. Chapter 12 offers consideration of corruption, doping and security to suggest that the scale of mega-events can create

temptations for organisers, athletes and governments to go way beyond Olympic ideals and enter what some might call 'the dark side of the Olympics' or sports mega-events more generally. The book contains new photographs taken by the authors, refreshed suggestions for further reading and all the boxes and figures have been revised and updated.

The book is divided into three parts again, although we have rearranged the contents. The first part, which broadly takes stock of 'where we are', provides answers to three broad questions: What are the main elements in the stories behind Rio 2016 and London 2012? What is the International Olympics Committee (IOC), the organisation that owns and protects the contemporary Olympic 'brand'? What are the main economic forces that have led to the television- and sponsor-driven commercialisation of sport, including the Olympic Games, in the past 35 years? Chapter 5 considers the relationship between urban development, tourism and the growth of concerns for establishing a sustainable legacy from hosting an Olympic Games. Winning the Games functions to enable a whole range of giant infrastructural projects that would otherwise struggle to win support. The Games stimulate the dreams of architects and mayors, builders and planners, leaders and entrepreneurs – these are critically assessed in this chapter.

The second part of the book, reflecting on 'where we have come from', provides a look back into the past to examine the historical context of the emergence and establishment of the modern Olympic Games. The five chapters in this part seek to explain where the Olympic Games came from, how they developed during the last decade of the nineteenth century and the twentieth century, as well as considering the growth of their political significance in the twentieth and twenty-first centuries.

Chapter 6 discusses the ways in which the ancient games were mythologised, in forms that provided the underpinnings of modern Olympism. It reviews attempts to establish modern multi-sport events (e.g. Penny Brookes' Much Wenlock Olympics and the Cotswold Games), of which De Coubertin's was only one. It traces the ways in which mythologies of Ancient Greece, the English public school system of the mid-nineteenth century, the post-1870 crisis of France and utopian internationalism all contributed to the formation of modern Olympism. It examines the various religious underpinnings of the modern Olympic 'faith'.

Chapter 7 examines the way the early Olympic Games as a cultural form were closely linked to world's fairs and how only in the television era was the Olympics able to become a full-fledged mega-event. This chapter traces that development, examining how the Olympic Games retained elements of their origins while they altered in relation to other significant political, economic and cultural processes. The next three chapters thus outline the political, economic and cultural processes that have shaped the current state of the Olympic Games. Although the Games were conceived partly as an internationalist meeting ground, from the start the tensions and rivalries between nations disrupted the aspirations of Olympism. The 1936 Games became notorious as the 'Nazi' Olympics, and in the Cold War era the Games became a symbolic battleground between East and West, communism and capitalism. Chapter 8 examines the inherent contradictions of national organisation, the Cold War era and the rise of individualism as impacting on the Olympic Games. It outlines the development and management of political tensions by the Olympic movement and the relation between the Olympic movement and Great Power diplomacy.

In the period between 1968 and 1984 the Games became the site of more focused symbolic political contestation in which the boycott became a significant political weapon. Chapter 9 examines the mythologising of key moments, such as the 'Black Power' salutes in the 1968 Games in Mexico, and raises questions about the process whereby symbolic politics have been marginalised in more recent Games. It examines the extent to which the Beijing Olympics marked a break with this more recent depoliticisation and assesses the future political terrain that the Olympic movement will be negotiating. It also outlines the ways in which, within the politics of bidding and hosting the games, boosters and sceptics have to articulate and negotiate issues of risk and global geopolitics.

Chapter 10 interrogates 'Olympism' in terms of the concepts of festivity, spectacle and the carnivalesque, returning to a question posed by one of the authors in the 1980s: can an event succeed in being both a spectacle and a festival (Whannel 1984)? It examines the rather problematic relation of the needs of festivity and security, the patchy history of the Cultural Olympiad and the tendency for the noble aspirations of bidding cities to fade before the Games arrive. This chapter thus raises questions about public space, popular cultural pleasures and Olympic legacies.

The third part of the book, 'where we are heading', is the shortest but contains some of our more critical assessments of the Olympics and the Olympic movement. Chapter 11 examines issues of access and equity – social class and the exclusion of professionals until 1974, the treatment of women, the composition of the IOC, race and racism and disability/para-sport. It examines the contrast between the rhetoric and the practice of Olympism. Women were excluded entirely from early Games, and only since the 1980s has the full programme of events begun to be opened to women. The commitment to amateurism, only abandoned since the early 1970s, gave the Games a distinctive social class character. The Paralympic Games, even after a long struggle for inclusion, are still staged as a separate event. The governance of the Olympics appears to be still dominated by a predominantly white, male, European, and in some cases aristocratic, group, while major corporations, most notably NBC and its parent General Electric, are in a position to exercise a shaping influence on the development of the Games. This chapter thus poses the question 'Who are the Games for?'

The final chapter, Chapter 12, examines the 'dark side' of the Olympics and sport and focuses on corruption and accountability, doping and security. It asks if Olympism is just part of the great myth of sport's inherent goodness and still meaningful in the contemporary world.

John Horne and Garry Whannel
Edinburgh and London
October 2015

NOTE

1 www.bbc.co.uk/sport/0/olympics/34266181?print=true (last accessed 21 September 2015).

ACKNOWLEDGEMENTS

Institutional and financial support for much of the research and travel upon which the first and second editions of this book are partially based has been gratefully received from the University of Central Lancashire (JH), the University of Edinburgh (JH) and the University of Bedfordshire (GW). The libraries of these institutions and also the British Library, the National Library of Scotland, the Bibliothèque Nationale, the Bibliothèque du Centre Pompidou and the Library of New South Wales have enabled access to difficult-to-find material. So, too, did the archivists in the Museum of London. Financial support and support in kind were also received from the Carnegie Trust for the Universities of Scotland, the Australian Centre for Olympic Studies at the University of Technology Sydney, the University of Western Sydney and the Government of Canada Faculty Research Programme. Unless otherwise stated, John or Garry took all the photographs in this book. We are lucky in having partners who themselves know that research is mostly fun and writing can be hell, and we thank Delia Lomax and Deborah Philips for their forbearance, support and love. We would also like to thank Simon Whitmore and his team at Routledge for their interest in our work and their patience.

There are four groups of people John would especially like to pay acknowledgement to, who in various ways have supported this work over the past 15 years or so. First are those with whom he has had the good fortune to work as co-researcher and co-author: Simon Darnell, Rick Gruneau, Jean Harvey, Graeme Hayes, Wolfram Manzenreiter, Parissa Safai and David Whitson. These collaborations have resulted in ideas, information and material that are incorporated into this text in various ways. Second are those people who have encouraged him in his work, by inviting him either to contribute to publications or to talk at conferences and other symposia, or both: Alan Bairner, Glauco Bienenstein, Anne-Marie Broudehoux, Richard Cashman, Chris Gaffney, Tony Hwang, John Karamichas, Gilmar Mascarenas, Carlos Vainer, Raquel Rolnik, Noel Salazar, John Schulz, Atsuo Sugimoto, Yoshio Takahashi and Steve Wagg. Third are those friends who have provided him with support by making available information, providing translations or images or being prepared to discuss some of the finer points of Olympic history, despite their very busy lives: Greg Andranovich, Jules Boykoff, Helena Galiza, Annette Hofmann, Shin Kawaguchi, Gerd von der Lippe, Nelma Gusmao de Oliveira, Tony Veal and Takayuki Yamashita. Fourth, but by no means least, are those students and researchers who have heard some of this before and helped him reformulate what he actually meant to say: Sadie Hollins, Andrew Rackley, Gabriel Silvestre, Fabiana Rodrigues de Sousa Mast and Donna Wong.

Garry would like to thank Alan Tomlinson, with whom he edited *Five Ring Circus* in 1984, and who did so much to fuel his own Olympic interests; and Taylor Downing, Michael Poole and Michael Jackson who provided journalistic contexts in which he could pursue that interest. He would also like to thank Alexis Weedon, Director of RIMAD (Research Institute for Media Art and Design) at the University of Bedfordshire; Raymond Boyle and the contributors to the special issue of *Convergence* (2010, 16: 3) devoted to Sport and New Media; members of the JOG Group (Journalism and the Olympic Games); the conference organisers who were good enough to include him, especially Robert K. Barney; colleagues and students at the University of Bedfordshire; and David Rowe of the University of Western Sydney for making him welcome and supporting his research into some aspects of the Olympics.

Conversations, interviews and chance encounters with many people over many years have fed Garry's continuing fascination with the Olympic Games. The list includes such diverse figures as Seb Coe, Sam Ramsamy, Ron Pickering, Adrian Metcalfe, John Rodda, Alex Gilady, Bruce Kidd, Keith Connor, Fanny Blankers-Koen, Wojciech Liponski, Nicos Filaretos, Michele Verdier and David Bedford. His own work on sport, culture and politics would not have been possible without fellow founders of the Centre for Sport Development Research, Jennifer Hargreaves and Ian McDonald. The work of Alina Bernstein in establishing the Media and Sport Section of the IAMCR (International Association for Media and Communication Research) has greatly strengthened our various networks. He owes thanks also to others with whom he has discussed sport, culture and politics – Joe Maguire, Toby Miller, Larry Wenner, Belinda Wheaton and Tony Veal.

As we noted in the first edition, in a list like this there are inevitably omissions – apologies to any other people we should have included!

ABBREVIATIONS

AAA	Amateur Athletic Association
AAC	Amateur Athletic Club
AIOWF	Association of the International Olympic Winter Sports Federations
ANOC	Association of National Olympic Committees
ANOCA	Association of National Olympic Committees of Africa
ASOIF	Association of Summer Olympic International Federations
BINGOs	business-oriented international non-government organisations
BME	black and minority ethnic
BOA	British Olympic Association
BOB	Beijing Olympic Broadcasting
BOC	Brazilian Olympic Committee
BRICS	Brazil, Russia, India, China and South Africa
BRT	bus rapid transit
BSIA	British Security Industry Authority
CBD	*Confederação Brasileira de Desportos*
CBF	*Confederação Brasileira de Futebol*
CCTV	China Central Television
cctv	closed circuit television
CIPFA	Chartered Institute of Public Finance and Accounts
CO2e	carbon dioxide equivalent
COHRE	Centre on Housing Rights and Evictions
CND	National Sport Council (Brazil)
CPSS	Command Perimeter Security System
CSL	Commission for a Sustainable London 2012
DCLG	Department for Communities and Local Government
DCMS	Department of Culture, Media and Sport
DWP	Department for Work and Pensions
EBU	European Broadcasting Union
EC	Evaluation Commission
EOC	European Olympic Committees
EOM	Municipal Olympic Company (Brazil)
FIFA	Fédération Internationale de Football Association
GANEFO	Games of the New Emerging Forces
GFP	Games Foundation Plan

GLA	Greater London Authority
HASC	Home Affairs Select Committee
IAAF	International Amateur Athletic Federation
IABA	International Amateur Boxing Association
IF	International Federation
IJF	International Judo Federation
ILTF	International Lawn Tennis Federation
IOA	International Olympic Academy
IOC	International Olympic Committee
IPC	International Paralympic Committee
ISL	International Sport and Leisure
LA21	Local Agenda 21
LAP	Legacy Action Plan
LDA	London Development Agency
LOCOG	London Organising Committee of the Olympic Games and Paralympic Games
LSI	Lucerne Sports International
MDG	Millennium Development Goals
MENASA	Middle East, North Africa and South Asia
MPC	Main Press Centre
NGO	non-governmental organisation
NOC	National Olympic Committee
OAG	Olympic Advisory Group
OCA	Olympic Council of Asia
OCOG	Organising Committee of the Olympic Games
ODA	Olympic Delivery Authority
ONOC	Oceania National Olympic Committees
OPSU	Olympic Programme Support Unit
PASO	Pan-American Sports Organisation
PPP	public–private partnership
PR	public relations
PRC	People's Republic of China
PSA	Public Service Agreement
RSI	Red Sports International
SANOC	South African National Olympic Committee
SANROC	South African Non-Racial Olympic Committee
SCSA	Supreme Council for Sport in Africa
SDG	Sustainable Development Goals
SDP	Sport for Development and Peace
TCC	transnational capitalist class
TOP	The Olympic Partner Programme
UPP	police pacifying units
WADA	World Anti-Doping Agency
WCA	Work Capability Assessment
ZHA	Zaha Hadid Architects

PART I

THE CONTEMPORARY OLYMPICS

CHAPTER 1

BREAKING NEW GROUND

RIO 2016

INTRODUCTION

After the Olympic and Paralympic Games in London in 2012, the sport historian Martin Polley (2014: 255) remarked that if 'the motto of London 2012 was "inspire a generation" for hundreds of authors this was easily recast as inspire a publication'. A similar situation is arising with Rio 2016. Ahead of the World Cup hosted in 2014, US journalist Dave Zirin published a book called *Brazil's Dance with the Devil* (Zirin 2014). In 2015, ahead of the next sports mega-event to take place in Brazil, journalist Juliana Barbassa has published *Dancing with the Devil in the City of God* (Barbassa 2015). Whereas Zirin's book attempted to provide an overview of the whole country, Barbassa's emphatically focuses on the city that will host the 2016 Summer Olympic and Paralympic Games, Rio de Janeiro – a city 'on the brink', as her subtitle suggests. The question is: on the brink of what? Her book deliberately alludes to both the opportunities and the challenges facing Rio as it hosts the XXXI Olympics.

The international mass media do like to highlight the challenges faced by countries, especially those outside the global North, when they stage global spectacles such as the Olympics. Hence, with less than a year to go to the opening ceremony, newspapers and broadcasters in the UK reported that the Rio Games faced a budget cut of one-third, the city was a potentially dangerous location for tourists and the environmental costs of the Games were increasing, as the Brazilian currency and economy has weakened (Gibson 2015; Davies 2015). This chapter attempts to provide insight into the background context – social, economic, political and sporting – behind the 2016 Games; it examines the relationship of Brazil to the Olympic movement and outlines the challenges faced in breaking new ground in Rio. It explores the unfolding politics of Rio de Janeiro and Brazil, both before and after hosting the 2014 FIFA World Cup. In addition, it examines debates about sport for development and the role of the Olympics in this, and how by 'learning from Barcelona', via urban and sport policy transfers, another of the so-called 'BRICS' nations (Brazil, Russia, India, China and South Africa) has sought to make use of sports mega-events.

RIO 2016 IN SOCIAL AND SPORTING CONTEXT

On the evening of Friday 5 August 2016, IOC President Thomas Bach will declare the official opening of the XXXI Olympic Games. At that stage the drama of the preparations for them will (probably) have been resolved and the city and the world will closely follow the performances of the world's top athletes. In this respect Rio 2016 will be no different to many other sports mega-events. Yet interest in the development of the wider economic and political system of the largest nation in South America has been a long-standing feature of scholarly research (see, for example, Levine and Crocitti 1999; McCann 2008). Academic interest in sport in South America has also been given a significant boost by the scheduled hosting of the two largest sports mega-events – the FIFA men's Football World Cup finals and the Summer Olympic and Paralympic Games – in Brazil and Rio de Janeiro in 2014 and 2016, respectively. This is not to say that research has not been conducted until recently, but to acknowledge that the English-language literature has started to increase, and looks certain to grow even more rapidly in the coming years (for earlier research, see Arbena 1999). As Polley suggested, the contemporary Olympics do 'inspire' many publications, including this new and revised edition of *Understanding the Olympics*.

In *Soccer Madness*, Lever (1995/1983: 6) contends that sport generally and, in Brazil, football specifically, has the 'paradoxical ability to reinforce societal cleavages while transcending them'. She argues that sport/football can 'create social order while preserving cultural identity', thus promoting rather than impeding goals of national development (Lever 1995: 22). Anthropologists, historians, human geographers, political scientists and sociologists, among other scholars, have begun to investigate a number of recurring topics that enable us to begin to understand these and other developments in South America. Football, by far and away the most popular sport throughout South America, features in articles about fans, elite migrant labour, professional organisations and globalisation (Gordon and Helal 2001; Raspaud and Bastos 2013; Vasconcellos Ribeiro and Dimeo 2009). Alvito (2007) notes, for example, that football in Brazil has faced the twin challenges of commercialisation and mediatisation for at least the past 30 years. Mega-events attract accounts about the history of South American involvement, involvement in the Football World Cup and the Olympics and also the impacts of hosting on marginalised communities (Curi 2008; Gaffney 2010; Silvestre and Oliveira 2012; Sánchez and Broudehoux 2013; also see Horne and Silvestre 2016 for discussion of wider analysis of sport and leisure in Brazil and South America).

In the past 30 years most of the developed and developing world have joined in the competitive marketing of places as social and economic opportunities seeking capital investment (de Oliveira 2015). Many 'Cariocas' (as Rio de Janeiro locals are called) glued themselves to their TV screens at 11 a.m. local time on 2 October 2009, awaiting the results of a decision about whether or not Rio de Janeiro would host the 2016 Olympic and Paralympic Games. On Copacabana beach, the proposed site of the 2016 beach volleyball competition, a huge party was scheduled whether or not Rio was selected. The decision to award the Olympics to Rio was very much the icing on a decade of steady development. Brazil had been one of the few economies, alongside the other so-called BRICS, that had remained stable and grew during the recession of 2008 and 2009.

The BRICS account for over 2.8 billion (40 per cent) of the world's population, but only command 25 per cent of global GDP, and hence they are also referred to as 'emerging economies'. Given the hosting of the Olympic Games by Beijing (2008), the

4

Commonwealth Games by Delhi (2010), the FIFA World Cup by South Africa (2010), the Winter Olympic Games by Sochi (2014) and the FIFA World Cup by Russia (2018), as well as the Brazilian involvement in staging the Pan American Games (2007), the FIFA World Cup (2014) and the Olympics (2016), some have suggested that a 'BRICS style' of hosting sports mega-events may be emerging (Curi *et al.* 2011). Curi *et al.* point out that between 1950 and 2007 no major international sports event was hosted in Rio de Janeiro, the city lost its status as capital to Brasilia in 1960, and when it did stage the 2007 Pan American Games they were the most expensive of that series of competitions ever held. The 2007 Pan American Games were marked by very tight security, including the erection of walls to separate games attendees from the local, poorer, population. Hence bidding to host these events has to be seen in a context where consumption-based development is seen as a solution to city-specific urban problems as much as national ones (Gaffney 2010).

While there were no groups organised in Rio specifically against the Olympic bid, there were several groups on the ground concerned with the legacy these Olympics would bring to Rio, and especially to the marginalised communities living in *favelas* (sometimes referred to as 'slums'). While eviction in low-income, informal areas has become a not-uncommon consequence of mega-event planning worldwide, housing rights violations have reached significant proportions during recent Olympics. It is in this way that sport, and sports mega-events such as the Olympics especially, may appear superficially as credible tools of development. Yet they do so in ways that do not challenge inequalities or neo-liberal development. In fact the hosting of sports mega-events may be a most convenient shell for the promotion of neo-liberal agendas, since they do not deviate from top-down notions of economic and social development.

SPORT AND POLITICS IN BRAZIL

> Brazil has been, in less than a century and half, a monarchy, a republic, and a federation. It has been ruled by parliament, civilian presidents, military juntas, general-presidents, and by a civilian dictator.
> (Rocha and McDonagh 2014: 61)

A number of journalistic accounts of sport, and especially football in Brazil, are available that discuss the connection between sport, nationalism and politics (see, for example: Humphrey 1986; Goldblatt 2014; Zirin 2014). Here we briefly refer to two of the key academic sources that these journalistic accounts rely on (Lever 1995/1983; Levine 1980) to provide a brief historical contextualisation of the relations between politics and sport in Brazil.

Levine (1980: 233) recognises the possibility of viewing sport, and especially football, as a form of opiate and distraction and thus an agency of social control. He also acknowledges the alternative view that sport provides a source of group identity and social integration, and thus can act as a unifier of local, regional and national populations. He argues, however, that in the case of Brazil, 'futebol's chief significance has been its use by the elite to bolster official ideology and to channel social energy in ways compatible with prevailing social values'. Thus he appears to adopt a perspective more in keeping with that of Antonio Gramsci, or 'hegemony theory' (Rowe 2004).

Lever (1995: 56), adopting a social integration perspective, argues that 'sport promoted national integration in Brazil long before other social organizations criss-crossed the nation'. By 1914 Brazil had a national federation of sports clubs, the *Confederação Brasileira de Desportos* (CBD), or 'Brazilian Sports Confederation', and the football club as an institution dates from the late nineteenth century. Levine (1980: 234) suggests that the development of football in Brazil falls into four broad periods: 1894–1904, the development of private urban clubs for foreigners (especially the British, German and Portuguese); 1905–1933, the amateur phase which nonetheless saw a marked growth in interest; 1933–1950, professionalisation and participation on the world stage, including the hosting of the fourth FIFA World Cup Finals in 1950; and since 1950, world-class recognition and the growth of commercialism. This remains a useful way of understanding the emergence of the sport in Brazil (for greater detail, see Bellos 2002; Gaffney 2008; Goldblatt 2014).

The first football clubs to be established in Rio reflected the influence of foreigners: Vasco da Gama established in 1898 at the Lusitania club for Portuguese merchants and bankers; Fluminense developed out of the British 'Rio Cricket and Athletic Association' in 1902; Botafogo were a spin-off from a rowing club (1904); and Flamengo, formerly another rowing club, was formed in 1915 when athletes defected from Fluminense. Thus are great sporting rivalries created within the boundaries of one city. Popular interest in the sport was also aided, as in other nations, by the growth of media reporting of the results by the newspaper press from the 1900s and radio from the 1930s.

Levine (1999: 44) notes how government expanded into everyday life, including sport, in Brazil in the 1930s. The federal government seized upon the Brazilian victory in the 1932 South American Cup, and a year later football became a national institution when it was professionalised under the auspices of the CBD. In 1941 the club network in Brazil was linked to the federal government by President Vargas' centralisation programme. A National Sport Council (CND) within the Ministry of Education and Culture was established to 'orient, finance, and encourage the practice of sport in all of Brazil' (Lever 1995: 56).

Lever (1995: 59) argues that from the beginning of the diffusion and adoption of modern sport, 'sport and government more than coexist; their relationship is better described as symbiotic'. While individual Brazilian athletes – such as tennis player Maria Bueno, who won four times at Forest Hills and three times at Wimbledon between 1959 and 1966, and racing driver Emerson Fittipaldi who was at his best in Formula One racing in the 1970s – may have been used to symbolise Brazilian greatness, Lever (1995: 55) states that it 'is through team sports, with their highly organised structure that precedes and outlives any particular set of athletes, that more than momentary unification of a nation is established'. She argues that in Brazil 'politicians have spurred the growth of both spectator and participant sport; sport, in return, has helped politicians court popularity and has helped the Brazilian government achieve its nationalistic goals' (Lever 1995: 59). In many ways, therefore, her argument can be seen as complementary to that of Levine.

6

The contemporary Olympics

Lever (1995: 59) additionally argues that the modern history of Brazil is 'one of social and economic change through authoritarian centralization'. Sport has played its part in this in various ways. The military coup d'état in 1964 saw the establishment of army presidents. In 1968, as repression intensified, the President, General Emílio Garrastazu Médici, began taking an interest in Flamengo and the national team. When Brazil won the FIFA World Cup for an unprecedented third time in Mexico in 1970, the team was flown directly from Mexico City to the capital Brasilia, and the players were personally received by Médici in the Planalto Palace (Levine 1980: 246). Two days of national celebration followed and shortly after the military took over control of the CBD (eventually renamed the *Confederação Brasileira de Futebol* (CBF) after a demand by FIFA in 1979).

Although there was considerable interest in football in Brazil, it is clear that less attention was paid to developing other 'Olympic sports' until relatively recently (Levine 1980: 249). For example, when it was suggested to President-designate General João Baptista de Oliveira Figueiredo that amateur sport should be given greater emphasis to improve Brazilian performance at the Olympic Games, he retorted that the Olympics were: 'political propaganda for nations who needed that sort of thing' (quoted in Levine 1980: 250). Brazil's achievements at the Summer Olympics continue to be middle-ranking, including never having secured a gold medal in either the men's or women's football competition. The top medal-producing sports have been volleyball, sailing and judo. It was not until 1984 that Brazil won its first Olympic medal in track and field events, when Joachim Cruz won the gold medal in the 800 m in Los Angeles, setting an Olympic record.

Brazilian athletes first participated at the Summer Olympic Games in Antwerp in 1920, and won a gold, silver and bronze medal (Rubio 2009: 32). However, it was not until London in 1948 that they won another medal. Brazilian athletes have also participated in the Winter Olympic Games since 1992, although they have yet to win a medal in winter sports. Perhaps it is not surprising that London 2012 was the year Brazil secured the largest medal haul to date – given the impetus through additional financing that Olympic sports has been given by hosting the Games in 2016 – although it was in Athens in 2004 that the country won the most gold medals (see Figure 1.1).

Since the re-democratisation process in the late 1980s, sports other than football have slowly attained greater prominence in the national political agenda, resulting in the

Year	Host city	Number of athletes	Gold	Silver	Bronze	Total	Medal table rank
1988	Seoul	171	1	2	3	6	24
1992	Barcelona	195	2	1	0	3	25
1996	Atlanta	225	3	3	9	15	25
2000	Sydney	205	0	6	6	12	53
2004	Athens	247	5	2	3	10	16
2008	Beijing	277	3	4	8	15	23
2012	London	258	3	5	9	17	22

Figure 1.1 Brazilian athletes, Olympic medals won and medal table rank: 1988–2012.

Source: adapted from http://olimpiadas.uol.com.br/2008/historia/ (last accessed 30 July 2015).

creation of a dedicated ministry under the government of President Luis Inacio ('Lula') da Silva of the Workers' Party. Attention and resources have been mostly oriented towards professional sports and were lately dominated by the hosting of mega-events (Schausteck de Almeida *et al.* 2012). The bidding campaigns for the FIFA 2014 World Cup and the 2016 Olympic Games were fully endorsed by the national government and in the passionate support of President Lula, who on the occasion of the awards declared that football was 'more than a sport for Brazilians, it is a national passion' and that with the Olympics 'Brazil gained its international citizenship . . . [t]he world has finally recognised it is Brazil's time' (BBC Sport 2007; Rohter 2010: 223). Such claims demonstrate the political capital to be explored in relation to two audiences: the Brazilian electorate and international opinion.

BRAZIL AND RIO HOSTING THE WORLD'S GAMES

In this section we focus attention on the political aspects of the preparation for the staging of two sports mega-events, the men's Football World Cup in 2014 and the Olympic and Paralympic Games in Rio in 2016. We briefly retrace the bidding and preparation history of the events while reflecting on their expected contributions and impacts, a debate that rose to global prominence with the international media coverage of scenes of nationwide protests in 2013.

The 2014 World Cup

Following the controversies surrounding the voting for the 2006 World Cup – when the South African bid was beaten by one vote after the sudden change of mind of one delegate – FIFA introduced a continental rotating system to designate host countries, starting with Africa and followed by South America (but then subsequently abandoned it). Since last hosting the event in 1950 the new rotation system provided an opportune occasion with which the then chairman of CBF, Ricardo Teixeira, worked in getting the support of the recently elected President Lula. In October 2007 Brazil was confirmed the host of the 2014 World Cup in the unusual situation that the cities that would stage the competition were still to be decided. From a shortlist of 18 cities 12 were finally chosen in May 2009 after FIFA conceded to a request to include more host cities than the usual eight or ten (Gaffney 2016).

The preparations for the World Cup were poised to be one of the main symbols of Lula's successor, Dilma Rousseff's, government, following the announcement of an overall programme package in Lula's last year in office. A suite of agreements with state and municipal authorities were signed, detailing works in stadiums, public transport, airports, tourism infrastructure and roads and highways. In order to facilitate and speed up the tendering of contracts, special regulations were enacted to flexibilise both the tendering process and the cap of municipal and state levels of indebtedness. The progress of works was at times obfuscated by the turbulence in the relationship between FIFA and the Brazilian government, leading to the approval of a general set of laws in relation to the organisation of the event. These included the application of guarantees previously signed by the Brazilian government in relation to tax exemptions, the approval of visas

8

and restrictions on ambush marketing, and also to other items that triggered heated debates such as concessionary tickets, licensing for the sale of alcohol at the venues and the activities of street vendors in the venue surroundings. Minor concessions were made, for example, such as half-priced tickets for students and the elderly, and agreeing to allow the traditional *baianas* to sell Afro-Brazilian food in Salvador.

The immediate run-up to the 2014 World Cup was plagued by delays, cost overruns, fatalities and nation-wide protests. The national government persisted with the discourse of expected benefits accruing from the event, with constant reference to the legacies that would benefit the majority of the population. There was mounting criticism from the press about the escalating budget figures, particularly the costs of stadia and their proposed post-event use. In one case, the predicted final figure for Brasilia's National Stadium was almost double the original estimate, while the future of the stadium post-World Cup remained uncertain, given the absence of a competitive team in the upper tiers of the Brazilian football competitions. A similar situation beckoned for the stadia in Natal, Cuiabá and Manaus. Up to the completion of the stadia, ten deaths of construction workers were registered as progress was rushed to meet deadlines. Half of the venues were unveiled for the Confederations Cup in 2013, the FIFA rehearsal tournament for the World Cup, despite ongoing works still visible at many of the venues. Up to that point the expected budget for World Cup-related expenditure had already increased to five times the original estimates. One year to go and facing mounting challenges in several planning areas, the organisation of the event found itself caught in the middle of a massive public protest that swept across the country.

In June 2013 public demonstrations in the streets of Brazilian cities, and heavy-handed police response, were widely covered by the international press. What had started as a local protest in São Paulo against an increase in bus fares, which brought some of its main thoroughfares to a halt, quickly triggered demonstrations elsewhere in the country after it was met by a disproportionate response by the police. Thousands poured into the streets of more than 350 cities to express not only their indignation at scenes of police brutality widely circulated in social networks on the internet, but also to release their discontent with corrupt politics and the neglected state of public services. While some expressed their anger with the continuous corruption scandals that marred national politics and Rousseff's (and Lula's) Workers' Party, many manifested their revolt against issues closer to their daily lives: the poor condition of the public health, education and transport systems in Brazil (Vainer 2016).

The emergence of the Workers' Party as the federal government in 2002 coincided with a period of strong economic growth, improvement of social indicators and rising levels of consumption by the poorer sections of Brazilian society that helped them to endure the global financial crisis relatively unscathed (Anderson 2011). The Workers' Party's continuance in power was sealed via a familiar political strategy in Brazil of securing support via shady deals. Exposed during the denouncement of a vote-buying scheme in 2005 that led to the sentencing of some of the party's top ranks, this long-evolving story was also represented on some of the banners on display during the June 2013 protests. Hence, although able to afford more consumer goods, the urban poor have endured an ambiguous existence of formal jobs in precarious conditions alongside poor public

Figure 1.2 A protestor in Rio dressed as Batman with a sign that says: 'We want FIFA-standard education and health, schools and hospitals'.

services. The two agendas thus converged around a related and immediate event: the FIFA Confederations Cup in 2013.

Protesting against the vilified 'FIFA standards' often evoked in official discourses to justify the spending on football venues, Brazilians demanded the same level of quality in the delivery of public services. The ever-rising budget for the event, the finding of irregularities and the suspension of projects served to confirm the general sentiment that only the powerful and rich would benefit. Long-standing campaign groups such as the *Comitês Populares da Copa* ('Popular Committees of the World Cup') highlighted the displacement of thousands of people from low-income communities by works related to the event, with estimates ranging between 170,000 and 250,000 people (Montenegro 2013), and the appropriation of public improvements by private companies as the operation of the venues was privatised (Gaffney 2014). Protest videos posted online went viral. The otherwise football-crazy image that characterised the portrayal of Brazilian fans was nowhere to be seen in the Confederations Cup tournament as chants of '*Não vai ter Copa!*' ('There won't be a World Cup') and '*Da Copa eu abro mão, quero meu dinheiro pra saúde e educação*' ('I give up the World Cup, I want my money to go into health and education') echoed in many of the host cities.

While some municipalities backtracked on their decision to raise transport fares, the federal government responded with a public announcement from President Rousseff acknowledging the demands but condemning acts of vandalism. National programmes and new governmental intentions for healthcare, education and transport were announced. If the measures managed to placate widespread demonstrations, other protests smaller in number continued to be carried over in the following months. This was accompanied by a wave of strikes in the professions – especially the police, teachers, road sweepers and public transport operators – for improved pay and working conditions. FIFA continued to refute criticism of its role by stating that it was Brazil's decision to bid for the event and to propose the projects associated with the stadia.

10

The total cost of expenditure announced by the Brazilian government on the eve of the World Cup in 2014 was $11.3 billion (the predicted total at the time of writing in October 2015 is now closer to $15 billion – see Boadle 2014). It was a far cry from initial government statements such as that of the Minister of Sports back in 2007 that it would be the 'World Cup of the private sector', meaning that essential works such as those destined for the venues would be covered by private companies. The final financial breakdown saw almost 83 per cent of the costs attributed to governmental spending or financed by state banks (Folha de São Paulo 2014). It was perhaps no wonder that, with the exception of one or two rather tame decorations celebrating the arrival of yet another World Cup, the vivid signs of popular excitement on the walls and streets of Brazilian cities that might have been expected with the hosting of a World Cup on home soil did not initially materialise in 2014. Gaffney (2016) explores the socio-economic impacts of hosting the 2014 FIFA World Cup throughout Brazil, stemming from substantive observations developed during extensive engagement with scholars, activists and media in Brazil, as well as a longitudinal study that dealt with the urban impacts of the World Cup in all 12 of the host cities. Gaffney found subtle regional variations between host cities, but argues that a condition of permanent crisis, emergency and exception led to a weakening of Brazilian democratic institutions, the deterioration of public spaces and the increased socio-economic polarisation of Brazilian society (see also Vainer 2016).

The Rio 2016 Olympic Games

The 2016 Rio de Janeiro Olympic project bears some resemblance to the 2014 World Cup, in which big politics and long-time serving sports leaders played a pivotal role in securing the rights to host the event for the first time in a South American country. However, distinct from the World Cup, in which football politics determined the urban agenda of hosting cities, it was the urban politics of Rio de Janeiro city that determined the Olympic project.

Rio de Janeiro had previously unsuccessfully attempted to be host for the 1936 and 1940 Olympic Games, and the separate equestrian competition of the 1956 Olympics. A new bid was prepared for the 2004 Olympic Games, this time as the outcome of an inter-urban policy exchange. The local elections of 1992 brought the conservative candidate Cesar Maia to government, promising to restore urban order and modernise public administration. An important element of Maia's agenda was to elaborate a strategic plan then in vogue in North American and European cities to set a vision for the city in collaboration with other representative groups. The initiative was pursued with the consulting services of policy-makers from Barcelona soon after the organisation of the 1992 Olympic Games. It was out of this relationship that the concept of a Rio Olympic bid was born, as a way to promote urban development and city marketing (Silvestre 2016).

Hastily prepared, the bid attempted to incorporate the general precepts of the 1992 Barcelona Olympic Games by earmarking declining urban areas for regeneration and a multi-cluster organisation for the event, using different areas of the city. The event was also expected to turn around the image of a city synonymous with rampant crime and police-led carnage. The bid generated great support from the public while new promises were announced, including a bold social development agenda aimed to improve living conditions by eradicating poverty and upgrading slums. However, the bid failed to impress the IOC inspectors and was not shortlisted in the final voting round. The result frustrated some of the key promoters of the bid, leaving re-elected Mayor Maia and the President of the Brazilian Olympic Committee, Carlos Nuzman, to pick up the pieces and to drastically rearrange the Olympic project.

Working his way through the Olympic system and becoming a member of the IOC, Nuzman translated the message that Brazil had to first prove its credentials by convincing Maia to support a bid to host the 2007 Pan American Games in Rio, the regional multi-sport competition for the Americas. Giving a relatively modest competition the 'Olympic treatment', the original estimates for the event quadrupled as a set of venues were specially built for it, including an Olympic stadium ('João Havelange Olympic Stadium' at Engenho de Dentro), a velodrome, an indoor arena and an aquatics centre. The spatial planning privileged the expanding and wealthy district of Barra da Tijuca with the athlete's village, adding to the local gated-community stock. Criticism, particularly in relation to the inflated costs, was largely held at bay as the experience was justified as an Olympic rehearsal with a new bid quickly announced for the 2016 Games (see Curi *et al.* 2011 for some of the criticisms).

Up to this point the national government had played a supporting and guarantor role. President Lula had confirmed in 2003 the commitment of his government with the pre-parations for the 2007 Pan American Games and his backing to a short-lived bid for the 2012 Olympics. The contribution of the federal government to the total budget for the 2007 event increased substantially in the run-up period as municipal finances were stretched. The 2016 bid then became more aligned with Brazilian foreign policy discourse, reflecting the country's increasingly prominent role, and having in President Lula an active international 'poster boy'. A team of seasoned consultants, with previous experience in the Sydney 2000 and London 2012 candidatures, helped highlight the acquired organi-sational expertise, geopolitics, booming national and local economies and branding opportunities in bringing the event for the first time to South America, tailoring the bid to its IOC audience. Rio was then selected in Copenhagen in October 2009 as the 2016 Olympic Games host.

The masterplan for the 2016 Games reinforced the concentration of venues and facilities at Barra da Tijuca, but whereas the Pan American Games brought little contribution to the city's internal system, new transport networks and the regeneration of the port area are part of the expected material legacies of 2016. The new city government of Mayor Eduardo Paes in 2009 reproduced at the local level the political coalition present at the state and national governments, which then facilitated a shared agenda to release municipal, state and federal land for the regeneration of the port area – a project known as 'Porto Maravilha' (Galicia 2015). Despite not featuring any sports facilities itself, the project has been strongly associated as a legacy of the event, with the Olympics providing a deadline for the conclusion of several works that will transform it into a new mixed-use district of corpo-rate towers, museums and residential area. The other highly visible programme associated with the Games is the construction of 250 km of segregated bus rapid transit (BRT) lanes and an extension of the underground railway (metro) system, which together will improve the link between Barra and other parts of the city.

12

Without proper disclosure of the details of the projects, a range of low-income communities learned of their displacement for Olympic-related works, as municipal staff turned up to mark their houses for demolition (Silvestre and Oliveira 2012). A study by the *Comitê Popular da Copa e das Olimpíadas do Rio de Janeiro* (Popular Committee for the World Cup and Olympics in Rio de Janeiro) (2013) estimated that almost 11,000 families had been affected by these works, and were offered temporary rental assistance, financial compensation or relocation to social housing estates in the western fringes of the city. Another element that has substantially affected the lives of the inhabitants of Rio's *favelas* is the security programme of police pacifying units (UPP) launched in 2008. Consisting of a joint effort between the Brazilian Army and the state's elite police squad, it attempts to occupy gang-controlled communities, driving away drug traffickers while constructing police bases inside some *favelas*. Despite not being directly linked with the mega-event projects, the geographical location of the UPP has been in close proximity to competition sites and tourist areas. Revelations of police abuse, the delayed arrival of public services, gentrification and the continuation of criminal activity have undermined initial positive reception by local residents.

The indignation of part of the population, together with rising living costs, thus helped to fuel the local June 2013 demonstrations, with some estimated 300,000 people taking to the streets of central Rio alone on 20 June (G1 2013). Some concessions were announced by the state governor – for example, backtracking on the decision to demolish the athletics and aquatics centre together with the museum of indigenous people at the Maracanã complex to make way for car parking spaces for the main stadium. The Rio Mayor, Eduardo Paes, announced that evictions were to be temporarily suspended until detailed studies were produced.

The same criticisms levelled at the World Cup for its lavish spending and also for worrying project delays were also directed at Rio's preparation for the Olympics, as a string of negative comments about the readiness of the venues became the focus of press coverage. Two years prior to the opening ceremony, Rio was reported to have just 10 per cent of facilities ready (Jenkins 2014) while the Olympic Park was a desolate site with no erected structures and the sports cluster of Deodoro was still awaiting tenders for development. Utilising sport for social development has been a notable feature of discourse about sport's social role for many decades, but in recent years it has developed into a specific conception of Sport for Development and Peace, or SDP. The hosting of sports mega-events has 'consistently traded' on the discourse of development, and this is a notable feature of Rio 2016 (Darnell and Millington 2016: 65). There have been some analyses of sport's role in dealing with social problems in Brazil and specifically Rio (Reis and Sousa-Mast 2012). The next section takes the story forward and discusses the way Rio has been made into an Olympic city. It outlines the locations of the 2016 Games and assesses debates over governance and the budget, security issues, transport, the environment and the social impacts of urban regeneration in Rio.

MAKING AN OLYMPIC CITY OUT OF RIO

The preparations for the 2016 Olympic Games are taking place in a particular context for Rio de Janeiro, which overlaps and intersects with other unfolding processes, as Silvestre

(2016) notes. The 2016 hosting decision occurred in conjunction with a period of economic growth that in combination with fiscal and distribution policies stimulated higher consumption levels. Locally, Rio was impacted by the growth of the oil and gas industry, with the installation of new national and foreign companies. A security policy implemented by the state of Rio ended the presence of armed groups in some *favelas* and stimulated a rise in property markets both inside them and in nearby areas. Finally, the city also played a key role in the hosting of the 2014 World Cup, with seven matches including the final played at Maracanã Stadium. Therefore 'it is difficult to fully disentangle the preparations for the 2016 Games from these dimensions' (Silvestre 2016).

Locations

The Olympic events will take place in four clusters around the city – Maracanã in the north, Deodoro to the west, Copacabana in the south and Barra de Tijuca in the south-west (see Figure 1.3).

The concentration of competitions and the extent of urban interventions vary considerably among them. In the Copacabana zone, where the main tourist district is located, changes are minimal. The outdoor competitions of rowing, beach volleyball and triathlon will use existing and temporary facilities with the city's iconic beaches and mountains as a backdrop. Another zone encompasses the stadia of Maracanã, recently revamped for the 2014 FIFA World Cup, and the João Havelange Olympic Stadium (known as 'Engenhão'), built for the 2007 Pan American Games, and home to Botafogo FC (see Figure 1.4). The latter has also had to be renovated despite being constructed relatively recently. A novel feature of the Rio Olympics will be the organisation of the opening and closing ceremonies at a different stadium (Maracanã) than where the athletics track and field competitions will be held (Engenhão).

Although the Maracanã, its surrounding sports complex and local area have been the site of struggles and protest since the mid-2000s, it is in the zones of Deodoro and Barra that the most substantial processes of urban change have been taking place (in Chapters 5 and 9 we discuss the increasing role of protest in the planning and realisation of sports mega-events – see Boykoff 2014b; Lenskyj 2000). In Deodoro, to Rio's west, the Olympic facilities will be located within *Vila Militar*, a planned community of the Brazilian Army. Military facilities will be used for the shooting and equestrian competitions, while training grounds will give way to the hockey and rugby arenas. These facilities are mostly existing or temporary and will not produce major changes in the area. However, other land belonging to the Brazilian Army will be transformed into the 'X-Park', dedicated to extreme sports, which will make use of the BMX tracks and the canoe slalom facility built for the Games. However, post-event plans are still vague and at the preliminary stage, particularly in terms of management and sustainability.

As a result of being the main Olympic cluster, Barra is the focus of most of the public policies and private investment. The lifting of certain planning restrictions has allowed the construction of taller Olympic-related housing and hotels. In the post-event scenario, access to the region will be improved with extended metro lines, duplicated highways and new BRT corridors linking Barra to the city centre and the international airport in the

14

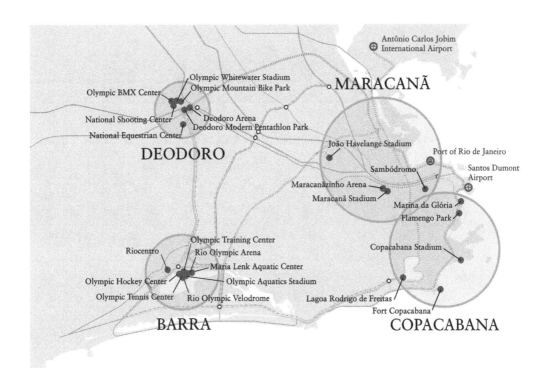

LIST OF VENUES

Olympic 'region'	Facilities
Barra (BR)	Olympic Park, including: Olympic Tennis Centre; Olympic Hockey Centre; Rio Olympic Velodrome; Handball Arena; Maria Lenk Aquatic Centre; Olympic Training Centre
	International Broadcasting Centre; Main Media Centre; Media Hotel; Olympic Athletes Village; and Golf Course
Deodoro (DR)	Olympic Whitewater Stadium; Olympic BMX Centre; Deodoro Arena; Deodoro Modern Pentathlon Park; National Equestrian Centre; National Shooting Centre; Olympic Mountain Bike Park
Copacabana (CB)	Copacabana Rowing Stadium; Marina da Gloria; Largo Rodrigo de Freitas
Maracanã (MN)	Maracanã Stadium; João Havelange Olympic Stadium; Maracanãzinho Arena; Sambadromo

Figure 1.3 Rio 2016 Summer Olympic and Paralympic venues.

Source: adapted from https://en.wikipedia.org/wiki/Venues_of_the_2016_Summer_Olympics_and_Paralympics (last accessed 25 September 2015).

Figure 1.4 A view from inside the new Maracanã Stadium.

north of the city. The Barra zone will be the centrepiece of the Games and 16 competitions will be held there. It is an area of great real estate speculation and where post-event plans have been most clearly defined. The Olympic Park is being developed on the former site of the Formula One racing circuit in a peninsula on the Jacarepaguá lagoon. It will house nine sports arenas, which will stage gymnastics, swimming, cycling, tennis, basketball, handball, fencing, wrestling and taekwondo, as well as the broadcasting and media centres. The spectre of white elephants has been a constant presence in public discourse and the post-event use of the arenas has been of concern. It is planned that the handball arena and equipment from the aquatics centre will be taken down after the event and reassembled for use at public schools and swimming pools.

The Olympic Park is being developed via a public–private partnership (PPP) in which a consortium of developers is responsible for the delivery of part of the venues and related infrastructure. After the event, 75 per cent of the land will be transferred to developers to make way for private housing, offices, hotels and shopping malls. The remaining 25 per cent will provide facilities for an Olympic Training Centre run by the Brazilian Olympic Committee (BOC) for the use of elite athletes. It is still unclear, however, how the centre will be funded and managed, and, given the underuse and poor maintenance of the venues built for the 2007 Pan American Games, doubts remain about its future.

16

The Athletes' Village is being developed next to the Olympic Park by the private sector, with a financial package provided by the state Federal Savings Bank. The project, a co-production by Brazilian construction companies Carvalho Hosken and Odebrecht, envisions the construction of 31 tower blocks of 17 stories each, totalling 3,604 units, accommodating 18,000 athletes and team members. After the Games the site will become a complex of gated communities called *Ilha Pura* ('Pure Island'), currently promoted as a new 'neighbourhood committed with good taste, luxury and sophistication' (Ilha Pura 2015). The quotation below from Carlos Carvalho is indicative of the politics of urban development related to the Olympics in Rio, and arguably elsewhere:

> We think that if the standards were lowered, we would be taking away from what the city – the new city – could represent on the global scene as a city of the elite, of good taste. Ilha Pura could not scratch this destiny that has been given to the region. For this reason, it needed to be noble housing, not housing for the poor.
>
> (Quoted in Watts 2015)

Athletes will also be able to make use of training grounds at the adjacent Athlete's Park and a private beach in a cordoned-off area of Barra beach. It remains to be seen what the demand is for Ilha Pura.

Governance and budget

Despite declarations of openness and transparency, the costs of staging an Olympic Games remain susceptible to different interpretations and more often than not several alterations. Figures produced as part of an Olympic candidature (bid) book are often rendered in USD, GBP or euros, and then when converted a few years later into other currencies – in the case of Rio 2016, Brazilian reais (BRL or R$) – the actual amounts can look discrepant. Rio's book for the Games submitted in 2008 estimated that it would cost a total of $14.42 billion, divided between the Organizing Committee for the Olympic and Paralympic Games (OCOG) budget for staging the Games (BRL4.4 billion or $2.82 billion) and a non-OCOG budget for delivering the related infrastructure and services (BRL18.11 billion or $11.6 billion). This was the highest budget of all candidate cities in 2009, but promotional material stressed Brazil's positioning during the global financial crisis as a 'small island in an ocean of negative economic results' (Ministério do Esporte 2009: 100; cited in Silvestre 2016). According to the frequently asked questions section of the Rio 2016 website in July 2015, the OCOG was relying on a budget of BRL5.6 billion. The website continued: 'The organizing Committee is not responsible for any works. The cost of venue and infrastructure works, adding up to R$ 23.2 billion, will be managed by the three government levels' – that is federal, state and municipal.[1]

While the OCOG intends to have its budget funded by private organisations, the three levels of Brazilian government have assured the IOC that they will cover any funding needed by the Organizing Committee, as is now expected of any Olympic host nation. Also in July 2015, according to journalist Jonathan Watts (2015), the total 'budget of 38.2bn reais (£7.9bn) is slightly lower than that of London and well below that of Beijing'.

Writing one year prior to the start of the Games, therefore, the costs appear to have increased by 34 per cent of the original budget.[2]

Initially it was proposed to create a body along the lines of the Olympic Delivery Authority, responsible for the London 2012 Games (see the next chapter). The Olympic Public Authority ('APO' in Portuguese) would be a public consortium formed by the federal, state and municipal governments with centralised powers to deliver the infrastructure and services necessary for the organisation of the event (the non-OCOG attributes). However, as Silvestre (2016) noted:

> political wrestling over responsibilities and legal obstacles to ensure complete powers weakened the remit of APO. While bureaucratic processes delayed the approval of the institution at the federal level, the municipality of Rio de Janeiro decided to create its own delivery authority, the Municipal Olympic Company (EOM).

Hence while both bodies are nominally credited with delivering the Games, in practice EOM operates as the main delivery body, while APO has the role of reporting on the federal government activities and the consolidated budget.

In January 2014, APO published the Rio 2016 Games 'Matrix of Responsibilities'. This document details the contribution of each level of government – city, state and federal – to organising and holding the event, listing projects as well as responsibilities for implementing and supplying resources. The information is organised by the clustering of construction works and services related to the Olympic regions: Barra da Tijuca (BR), Deodoro (DR), Maracanã (MN) and Copacabana (CB). Described as a 'living document' to be continually reviewed and updated, the Matrix would be published biannually, with the aim of ensuring transparency and accountability.[3]

Six months after the first version was released, the APO announced in the second version that the Matrix was well in advance and 71 per cent of the total of 52 projects undertaken for the Games had already had their contracts signed, and construction work was underway. According to the update:

> private investments continue to lead the financing of projects, corresponding to R$ 4.2 billion (65 per cent) of the total, with the rest of the resources coming from the public sector. 'Public organisations are committed to the staging of a lean and efficient Olympics' stated the APO president.[4]

The list of responsibilities for 'the organisation and realisation' of Rio 2016 in each of the four Olympic regions is outlined in Figure 1.5. As can be seen by the number of projects and size of the anticipated spend, Barra is where most of the building is taking place. Also as can be seen, the total cost of over BRL6.5 billion is considerably more than the figure stated on the Rio 2016 website mentioned earlier. This is just one of the reasons why sceptics raise critical questions about the financing of sports mega-events, including Rio 2016.

Olympic promoters respond to criticism in several ways. For example, as if to head off concerns about delays in completing the projects at Barra, in July 2015 the Rio municipal

Olympic 'region'	Number of projects	Types of project	Resources and execution	Estimated cost*
Barra (BR)	25	Olympic Park; Tennis Centre; Velodrome; Handball Arena; Aquatic Centre	Federal government and city government	R$5,537.9m
		International Broadcasting Centre; Main Media Centre; Media Hotel; Athletes Village; Golf Course	City government and private; private	
Deodoro (DR)	15	Canoe Slalom Stadium; BMX Centre; Fencing Arena; Field Hockey Centre; Mountain Bike; Pentathlon; Rugby; Equestrian; Sports Shooting Centre	Federal government and city government	R$835.8m
Copacabana (CB)	4	Rowing Stadium; adaptation of marina	Federal, state and city	R$45.0m
Maracanã (MN)	8	Adaptation of: Sambadromo, Olympic Stadium and Maracanãzinho Arena	Federal, state, city and private	R$93.0m
Totals	52			R$6,511.7m

Figure 1.5 Rio 2016: projects, responsibilities and estimated costs.

Source: adapted from www.brasil2016.gov.br/en/news/olympic-public-authority-apo-publishes-update-responsibility-matrix (last accessed 28 July 2015).

Note
*At July 2014; some costs still to be determined.

government released an updated version of its video, mixing footage of construction work at 'Barra Olympic Park' with computer-generated images of how the site would look at Games time.[5] Olympic promoters also refute criticisms of the rising Olympic budget by citing statistics of the participation of the private sector. Accordingly, as mentioned earlier, over 60 per cent of the costs were expected to be covered by private funding. These are largely represented by the construction of the Olympic Village, the new golf course and the PPPs behind the construction of the Olympic Park and the regeneration programme of the port area.

As Silvestre (2016) notes, however, 'despite being touted as enterprises "where there is not a single cent from the public purse" . . . interest from developers was only possible with the alteration of planning restrictions and the transfer of land ownership'. The city previously owned the Formula One circuit on which the Barra Olympic Park is being constructed and 75 per cent of that will be transferred to private companies for commercial exploitation, including private housing, hotels and shopping malls. The compensation and relocation of the hundreds of families living next to the Park in Vila Autódromo and the construction of a new racing track at a protected greenfield site in Deodoro are considered as 'existing costs' resulting from the destruction of the Jacarepaguá circuit. However, the costs of evictions are not included in the Olympic budget and stand as reminders of the need for close scrutiny and inclusion of both the social and environmental costs of 'breaking new ground' in Rio (and anywhere else that hosts an Olympic Games).

Security and safety

Even though the 2007 Pan American Games held in Rio were considered to be tightly controlled (Curi *et al.* 2011), in light of continuing IOC evaluations of Rio's security and safety as problematic, an extensive security programme was introduced which, despite not being designed specifically in response to the hosting of mega-events, has become closely implicated with them (Freeman 2014). Starting in December 2008 the UPP programme has sought to take territorial control of *favelas* from organised criminal groups with the installation of police stations and implementing community policing (Alves and Evanson 2011). Prior announcement of an intervention seeks to influence drug gangs to leave the area, thus avoiding armed conflicts with the arrival of the elite police forces. By the summer of 2015 some 40 *favelas* had been targeted and a reduction of violent crimes occurred in the first four years of the programme (see Silvestre 2016; Freeman 2014).

However, as Cano *et al.* (2012) have noted, the selection of *favelas* was not supported by indicators such as crime statistics. Rather, it was highly suggestive of forming a 'security belt' around the Maracanã Stadium and near other Olympic and tourists sites, thus 'ignoring the most violent areas of the metropolitan region, which are the Baixada Fluminense and the North End of Rio' (Cano *et al.* 2012: 194). Other research confirms that the hosting of the World Cup and the Olympics were determinants in guiding decisions over the expansion of UPP operations (see Silvestre 2016). Recent escalating violence and police abuse at some of the 'pacified *favelas*' has made residents doubtful of the longevity of the programme after the event (Puff 2014).

Transport

Having Barra de Tijuca as the main stage of the Games suggested that improved access to the area and transportation was another theme in which the city trailed behind other bids. The 2016 bid promised the creation of a 'High Performance Transport Ring' and introduced the concept of the BRT system as a feasible way to connect the four Olympic clusters and deliver a new transport network in time for the event (Rio 2016 OCOG 2009). Barra will act as the nodal point of the three segregated bus corridors tied to the Olympic deadline. Totalling 117 km, they consist of the *Transoeste* corridor linking Barra to the West End and a new metro terminal; the *Transcarioca* line, which cuts through the North End towards the international airport; and the *Transolimpica*, linking the Olympic Park with Deodoro.

Critics meanwhile point to the marginalisation of the metro and rail expansion and that the system presents only temporary results as it can be flooded quickly. The experience of the *Transoeste* and *Transcarioca* corridors already in operation seem to corroborate the latter argument. Press coverage of the systems inaugurated in 2012 and 2014, respectively, document overcrowding and safety worries as routine occurrences (Silvestre 2016).

The environment

Perhaps the greatest gamble of Rio's Olympic-dependent programme of interventions has been the clean-up of the waters of Guanabara Bay in order to provide the best conditions for the sailing competitions. Water pollution has grown exponentially since the 1960s due to industrial activity and the discharge of raw sewage from the 16 municipalities of the Rio de Janeiro Metropolitan Region on the shores of the bay. The Olympic bid set out the objective to treat 80 per cent of the sewage by 2016, but recent figures suggest a more modest outcome is likely.

A state-led sanitation plan has been in place since 1995, but it has been marred by the lack of coordination among stakeholders and funding discontinuities, and by 2007 it presented a level of 12 per cent of treated sewage (Rio 2016 OCOG 2014; Neves 2015). Thus the hosting of the Games presented the opportunity to leverage funding and efforts to accelerate the sanitation policy and improve environmental conditions for the Rio population of 8.5 million people. Despite showing progress leading to the treatment of 50 per cent of sewage in 2013 (Rio 2016 OCOG 2014), in the selection of public policies for the 'Legacy Plan' a modest set of programmes totalling R$124.67 million was included (Silvestre 2016). These related to sewerage works in the central Rio area, river barriers and collecting barges. The latter two are mitigation efforts to avoid garbage floating near the competition areas, and post-event targets remain uncertain (Brooks and Barchfield 2015).

Reviewed targets also compromised the reforestation pledge to compensate for carbon emissions resulting from works for the Games. After expanding the original plan of planting 24 million trees by a further ten million, a readjusted figure of merely 8.1 million was announced (Silvestre 2016). The figure contrasts with the deforestation of 270 m² of Atlantic rainforest for the construction of the *Transolímpica* corridor and the duplication of the *Joá* elevated expressway (Silvestre 2016).

Finally, but by no means least, the construction of the Olympic golf course has been identified as 'emblematic of the ways in which Rio's preparations for the 2016 Games are deeply problematic' and responsible for the loss of natural environment (Hodges 2014). The sport, alongside rugby, was included in the Summer Games by the IOC after candidate cities for 2016 had submitted their final bids. The Rio de Janeiro Olympic golf course is located on the shores of the Marapendi Lagoon in Barra, in an area previously protected as a site of natural beauty and 'home to rare butterflies, pines and other species not found anywhere else in the world' (Watts 2015). Alleging financial and logistics reasons for not using the two existing private golf clubs, the municipality partnered with a private developer owning land north of the preservation area to build a course from scratch (Silvestre 2016). According to the terms of the PPP, the developer is responsible for the construction and maintenance costs of the venue. In return the municipality reviewed planning restrictions to allow taller luxury buildings to be built on the private land. After the event the venue will be operated as a public golf course for a period of 20 years before returning to the private owner (Silvestre 2016). A year before the Games, golf course activists, in the shape of Rio's Occupy Golf movement, continued to contest these decisions.

The social impacts and consequences of Olympic-related urban regeneration

Historical episodes of profound urban transformation in Rio have invariably produced substantial costs to the city's poor (Meade 1997; McCann 2014; Perlman 2010). Between 1902 and 1906 Mayor Francisco Pereira Passos is credited with the wholesale transformation of Rio's central area, a feat likened to that of Baron Haussmann in Paris (Benchimol 1990). During the Pereira Passos reforms, tenement houses were targeted, leading to the displacement of the (poorest) residents to nearby hills and substandard housing beside the railway tracks. Another period of intense displacement took place in the 1960s during Rio Governor Carlos Lacerda's term of office. His pledge for transforming the urban space also translated into the wholesale removal of *favelas* in the South End of the city, with families relocated to social housing projects such as *Cidade de Deus* in the then distant region of Barra (Silvestre 2016). This historical legacy has been repeated with the hosting of the 2016 Games contributing to the displacement of thousands of residents from *favelas* and low-income neighbourhoods.

The social impacts associated with the hosting of major events are extensive and well documented (Ritchie and Hall 1999; Lenskyj 2002, 2008; Silvestre 2008; Minnaert 2012; Hayes and Horne 2011), with the displacement of residents representing the most dramatic impact (Olds 1998; COHRE 2007; Porter *et al.* 2009; Rolnik 2009). The preparations for the Rio 2016 Games have accumulated a problematic track record in this respect, as substantial parts of, and in some cases entire, *favelas* have been removed to make way for the works associated with the Games. Faulhaber and Azevedo (2015) examined all the official requests for expropriation since Mayor Paes took office in 2009 and discovered a total of 20,229 households had been affected. The reasons for displacement included works for the Olympic Park, the BRT corridors, works carried out by the secretariat of housing and other secretariats, and those considered 'at risk'. The figure places Eduardo Paes' mandate as responsible for the largest number of evictions in Rio ever, ahead of even Lacerda and Passos.

The case of removal is even more dramatic when the experience of those affected is exposed. Silvestre and Oliveira (2012) documented the initial cases of displacement caused by works for the Transoeste BRT along Americas Avenida in the Barra Region, which became standard practice for other removals. After an area was declared for 'public utility' and a list of properties was published, city officials promptly visited a *favela* to inform residents of their eviction and to mark houses with painted signs (see Figure 1.6). 'SMH' – the initials of the housing department of Rio de Janeiro – was painted onto the walls of homes in *favelas* marked for demolition as 'a sort of officially sanctioned graffiti' (Bowater 2015).

Residents are oriented to either accept financial compensation, which only takes the built structure into account, or to be relocated to housing projects mostly situated in the city's western edge – otherwise they risk being left empty-handed. Compensation is often insufficient to acquire a similar dwelling, even at local *favelas*, and the move to distant social housing brings financial and social hardship due to added commuting costs and the abrupt rupture of the social fabric. Those who accept the municipality's offers have their

Figure 1.6 SMH sprayed on a house in Morro Providencia.

houses immediately cleared, leaving remaining residents to live among rubble and litter. Delay to compensate or relocate has exposed families to vulnerable situations, having to live with family and friends or being rendered homeless (Silvestre and Oliveira 2012).

In the first edition of this book we discussed the case of the *favela* of Vila Autódromo (Horne and Whannel 2012: 138–145) in some detail. Since 2010 one of us (JH) has visited Vila Autódromo on several occasions and interviewed residents and members of the residents' association. Official 'Rio 2016' discourse claims that the removal of the *favela* of Vila Autódromo is the only case directly linked with the Games (Anon 2012; Rio 2016 OCOG 2014). It is argued that infrastructure-induced displacement, such as the BRT corridors, are the result of policies that would be carried out regardless of hosting the event (Rio 2016 OCOG 2014). Vila Autódromo is located on the edge of the former Jacarepaguá Formula One circuit, initially settled by fishermen in the 1960s and expanded with the arrival of the workforce employed for the construction of the same circuit and nearby Riocentro convention centre in the following decade (see Figure 1.7).

Since the early 1990s the *favela* has been subject to continuous threats of removal, despite having their right to stay recognised by the state of Rio, the landowner of the circuit, in the 1990s. Ownership was transferred to the municipality in 1998 and since then the

Figure 1.7 Vila Autódromo 'Welcome to the community' sign.

threats intensified, first with the hosting of the Pan American Games and finally with the Olympic award. Since 2010 residents have fought against removal (see Figure 1.8).

The singular case of Vila Autódromo among other *favelas* prompted the assistance of local architecture and planning schools to help the residents' association to develop a

Figure 1.8 A banner in the residents association proclaiming the slogans 'Long live Vila Autódromo', 'Rio without forced removals', and 'Our community is not for sale!'

Figure 1.9 Celebration party for the award given to the alternative plan for Vila Autódromo.

bottom-up alternative proposal for the site's redevelopment (AMPVA 2012). In demonstrating that the upgrading of the *favela* did not compromise the work for the Olympic Park, and that it would cost less than the compensation and relocation to another site, the plan won the Deutsche Bank Urban Age Award in 2013 (Tanaka 2014; see Figure 1.9).

However, the municipality was adamant that it would clear the site, which was now included in the PPP contract for the development of the Olympic Park. Different reasons – ranging from exposure to natural hazards, environmental damage, event security, the construction of the Main Press Centre (MPC), the BRT corridor and the duplication of access roads – were alleged at different times without the details and plans being fully disclosing, despite public requests (Silvestre 2016). In contrast to the options offered for other displaced residents, relocation was to a housing project only 1.5 km away. However, the six-year-long intimidation process and the resulting psychological stress, common in other *favelas* subjected to similar removals and evictions, led most of the residents of Vila Autódromo to accept the deal, leaving only a small group to challenge the municipality's plan (see Figure 1.10).

In June 2015 violent clashes with the police gained world-wide attention with the remaining residents fighting for their right to stay. One Brazilian journalist commented: 'Já temos um

Figure 1.10 The demolition of Vila Autódromo.

vergonhoso recorde olímpico antes mesmo da abertura dos Jogos' ('We have a shameful Olympic record even before the opening of the Games').[6] Three months later, in October 2015, further 'lightning evictions' took place and more homes at Vila Autódromo were demolished, leaving fewer than 100 families where there used to be 600.[7]

CONCLUSION

The year 2014 marked several anniversaries for Brazil. It was 50 years since a military coup d'état brought about a 21-year period of dictatorship, and 29 years since its replacement and re-democratisation. During this time, and before, sport has remained firmly connected to politics in Brazil. When Lula became President in 2002 he inherited several problems from his predecessor, Fernando Henrique Cardoso. Public debt had doubled, the current account deficit was twice the average for South America, interest rates were over 20 per cent and the Brazilian currency was depreciating rapidly (Anderson 2011). While Lula introduced policies that materially impacted on the poorer sections of society, such as the 'Bolsa Familia', which involves a monthly cash transfer to poor mothers against proof that they were sending their children to school and getting regular health checks, he also became aware of the potential value of aligning with those interested in hosting sports mega-events.

What was initially thought of as a timely opportunity for domestic and foreign politics, as well as for personal benefit for those at the heart of the project, the 2014 FIFA World Cup turned into an anathema. Anger directed towards FIFA and their expected record profit from the mega-event affected the problematic reputation of the world governing body of football even more, while it continued to struggle with several corruption scandals. International press coverage highlighted many problems with the preparations for the event and the contrasts between the lavish stadiums and precarious social conditions of many Brazilians. However, the forecasts of a doomed event did not materialise, at least not from where it was expected. The press, FIFA, athletes and fans alike positively reviewed the general running of the event. Contrary to the scenes of the previous year, protests did not generate the same amount of support and were fewer and smaller, if still suppressed by a strong police presence. It was rather on the pitch that Brazilian hopes for some positive vision were crushed, including the biggest defeat in the history of the *seleção*, 7–1 by the eventual World Cup winners, Germany. As Alex Bellos (2014: 388–389) had noted before the competition:

> The parallels with 1950 are strong. Brazil has more swagger than it did but it remains an insecure country, desperate to show the world that it is a serious, competent and modern nation. Its own self image could again depend on a single goal.

Or, we might add with the benefit of hindsight, maybe 7!

In 2016, however, the Summer Olympic and Paralympic Games will take place in Rio, and so a second opportunity awaits Brazilian hosts to demonstrate to the world their capacity to stage the biggest multi-sport mega-event. As we have suggested, the global impacts on the local via urban politics (Sanchez *et al*. 2014) and globalisation brings with it an amplification of existing contradictions in society; in contemporary Rio this is especially the case (Barbassa 2015). Writing less than a year before the start of the Games, there are two contrasting views of progress towards the next Summer Olympics that also serve to highlight the contradictions of Rio 2016. Mayor Paes' election has rescued dreams of emulating Barcelona in the global South by associating mobility and urban regeneration projects with the Olympics. The mega-event puts particular emphasis on a wealthy area of the city, which despite representing the possibility of a more compact Games, has marginalised the rest of the city. Barra de Tijuca will strengthen its location as an urban zone with improved public transport access and new housing for the middle classes. However, not only will parts of the city be profoundly transformed, but Paes will also be responsible for having displaced more residents than former Mayor Passos and the Lacerda government of the dictatorship era. As in previous grand projects, the majority of the population living in the north and west zones, along with the Baixada, will continue to be overlooked and endure long commutes in crowded trains and buses.

The Brazilian Ministry of Sport announced in July 2015 that the Brazilian team campaign at the Pan American Games in Toronto succeeded in winning 41 gold medals and third place in the final medal table. The cost, an estimated BRL3.1 billion in public money between 2012 and June 2015, was half the investment for the Olympic cycle before the London Games. In the same month, a gathering in front of Rio's City Hall was being planned for 5 August 2015, one year before the opening of the Olympics in 2016, on the theme of 'Olimpíada Para Quem' ('Olympics for Whom?'). According to the organisers, the plenary was to protest against the neglect, disrespect and violations of human rights promoted by the Municipality of Rio de Janeiro, with the connivance of the IOC. Chega de violações! ('No more violations!') was one of the slogans of the organisers. Concerned that 'the city is sold as a luxury commodity for privileged groups', the event would mark the launch of a public campaign denouncing removals, human rights violations, repression of the work of street vendors, closing of public sport facilities, militarisation of the city, police violence, privatisation and public–private partnership agreements involving public facilities, street sweepers and the dismissal of teachers, treating sport as a business that favours large companies and contractors and real estate, and finally, the lack of transparency and participation. Capturing this mood, some academics have described the 2014 World Cup and the 2016 Olympics as 'Rio's ruinous mega-events' (Braathen *et al.* 2015).

NOTES

1 www.rio2016.com/en/faq/1784 (last accessed 31 July 2015).
2 www.rio2016.com/en/news/news/olympic-public-authority-publishes-rio-2016-games-matrix-of-responsibilities (last accessed 8 August 2015).
3 www.rio2016.com/en/news/news/olympic-public-authority-publishes-rio-2016-games-matrix-of-responsibilities (last accessed 28 July 2015).
4 www.brasil2016.gov.br/en/news/olympic-public-authority-apo-publishes-update-responsibility-matrix (last accessed 28 July 2015).
5 www.apo.gov.br/index.php/new-video-shows-construction-progress-at-barra-olympic-park (last accessed 28 July 2015).
6 http://blogdomariomagalhaes.blogosfera.uol.com.br/2015/07/28/editora-rebate-eduardo-paes-que-chamou-de-asneira-livro-sobre-remocoes (last accessed 28 July 2015).
7 www.rioonwatch.org/?p=24921 (last accessed 24 October 2015).

FURTHER READING

Barbassa, J. (2015) *Dancing with the Devil in the City of God: Rio de Janeiro on the Brink*, New York: Touchstone.
Braathen, E., Mascarenas, G. and Sorboe, C. (2015) 'Rio's ruinous mega-events', in P. Bond and A. Garcia (eds) *BRICS: An Anti-capitalist Critique*, London: Pluto, pp. 186–199.
Broudehoux, A.-M. (2016) 'Mega-events, urban image construction and the politics of exclusion', in R. Gruneau and J. Horne (eds) *Mega-Events and Globalization: Capital and Spectacle in a Changing World Order*, London: Routledge, pp. 113–130.

28

CHAPTER 2

LONDON, THE GAMES AND THE LEGACIES

In 2012 London staged the Olympic Games for the third time, the first city to do so. The facilities were built, in time and under budget, the transport systems worked smoothly, the sun came out and the host country won a large number of medals. Of course no one could have known, seven years earlier, when London was awarded the 2012 Games, that all would turn out well. In this chapter we chart the road to 2012, and survey the debates about legacy that are well underway.

On 6 July 2005, on a hot and humid night in Singapore, the International Olympic Committee (IOC) announced the winner – London had beaten Paris by 54 votes to 50. The following morning, in London, four bombs were exploded, apparently by jihadists – three on tube trains, one on a bus. It made for a sombre start to the journey towards 2012.

There were two main organisations involved in the London Games – the London Organising Committee for the Olympic Games (LOCOG) and the Olympic Delivery Authority (ODA). LOCOG was responsible for running the Games, while the ODA was responsible for the provision of the infrastructure. Olympic finances divide into two elements – the cost of running the Games and the cost of providing the facilities. The budget for running the Games assumes that a share of revenue from television, sponsorship, ticket sales, and merchandising will cover running costs. Infrastructure spending is provided by the host city and country.

The original estimate of £3.4 billion had rapidly soared, it emerged in 2007, to £9.3 billion.[1] This sum was four times as much as Sydney 2000, almost twice as much as Athens 2004, but one-third that of Beijing 2008. However, it can be difficult to compare costs (see Preuss 2004). Every Olympic Games has its own accounting conventions; the circumstances vary from country to country; and exchange rates and differing levels of inflation complicate the calculations. The extent to which Olympic-related infrastructural costs are included or excluded varies from Games to Games. Typically, governments will try to minimise the apparent costs by ensuring that some of the expenditure is hidden in general government budgets. It is clear, though, that there has been a steady rise, above inflation, since the Second World War, with some aberrations in this general pattern.

HOW DID LONDON COME TO BE AWARDED THE GAMES?

Since 1980, there were several attempts to bring the Olympic Games to the UK again. Indeed, the UK is only the second nation to be awarded a third Olympic Games, and

29

Year	City	Cost ($ millions)
1948	London	0.76
1956	Melbourne	5.4
1964	Tokyo	72
1968	Mexico City	176
1976	Montreal	1,500
1984	Los Angeles	412
1996	Atlanta	1,700
2000	Sydney	3,000
2004	Athens	7,200
2008	Beijing	40,000*
2012	London	13,500**

Figure 2.1 The cost of staging selected Summer Olympic Games, 1948–2012.

Source: CNBC *European Business*, March 2009.

Notes
Figures not adjusted for inflation.
* Estimate based on projected infrastructure investment in roads, railways, power and environmental projects.
** Projected budget.

London is the first city to stage a third Games. Over the years, 16 of the 29 Games awarded have been in Europe, and as yet Africa has not staged an Olympic Games.

Running an Olympic bid is a lengthy and expensive operation, which requires the cooperation and active support of both national and city governments. Obtaining such support requires delicate diplomacy and extensive lobbying. In the process, typically, a variety of separate interest groups with divergent agendas are drawn together. Staging an Olympic

Europe	Americas	Asia	Australasia/Oceania
Athens 1896	St Louis 1904	Tokyo 1964	Melbourne 1956
Paris 1900	Los Angeles 1932	Seoul 1988	Sydney 2000
London 1908	Mexico City 1968	Beijing 2008	
Stockholm 1912	Montreal 1976	Tokyo 2020	
Antwerp 1920	Los Angeles 1984		
Paris 1924	Atlanta 1996		
Amsterdam 1928	Rio de Janeiro 2016		
Berlin 1936			
London 1948			
Helsinki 1952			
Rome 1960			
Munich 1972			
Moscow 1980			
Barcelona 1992			
Athens 2004			
London 2012			

Figure 2.2 Cities staging the Summer Olympic Games, by continent.

The contemporary Olympics

Games requires extensive public investment in infrastructure. It is increasingly hard to justify this expenditure simply on the grounds of hosting a 15-day event, however global its appeal. So claims for long-term legacy have to be developed.

Governments and political parties may be attracted to the grandeur and high visibility, and to the potential positive impact on the unity and enthusiasm of the people as a whole. Urban planners may perceive an Olympic project, even if the bid is ultimately unsuccessful, as a means of uncorking funding for strategic projects – new road and rail links, industrial development and housing developments. Architects will be attracted by the possibility of commissions for iconic stadiums and other buildings. Builders and associated contractors will see the potential for large contracts. Local politicians will sense an opportunity for new parks and sporting facilities and for local employment. Most significantly, the establishment of new transport infrastructure and the high profile of the Olympic project attract associated development – speculative housing, industrial development and shopping malls. A well-managed Olympic bid will endeavour to bring together, sometimes in teeth-gritting harmony, all these elements.

It was not always thus. After Athens in 1896, the next three Olympics were staged as adjuncts to international exhibitions and trade fairs. It was not until the 1920s that the profile of the event began to grow. Governments began to perceive the Games as a display of national prowess – most notoriously in the 'Nazi' Olympics in 1936, a public promotion of Aryan supremacy and German power. In the Cold War era the Olympics became a symbolic battleground. The spread of television from the 1960s onwards escalated the public visibility of the Games and produced an ever-rising revenue stream. However, the costs of the Games also began growing. The Montreal Games in 1976 went so far over budget that the citizens were paying off the costs until the end of the century. Cities became reluctant to mount bids, and in the late 1970s the only bidders to stage the 1984 Games were Los Angeles and Tehran. The overthrow of the Shah of Iran in 1979 in an Islamic revolution brought an end to Iran's bid, leaving Los Angeles as the only bidder. The citizens of Los Angeles were so concerned about potential costs that they voted to deny the Games public money. Faced with no alternative bidder, the IOC was forced to accept the supposedly private Games, to be run by a private not-for-profit organising committee. It became vital for this committee, who would be personally liable for any losses, to minimise expenditure and tap new forms of revenue.

Los Angeles produced a myth – that the Olympic Games could break even, and even make a small 'surplus' (the IOC disapprove of the word 'profit'). In fact, there was extensive hidden public support in the form of transport infrastructure, policing and security. No Games since 1984 has successfully broken even, if the full costs are properly accounted for. The presentation of Olympic Games accounts systematically separates the cost of running the Games and the infrastructural costs involved in preparing for the Games. The accounts can show that the share of television rights payments, sponsorship revenue, ticket sales and other marketing received by the organising committee covers the cost of staging the Games. It does not, however, cover the costs, generally much larger, of building stadia and associated facilities, which must be borne by the hosting city and country. It is this consideration that has prompted careful thought and debate in countries proposing to bid to stage an Olympic Games. Decisions have to be taken as to whether such expenditure can be justified.

BRITISH OLYMPIC BIDS

London staged the 1908 Games, stepping in at relatively short notice after Italy withdrew. After the Second World War, London once again took up the challenge of staging a Games at short notice. In the context of war devastation, rationing and general shortages, the 1948 Olympics were staged as economically as possible, and have subsequently been dubbed the 'Austerity Games'. The UK did not again contemplate campaigning to stage the Games until the late 1970s. An abortive London bid to stage the 1988 Games presaged a series of failed bids, before eventual success in 2005.

The mythologising of the Los Angeles Games 'surplus' attracted far greater enthusiasm for bidding around the world. In the mid-1980s, six cities (Paris, Birmingham, Belgrade, Brisbane, Barcelona and Amsterdam) entered the race to stage the 1992 Olympic Games. Olympic insiders, though, were convinced that Barcelona would win, recognising the power and influence of IOC President Juan Antonio Samaranch, who was from Barcelona. The intense competition meant that budgets for bidding rose dramatically, with the cities spending an average of $10 million each. Lavish receptions were hosted, IOC members were showered with expensive gifts and free travel, and the culture that later led to IOC members being expelled for accepting inducements and bribes for votes began to take hold. In the event, the Games, as widely predicted, were awarded to Barcelona. The British candidate to host the 1996 and 2000 Games was Manchester, whose bidding team was led by Bob Scott, a flamboyant theatre entrepreneur, who acknowledged that 'If you put up Manchester . . . the world then comes to the conclusion that Britain has decided to send out its second XI and is not taking the competition seriously' (*Daily Telegraph* 26 May 2003).

Atlanta was awarded the 1996 Games and Sydney given the 2000 Games. The experience gained during these two Olympic bids fed into Manchester's successful bid to stage the 2002 Commonwealth Games, headed by Scott. It had become very clear during the 1990s that the IOC could only be attracted to the UK by a London bid.

A London bid?

The re-establishment of a London-wide authority, development strategies for East London and the Thames estuary region, and the development of the Channel Tunnel rail link were all relevant factors framing London's Olympic bid. The socially deprived area of East London had poor transport links and extensive derelict industrial sites. One of the biggest sites in the area, in Stratford, contained a railway yard, largely disused, a range of light industry, much of it derelict, and a complex network of rivers, canals, streams, sewer pipes and other waterways. The government began redeveloping the docklands during the 1980s, establishing the Docklands Development Corporation, and the 'Thames Gateway' scheme. The Channel Tunnel had opened in 1994, and the projected high-speed Channel Tunnel rail link, running through Stratford, was opened in 2007. By 1995 the Thames Gateway Task Force had drawn up plans for 30,000 new homes and 50,000 new jobs to be established in the 'Thames Corridor' by 2021 (Poynter 2005). London finally regained a form of central strategic body in 2000 with the creation of the Greater London Authority.

The British Olympic Association (BOA) decided in 1997 that if there was to be another UK bid, it would have to come from London (*Daily Telegraph* 26 May 2003). They commissioned a feasibility study, a 395-page document, published in 2001. It proposed sites in the west and east of London as options for the Olympic site, but London Mayor Ken Livingstone insisted that the East London option was the most viable because of the regeneration opportunity it created. By late 2001 the BOA and Livingstone agreed that a Wembley site was impractical and that, in Stratford, a stadium and village could be built close together and near good transport links (*Daily Telegraph* 9 October 2003). The proposed bid appeared to be massively popular with the public. In 2002 it enjoyed 82 per cent support and no region showed less than 75 per cent support (Karamichas 2013: 171). In May 2003, the government declared it would back the London bid.

In June 2003 Livingstone appointed Barbara Cassani as Chair of the 'Bidding Committee' (*Daily Telegraph* 9 October 2003). Cassani, an American, was former chief executive of the low-cost airline Go, but had little experience of the world of international sport organisation – which remains doggedly male, clubbish and rooted in late-night conviviality. Although Cassani was praised for her team-building work, she proved not to be adept at or enthusiastic about the necessary lobbying work. The full bid proposal was submitted in January 2004. By May the IOC announced the shortlist – London, Paris, New York, Madrid and Moscow. Cassani resigned, to be replaced by ex-Olympic medallist Sebastian Coe, now Lord Coe. It proved to be a key turning point. Coe's knowledge of the world of sport organisation in general and the IOC in particular was a considerable asset. As an ex-Conservative MP, he also knew how to operate in Westminster circles. The fact that IOC ex-President Samaranch had great affection for him was also an advantage. For the last year before the vote, the London bid was steered and managed with confidence and shrewdness.

The political context of the London bid made for potential tensions between political parties, between city and country and between sport organisations and political organisations. These tensions were best embodied in the three figures of Sebastian Coe (as noted, an ex-Conservative MP), Tessa Jowell (a Labour MP and Blair loyalist) and Ken Livingstone (a left-wing maverick). It speaks volumes about the enormous symbolic power of an Olympic bid that this frail coalition was able to hold together.

A concerted campaign began to build and maintain public support, as any suggestion of an ambivalent or hostile public can damage the chances of success. The final bidding document was presented to the IOC in November 2004. During the first half of 2005 the IOC Evaluation Committee visited all the remaining bidding cities. By June 2005 it was clear that London and Paris were ahead of Madrid and New York, but not by much.

It is always hard to interpret IOC votes, given the small unrepresentative electorate, and the secret ballot. Candidate cities have just over 100 delegates to lobby. There have been allegations of corruption since the 1980s, when banquets, lavish gifts, free air travel and other perks were showered on IOC members. Eventually, associated with the Salt Lake City bid for the Winter Games, bribery allegations were substantiated and several IOC members were expelled. Faced with such a public humiliation, the IOC had to introduce more stringent regulations to try to curb the excesses. Nevertheless, it is clear that a lot can happen behind the scenes that does not become public. The line at which hard-nosed

33

political dealing becomes corrupt can be a blurred one, not least because of the non-representative and secret nature of the decision-making process, which, in theory at least, would allow an IOC member to offer his vote to several candidate cities.

All that said, London produced a very credible plan, submitted a thorough and convincing bid (apart from the questionable financial plan) and by all accounts staged an impressive presentation. The bid has to be of a high technical standard, the IOC has to be assured of a high level of enthusiasm in a bidding city and the presentation should impress. These things, however, can avoid failure but not in themselves assure success. Members and their wives (for the vast majority of members, still, are male) are likely to favour spending two weeks (in highly pampered circumstances, in the finest hotels, with luxury travel) in an attractive city. London has become an attractive city – but so is Paris.

The very well planned use of then Prime Minister Tony Blair may also have had a last-minute influence. The Olympic Session came at a very awkward time for world leaders, coinciding as it did with the G8 Conference in Scotland. But whereas Chirac paid only a fleeting visit to Singapore, Blair devoted a whole day to an exhausting series of 15-minute meetings with key IOC members. He was meticulously briefed by the London team, who were full of praise for his efforts; for example he made time to give an interview to Olympic insider website 'Around the Rings' (see Sugden and Tomlinson 2012: 7). It was strangely like a Sebastian Coe race – a few problems at the beginning, then gradually becoming well positioned and putting in a devastating late sprint.

RUNNING THE GAMES

All Olympic Games organisers face the same problem: when the bid is won they begin their work in the bright sunshine of great publicity, but then for the next six years they have to face a blizzard of critical coverage. For much of the build-up there are generally only two storylines – that facilities will not be ready on time, and that everything will cost too much. Major construction work included stadia (main stadium, aquatic centre, velodrome, hand-ball arena), the Media Centre and International Broadcasting Centre, and the Olympic Village (*Guardian* 3 July 2009). In 2007 the *Evening Standard* (28 February 2007) ran a dramatic front page which proclaimed 'OLYMPICS BILL SOARS TO £10bn'. It triggered a political storm, and the impression was created that the original budget had been a slipshod affair, possibly put together by people who did not really believe they were likely to win.

At the Closing Ceremony of the 2008 Beijing Olympic Games in August the Olympic Flag was passed from the Mayor of Beijing to the (new) Mayor of London, Boris Johnson, and London moved into the spotlight. The world financial crisis began to unfold, and the impact of incalculable levels of toxic debt forced governments around the world to allocate unprecedented sums to prop up the banking system. Although the recession clearly created additional problems for the London Games, it also had some positive aspects in presentational terms. The recession presented a scapegoat. Any further cost over-runs or cuts in the scope of plans could be blamed on the unpredicted financial crisis. In 2007, £10 billion appeared to the public a huge sum, which it is, but once the governments of the world had found it necessary to commit massive amounts to bail out the banks, £10 billion seemed a rather trivial sum by comparison.

The London 2012 Olympic Games encountered relatively little opposition from protest groups. Their main concerns were the high cost; the role of corporate sponsors; seizure of space for Olympic purposes; and excessive Olympics-induced security (see Boykoff 2014b). The few diverse groups that were active had a range of issues but never really found an effective common framework. Protests over the Manor Farm Allotments and the Clays Lane housing estate gained some exposure. The more imaginative protests, generated by local artists and documented in *The Art of Dissent* (Powell and Marrero-Guillamón 2012), took place along and in relation to the 11-mile blue fence that encircled the site during construction (also see Chapter 10).

For much of 2012 the apparent mood of expectation seemed tinged with anxieties over security, transport congestion and organisation. In the last few days the sun came out, the Opening Ceremony was widely admired, transport systems coped admirably and once Team GB started winning medals the mood became euphoric. The Games were broadly seen as a success – facilities produced on time and under budget, systems all worked properly, organisation was smooth, the volunteers won warm praise and the UK won

Figure 2.3
Jessica Ennis poster in Oxford Street (2012), towering over onlookers. Jessica Ennis was, both metaphorically and literally, the 'poster girl' of the London 2012 Games.

35

plenty of medals. Oppositional voices were muted, although research carried out on East Midlands respondents detected some criticism. Some respondents felt it was an elite, south of England, middle-class event for which tickets were too expensive. Others felt McDonald's sponsorship was inappropriate (see Mackintosh *et al.* 2015). Overall, though, all the evidence suggested that the public warmly received the event.

Responses, judgements and assessments

In a subsequent government review, the London 2012 Olympic Games and Paralympic Games were pronounced

> a resounding success . . . the construction programme was delivered on time and within budget, and the Games themselves ran extremely smoothly . . . the opening and closing ceremonies were very well received and the contribution of tens of thousands of volunteers has been widely and rightly praised.
> (House of Commons Committee of Public Accounts 2013)

The main problematic issue highlighted by the review was security, described as a 'notable blemish' and 'a sorry episode'.

According to security consultant Hugo Rosemont, G4S initially contracted to provide 2,000 personnel, among other services, but in December 2011 it signed a 'variation of the contract' to increase the requirement of new staff on the company to 10,400 officers. On 11 July 2012, G4S informed the authorities that it would be unable to supply all of the 10,400 officers it was contracted for. The Home Affairs Select Committee (HASC) concluded that the blame for the failure to deliver the contract to supply sufficient numbers of venue security staff for the London 2012 Olympic Games lies 'firmly and solely' with private security company G4S. Rosemont argues that while G4S were blamed, the government needed to shoulder some of the responsibility. The 'delays in establishing an accurate picture of the number of staff who would be required' were not the responsibility of G4S. It was the government, not G4S, who were ultimately accountable for the Games' security (Rosemont 2012).

In the *Daily Telegraph*'s 2013 account, in March 2011 G4S had contracted to be the official security services provider for London 2012, providing training and management for the 10,000-strong security workforce. By December, the government announced that 23,700 security guards, double the original estimate, would be needed. The security budget had now risen from £282m to £553m. G4S's management fee rose from £7.3m to £60m. On 11 July 2012, a fortnight before the start of the Games, G4S announced that it would be unable to deliver all the numbers needed, forcing Defence Secretary Philip Hammond to allocate 3,500 soldiers to the Games. After extensive negotiations, G4S subsequently had to pay around £70m in compensation, and in May 2013 Chief Executive Nick Buckles resigned (*Daily Telegraph* 21 May 2013).

The House of Commons Committee of Public Accounts took a dim view of all this, judging that the security costs were massively under-budgeted before 2011, and that G4S failed to deliver fully on their commitment, which required the Police and Army to step in at very short notice. The 2007 Public Sector Funding Package had contained no specific provision for venue security, and there was just £29 million in LOCOG's own budget (House of Commons, 2013). LOCOG, the Home Office and the Department for Culture, Media and Sport all claimed that estimates had been made on best information available at the time, that the over-riding security regime changed in the years running up to the Games and that detailed operational planning could only take place in 2011 once the detail of venue specifications and event scheduling was known. The Commons Accounts Committee remained unconvinced by these arguments.

On ticketing, the House of Commons Accounts Committee expressed concern at the large number of unused accredited seats and the small proportion available to the public for major events. Only 51 per cent of tickets for the men's 100 metres final were available to the UK public and only 47 per cent of tickets for the track cycling. On unused accredited seats, the Committee believed that the 12–15 per cent set aside proved to be excessive and the empty seats added to the disappointment of those who could not buy tickets for sold-out events. It suggested that the demands of international sports bodies and media organisations for large numbers of accredited seats should be challenged (House of Commons Committee of Public Accounts 2013). Apart from the issues of security and ticketing, however, the official verdict on the staging of the Games was largely very positive.

But how much did it really cost?

The mantra that the Games came in on time and under budget has been repeated often enough that it has come to seem accepted common sense. But all may not be as it seems. Confusion has been engineered between the original budget in the bid book and the revised budget revealed in 2007. In November 2012 a House of Lords Library Note summarised the position by saying that official estimates of the cost of hosting the Olympics had more than doubled, from the time the bid was made to the present day. (House of Lords Library, 2012). In 2003 the total costs were estimated at £4 billion – £2.992 billion core Olympic costs plus £1.044 billion for infrastructure on the Olympic Park. It was planned that these costs would be covered by a public sector funding package of £2.375 billion for the core Olympic costs, £1.044 billion Exchequer funding for the infrastructure, plus an anticipated £738 million from the private sector. However, in 2007 the revised budget totalled £9.325 billion. The National Audit Office noted that public sector funding had almost tripled, while private sector contributions had fallen to less than 2 per cent. On 23 October 2012 the government calculated that the final costs of the Olympics would be £8.921 billion, a saving of £377 million on the £9.298 billion budget (House of Lords Library 2012).

However, the House of Commons Public Accounts Committee report in 2012 suggested that the overall cost to the public purse would be £11 billion due to significant public sector costs not included in the Public Sector Funding Package. These costs included £766 million to purchase the Olympic Park land and around £826 million for legacy projects and expenditure on Games-related activities by government departments (House of Lords Library 2012). Sky Sports (January 2012) estimated a £12 billion cost, based on including a range of extra public spending such as more anti-doping control officers, the torch relay, paying Tube workers not to strike, the cost of the Olympic Park Legacy Company, legal bills over the stadium tenancy decision, extra cash to UK Sport and legal costs associated with land purchases. In addition, if the calculations also included additional policing costs, transport projects and counter-terrorism efforts, the Olympics cost over £24 billion, ten times the original calculation (House of Lords Library 2012).

Olympic accounting presents problems – for over 40 per cent of the Games staged since 1960 there is no clear final budget figure: 'for 41 per cent of Olympic Games between 1960 and 2010 no one asked how well the budget held for these Games, thus hampering learning regarding how to develop more reliable budgets for the Games' (Flyvbjerg and Stewart 2012). One thing is clear though: every Games, without exception, has experienced cost overruns, averaging 179 per cent in real terms. In fact, Flyvbjerg and Stewart (2012) say cost overruns in the Olympic Games appear to be substantially higher than in other types of mega-projects. Their research found average cost overruns in major transportation projects of between 20 and 45 per cent, and similar studies on major IT projects found average overruns of 27 per cent, both in real terms. Their data appear to show that cost overruns have decreased over time. For Games after 1999, cost overruns are significantly less than for Games before 1999. However, London 2012 appears to be reversing the trend. It is not self-evident that the claim that the London 2012 Games were brought in under budget entirely stands up to close scrutiny.

THE TROUBLING QUESTION OF LEGACIES

So if the Games themselves were judged a success, the issue switches to the legacy – are there long-term benefits in return for the £10 billion expenditure, and if so, what are they and how might they be assessed? As far as government is concerned, although many central and local government organisations have responsibility for projects in the legacy programme, the Cabinet Office is responsible for coordinating and assuring delivery of the legacy as a whole. The Commons Accounts Committee declared that it is important that the Cabinet Office provides strong leadership to maintain momentum and focus (House of Commons Committee of Public Accounts 2013).

The most important thing to understand about 'legacy' is that it is a profoundly ideological term – it has become necessary, when hosting mega-events, to claim that *there will be a legacy*. It is politically almost impossible to justify spending £10–20 billion for a month-long party, however lavish – there have to appear to be long-term benefits too. Sebastian Coe himself was quite clear on the issue in 2006, when he declared: 'Legacy is absolutely epi-central to the plans for 2012. Legacy is probably nine-tenths of what this process is about, not just 16 days of Olympic sport.'[2] However, by 2012 he was also clear that deliverance was not his responsibility:

> I don't want this to sound like this is not my job, but actually it isn't. We created the best platform in living memory to create the environment for that to happen. This begins after 2012. We finish and go off and do whatever we do.[3]

Here, then, is the dilemma – for all the fine promises of legacy, when the circus leaves town, the organising committee shuts up shop, the budget for staging the Games has been used up, and all too often in the past no public bodies are prepared to shoulder the responsibilities, and more significantly the costs, of ensuring that legacy promises can be fulfilled. Legacy is at its root an ideological concept – it is constructed as a vision of what can happen in the future. By the time any meaningful judgements can be made, the original proponents have left the stage. Vijay (2015) refers to 'the stark contradiction between the *temporary* nature of the Games and the supposed *permanence* of their effects'. He recognises that it is precisely because

> the Olympics are so temporary, so costly, so obviously unsustainable, and even ruinous that they must lay claim to the temporal ground of legacy, sustainability, certainty, and permanence, with the rhetoric of the legacy justifying and occasioning the creation of the Games.
>
> (Vijay 2015: 441)

While the IOC approves of the concept of legacy and likes it to be present in a bid, the proposed legacy is not a major factor in the success of a bid. The IOC is primarily concerned that the Games are successful – aesthetically, competitively and commercially. They desire that the value of the Olympic brand is enhanced and its value to television and sponsors – the main paymasters – is enhanced or at least maintained. They hope thereby that adequate numbers of cities will, in the future, be prepared to spend the millions required to mount bids to stage the Games. If, through choice of city, the prestige of the Games and the IOC, and their relevance to globalising processes and the geopolitical environment, can be asserted, all the better. This is not to say that there are, or will be, no relevant legacies – but it is to assert that, given the need to establish an ideology of legacy, that any such claims to legacy should be subject to close scrutiny.

Horne (2016) argues that London was the first true 'legacy' Olympics. The IOC had not used the concept widely before, staging its first conference on legacy in 2002, just two years before London submitted its bid book. Since then, he suggests, it has become essential that a bidding city spell out at the bid stage how legacy will be implemented. Horne (2016) also suggests two distinctions with respect to legacies when considering the political implications – that they can be *tangible* and *intangible*, and also *universal* and *selective* (for further discussion see Cashman and Horne 2013). Legacies related to sports mega-events can be tangible, related to changes to the material infrastructure or economic performance of the city or nation, or intangible, for example emotional responses to a mega-event, whether individual or collective.

> Tangible legacies refer to substantial and long standing changes to the urban infrastructure – the building of iconic stadia being one of the most notable when it comes to sports mega-events. The intangible legacies of sports mega-events refer predominantly to popular memories, evocations and analyses of specific moments and incidents associated with an event.
>
> (Horne 2016)

Legacies can also be *selective* and *universal*:

> *Selective legacies* are particular, individualist, and elitist, and tend to serve the interests of those dominating powerful political and economic positions in society. *Universal legacies* are communal, collectivist, and inherently democratic, available

to all by virtue of being made freely accessible. A problem for sports mega-events is that they largely generate *tangible legacies* that are *selective* and *intangible legacies* that are *universal*.

(Horne 2016)

The first problem is to establish precisely what legacy promises were made, which involves distinguishing between firm and specific commitments, for which it might well eventually be possible to assess the degree of success; and the more vague, ill-defined rhetorical claims, which can rarely be neatly assessed. There are the promises made in the bid book, those made during the campaign, and those outlined in the framework as redefined by the government. These were the five legacy promises that the government declared, in the government's Legacy Action Plan (LAP), which constitute one yardstick by which we might assess post-Games developments:

- making the UK a world-leading sporting nation;
- transforming the heart of East London;
- inspiring a new generation of young people to take part in volunteering, cultural and physical activity;
- making the Olympic Park a blueprint for sustainable living;
- demonstrating that the UK is a creative, inclusive and welcoming place to live in, visit and for business.

An additional sixth legacy promise was added later in recognition of London 2012, involving both the Summer Olympic and Paralympic Games – 'to develop the opportunities and choices for disabled people' (see Cashman and Horne 2013: 54–55).

An interesting question to ask is how, if at all, such statements can be falsified – how, for example, might evidence clearly indicate that the UK is or is not 'a creative, inclusive and welcoming place'? There was a 2013 report, *Meta-Evaluation of the Impacts and Legacy of the London 2012 Olympic Games*, offering an assessment to the Department of Culture, Media and Sport (DMCS), with extensive detail. However, you only have to read the relentlessly upbeat tone of the chapter headings to sense that the whole enterprise was geared to search for positive evidence:

1 The Games have provided a substantial boost to the UK economy
2 More of us are participating in sport because of the Games
3 The Games inspired a generation of children and young people
4 The Games were the catalyst for improved elite sporting performance in the UK
5 The Games supported the growth of the UK tourism industry
6 The Games set new standards for sustainability
7 The Games improved attitudes to disability and provided new opportunities for disabled people to participate in society
8 Communities across the UK engaged with the Games
9 The Games have increased enthusiasm for volunteering
10 The Games accelerated the physical transformation of East London
11 Socio-economic change in East London has been shaped by the Games
12 The Games delivered many strategic benefits and lessons learnt

(Source: Grant Thornton UK, 2013)

So, it's all good! Except that in 2014 National Public Radio published a rather devastating critique. The report, they acknowledged, concluded that by last summer Britain had already earned at least $1 billion more than the $15 billion it spent on the 2012 Summer Games. Forecasts for the future went into the tens of billions of dollars. The government commissioned the report in a $2 million contract with the firm Grant Thornton. Peer reviewer Stefan Szymanski (Professor of Sports Management and Economics at the University of Michigan) told NPR, 'I thought this was tantamount to a whitewash. . . . The report provided a very bullish view, refused to comment on any of the negatives, or even to really qualify any of the results, and I was very unhappy about this.' Szymanski was sent the final draft with one week to make comments, and was not allowed to access the underlying economic model, which Szymanski regarded as 'extremely unusual'. Szymanski contacted the author of the report to say that he was uncomfortable about 'the triumphalist tone of the report, which does not reflect what the data is saying'. Szymanski, who was the only person with expertise in statistical number crunching who looked at this study before it was published, described it as a 'political document' that ignored extensive economic research showing Olympics are almost always unprofitable (Shapiro 2014). This critique has not received the wider circulation it warrants.

In fact, the Olympic operation from 2004 onwards appears to have been a massively successful exercise in news management with only a few glitches. The revelation of the tripling of the budget could have been handled better, but the under-budget claim has escaped serious scrutiny to become accepted common sense. With reference to the main stadium, the relative absence of negative publicity about the total failure to consider end usage properly at an early stage is striking. Some promises are not assessed, but simply disappear from the discussion. For example, the London Olympic Institute, proposed, with much publicity in June 2005, had, by 2011, been abandoned and airbrushed from history so effectively that it is now hard to unearth how events unfolded. By 2013 the plan to open an Olympic Museum also appeared to have been dropped.[4] The London Pleasure Gardens, an entertainment complex on the Royal Albert Dock, designed to appeal to crowds leaving the Excel arenas, into which Newham Council invested £3 million, went into liquidation on 3 August 2012, less than five weeks after opening (*Newham Recorder* 3 August 2012).

One sensed at times an almost paranoiac desire to micro-manage impressions. One of us wrote a piece for a collection on London 2012 being overseen by LOCOG. Lengthy memos were sent detailing things that could not be stated. It was not allowed, bizarrely, to describe Ken Livingstone as a 'left-wing maverick', although (prior to Jeremy Corbyn's rise to prominence as Labour Party leader in 2015) a Google search for 'left wing maverick' invariably returned the name Ken Livingstone. The LOCOG overseer of the project also insisted that it could not be said that Mike Lee had written a particular Sebastian Coe speech. But the submitted chapter had made no such claim, and indeed did not even allude to the speech. A hidden hand, it was subsequently confirmed to us, was managing the news with forensic detail, and, we would suggest, considerable paranoia.

Once the games concluded, LOCOG and the ODA effectively wound up their operations. Responsibility for legacy was handed to a new body – the London Legacy Development Corporation, formed in April 2012. This body defined its responsibilities as 'the creation

41

of Queen Elizabeth Olympic Park to develop a dynamic new heart for east London, creating opportunities for local people and driving innovation and growth in London and the UK'. The Legacy Corporation, then, is responsible for 'the long-term planning, development, management and maintenance of the Park and its impact on the surrounding area after the London 2012 Games'.[5] The Mayor of London has indicated that he considers the Games, and ensuring their legacy, 'will be London's single most important regeneration project for the next 25 years' (DCLG 2015).

One of the problems of assessing legacy is that so many people seem to be doing it – the London Development Agency (LDA), Greater London Authority (GLA) and the DCMS, as well as the London 2012 Host Boroughs. In March 2015 the Department for Communities and Local Government published the *London 2012 Olympics Regeneration Legacy Evaluation Framework*, written by AMION Consulting Limited, the purpose of which was to develop a bespoke Evaluation Framework for the regeneration legacy impacts of the London 2012 Olympics and Paralympic Games. The report recognises that it will be necessary to consider how to integrate this Framework with the other London 2012 regeneration evaluation initiatives that are being undertaken, and acknowledged that answers would not be fully available for several years. True enough, although three years after 2012 seems a rather slow start on devising a framework. In 2015 much of the rhetoric seems still to be about the future, while cutbacks in local authority finance bite right down to the bone. It is possible, sometimes, to get the sense that beneath the grandiose talk and endless maze of evaluations, frameworks and overviews, nothing much is happening to transform the lives of the local community.

The Olympic facilities

According to the IOC, most Olympic venues will be available for both elite and community sporting events after the Games: the Olympic Stadium will host cultural and community events as well as the 2017 World Athletics Championships; the Aquatics Centre will be open to clubs, schools and the general public, as well as elite athletes; the Copper Box will become a multi-use sports centre for the community, and a venue for elite training and competition; and Eton Manor will become a major community sports centre, featuring football pitches, tennis courts and a hockey centre (IOC 2012). On the face of it, then, this is a very positive scenario. The swimming pool has indeed been opened to the public for reasonable prices. It is a beautiful design; but elegant though it is, the building may not be without flaws – the LLDC is currently (autumn 2015) advertising a contract to supply anti-glare blinds for the west side. The high roof and resultant extra heating costs may mean that it is expensive to maintain – only time will tell.[6]

One of the biggest problems of Olympic legacy over the years has proved to be the subsequent use of the major facilities, and especially the main stadium. Famously, the Montreal public only finished paying for the 1976 Games in 2006, and only in the last few years has the main stadium there begun to find a purpose after many attempts and two changes of roof. The hard reality is that very few cities can actually find enough events to fill an 80,000-seat stadium on a regular basis. Only top-level football, in a very few cities, has this crowd-pulling ability. So around the world, Olympic and other mega-event facilities are under-used, under-funded or semi-derelict. The 2004 Olympics in Athens

42

Figure 2.4 The Aquatics Centre, seen from the ArcelorMittal Tower. The elegant lines of architect Zaha Hadid could not be fully appreciated during the games due to banks of extra seating on either side, since removed.

left the country saddled with more than a dozen once-glorious sporting venues that are now abandoned or barely used – yet still cost millions for upkeep and security. Huge cost overruns contributed to the debt woes that have wrecked the Greek economy.

(Newman 2012)

The iconic venues of the Beijing Olympics in 2008, the Bird's Nest and Water Cube, are also under-used today. Newman argues that the need 'to showcase thousands of athletes competing in more than two dozen sports may simply be incompatible with smart economic development' (Newman 2012). Surprisingly, even in the Candidature File (the so-called bid book) submitted in 2004, despite copious details on many aspects of the Games, the commitments to legacy are couched in relatively general terms.

The main stadium

The sad story of the mismanagement of the main stadium is a catalogue of errors. The original plans seem to have given little or no thought to an end-user. Even when the idea crystallised that it should be a largely temporary structure, to be reduced to a 25,000-seat stadium after the Games, largely for the use of athletics, the plan seemingly did not get proper critical scrutiny; the most basic knowledge of the audience for athletics would show that athletics events could not provide the regular revenues needed to set against main-tenance costs. As long ago as 2006/2007, a memo from Newham Council suggested that the stadium should have a football club end-user, that 25,000 was too small, and that West Ham would be an appropriate end-user.[7] Sebastian Coe's determination to retain an athletics track is, given his own history, utterly understandable. However, heart ruled the head, and there was a failure to learn from the previous attempt to combine athletics and football at Wembley, and the problems associated with the never-realised Pickett's Lock stadium plans.

Even when it had become obvious to most observers that the only viable end-user was a major football team, that realistically there were only two possible candidates, that talks

43

Figure 2.5 The Olympic stadium, with modified roof, seen from the ArcelorMittal Tower in June 2015.

might usefully be held at an early stage, in order that a stadium design might accommodate both the needs of an Olympic Stadium and a subsequent football stadium, nothing meaningful was done to alter the original stadium plans. Once a football end-user was agreed, a long, elaborate, yet poorly considered tendering process ended in litigation that sabotaged the original scheme of a football club as co-owner. Instead, the tenancy was handed to West Ham at a bargain basement cost, in circumstances that would require extensive and expensive modifications to remake the stadium.

A new company, E20, a joint venture between LLDC and Newham Council, had to be set up to manage the stadium. E20 awarded a £154m contract to Balfour Beatty to convert the Olympic Stadium (*Evening Standard* 6 January 2014: 43). Newham made a £40m loan to the project as its share of the costs. The tenancy agreement eventually agreed appears to have offered West Ham very favourable terms. West Ham will pay £2.5m rent and a one-off fee of £15m (*Guardian* 7 January 2014: 21). The existing capacity of Upton Park is 35,345, and in season 2014/2015 the average crowd was 34,871. To make a rough calculation, assuming an average ticket price of £35 this would yield revenues of around £1,220,000 per match, about £23m per season. If they increased their average crowd to 54,000 this would yield revenues of around £1,900,000 per match, about £35m per season. This equates to extra revenue of £12m against rent of £2.5m. Even if average crowds only went up to 40,000, extra revenue would still be £3m, comfortably above the rental. Once again, public investment has fed into private profit. At present the actual details of the contract are secret, although an FOI request for disclosure has been submitted, and an appeal against disclosure has been filed. Meanwhile, West Ham's current ground, Upton Park, will be demolished to make way for a luxury development that will include *no* social housing.

The small sum being paid in rent seems barely enough to cover the upkeep and maintenance of the stadium – it costs £11m per year to maintain the Birds Nest stadium in Beijing. As David Conn has argued, 'The real Olympic legacy winners, of course, are West Ham United . . . Karren Brady . . . negotiated this stadium deal of the century with

Figure 2.6 'What's next?' poster outside Olympic stadium in June 2015, portraying fans of West Ham United FC, the new tenants of the stadium.

London's mayor, Boris Johnson, and has since been made a Conservative peer – Baroness Brady of Knightsbridge' (David Conn, *Guardian*, 8 April 2015). The Balfour Beatty contract, of course, is only part of the extra expenditure – according to *The Economist*, around £250m has been pumped into renovating the stadium, and the government has now pledged another £141m to the Olympicopolis – a cultural and educational district on the Queen Elizabeth Olympic Park (*The Economist* 4 August 2015). A new charity, Foundation for FutureLondon, has been created to help realise the potential of Olympicopolis and Queen Elizabeth Olympic Park. The charity aims to ensure, through the promotion of arts, culture, science and education, that the arrival of world-class institutions can successfully raise expectation and aspiration and provide the stepping stones towards a wider aspiration for East London. The Foundation for FutureLondon will work closely with the partners of the 'Olympicopolis' project on Stratford Waterfront – home to a new branch of the Victoria and Albert Museum, a new campus for the University of the Arts London, a new theatre for Sadler's Wells and possibly the first permanent home for the Smithsonian Institution outside the US. The charity will also work with University College London on its new campus to the south of the ArcelorMittal Orbit structure.

Figure 2.7 The RUN sculpture, June 2015, in front of the Copper Box.

The Legacy List, launched in 2011 to build on the arts and cultural legacy of the London 2012 Olympic and Paralympic Games, will merge with the Foundation for FutureLondon and will continue to deliver an arts and culture programme on the Park and locally. Some members of The Legacy List's Board will move to become Trustees of the Foundation.[8] However, it is striking how many of these plans are still in the future, even after ten years to prepare. The Media Centre, for example, is still seeking tenants to fill its considerable floor space. The ArcelorMittal Orbit, a tower-like viewing platform, lost £520,000 in 2014–2015, a loss of £10,000 per week (LLDC Annual Report 2014–2015). The Olympic Park has some very elegant landscaped gardening, but of a type that will prove to be very high maintenance.

The major problem with the spending of large sums on iconic Olympic facilities is very clear and has been for many years. If the aim were to build facilities that are needed in the long term, for spectator sport and/or communal use, you would simply not build the sort of facilities that are constructed for most Olympic Games. The main stadium for London was designed without any proper consideration of the needs of a potential end-user, resulting in a very expensive refit. The swimming pool may win many design awards, but the high ceiling and resultant extra cubic metres of air that needs to be heated in turn means expensive maintenance costs. If participation is the legacy aim, then the money might better have been spent on cheaper pools throughout the country, or maintaining and subsidising our many existing pools.

The local community

In the bid rhetoric, the local community loomed large. It is certainly the case that the inner-city boroughs of the East End of London are among the poorest in the country. According to the Gini co-efficient, which measures degrees of equality/inequality in a country, the UK shows up as worse than almost any other developed country. According to IMF economists, nearly 30 per cent of income went to the top 5 per cent of earners. The OECD says that the UK has the worst social mobility of developed nations (Karamichas 2013: 169). So plenty needs to be done. Newham has the highest overcrowding rate in the country at 25 per cent, the third highest child poverty rates in London, the second highest unemployment rates and one-third of its residents are in low-paid work – the highest proportion of any London borough.[9] There is a chronic shortage of social rental housing in the area (Watt 2013). Two 'Olympic Boroughs' – Newham and Dagenham and Redbridge – have the lowest physical activity rates in the whole of England, with 39 per cent and 38 per cent of people physically inactive (Campbell 2014).

According to the IOC, locating the Games in East London revitalised an industrial wasteland and set the stage for future economic growth. Prior to construction, the ODA excavated and cleaned more than 2.3 million cubic metres of contaminated soil and the UK government have invested £300 million to transform the Olympic site into the 'Queen Elizabeth Olympic Park', which will include housing, new schools, health centres, business space and sports venues (IOC 2012). Assessing legacy properly cannot be done for a decade, but it is worth reviewing the situation in East London.

Housing

The bid claimed that 'the legacy would lead to the regeneration of an entire community for the direct benefit of everyone who lives there', but the actual commitments and specific details were vague (see Bernstock 2014: 195). The IOC proclaimed that the Olympic Village would be converted into more than 2,800 flats, and five new neighbourhoods would be established around the Park, to include 11,000 residences, one-third of which would be affordable housing (IOC 2012). However, this figure of 2,800 marked a significant reduction from the 2004 GLA plan for up to 4,600 homes. Bernstock (2014) said that the actual legacy linked to the Athletes' Village had been substantially reduced. Undoubtedly the East Village development could be a very pleasant place to live. It has green spaces and, thanks to money spent by its developers on surveillance and security, very low crime. It is also eerily quiet, as its streets are not really a route between any other places – and with many of the young professionals who have moved in out at work all day there is little passing trade and therefore not much to encourage the promised retail businesses to move in.

Additional housing is certainly needed in East London. According to *The Economist*, Newham and Tower Hamlets, among the poorest local authorities in the country, have the fastest population growth in London, rising by 39 per cent and 45 per cent between 2001

47

Figure 2.8 East Village Living shop window (June 2015) promoting attractions to come when buildings are occupied.

and 2015. The East Village development is divided equally between social and private housing, but the other developments are mostly private: in Chobham Manor, only 28 per cent of homes will be 'affordable' and as 'the government's definition of affordable has risen to 80% of the market rent, few locals will be able to stump up the cash' (*The Economist* 4 August 2015). Eighty per cent of the market rent equates to 40–50 per cent of median income (around £28,000) of residents of the Olympic Boroughs.

The poorest residents may have little hope of benefiting from the new homes on the Olympic Park, and are more likely to be victims of the growing class cleansing being forced by government policies. In 2014, 29 young single mothers and mums-to-be were facing eviction from the Focus E15 foyer nearby – a temporary social housing block with skills and childcare provision on hand. The London Borough of Newham has suggested they consider leaving the city and moving to Hastings or Birmingham. If these offers are rejected, the mothers can be declared 'intentionally homeless' and forgotten altogether (GamesMonitor 3 February 2014).

Across London, a social cleansing process is underway, driven by a chronic shortage of cheap housing, sharp rent increases in the private rented sector, government cuts to benefit caps and other changes to the welfare system. Councils in affluent areas routinely arrange to house their homeless in poorer boroughs. This increases the pressure on housing stock and the poorer boroughs resort to moving families out of London altogether. During 2015, at least 20 London boroughs moved poor families out to places such as Luton, Basildon, Thurrock and Milton Keynes (BBC News 26 October 2015).

The success of the Olympics led to a wave of speculative building, and increases in property values in the area make it more attractive to affluent outsiders. An estate agent quoted in the *Daily Telegraph* (2 March 2012) said

> In the longer term it is possible that we will see increasing amounts of overseas wealth flowing into the area, not just from investors buying new-build properties

48

but also 'displaced' west Londoners taking the value of their property east and getting much more for their money.

Bernstock (2014) did not find evidence for this effect, but Kavestos estimated that properties in host boroughs are sold between 2.1 per cent and 3.3 per cent higher, depending on the definition of the impact area, and he cited a similar study which suggested that properties up to three miles away from the main Olympic stadium were selling for 5 per cent higher. Bernstock says that 'the real risk is that the area will be regenerated but with very little benefit to those existing communities' (Bernstock 2014: 202). The global market in real estate is a significant driver of the London economy. It is the market and not public strategy that is determining what is happening to property in London, and without a legislative intervention to change the structure of property transactions this process will continue, to the detriment of the lives of lower-income Londoners.

Shops

Here is one legacy that is all too clear: no-one who visited the Olympic Park will have failed to notice the large Westfield Shopping Mall, through which it was necessary to walk to get to the Olympic Park. Its up-market ambience contrasts dramatically with the shabby but cheap indoor mall across the street. The two Westfield Shopping Mall sites in London – Shepherds Bush and Stratford – made almost £2 billion in sales in 2013. Westfield plan a further development in Croydon in a joint venture with Hammerson (*Evening Standard* 26 February 2014: 34). Hammerson have previously been involved in developments at Brent Cross and the Bullring in Birmingham. Spitalfields Market was also developed with Hammerson involvement. Westfield Shepherds Bush was a joint venture with Hammerson. In a survey conducted by the Association of Foreign Investors in Real Estate, London was named top city for foreign property investors and was the only non-US city in the top five (*Evening Standard* 6 January 2014: 43). Westfield has provided a large up-market shopping mall, but in the rest of Stratford it is very hard to see any upgrading of retail facilities at all.

Jobs

Games preparations were, according to the IOC, a major factor behind a 1.2 per cent reduction in London's unemployment rate in early 2012. The 2012 Games were expected to create 17,900 additional jobs per year between 2012 and 2015. The six Host Boroughs close to the Olympic Park provided nearly one-quarter of the workforce throughout the project. For example, the Host Borough of Newham had 4,364 residents employed by LOCOG or by their contractors and a further 5,518 employed indirectly on the Games in the lead-up and at Games time. The IOC also claimed credit for the job boost from the Westfield Stratford shopping centre, which created 10,000 permanent new jobs from day one, including 2,000 for local people who were previously unemployed, although the Westfield enterprise had little to do with the Games (IOC 2012). The Olympic Park is a living wage employer, and as well as encouraging apprenticeships for local workers in construction, Birkbeck College were persuaded to open a site in Stratford, offering part-time education to enhance the job prospects of local residents.

But a UKTI report in July 2013 found that employment programmes by Boris Johnson, Mayor of London, had failed to deliver long-term Olympic jobs for the capital, with only a fraction of people going into the jobs predicted (BBC 19 July 2013). Only 10 per cent of the 48,000 jobs created by the London Olympics, for example, went to previously unemployed people (Abend 2014). The games did provide a boost for local jobs, if mostly temporary ones, according to Helen Seraphin at Workplace, a job centre funded by Newham Council. But not all boroughs felt the same effects. Although the unemployment rate fell in both boroughs, from about 13 per cent in 2012 to 9 per cent in 2015, it was still higher than the average unemployment rate in London (*The Economist* 4 August 2015). Much of the employment lift was not localised and was in specialist jobs, for example in security, where UK companies won 60 contracts for the Sochi 2014 Winter Olympics and 2018 Russia World Cup.[10] Indeed, apart from construction and retailing, it is hard to see where new employment prospects in the Olympic Boroughs are coming from.

Much other Olympic-related employment was temporary, as part of what Ameeth Vijay (2015: 439) termed the 'pop-up culture':

> The aesthetic of the temporary, in planning and culture, found its economic equivalent in the short-term employment boost in the lead up to the Games, which included work for migrant workers hired to maintain the facilities and sleeping ten to a room in portable cabins. . . . This temporariness is part of a longer trend, with temporary job placements rising 7% every year. Currently, over 1 million British workers are on zero-hour contracts – a vast reserve of contingent labor that has no certainty in work or income.

The Olympic Games, despite its enormous revenues, makes extensive use of volunteers; 70,000 people served as Games Maker volunteers – 40 per cent of whom volunteered for the first time ever. The 'Games Makers' were a feature of the 2012 Games that attracted considerable positive feedback from the public. However, as social analyst Ameeth Vijay (2015: 440) recognised, there are wider implications in the volunteer movement, for our attitudes to labour in this age of the growth of the zero-hours contract.

> This army of volunteers, including those who participated in the celebration of the opening ceremonies, is a caricature of the pop-up labor market. The temporary is thus neoliberal temporality in practice, produced by demands for flexible labor, without rights, guaranteed benefits, or even citizenship.

National legacies

Sport participation

Increasing participation, inspiring the young and hence enhancing the health of the nation was a significant theme of the London 2012 bid. The ambition was high and the claims enthusiastic. Funds were committed and organisations established. *International Inspiration*, an ambitious plan to involve young people all over the world in sport, engaged

50

12 million young people in 21 countries. The Department of Education provided £65 million physical education teachers to organise competitive sports, embed best practice and train primary school teachers. Across England, 12,000 schools participated in the *2012 School Games*. The *Join In Trust* project, supported by a government grant and sponsored by BT, encouraged people to try out sport or volunteer, as a legacy of the Games. The first Join In weekend, in August 2012, featured over 6,000 events. Sport England's £135 million *Places People Play* initiative will fund upgrades for sports venues and support a regional network of sport and leisure facilities. *Sportivate*, a £56 million Lottery-funded London 2012 legacy project involving a nation-wide campaign that encourages young people to try new sports by offering six-week coaching sessions was launched in June 2011 as a four-year programme aimed at 14–25-year-olds but, due to its success, additional funding of £10m per year has been invested, allowing the programme to run until March 2017. The *London Mayor's Participation Programme*, now known as the *Mayor's Sports Legacy Programme*, is upgrading sports facilities throughout the city, and is spending £2.25m in 2016. The official London 2012 education programme, *Get Set*, operated over a four-year period across the UK, providing flexible teaching resources for over 25,000 schools and 6.5 million young people to assist them in learning more about the London 2012 Games, the Olympic and Paralympic values and global citizenship; 85 per cent of UK schools signed up to this programme (IOC 2012).

Commercial corporations have been keen to sign up to be involved with some of the more high-profile projects – BT are a founding sponsor of Join In, Sainsbury's sponsor the School Games and Adidas UK funded a £1m programme, *Adizones*, in 2008, in the Olympic Boroughs, as a pilot scheme for which the DES subsequently contributed £3m with match-funding from local authorities, schools, colleges, the Police, community trusts and other partners, to roll these out nationally.

So the apparent lack of significant growth in sport participation, despite all these schemes, organisations and funding, comes as something of a setback. The strategy of nurturing elite sport, in the hope medal success leads to participation increases, seems flawed. In return for almost £1bn given to 46 national governing bodies since 2009, just five – athletics, boxing, cycling, mountaineering and table tennis – have managed to achieve a statistically significant increase in the number of people playing every month since the bid was won (*Guardian* 6 July 2015: 8–9).

Although 1.4m more people are participating now than when the bid to host the Games was won in 2005, the struggle to make the nation more active since 2012 is in stark contrast to the success Britain has enjoyed in elite sport. Almost 250,000 people stopped taking part in regular activity in the first six months of 2015. In total, 144,200 fewer people visited their local pool in the same period. According to Sport England, the percentage of those on the lowest incomes participating in sport has hit the lowest level since records began in 2005 (Dan Roan, *BBC*, 3 August 2015). The number of Britons exerting themselves at least once per week fell by 200,000 between 2012 and 2014. The numbers playing sport for at least 30 minutes per week dropped by 125,100 to 15.6m (*The Economist* 4 August 2015). The gender gap remains wide – 1.75m more men than women participate. There has been a decline of 121,700 to 1.58m in participation in sport for the disabled (*Guardian* 30 January 2015: 2).

Owen Gibson commented:

> a properly integrated, properly funded, cross-departmental plan for sport and
> wellbeing remains as frustratingly elusive as ever. Meanwhile childhood obesity
> rates continue to rise, PE in schools continues to decline, provision of facilities
> remains frustratingly patchy and participation figures suggest a widening gap
> between the sporting haves and have nots.
>
> (*Guardian* 25 March 2015)

The government austerity programme and curbs on local authority spending have impacted
on sport provision. CIPFA (Chartered Institute of Public Finance and Accounts) calculates
that the local authority budget specifically for sport has fallen by 25 per cent in five years.
In six years Newcastle's budget was cut by 45 per cent, with more to come. When the
coalition came to power it cut Labour's free swimming scheme. In ten years there has been
a drop of 729,000 people regularly swimming. During the 1997–2010 Labour governments, the numbers of children doing at least two hours of physical education in school
rose from 25 per cent in 1997 to 93 per cent in 2010. After years of growth in physical
education fostered by the Labour government, one of Minister of Education Michael
Gove's first acts was to abolish the School Sport Partnership, ending £162m of ring-fenced
funding. Gove also removed the requirement for schools to document the amount of time
spent on sport, which will make it considerably harder to track developments in future
(*Guardian* 6 July 2015: 8–9). Only 7 per cent of UK children go to private schools, but
these schools provided 41 per cent of Team GB in the 2012 Games.

In a way, none of this should be surprising. It has been clear for 30 years that sport participation relates to structural aspects – class patterns, gender relations, income inequalities
– that are not so easily changed. Campaigns to encourage greater participation have
never enjoyed much success. Far too much confidence was placed in the ability of the
Olympics and UK medal success to inspire. Even before the bid success in 2005, according
to David Conn, research by Tony Blair's policy unit had confirmed that hosting a television mega-event does not greatly encourage people to participate more regularly or in
greater numbers (David Conn, *Guardian* 16 June 2015).

Of course, once you have declared that there will be a legacy, a whole tier of reports and
documentation has to be created to confirm that the legacy is happening. To read these
reports is to enter an *Alice in Wonderland* world – they have all the formal style of impartial
and evidence-based studies, yet their rhetorical style is that of the PR company. They
are not exercises in rational and independent assessment, but rather exercises in self-
delusion, denial and sleight of hand. As Crompton (2006: 67) has commented, 'most
economic impact studies are commissioned to legitimize a political position rather than
to search for economic truth.'

One task for the critical commentator might be to inject a little reality, perspective, context
and history into this debate. One thing is clear: staging a mega-event is not a magic panacea
that can resolve problems borne out of long-term structural inequalities. Sport participation for at least the last 30 years has been an uneven process – the affluent participate
at higher rates than the poor, the young participate more than the old, men participate at
higher rates than women. A succession of government and sport organisation initiatives

have done little to alter these patterns, which are rooted in social structures, relations and cultural habits that are not easy to transform. The apparent growth in participation registered in some reports is quite small, undramatic and not easy to attribute causally to the Olympic Games. The more recent decline in participation rates is also not dramatic.

While the Olympic Games is a high-profile event, other factors, less visible, such as the reduction in local council budgets and school sport, can have a greater impact. For the last 30 years casual exercise (walking, swimming, cycling for leisure) have attracted far greater participation than most organised competitive sport. There is nothing intrinsically wrong with this, if the key policy goal is to foster a physically active population. Yet faced with budget reductions of up to 50 per cent over five years, local councils have been cutting to the bone – with libraries, leisure centres and pools perceived as less damaging cuts than the essential social services. Clearly this will be likely to impact upon swimming participation rates.

Environment

Karamichas (2013: 2) has examined the extent to which an Olympic Games leads to the Ecological Modernisation (EM) of the host nation, an outcome that is strongly promoted by the IOC. He suggests that at first the IOC was very slow to take on environmental concerns, but in 1996 environmental protection was added to the Olympic Charter and through Local Agenda 21 (LA21) environmental factors are now incorporated into planning, organisational and legacy concerns of hosts. The IOC has proclaimed that the London Games set new standards for sustainable construction and development practices by integrating sustainability goals into all aspects of Games preparations. Certainly, as in other areas, ambitions were high and substantial commitments made.

Without doubt, some of the achievements have been impressive. The Stratford site in 2005 was predominantly ramshackle, full of decaying and abandoned industrial structures, disused railway lines and toxic waste. The River Lea was so polluted that in the memorable words of comedian Rich Hall, 'you can develop film in it'. In the wake of the Games there is landscaped parkland, with river walks, playgrounds and trees.

To reduce the environmental impact of the massive construction project, workers dredged the River Lea to create a canal network that was used to transport construction materials to the site. More than 98 per cent of the demolition waste from decrepit buildings that were torn down was recycled. Organisers are also developing 45 hectares of habitat, with a ten-year ecological management plan to encourage biodiversity. Around 300,000 plants were planted in the Olympic Park's wetlands area. Over 1,000 new trees were planted in East London (IOC 2012). The BMX track incorporated 14,000 cubic metres of soil that was excavated, cleaned and reused from other Olympic Park construction sites. The Copper Box was covered with recycled copper and reduces water use by 40 per cent by recycling rainwater. The Velodrome was built with 100 per cent sustainably sourced timber. A unique mesh system holds the roof in place with a third less steel than in a conventional structure. The building is naturally ventilated, eliminating the need for air conditioning. The 29,000 m² Main Press Centre featured a 'brown' roof made of moss, logs and other materials to create a wildlife habitat. It is to be converted to commercial office space. The Energy Centre employed innovative biomass boilers that burned woodchips and other sustainable fuels to supply heating and cooling to buildings throughout the Olympic Park. It will continue to serve the community now that the Games are over (IOC 2012).

For the first time, an independent commission was established to monitor and publicly evaluate sustainability efforts. The Commission for a Sustainable London 2012 rated the overall effort 'a great success' (IOC 2012). On its own website, the Commission for a Sustainable London 2012 provided assurance to the Olympic Board and the public on how the bodies delivering the London 2012 Olympic and Paralympic Games and legacy were meeting their sustainability commitments. It is hard to have full confidence in the effective and questioning oversight that is provided by a body that defines its own mission as 'providing assurance'. The Commission was hosted by the GLA and was based at City Hall, and was funded by the ODA (30 per cent), GLA (20 per cent), GOE (20 per cent) and LOCOG (30 per cent). So it was housed by and funded by the very bodies for which it is supposed to function as a watchdog. These same bodies decided to wind up the Commission in March 2013, a year earlier than originally scheduled. So, this is a watchdog without much bite.

However, bearing in mind the cost of the Games, and the ways in which the whole project can inflect strategic planning for a city in particular ways, there are also questions to be raised about sustainability. Hayes and Horne (2011) argue that the approach to sustainable development is essentially top-down; its operational scope is very limited, and 'the extent of civic engagement in its production has been extremely narrow'. They ask to what extent 'a six-year scheme of construction for a four-week festival of sport can rightly lay claim to being "the most sustainable Games ever"?' and suggest that the concept of a 'sustainable Games' is less a benign paradox than a 'systemic contradiction of advanced late-modern capitalist democracies'. Hayes and Horne argue that the Games is a fundamentally unsustainable event, because the Games functions temporally to engineer a crisis of deliberative structures: the needs of the Games tend to override the normal participatory democratic structures (Hayes and Horne 2011: 759–761)

Business opportunities and economic impact

According to the IOC, the economic benefits of the Games are considerable. Grand and sweeping claims are made. VISA projects that the economic impact of the Games will total £5.3 billion by 2015, not including pre-Games impacts (IOC 2012). Factoring in pre-Games construction and other early Games-related economic activity, an Oxford Economics (2012) study commissioned by the Lloyds banking group estimates that the Games will generate £16.5 billion for the British economy from 2005 to 2017. During July and August 2012, visitors spent about £760 million in the UK, averaging £1,290 per person – almost double the normal amount. Expenditure from overseas visitors in August 2012, including Games ticket sales, totalled £4.5 billion (IOC 2012). Games-related projects generated thousands of jobs during the worst global recession in more than 60 years, and economists expect continued economic benefits long after the Games (IOC 2012). But how in reality are these economic impact figures compiled? Far too many impact studies seem to be conducted by people or organisations that are not genuinely independent from the process of provision.

54

As regards post-Games income, there is an agreement in place whereby the first £223 million of receipts from the Olympic Park goes to the GLA; the Lottery receives 75 per cent of the next £900 million of receipts (i.e. up to £675 million), with the other 25 per cent going to the GLA; and any receipts over £1,123 million are shared equally between the GLA and the Exchequer. Ownership of the Olympic Park land and assets rests with the LLDC, which is a mayoral body, and is responsible for deciding what is sold, when and for how much (House of Commons Committee of Public Accounts 2013). In 2007 the Labour government took £425 million from the Big Lottery Fund to help finance the Olympic Games, promising that the fund would be reimbursed by sales of Olympic assets. In 2015 the government suggests that that repayment may take until 2030 or beyond.[11]

If there is one area in which bullish claims have been made it is for the economic impact of the Games. According to the IOC, about 98 per cent of the £7 billion worth of ODA contracts, and about 94 per cent of LOCOG's £1 billion worth of contracts, went to UK businesses. The success of 2012 created opportunities for UK companies to service other mega-events – Rio 2016 and Sochi 2014 Olympic Games, as well as the Qatar 2022 World Cup (IOC 2012).

Indeed great claims are made for the business and economic benefits: in July 2013, a government report suggested that the Games had already boosted the UK economy by £9.9bn.[12] In November 2013, UKTI (government trade and investment), given the task of realising £11bn of economic benefit from the Games within four years, announced it had already hit the target (*Guardian* 16 November 2013). The figures included £130m supplying goods and services to Brazil and Rio – but how do we know with certainty that these are directly due to London hosting the Games? It is not clear how these things are quantified and evaluated.

These claims have been met with scepticism by some economists. Stefan Szymanski said it was impossible to tell how much of the economic activity could be put down to the Games. 'It's almost like a bit of creative accounting. There's no way of testing whether what they're saying is really true.' Jonathan Portes, Director of the National Institute of Economic and Social Research and a former Chief Economist at the Cabinet Office, said attributing the economic benefits to the Olympics was 'a little far-fetched to say the least'. The Federation of Small Businesses said the impact of the Games had been a disappointment. 'The contracts we were expecting really didn't materialise', said National Policy Chairman Mike Cherry (BBC 19 July 2013). Rose and Spiegel (2011) found that staging the Games can boost trade by up to 20 per cent, but interestingly merely bidding has a similar effect. Indeed, if true this would confirm the view of some Olympic analysts, that in terms of raising the profile of a city, the best value lies in bidding *but not winning!*

What is clear is that staging the Games is of benefit to the British members of the Olympic consultocracy, a 'caravan' (Cashman and Harris 2012) that 'wanders nomadically from Games to Games' (Jennings 2012: 3). It is easy to see the value of new sports venues, transport infrastructure and other tangible Games-related assets, but the Games also provide other lasting benefits that are harder to see and measure (IOC 2012). According

55

to a poll by Freeview for the British Pride Index, three-quarters of UK residents felt proud to be British at the end of the Games. Many speculated that the UK's success at the Olympics – which 88 per cent of the UK's population is thought to have watched – is responsible for the surge of national pride (IOC 2012). Four years later and the agenda has moved on. Other issues dominate the public discussion and these rather intangible effects seem less significant than they may have done in 2012. The IOC quote research to suggest 74 per cent of UK adults agree that the Paralympic Games has shown the world how to treat people with disabilities with respect and equality (IOC 2012). There seems little doubt that the 2012 Paralympic Games did have a considerable impact in raising the profile of, and enhancing the image of, people with disabilities. Yet in the years since, British people with disabilities have been subjected to humiliating re-testing to establish their right to disability benefit payments or, more accurately, to attempt to challenge their right (see Chapter 11).

The various areas in which the promises of legacy are not being fully realised are not for the most part due to a lack of will, although lack of sufficient funds may well be an issue. The main reasons for inadequate delivery lie in the nature of the promises themselves. For example, the belief that staging an Olympic Games might somehow magically transform participation patterns that have been relatively stable for 40 years. The low levels of, and unequal patterns of, participation in active physical leisure have proved remarkably resistant to the nudging and urging of social policy and Sport Council campaigning. These patterns have been produced by deep-rooted social and historical forces, not readily dealt with and certainly not through the impact of a single mega-event.

LOCOG was a private company and the commercial transactions it was involved in were not generally open to public scrutiny due to the 'non-disclosure agreement' its employees and contractors were required to sign. Nichols and Ralston (2015) argue that this greatly limited the knowledge transfer legacy of London 2012, and can be considered as a liberty cost of 'regulatory capitalism'.

Vijay (2015) argues that the rhetoric of legacy 'could be sustained only through an implication that the Olympic site – and East London as a whole – was in a state of ruin, a state which could be ameliorated through the production of this sporting mega-event'. I think one needs to distinguish between the site and East London as a whole. The site, notwithstanding Iain Sinclair's rather wistful nostalgic desire for the rough chaos of what used to be, could fairly be described as a ruin. It was a tangle of old railway lines, waterways, decaying industrial detritus and small-scale light industry, heavily polluted with toxic waste. The Olympic Park marks an improvement. If money was targeted at environmental improvement rather than at staging a mega-event, then would it have been more cost effective? Probably. Would the money have been forthcoming? Probably not. With regard to East London, it was and is decisively not a ruin. However, it was and is one of the most socially and economically disadvantaged areas of the country. Aside from the establishment of a pleasant park and a lot of housing, which is largely not affordable by, or designed for, the disadvantaged citizens of the local boroughs, has the Olympics really left a significant impact on the area? Readers who want to explore these complex issues in more detail should turn to the remarkable multi-dimensional study of the area and the Olympics by urban sociologist Phil Cohen (2013).

NOTES

1   http://researchbriefings.parliament.uk/ResearchBriefing/Summary/LLN-2012-037 (last accessed 17 October 2015).
2   Lord Sebastian Coe, CEO, LOCOG, May 2006, www.theguardian.com/sport/2006/may/04/Olympics2012.politics (last accessed 23 October 2015).
3   Sebastian Coe, March 2012, www.theguardian.com/sport/2012/mar/09/coe-sport-england-olympic-legacy; (last accessed 23 October 2015).
4   www.insidethegames.biz/articles/1015224/exclusive-london-olympic-museum-plans-shelved (last accessed 23 October 2015).
5   http://queenelizabetholympicpark.co.uk/our-story/the-legacy-corporation (last accessed 23 October 2015).
6   See www.delta-esourcing.com/tenders/UK-GB-Stratford,-London:-London-Aquatics-Centre-Blinds/GBG29X493Z (last accessed 23 October 2015).
7   In Culture, Media and Sport Committee, *London 2012 Olympic Games and Paralympic Games: funding and legacy*: Second Report of Session 2006–07: Memorandum submitted by the London Borough of Newham.
8   Foundation for FutureLondon (www.future.london), not to be confused with the Future of London Network (last accessed 23 October 2015).
9   www.gamesmonitor.org.uk/node/2212 (last accessed 23 October 2015).
10 'Securing the Olympic legacy', *Intersec: The Journal of International Security*.
11 Directory of Social Change, www.gamesmonitor.org.uk/node/2252 (last accessed 23 October 2015).
12 BBC 19 July 2013, www.bbc.co.uk/news/uk-23370270 (last accessed 23 October 2015).

FURTHER READING

Cohen, P. (2013) *On the Wrong Side of the Track? East London and the Post Olympics*, London: Lawrence & Wishart.
Cohen, P. and Watt, P. (eds) (2016) *A Hollow Legacy? London 2012 and the Post Olympic City*, London: Palgrave.
Fussey, P., Coaffee, J., Armstrong, G. and Hobbs, D. (2011) *Securing and Sustaining the Olympic City: Reconfiguring London for 2012 and Beyond*, London: Ashgate.
Gold, J. and Gold, M. (2016) *Olympic Cities: City Agendas, Planning and the World's Games 1896–2016* (3rd edition), London: Routledge.
Hayes, G. and Karamichas, J. (2012) *Olympic Games, Mega-events and Civil Societies: Globalization, Environment, Resistance*, Basingstoke: Palgrave Macmillan.

CHAPTER 3

THE IOC, POLITICAL ECONOMY
AND THE GAMES BIDDING PROCESS

A broad division exists between 'romantic idealists' and scathing critics of Olympism. The romantic idealists tend to believe that the Olympic Games can bring about greater internationalism, peace and fraternity; they refer to it as a movement or a 'family', and treat Olympism as a quasi-religion or civil religion. The scathing critics believe it encourages organisations and individuals – whom they see as corrupt 'chancers on the make' to line their own pockets – inducing potential hosts to spend millions of dollars to bid and persuade just over 100 people to vote for them, all amidst a prevailing lack of transparency. As Jennings (2012: 461) and Chatziefstathiou (2012) suggest, Baron Pierre de Coubertin can thus be understood as 'the Renovator', 'visionary', 'social marketer' or 'skilful manoeuvrer' behind the foundation of the modern Olympics, depending on your perspective.

For the past 25 years the IOC has enjoyed a no-cost promotion strategy, constantly in the glare of the world's mass media; in any single year several future Olympic venues and hosts still to be decided are known about. For example, writing in October 2015 the next two Summer and Winter Olympic host cities are known, and already five candidate cities have been identified to compete to host the 2024 Summer Olympic and Paralympic Games. In the odd years when there is not an Olympic Games taking place, a decision will be made at an IOC Session or Congress about where either a Winter or a Summer Olympics will be held in seven years' time (see the Timeline, pp. xi-xiii). As Jennings (2012: 461) suggests, in the 1890s 'it was the titled and wealthy bourgeois, today the multinationals seeking a Trojan horse to penetrate and subdue new markets' that perhaps benefit from the global spread of Olympism.

This chapter examines: the nature of the IOC and its relationship to the other components of international sport; the political economy of the Olympic movement and the sports business; and the nature of the bidding process. The chapter seeks to place specific Olympic Games in relation to the structure of the Olympic movement and the various institutions of international sport. It provides a schematic economic overview of the finances of the Olympic movement, and it analyses the peculiarly contradictory nature of the IOC in terms of its historical formation, its awkward adjustments to modernity and enterprise, and its extraordinary commercial success with one of the world's strongest brands. This chapter seeks to explore and explain the Olympic Games – and the IOC in particular – by positioning them in their social, cultural, economic and political contexts. As Gruneau and Neubauer (2012: 154) suggest, we believe that just as 'broad political and economic forces and local issues' shape each Olympic Games, so too does the organisation of the IOC have to respond to changing circumstances. The minutiae of the IOC and the Olympic movement, however, are dealt with in detail elsewhere (see, for example, Chappelet and Kubler-Mabbott 2008; Girginov and Parry 2005; Girginov 2010; Toohey and Veal 2007).

The chapter is in three parts. First, we consider the relationship of the IOC to other components of international sport, the nature of the IOC and its origins, and argue that it experienced a contradictory formation – having to adjust to both modernity and capitalist enterprise. In the past 25 years this involvement with more commercial stakeholders – sponsors and media corporations especially – has raised issues of 'governance' that will continue to influence the future of the IOC and the Olympic movement more generally (see Girginov 2013 for discussion of some of the intricacies of Olympic governance). Here, we seek to establish the kind of organisation that the IOC is, and how it is similar to and different from other sporting organisations – including how its members and Olympic cities are chosen. Second, we look at the changing political economy of the Olympic Games. Some of this is covered in Chapter 4 – especially the 1980s and the relationships between João Havelange (President of FIFA), Horst Dassler (CEO of Adidas) and Juan Antonio Samaranch (President of the IOC) – but here we will discuss the origins of the arrangements that have come to dominate the Olympics over the past three decades. We also consider the position of the Winter Olympic Games in this changing political economy.

Third, we discuss various issues confronting the IOC and how they have been dealt with – especially candidate cities and the bidding process, and relationships between National Olympic Committees (NOCs), International Federations (IFs) and individual members of the IOC. Since the first edition of this book, a new IOC President, Thomas Bach, has attempted to deal with some old and recurring problems for the organisation, including greater reluctance on the part of the citizens of some nations to host or even bid for the Olympics, especially the Winter Games, doping and lingering concerns about corruption, social responsibility and equity. In December 2014, following a year-long consultation process, 40 (20 + 20) recommendations were unanimously accepted by the IOC at its 127th Session in Monaco.[1] These formed the basis for what was called a 'strategic roadmap' for the Olympics for the next 15 years, 'Olympic Agenda 2020', which we discuss later in this chapter. We also offer consideration of the politics of IOC members, especially the Presidents, many of whom seem to have been largely right-wing, with some fascist sympathisers. Avery Brundage (IOC President 1952–1972) has been rightly criticised by many, mostly for his hard line on amateurism rather than his anti-communism, and this has made the others appear rather apolitical and saintly by comparison – but whether this is accurate needs exploring.

WHAT IS THE IOC?

The IOC was and remains an extraordinary association; not representative of nations, but with a membership that chooses its own members by the rules and within limits set by the organisation itself. The IOC remains a club based on the eighteenth-century aristocratic notions of membership associated with a gentlemen's club. This involves procedures such as the self-selection of members, the potential blackballing of applicants who wish to become members (that is, non-selection on the basis of objections by a few rather than by a majority) and clubability (that is, new members have to fit in socially). In all these ways the cohesion of the group, club or association was forged. Occurring at the end of the nineteenth century, 'The universalism and humanism of the concepts and ideology of de Coubertin and the Olympic movement . . . made the movement's interests and institution building appear compatible and convergent with broader processes of international institution building' (Roche 2000: 108). In many ways the IOC helped in the process of the invention of traditions, nation building and the imagining of communities that authors such as Anderson, Hobsbawm and Ranger have written about (see Chapter 6). The IOC, for example, was interested in associating itself with the League of Nations formed after the end of the First World War.

The organisation was not a disinterested party in the formation of nations, however. Hoberman (1995: 16ff.) suggests that the fact that the Scouting and the Olympic movements (in contrast with the Esperanto movement and the Red Cross) sought aristocratic affiliations and royal patronage indicates the degree to which they were ideologically interested in reconciling social classes. In 1908, 'European nobility made up 68 per cent of the membership of the IOC, a figure which had declined to 41 per cent by 1924' (Hoberman 1995: 16). He argues that during the 1930s the Olympic movement was essentially 'a right-wing internationalism effectively co-opted by the Nazis and their French and German sympathisers' (Hoberman 1995: 17).

At the time of writing (October 2015) the IOC currently has 100 members, 33 honorary members and 1 honour member (the former US Secretary of State, Henry Kissinger). The previous President, Jacques Rogge, is Honorary President.[2] The IOC appoints its own members, and members represent the IOC in their countries and are not their country's delegates in the IOC ('Members of the IOC represent and promote the interests of the IOC and of the Olympic movement in their countries and in the organisations of the Olympic movement in which they serve' – IOC 2014a: 33).[3] Of the current 100 members, 23 are women; 8 were elected 30 or more years ago; 10 have royal or aristocratic titles; 36 have participated in at least one Olympic Games; and 28 have won Olympic medals. The geographical distribution of the IOC membership reflects the European origins of the organisation: Europe 45 per cent, Asia 19 per cent, Africa 16 per cent, America 15 per cent and Oceania 5 per cent. Of the 33 'honorary members', five have royal or aristocratic titles and three are women. Age limits have often been the subject of debate among IOC members. The average age in 1894 was just over 38 years, with the eldest member being 59 years old. The age limit was fixed at 72 years in 1966 and raised to 75 in 1975. By 1980 the average age of the then 81 IOC members was over 67 years, with the eldest member 94 years old. The age limit was raised again to 80 in 1995, although the average age fell to nearly 62 years. From the 110th Session of the IOC in 1999 the age limit was reduced to 70 for all newly appointed members. At the 127th Session of the IOC in December 2014 one of the recommendations accepted unanimously was to allow 'a one-time extension of an IOC member's term of office for a maximum of four years, beyond the current age limit of 70', for a 'maximum of five cases at a given time'.[4]

Since formation there have been just nine IOC presidents. Initially, Coubertin had sought to alternate the presidency according to host city, but after the Paris Olympic Games in

Name	Member	President	Country
Pierre de Coubertin	1894–1925	1896–1925	France
Ernest Callot	1894–1913		France
Demetrios Bikelas*	1894–1897	1894–1896	Greece
Alexander Butowsky	1894–1900		Russia
Viktor Balck	1894–1921		Sweden
William M. Sloane	1894–1925		US
Jiri Guth-Jarkovsky	1894–1943		Bohemia
Arthur Russell, Lord Ampthill	1894–1898		UK
Charles Herbert	1894–1906		UK
Jose Benjamin Zubiaur	1894–1907		Argentina
Leonard Cuff	1894–1905		New Zealand
Comte Lucchesi Palli	1894–1895		Italy
Comte Maxime de Bousies	1894–1901		Belgium
Riccardo Carafa, Duke d'Andria	1894–1898		Italy

Figure 3.1 Founder members of the IOC in 1894.

Source: adapted from Guttmann 1984: 263; Toohey and Veal 2007.

Note
*Sometimes rendered in English as Vikelas.

1900 he was elected for a longer term and retained the presidency until 1925. The Olympic Charter published in 2014 (and ratified without change in 2015) stipulated a maximum term of eight years of office, with the possibility of one renewable period of four years. Hence the present incumbent, in office since 2013, Thomas Bach, will step down in 2021 – unless there is an extension to his period of office for four more years.

The IOC took its basic organisational shape during the inter-war period. The Executive Board of the IOC, originally founded in 1921, currently consists of the President, four Vice-Presidents and ten other members. All the members of the Executive Board are elected at an IOC Session, by secret ballot, by a majority of votes cast, for a four-year term. Among many responsibilities today, the IOC Executive Board oversees and approves the marketing policy developed and proposed by the IOC Marketing Commission at the IOC Session. As mentioned earlier, the IOC has always been self-recruiting, and views members as champions for the Olympic movement in their own nations, rather than as representatives of their countries at the IOC. Meanwhile, NOCs organise national teams for games events, and where they are hosts they take a leading role in organising events, although they are not formally represented on the IOC.

The Olympic Foundation is chaired by the IOC President, while an IOC Olympic Museum in Lausanne, which former President Juan Antonio Samaranch established, acts as a universal repository of the written, visual and graphic memory of the Olympic Games. It cost $70 million to build, but over 80 per cent of the funds came from donors or sponsors. As the Olympic Games are a multi-sport event it also required an international level of organisation in the constituent sports. Some IFs had already been established, such as the International Federation of Gymnastics in 1881, the International Rugby Football Board in 1886 and the International Rowing Federation in 1892. The IOC connected 'nationally powerful national level governing bodies of sport and permitted internationally standardised rules and regulations for international events to be developed, recognised and diffused' (Roche 2000: 109).

These networks began to emerge after 1896, but especially following the 1908 Games held in London when the organisers – the British Olympic Committee (now the British Olympic Association (BOA)) and the Amateur Athletic Association (AAA) – were accused of bias by the Americans. The International Amateur Athletic Federation (IAAF) was established the year after the Stockholm Olympics in 1913.

During the 1918–1939 period the IOC 'established itself as the primary authority and actor concerned with international sport, its games event became the pre-eminent sport event and its four-year calendar structured world sport' (Roche 2000: 109). Roche acknowledges that it also 'retained class-ist, sexist and racist attitudes from its late nineteenth century origins' (Roche 2000: 110). Roche asserts that, since the Second World War, the Olympic movement has 'on balance, been a significant force in the promotion of a genuine univer- salist humanistic ideology', showing a great deal of adaptation to 'pressures generated in its international political environment' (2000: 110–111).

The first version of the Olympic Charter appeared in 1908. The latest version was published in August 2015, with a few minor amendments from one agreed in December 2014 that has more wide-ranging changes. The charter sets out the 'fundamental principles and values of Olympism' and defines the 'rights and obligations of Olympic organisations', which are 'required to comply with the Olympic Charter' (see Box 3.1). Other amendments to the Olympic Charter agreed at the 127th Session of the IOC in 2014 can be found online at www.olympic.org/about-ioc-institution?tab=organisation (last accessed 3 August 2015).

Olympism is the 'philosophy' and movement devised by Coubertin. It refers to 'a philosophy of life, exalting and combining in a balanced whole the qualities of body, will and mind'. It attempts to blend 'sport with culture and education' and promote a way of life based on 'the joy found in effort, the educational value of good example and respect for universal

Name	Period	Country
Demetrios Vikelas	1894–1896	Greece
de Coubertin, Baron	1896–1925	France
Henri de Baillet-Latour, Count	1925–1942	France
J. Sigfrid Edstrom	1942–1952	Sweden
Avery Brundage	1952–1972	US
Michael Morris, Lord Killanin	1972–1980	Ireland
Juan Antonio Samaranch, Marquess	1980–2001	Spain
Jacques Rogge, Count	2001–2013	Belgium
Thomas Bach	2013–2021*	Germany

Figure 3.2 The nine presidents of the IOC, 1894–2021.

Source: adapted from Toohey and Veal, 2007: 49; Chappelet and Kubler-Mabbott 2008: 23.

Note
* with the possibility of an additional four-year term

62

fundamental ethical principles'. Such a combination of humanistic ideals with the celebration of physical activity was unusual in the Western philosophical tradition until the English public school developed athleticism. The Olympic movement is unique in sport, comprising a philosophy and a *movement* that encompasses organisations, athletes and other persons who agree to be guided by the Olympic Charter. The criterion for membership is recognition by the IOC. The Olympic movement therefore seeks to transcend sport and contribute to world peace and human rights. It also has the implication that since the Olympic movement has a *moral* stance based on its ideals/standards, it is open to criticism when it deviates from its own standards. As sport historian and Olympic scholar Bruce Kidd (2010: 158) writes more generally, 'the moral claims of sport legitimize it as a site of struggle'. This is very true of the Olympic movement, Olympism and the IOC.

The Olympic Games involves around 36 different sports: 26–28 in the Summer Games and 7–8 in the Winter Games. The IOC, which can now comprise up to 115 members, sits in the middle of a complex network or system. On one side there are the IFs of individual sports, representing about 200 national governing bodies. On the other there are another 205 NOCs.[5] Formal negotiations between the IFs and the NOCs and the IOC take place through bilateral meetings. IOC members are just that – members of the IOC; they are not representatives or delegates of a particular sport or country *to* the IOC.

Cultural non-governmental organisations (NGOs) first developed in the last third of the nineteenth century. The international cultural NGOs that developed then were fragile international networks and associations. As Roche (2000: 97) remarks, the creation of specialised governing bodies or IFs for different sports occurred

> in tandem with the development in the 1890s of a generalist and pluralist international sport movement, namely the Olympic movement, led by Coubertin and the IOC and oriented to the promotion of its sport ideology and the development of its multi-sport games event.

In the period between the two world wars (1918–1939) the Olympic 'model' was important in generating alternative visions of international sport ideology, multi-sport movements and events. These included the Workers' Olympics, Women's Olympics and the British Empire Games (since 1978 called the 'Commonwealth Games').

Many IFs allied with the Olympic movement and organised world championships within the Olympic Games event. The Fédération Internationale de Football Association (FIFA), formed in 1904 in Paris, helped the Olympic Games organisers (the Olympic Games host NOC and the host city) to stage international football world championships in each Olympic Games until the 1920s. Conflicts between FIFA and the IOC over the size and professionalism of the sport led to FIFA's decision to stage its own 'world cup' from 1930, 'intermediate to the Olympic four-year cycle' (Roche 2000: 97).

Unlike the international expositions from which the Olympic Games event had emerged (see Chapters 6 and 7), the processes of formalisation, rationalisation and bureaucratisation occurred much more rapidly. Rituals also became a feature of Olympic events during the inter-war period. The main stadium, according to Roche,

> effectively becomes 'diplomatic territory' and a de facto 'sacred site' for the duration of the games. The stadium contains the Olympic flame, the Olympic flag, the flags of the other nations and . . . no advertising or commercial imagery to detract from the impact of the Olympic symbols.

> (Roche 2000: 98)

As we noted above, the IOC has only had nine presidents since its inception in 1894, and four of them account for nearly 90 years in office. Most have come from small European countries (Brundage was the exceptional non-European). Five of the nine have belonged to nobility, although Samaranch and Rogge received their titles after taking up office. In an IOC handbook produced for sponsors of the Olympic Games in the 1990s, the many different forms of address for the then 89 IOC members were listed. Indicative of the unrepresentative nature of the IOC membership, these included: 'Monsieur le President/ Dear Mr President' (Samaranch), 'Dear General', 'Dear Colonel', 'Your Excellency', 'Professeur', 'Your Royal Highness', 'Your Serene Highness', 'Altesse', 'Monseigneur', as well as 'Dear Mr', 'Madame', and one 'Dear Ms' (Anita Defrantz, former Olympic athlete and IOC Executive Board member).

Founded by Coubertin in 1894, the IOC is the 'supreme authority' of the Olympic movement with the mission 'To promote Olympism throughout the world and to lead the Olympic movement.' With its headquarters in Lausanne, Switzerland, the IOC as an organisation has expanded considerably since the 1980s to more than 400 staff (Chappelet and Kubler-Mabbott 2008: 27–34). The IOC benefits from the low taxation regulations in Switzerland that enable it to keep more of its income than it would in any comparable country. The headquarters of FIFA and UEFA are also in Switzerland for similar reasons. The IOC has adopted several roles relating to various aspects of sport: ethics in sport, the education of youth through sport, encouraging the spirit of fair play, encouraging/ supporting sport and sports competitions, the promotion of women in sport, the fight against doping in sport, protecting the health of athletes, placing sport at the service of humanity to promote peace, ending any form of discrimination affecting the Olympic movement, promoting the social and professional future of athletes, sport for all, sustainable development in sport and a positive legacy for host cities and countries, blending sport with culture and education and supporting the International Olympic Academy (IOA) in Olympia, Greece and other Olympic education projects. A year after Coubertin's death (1938) and following his own wish, his heart was placed inside a commemorative stele in Olympia. This rekindled the idea for the establishment of a centre for the Olympic Games in Olympia, and the IOA was officially inaugurated on 14 June 1961. Today, some 40 different events take place every year on the premises of the IOA in Olympia.

To oversee these roles the IOC operates a number of 'commissions' (Toohey and Veal 2007: 54). In 2015 these were overhauled as part of the Agenda 2020 reforms. President Bach introduced changes that saw an increase in the number of places taken by women, rising to 32 per cent, and the number of chairpersons from Africa and Asia increasing to 34 per cent.[6] The former Sport and Environment Commission was renamed the Sustainability and Legacy Commission in line with the growing influence of these two words in mega-event discourse. The former Culture and Olympic Education Commission was split into two separate commissions – the Olympic Education Commission and the Culture and Olympic Heritage Commission. The Medical Commission was renamed the Medical and Scientific Commission but still assists in the implementation of the Olympic Medical Code regarding the policing of prohibited drug use. A new Communications Commission was established to support the promotion of Olympic values. A new Olympic (Broadcast) Channel is being created as a result of Agenda 2020, and an Olympic Channel Commission was also established to support it. The International Relations Commission was renamed the Public Affairs and Social Development through Sport Commission, reflecting the growth of interest in linking with the United Nations to promote sport and Olympism for social development purposes. The Women and Sport Commission that focused on the promotion of equal opportunities for girls and women to participate in sport and physical activity was renamed the Women *in* Sport Commission.

Several commissions remained unchanged: the Coordination Commissions for the Olympic Games still provide the link between the IOC and host city OCOGs, IFs and NOCs; the Ethics Commission, which establishes ethical rules for IOC and Olympic activities; the Finance Commission still oversees accounting and finance of the IOC; and the Marketing Commission advises the IOC on sources of 'financing and revenue' as well as on marketing. The Athletes' Commission represents the views of athletes to the IOC, and is composed of retired and active Olympic athletes. The Olympic Solidarity Commission is charged with overseeing the distribution of IOC funds to NOCs in less wealthy countries.

THE POLITICAL ECONOMY OF THE IOC

There have been three main phases in the development of the Olympic Games according to Alan Tomlinson (2005a: 60):

1   1896–1928: 'a grand socio-political project with a modest economic profile';
2   1932–1984: 'a markedly political intensification of the event at the heart of international political developments';
3   1984 onward: 'fuelled by the global reach of capital . . . in the international economy of a global culture'.

It is this last phase that we focus on in this chapter – since the mid-1980s – when funding of the Olympics and the Olympic movement have derived mainly from the sale of broadcasting rights and worldwide exclusive sponsorship arrangements. As the only candidate city for the 1984 Games, Los Angeles Olympic organisers 'were able to negotiate unprecedented concessions from the IOC, including control over all aspects of Olympic planning and the right to keep all media and sponsorship revenues' (Gruneau and Neubauer 2012: 147). Furthermore, they argue that no 'local Olympic organizing committee has since had the monopolistic control over revenue production enjoyed by the LAOOC' (Gruneau and Neubauer 2012: 155). The IOC has 'been the overwhelming beneficiary of Olympic commercialism, reaping windfall profits from sponsorship and media revenues over the past two decades while allowing local organizing committees to bear all the financial risks' (Gruneau and Neubauer 2012: 155). As such, sports mega-events like the Olympics and the men's Football World Cup have become franchise operations, similar to the fast-food corporation McDonald's, one of the major sponsors of both (Bose 2012; Stewart 2012). Gruneau and Neubauer (2012: 134–135) also suggest one of the most significant (unintended) legacies of the Los Angeles Olympics in 1984 was the legitimation of 'a sweeping neoliberal political project in the United States, with repercussions that have been felt across the globe' ever since. In this respect the 1984 Los Angeles Olympics 'have left an indelible mark on the international political landscape' (Gruneau and Neubauer 2012: 156).

Over the course of the nearly 120 years since the IOC was formed, various symbols and ceremonial features have been developed. These include the five rings symbol (the Olympic Symbol), arguably the most widely recognised logo in the world, which dates from 1913. These rings may represent the five continents, but they have no ancient Olympic Games connection. The Olympic Flag was created in 1914 and first used at the Antwerp Games in 1920. There is some speculation about how the flag, generally handed from host city to host city, got from Berlin in 1936 to London in 1948.

The Olympic motto – *citius, altius, fortius* (faster, higher, stronger) – was derived from 1886 and the credo of Pierre Didon, a Dominican priest whom Coubertin knew. The Olympic anthem derives from a Greek poem: 'Ancient, eternal and immortal spirit', put to music by Spyros Samaras. First performed in 1896, it was only officially adopted in 1958. Olympic emblems and mascots (since 1972) are designed for each Games. The Olympic flame, torch and relay, while appearing to have great lineage, only date from the Amsterdam Games in 1928 (IOC 2014a). From 1936, the flame was lit at Olympia from 'the sun's rays'. The torch relay to the host city became a major event but, following 2008, it is unlikely that it will ever follow such an international route again (Horne and Whannel 2010). Despite the rise and fall of the torch relay in terms of distance and countries covered (see Figure 3.3) it has become a major way in which sponsors can associate their brand with the otherwise commercially untainted Olympic 'brand'.

Once it has arrived at the Olympic stadium the flame burns throughout the Games. Medal ceremonies in their current format were introduced in 1932 at the Summer Games in Los Angeles and Winter Games in Lake Placid. These involved medals awarded at ceremonies 'on site' at the events and the use of the three-level podium. Finally, the Olympic Order mimics national honours systems and is for individuals who have either achieved remarkable merit in the sporting world or rendered outstanding service to the Olympic movement.

In the past 30 years, protecting the 'brand' and image of these 'properties' has become of paramount importance. As the Olympic Charter (IOC 2014a: 22) states:

> The Olympic Games are the exclusive property of the IOC, which owns all rights and data relating thereto, in particular, and without limitation, all rights relating

Year/host city	Distance travelled (km)	Number of torchbearers
1992 Barcelona	6,307	9,849
1996 Atlanta	26,875	12,467
2000 Sydney	45,693	13,400
2004 Athens	84,600	11,300
2008 Beijing	137,000	21,800
2012 London	15,775	8,000

Figure 3.3 Summer Olympic Games torch relays: 1992–2012.

Source: adapted from *Torches and Torch Relays of the Summer Games from Berlin 1936 to London 2012*, Lausanne: Olympic Studies Centre.

to their organisation, exploitation, broadcasting, recording, representation, reproduction, access and dissemination in any form and by any means or mechanism whatsoever, whether now existing or developed in the future.

Hence the symbol, flag, motto, anthem, identifications (including but not limited to 'Olympic Games' and 'Games of the Olympiad'), designations, and emblems, flame and torches are collectively or individually referred to as 'Olympic properties'. All rights to any and all Olympic properties, as well as all rights to the use thereof, belong exclusively to the IOC, including but not limited to the use for any profit-making, commercial or advertising purposes. These rights are protected by law, particularly in Olympic Games host countries.

In addition to broadcasting partnerships the IOC manages The Olympic Partner (TOP) world-wide sponsorship programme and the IOC official supplier and licensing programme. Since 1985, when the TOP programme started, the financial health of the IOC has been secured by the first two sources – television rights payments and global sponsorship deals. As an article in *The Economist* put it ahead of the Atlanta Summer Olympics in 1996, 'The zillion dollar games' have developed because 'the power of corporate hype linked with global television is a marvellous machine for promoting sports'. As outlined in more detail in the next chapter, the IOC refers to its financial operations in terms of an 'Olympic quadrennium' – a four-year period (from 1 January to 31 December). Television rights account for slightly less than 50 per cent of IOC revenue. Despite increasing attention being paid to digital and social media, it is likely that television income will continue to increase and thus the majority of Olympic income will come from corporate sources.

The IOC provides TOP programme contributions and Olympic broadcast revenue to the OCOGs to support the staging of the Olympic Games and Olympic Winter Games. Long-term broadcast and sponsorship programmes enable the IOC to provide the majority of the OCOG's operational budget well in advance of the Games, with revenues effectively guaranteed prior to the selection of the host city. The two OCOGs of each Olympic quadrennium share approximately 50 per cent of TOP programme revenue and value-in-kind contributions, with approximately 30 per cent provided to the Summer OCOG and 20 per cent to the Winter OCOG. The OCOGs in turn generate substantial revenue from the domestic marketing programmes they manage within their host country, including domestic sponsorship, ticketing and licensing. NOCs – of which there are over 200 – receive financial support for the training and development of Olympic teams and Olympic athletes. The IOC distributes TOP programme revenue to each of the NOCs throughout the world.

Although there appear to have been many positive developments since the Los Angeles Olympics, many academics at the time (see the contributors to Tomlinson and Whannel 1984) and since have been critical of the increasing commercialisation of the Games and the likely impact this has had on the event (e.g. Donnelly 1996; Whitson 1998). Portrayed as 'gloom merchants' and 'naysayers' by those involved with the Olympics and associated sports federations, these criticisms are not simply voiced by people who want to put an end to the Olympics. With the increasing involvement of powerful global brands as Olympic sponsors has come attendant commercial rights legislation – to provide exclusivity to their association with the Olympic symbols (the interlocked rings, the name of the

Games, etc.) and to avoid 'ambush marketing', which is the unauthorised commercial connection of a company with the Olympics, which the corporations pay millions of dollars to obtain. Yet this is seen as overly restrictive by smaller businesses and organisations. The Olympic Games also provide a major attraction to sponsors at a national level and thus drain resources from other non-Olympic sports and cultural activities during the build-up to the event. Criticisms of the IOC as an organisation have impacted on some of its practices, as can be seen by the 20 + 20 recommendations and Agenda 2020 'roadmap'. This is most evident in the changes introduced to the bidding process and Olympic host city selection since the late 1990s and again in 2015.

THE BIDDING PROCESS AND HOST CITY SELECTION

> In this city, you were either working for the Olympics, or you were dreading them – there was no middle ground.
>
> (Manuel Vázquez Montalbán, *An Olympic Death*, 2004 [1991]: 34)

Following the Salt Lake City bid scandal and subsequent reforms in the late 1990s, technically the procedure for bidding and selecting an Olympic host city now appears quite straightforward. If more than one city within a country wishes to bid to host the Games, the country's NOC selects one. Cities submit bids to the IOC eight or nine years in advance of the Games. An Evaluation Commission (EC) is appointed that reports to the IOC on the bidding cities and progress (only EC members can visit bid cities). The IOC selects a successful bidder seven years in advance of the Games – so in 2017 the IOC will vote on the Summer Games of 2024, and in 2019 it will vote on the Winter Games of 2026, etc.

Bids must provide information on the following topics: motivation, overall concept and public opinion, political support, finance, venues and programme, accommodation (athlete/media villages, hotel accommodation for IOC members, etc.), transport, security and other general conditions (demographics, environment, climate) and experience of running large-scale (if not mega-) events. In addition, a cultural programme is a requirement of each Games, to help 'promote harmonious relations, mutual understanding and friendship among the participants and others attending the Olympic Games' (Olympic Charter). The 'Host City Contract' – between the IOC, the host city and the NOC – is vitally important. All responsibilities and liabilities are vested in hosts, underpinned by stringent 'Rules of Conduct'.

As we have seen, the IOC remains a private organisation, which only accepts invited members. The voting membership of the IOC currently consists of 100 people, including the President Thomas Bach, but only slightly more than one-fifth of these are women. The IOC contains several members of royal families and corporate leaders and people holding an executive or senior leadership position within an IF or an NOC, including Sepp Blatter from FIFA. It thus remains subject to accusations of lack of transparency while it claims to be a movement and a 'family' based on a philosophy beyond politics (Lenskyj 2012; Jennings 2012). Alongside the myths and ideology of Olympism – with elements such as the creed and the motto borrowed from Christianity (Catholicism and Protestantism) – it is not surprising that quasi-religious claims are often made, such as upholding the 'spirit'

69

of the Games. On the other hand, critics prefer to portray the Olympics nowadays as an 'industry', a 'machine' and even a 'disease' that creates a blight on the cities and their populations that act as its hosts. These discursive differences manifest themselves in the politics of hosting, and especially in the public relations wars, which we consider next.

Olympic Agenda 2020 in context

As we have suggested, since his election as President in 2013 Thomas Bach has overseen several developments in the IOC and the Olympic movement. The Olympic Agenda 2020 – 'a strategic roadmap for the future of the Olympic movement' – was adopted in December 2014 at the 127th IOC Session in Monaco with 96 out of the 100 current IOC members in attendance. Related revisions to the Olympic Charter were adopted with effect from 8 December 2014. In May 2015 changes to the IOC commissions, with nearly one-third of commission members being women, were announced.

Several of the Agenda 2020 reforms appear to be in response to growing criticisms of the staging of sports mega-events in general, and not just the IOC, that have left the allure of hosting sports mega-events somewhat tarnished. These include: scandals associated with alleged vote rigging in FIFA, that actually involve some members of the IOC; continuing allegations of widespread doping and inaction on the part of IFs to investigate it, including in track and field athletics, for some the 'jewel in the crown' of the Summer Olympics; abuses of human rights by nations hosting sports mega-events, in contradiction of the IOC Charter; and the long-standing concern over 'white elephants' and the costs of staging sports mega-events at a time many governments are pursuing 'austerity' economic and political policies.

Given the increasing reluctance of urban populations in democracies to host sports mega-events, it appears that the analyses of earlier and more recent academic work on the politics of sports mega-events, informed by and informing the work of activists, may have begun to have some effect (Lenskyj 2008; Boykoff 2014a, 2014b). Lauermann (2015) identifies two recent 'trends in the urban politics of mega-events'. First has been the role of academic and non-academic critics of mega-events who have attempted to counter bids and 'contest the ways in which the professionalization of the industry impacts local decision-making'. Second has been the impact of questions raised by anti-bid activists, not just about the division of costs and benefits of mega-events, but also about 'the legitimacy of event-led development models' on cities contemplating bidding for them. These developments would go some way to explaining the declining interest in hosting the Winter Olympic Games as evidenced by four European cities – Norway's Oslo, Poland's Krakow, Sweden's Stockholm and Ukraine's Lviv – withdrawing from the bidding to leave only Beijing and Almaty as the remaining candidates for the 2022 edition. Equally, the withdrawal of Boston from being the nominated city from the United States Olympic Committee (USOC) to bid to host the 2024 Summer Olympics (replaced by the city of Los Angeles which perennially seeks nomination as an Olympic host candidate city) can be understood as a response to anti-bid pressure as well as concerns over public funding of such an event.

Hence a number of the 40 recommendations in Agenda 2020 relate to these concerns: for example, complying with the basic principles of good governance, supporting autonomy and increasing transparency, shaping the bidding process as an invitation, reducing the cost of bidding and including sustainability in all aspects of the Olympic Games. Other elements in Agenda 2020 include the fostering of gender equality and strengthening the 6th 'Fundamental Principle of Olympism' to include sexual orientation and addressing the IOC membership age limit (Gibson 2014). Other changes agreed included the launching of an Olympic Channel, the reviewing of the scope and composition of IOC commissions and the setting out of a framework for the Olympic programme that would allow more flexibility into the programme for hosts wishing to include sports popular in their country.

The costs of preparing a hosting bid – let alone staging an Olympic Games – are considerable (Toohey and Veal 2007: 131–132, after Preuss 2004). Nonetheless, Olympic economist Holger Preuss (2004: 275) calculates that every Summer Games since 1972 has made a surplus: 'When investments are eliminated from the final balance sheets of the OCOGs and operational expenditures are set against OCOG revenues, it can be stated that all the OCOGs under review [1972–2008] succeeded in making a financial profit.' Preuss operates with a 'decision model' that differentiates between 'Games-related and non-Games-related costs for facilities used during the Olympics'. On that basis, he argues 'an OCOG *should* only have to cover the costs for temporary facilities, overlay and rent' (Preuss 2004: 275, emphasis added). He can only do this by discounting as an Olympic cost many substantial infrastructure projects that have taken place at the same time as or preceding an Olympics – such as a refurbished airport, transport links and other forms of urban redevelopment. This separation of operational from capital investment costs associated with the Olympic Games results from a conventional economist's approach to modelling. As Toohey and Veal state:

> The arguments concerning apportionment of investment costs can also be raised in relation to sporting venues, since they also will continue to be used for other sporting events and by local citizens long after the Olympic Games are over. Thus the overall capital costs of sporting infrastructure investments should *ideally* be excluded when estimating the cost of running an Olympic Games event.
> (Toohey and Veal 2007: 133, emphasis added)

With this method of economic modelling, the $2.2 billion deficit for Montreal in 1976 can be transformed into a $0.64 billion surplus (Preuss 2004: 277). This economic approach makes two further important assumptions: (1) the venues will be used and (2) local citizens will use them. This is 'ideal type' modelling. But what about real-world opportunities, costs and impacts?

Mega-events such as the Olympic Games provide multiple meanings for different groups of people – as they happen, when they have taken place and, perhaps especially, as they are being bid for. Hence we know that advocates of hosting the Olympics will deploy a range of discursive strategies to win over public opinion. The main issues around which the hosting of the Olympics has been debated involve the burden of the costs and the distribution of the benefits. Research points to the uneven impacts of the Olympics. Despite much media acclamation, and the accolade 'the best Games ever' being proclaimed at the closing ceremony by the outgoing IOC President Juan Antonio Samaranch, the 2000 Olympics in Sydney generated substantial negative impacts on local residents and the environment – giving evidence to the claim that there is potential for conflict between economic and social benefits realised from hosting sports events. Since the late 1970s (and the Montreal Olympics in 1976 especially), a major concern in considerations of the Olympics has been this gap between the forecast and the actual impacts on the economy, society and culture. That there is likely to be such a gap is now fairly predictable. Pro-hosting advocates tend to gather and project optimistic estimates, while anti-hosting groups articulate concerns. More generally there has been an over-estimation of the benefits and an under-estimation of the costs of mega-events (Flybjerg 2014; Zimbalist 2015).

The positive achievements claimed by Games boosters include increased employment, a boost for tourism, opportunities for civil engagement – through volunteering (unpaid work) – and emulation in terms of increased active involvement in physical activity. In addition there is a 'trickle-down' assumption that suggests that industries and other parts of the host city's nation will benefit from the economic upturn and demand for goods and services stimulated by the hosting of the Olympics. Certainly recent past and selected future Olympic hosts have made these arguments. One of the main problems regarding the assessment of the costs and benefits of mega-events relates to the quality of data obtained from impact analyses.

Economic impact studies often claim to show that the investment of public money is worthwhile in the light of the economic activity generated by having professional sports teams or mega-events in cities. Yet here much depends on predictions of expenditure by sports-related tourism. Research shows that many positive studies have often been methodologically flawed and that the real economic benefit of such visitor spending is often well below that specified. According to the European Tour Operators Association (*Olympics and Tourism: Update on Olympics Report 2006*), the Olympic Games are 'an abnormality that is profoundly disruptive' of normal patterns of tourism. Another measure of economic impact – on the creation of new jobs in the local economy – has often been politically driven to justify the expenditure on new facilities, and hence the results are equally questionable.

With respect to social regeneration, it has been noted that there is an absence of systematic and robust empirical evidence about the social impacts of sports-related projects. Some research suggests that there may be positive impacts from greater community visibility, enhanced community image, the stimulation of other economic development and increases in 'psychic income' – collective morale, pride and confidence. Most non-academic commentators appear to agree that there will be a positive outcome with respect to health promotion, crime reduction, education and employment and general 'social inclusion' but without actually having the evidence to support the view. One problem is that there have not been many systematic research projects carried out into this, nor have the methodologies needed to investigate them been adequately developed. Another is that when evidence is forthcoming it is often rejected by Games boosters as biased and not impartial.

Since the early 1990s, when investigative reporting by journalists and social researchers uncovered details of corruption in the Olympic movement, and such news began to damage the reputation of the IOC, the organisation and OCOGs have engaged public relations (PR) companies and spin doctors to assist in managing media messages and the global and

72

local image of the Olympics. News and image management, spin doctoring and PR have become key features in any major public policy development in the UK and throughout the rest of the world.

Clearly the mass media are centrally important in discussing PR 'wars'. Are the media 'boosters' or 'sceptics'? It depends. The private sector media – in the UK the newspaper press and independent TV for example – could be critical if it suited their interests. The public sector – especially the BBC in the UK – tended to help to sell the 2012 bid, for example, and the associated hosting to an uncertain public. The BBC provided saturation coverage of the 2008 Beijing Olympics, sending over 440 journalists and reporters – an unprecedented number. For London 2012 the number increased to 765, with several hundred others on standby (Boyle and Haynes 2014: 85). BBC sports reporting can sometimes be accused of adoration that leans towards idolatry of professional and elite athletes. This in turn creates an expectant audience. Irrespective of occasional critical comments and blogs by journalists, the BBC remained a major booster for the London Games. Whether the BBC will be able to retain its 'Olympic Broadcaster' status from 2024 remains to be seen.

Just as reputation and symbolic power have become increasingly valuable resources for elected politicians, so too are they vital for international sports organisations and IFs. The IOC, for example, expects to see evidence of strong public support in any country that applies to host the Olympics. In this environment 'crisis communications', in response to bad publicity during 'spin wars', have become part of the PR role. It has been argued that PR's job is essentially to secure or 'manufacture' the consent of the public, which covers both active support and passive acquiescence for economic and social policies and developments. More broadly, Miller and Dinan (2007: 13) argue that PR's role has become 'to position private interests as being the same as public interests' and in so doing undermine the meaning of a public interest separate from that of private corporations. In this respect PR is concerned with bringing other private businesses and civic leaders 'onside' as well as members of the general public. As it has developed, a PR company's task is often to predict and thus ward off damaging attacks, especially in debates in the public sphere about urban development, such as the hosting of the Olympics. Hence an advertisement in the *Guardian* from the London 2012 Olympic Delivery Authority (ODA) asked for 'Community Relations Executives' who would act as:

> the main link between the ODA project teams, contractors and local residents with special regard to the construction impact and have the ability to win the trust of sceptical local audiences through strong interpersonal, influencing and communications skills.
>
> (*Guardian* 24 March 2007, 'Work' section: 12)

Events like the Olympic Games, the Football World Cup and other sports mega-events act as socio-cultural reference points, and reveal both the appeal and elusiveness of sport. In the age of global television, moreover, the capacity of major sports events to shape and project images of the host city or nation, both domestically and globally, makes them a highly attractive instrument for political and economic elites. It is in this context that the pursuit of hosting sports mega-events has become an increasingly popular strategy of governments, corporations and civic 'boosters' world-wide, who argue that major economic, developmental, political and socio-cultural benefits will flow from them, easily justifying the costs and risks involved (Horne and Manzenreiter 2006). Numerous studies fuel the popular belief that sport has a positive impact on the local community and the regional economy. Sport has been seen as a generator of national and local economic and social development. Economically it has been viewed as an industry around which cities can devise urban regeneration strategies. Socially it has been viewed as a tool for the development of urban communities, and the reduction of social exclusion and crime. Hence the increased participation in the 'Olympic City Bidding Game' (Roche 2000: 150) in the past 25 years (see Figure 3.4).

Compared with this conventional – or dominant – view of the Olympic Games and the Olympic movement, a different series of conclusions derived from a book and documentary film about the 2010 Vancouver Winter Olympics (Shaw 2008; Schmidt 2007) are worthy of consideration. The Olympics can be seen as a tool used by business corporations and governments (local, regional and sometimes national) to develop areas of cities or the countryside. They permit corporate land grabs by developers. Five major construction projects took place in association with the 2010 Winter Games: the building of the Canada Line (formerly known as the RAV – Richmond Airport–Vancouver Line) connecting the airport and downtown Vancouver; the athletes' village; a convention centre; developments in the Callaghan Valley west of Whistler (the main skiing area where the Olympic snowsport events would take place); and the building of an extension to the 'Sea to Sky Highway' through Eagleridge Bluffs, in West Vancouver, to enable shorter road times between Vancouver and Whistler. The view of one of the contributors to the film was that it was a disaster for any city on the planet to host the Olympics. Host city populations face increased taxes to pay for the 'party'. The poor and the homeless face criminalisation and/or eviction as downtown areas are gentrified (improved to appeal to more affluent visitors or full-time residents). The hosting of such a mega-event skews all other economic and social priorities and means the loss of the opportunity to do other things with public resources spent on the Games. The IOC markets sport as a product, pays no taxes and demands full compliance with its exacting terms and conditions, including governmental guarantees about meeting financial shortfalls. The end results are 'fat-cat' projects and media spectacles benefiting mostly the corporations that sponsor the Games, the property developers that receive public subsidies and the IOC – which secures millions of dollars from television corporations and global sponsors. These ideas have been summed up in recent writing by Boykoff (2014a), who argues that the Olympics have helped develop a distinctive form of capitalism: 'celebration capitalism'.

Similar criticisms have been made about the 2016 Summer Olympics to be staged in Rio de Janeiro. In October 2009, when Rio was awarded the right to host the 2016 Summer Olympics, in the face of apparently strong competition from a Chicago bid that had been enthusiastically endorsed by US President Barack Obama, it was heralded by the Brazilian President Lula as a sign that his country had moved from being a second-class to a first-class nation (Horne and Silvestre 2016; Clift and Andrews 2012). The decision to stage an Olympic Games in South America for the first time was, according to Dick Pound, a Canadian IOC member, 'not an anti-America thing or an anti-Obama thing. It's a sports competition, not true politics' (*Sunday Morning Post*, 4 October 2009). But

The contemporary Olympics

Summer Games

Year	Host	Other bidders
1976	Montreal	Los Angeles, Moscow
1980	Moscow	Los Angeles
1984	Los Angeles	
1988	Seoul	Nagoya
1992	Barcelona	Amsterdam, Belgrade, Birmingham, Brisbane, Paris
1996	Atlanta	Athens, Belgrade, Manchester, Melbourne, Toronto
2000	Sydney	Beijing, Berlin, Istanbul, Manchester
2004	Athens	Buenos Aires, Cape Town, Istanbul, Lille, Rio de Janeiro, Rome, San Juan, Seville, Stockholm, St. Petersburg
2008	Beijing	Istanbul, Osaka, Paris, Toronto
2012	London	Madrid, Moscow, New York, Paris
2016	Rio de Janeiro	Chicago, Madrid, Tokyo
2020	Tokyo	Istanbul, Madrid
2024	To be decided at the IOC Session in Lima in 2017 (Budapest, Paris, Rome, Los Angeles)	

Winter Games

Year	Host	Other bidders
1976	Innsbruck	Denver,* Sion, Tampere/Are, Vancouver
1980	Lake Placid	Vancouver-Garibaldi**
1984	Sarajevo	Sapporo, Falun-Goteborg
1988	Calgary	Falun, Cortina d'Ampezzo
1992	Albertville	Anchorage, Berchtesgaden, Cortina d'Ampezzo, Lillehammer, Falun, Sofia
1994	Lillehammer	Anchorage, Oestersunde/Are, Sofia
1998	Nagano	Aoste, Jacca, Oestersunde, Salt Lake City
2002	Salt Lake City	Oestersunde, Quebec City, Sion
2006	Torino	Helsinki, Klagenfurt, Poprad-Tatry, Sion, Zakopane
2010	Vancouver–Whistler	PyeongChang, Salzburg
2014	Soichi	PyeongChang, Salzburg
2018	PyeongChang	Annecy, Munich
2022	Beijing	Almaty

Figure 3.4 The Olympic Summer and Winter City bidding game, 1976–2024.

Source: adapted and updated from Roche 2000: 150–157.

Notes
*Awarded to Denver but rejected following citizens' plebiscite in 1972.
** Withdrew before final vote.

the opportunities that the successful bid has created for specific construction industry corporations in Brazil to develop parts of the Rio infrastructure, and the impacts this has had upon local communities, are now evident, as we discussed in Chapter 1. Clearly, when considering the politics of the Olympic Games the role and impartiality of the researcher can be called into question, as Montalbán suggested in the quotation cited earlier (he was originally writing just before Barcelona hosted the Olympics in 1992); researchers may find that there is no middle ground.

Despite Preuss' economic modelling, hosting the 1976 Summer Olympics resulted in huge losses and debts for the city of Montreal. The debt incurred on the interest for the loans to build what turned out to be largely 'white elephant' sports infrastructure was only finally paid off in November 2006 – costing Montreal's taxpayers well over CA\$2 billion in capital and interest costs, without anything like commensurate benefits. Rather than experiencing a post-Olympic boom, the economy of Montreal in the mid-1970s went into a steep decline that would last for almost two decades. No wonder, then, that when the Los Angeles Olympics took place in 1984 there had been no other city seriously bidding to host the event (Whitson and Horne 2006).

Today, established cities in advanced capitalist societies and cities in developing economies alike still line up to consider the possibility of hosting the Olympic Games. At the time of writing the hosts for the next four Olympic Games (2016, 2018, 2020 and 2022) are known and four cities – Budapest, Los Angeles, Paris and Rome – are expected to submit 'bid books' for the competition to host the Summer Games in 2024. At any one time, then, several cities are anticipating hosting an Olympics and many others are waiting to discover if it will be their turn. The change in the allure of hosting the Olympics has come about partly because of the success that the LA 1984 Games appeared to be – in terms of making a substantial financial surplus or profit of over \$200 million, laying a solid economic foundation for a support system for athletes in the US and putting on a television spectacular involving many of the world's athletes. The attraction of hosting has also come about because of changes that the IOC has made to the process of selecting cities following investigative journalists' revelations of insider corruption in the 1980s and 1990s (see Simson and Jennings 1992; and http://transparency insportblog.blogspot.co.uk). The major inducement to engage in Olympic hosting now, as opposed to in the 1980s, is of course financial. The sponsorship and television rights money that the IOC has negotiated covers most of the *operating* costs of the Olympic Games – \$2–2.5 billion for the Summer 'edition'. In addition, large television audiences have meant that television corporations and broadcasting unions have been prepared to pay increasing sums of money for exclusive coverage of the Olympics to the IOC, which has helped them to offset the operational costs of the Games (discussed in the next chapter).

Critics, critiques and challenges

Since the 1980s, critiques of the Olympics have developed and its contradictions have been exposed by both academic scholars and investigative journalists who have sought to promote greater transparency in sport. The credibility and integrity of the IOC and other international sports organisations (especially FIFA) have been further challenged following proven allegations of doping, physical and psychological violence and corruption. Revelations of doping (perhaps reaching a nadir in 1988 with Ben Johnson and the 100 metres final), bribery and opaque IOC procedures created the environment for serious challenges to the IOC. The romantic idealists (for example Bruce Kidd 1992) and John

MacAloon 1981) faced the scathing critics (such as John Hoberman 1995; Arnd Krüger 1993; and Helen Lenskyj 2000, 2002, 2008).

Different types of criticism have been made about the Olympics. It has been criticised for the rise of excessive commercialism, for hypocrisy and the betrayal of Olympic ideals, and for the promotion of excessive nationalism. Andrew Jennings was an early journalist critic of corruption in the bidding process, the suppression of negative drug test results, bribery in individual contests, the manipulation of press coverage, President Samaranch's links with the fascist Franco regime in his native Spain, the IOC members' acceptance of lavish gifts and the general impact of increased commercialisation. In the academic sphere French Marxist critic Jean-Marie Brohm was joined by Canadian Rick Gruneau and Alan Tomlinson and Garry Whannel in the 1980s.

Local opposition to the Games has also developed on the basis of concerns over: the huge amount of public expenditure for a very brief athletics and sport festival; persons displaced by development; rent increases; environmental and social impacts; and the lack of public consultation or ability to participate in decisions. So the Olympics have shifted from being seen as a movement (Coubertin) to an industry (Lenskyj) and more recently as a system (Chappelet). Based on an idealistic ideology, as a movement the Olympics are seen as an organic, functional, civic religion. Conceived of as an industry – commercial, dysfunctional and corporate – materialist critics consider the ideals of the Olympic movement to be compromised by the growth of involvement with corporate sponsors and media organisations. Viewed more pragmatically as a system – a network of distributed parts, hubs and switches, but also unstable – the Olympics can be viewed as continuing to exhibit contradictory tendencies.

Talk about legacies across various dimensions has become an established part of Olympic hosting as we discussed in the previous chapter. Hence economic benefits (direct and indirect), improvements to the built environment (non-sporting, e.g. transport infrastructure), information and education (concerning sport and culture), public life, politics and culture, sport, elite performance, mass participation, the 'trickle-down' effect, financial support, the built sporting infrastructure, and sporting symbols, memory and history are all considered as potentially positive aspects of hosting an Olympics or other mega-event (Cashman 2006). Yet critics still ask if the response of the IOC and the Olympic movement was to treat the problems of the 1980s and 1990s as a crisis of communication rather than as a crisis of ethics and morals (Jennings 2000). That is, to what extent has the Olympic movement lost its integrity and distinctive role in world sport? Undoubtedly there are continuing contradictions of Olympism around various binaries. As Gruneau (2002) suggests with respect to sports mega-events, three important questions are sometimes overlooked: Who benefits? Who is excluded? What scope is there for contestation? We attempt to identify some answers to these questions elsewhere in this book.

CONCLUSION

The IOC claims that the Games offer inspiration as a movement, a family and a philosophy, derived in many respects from Pierre de Coubertin's Christian beliefs and his relationship

77

to organised religion of the late nineteenth and early twentieth centuries. Being critical of the Olympic Games can therefore be likened to 'farting loudly during High Mass in the Vatican' (Shaw 2008: 154). Yet the Olympic movement creates attention for itself by inviting criticism when it deviates from its own proclaimed ethical standards. Hence, in the first part of this chapter we considered the IOC as a contradictory formation – having to adjust to both capitalist modernity and enterprise culture. The contradictions led to charges of hypocrisy by critics, and concerns about issues of 'governance' by those seeking to influence the future of the IOC. Developments in capitalism over the past 30 years provide the background against which the allure of hosting the Olympic Games has grown. Despite recent setbacks, with respect to the Winter Olympics especially, the number of cities wishing to host another Summer Games appears undiminished. The IOC lists a global network of nearly 40 study centres interested in investigating the Olympic movement and ideals.

Developments in contemporary capitalism also shape the changing political economy of the Olympic Games and thus create the conditions in which criticism of the events develops. As Shaw (2008: 168) states, 'In our consumer culture, mega events, Olympics included, use sports as a platform to sell stuff.' The negative 'legacies' associated with the Games include social polarisation, eviction and displacement of marginal populations, public resources being used for private benefit, global rather than local benefit and the creation of playgrounds for the affluent. When normal political routes and legal processes are short-circuited by governments and local organisers anxious to get work completed on time, it is not surprising that critics consider tactics that they hope may create the biggest public relations impact. Different examples of 'seizing the platform' (Price 2008) become available as protest and event coalitions and activism develops. The mass media are of central importance in defining mega-events as valuable and giving them their political potency. We turn to the relationship between the Olympics and the media in the next chapter.

NOTES

1 www.olympic.org/Documents/Olympic_Agenda_2020/Olympic_Agenda_2020-20-20_ Recommendations-ENG.pdf (last accessed 28 August 2015).
2 www.olympic.org/ioc-members-list (last accessed 28 August 2015).
3 www.olympic.org/Documents/olympic_charter_en.pdf (last accessed 28 August 2015).
4 See Recommendation 37, page 19, www.olympic.org/Documents/Olympic_Agenda_ 2020/Olympic_Agenda_2020-20-20_Recommendations-ENG.pdf (last accessed 28 August 2015).
5 www.olympic.org/ioc-governance-national-olympic-committees?tab=mission (last accessed 28 August 2015).
6 www.olympic.org/news/olympic-agenda-2020-triggers-significant-changes-to-ioc-commissions-president-bach-nominates-more-women-and-broader-geographical-representation/246159 (last accessed 3 August 2015).

FURTHER READING

Chappelet, J.-L. and Kubler-Mabbott, B. (2008) *The International Olympic Committee and the Olympic System: The Governance of World Sport*, London: Routledge.

Lenskyj, H. (2008) *Olympic Industry Resistance*, Albany, NY: SUNY Press.

Toohey, K. and Veal, A. (2007) *The Olympic Games: A Social Science Perspective* (2nd edition), Oxford: CABI.

Vázquez Montalbán, M. (2004 [1991]) *An Olympic Death*, London: Serpent's Tail.

CHAPTER 4

TELEVISION AND THE COMMERCIALISATION OF THE OLYMPIC GAMES

The Olympic Games could never have attained global impact without television. The Games, as they now exist, are a product of television's power to produce and distribute live global spectacle. Indeed the Games are perhaps *better* understood as a television event than as a sporting one. Of the Olympic sports, only athletics, tennis, football, basketball and boxing have any significantly large spectator following outside the Olympic Games – and in the case of tennis, football, basketball and boxing, the Olympics is only a minor part of their sporting calendar and competitive formats. In our rough estimate, the other 21 sports included in 2012 typically account for only around 5 per cent of television sport hours on terrestrial television in the UK. The Olympics aside, athletics cannot compete for popularity or financial strength with the major commercialised sports such as football, basketball, golf, tennis, motor racing and American football. The majority of people who watch the Olympic Games do not otherwise follow regularly even the sports that are most prominently featured on Olympic television – athletics, swimming and gymnastics.

Nor can the Olympic sports, for the most part, claim a broad base of participants. Although a fair proportion of Olympic sports can claim a degree of participation, in the UK at least, only football, running, swimming and cycling would count as mass participation activities, and then only if one includes swimming, running or cycling for leisure rather than for competition. According to Sport England's Active People Survey (2014) there has been a small increase in overall participation between 2005 and 2014 (from 34.2 per cent to 36.2 per cent). The majority of the population cites no active participation: 2005 – 58.8 per cent, 2014 – 57.2 per cent (participation is defined in this survey as taking part in one session per week; at least four sessions of at least moderate intensity for at least 30 minutes in the previous 28 days). Typically, less than 2 per cent of the population regularly plays tennis and less than 1 per cent ride horses.[1] So the Olympics do not appear to be popular because of the regular following of its major sports either as spectators or as participants. Rather, it is because it is a spectacular television show, with the badge of being the world's best. Indeed, football's World Cup has a far stronger claim to have a non-television basis to its popularity, with millions around the world involved both as spectators and participants. So, we would argue, it is partly as a spectacular television event that the Olympic Games can be productively understood. As such, it has been shaped by the forces of commodification, globalisation and digitalisation; and it is increasingly shaped by the convergence of the once distinct technologies of television, computers and the internet. This chapter outlines the financial relations between television, sponsorship and the Olympic Games, presents a periodised historical outline of the relations between

80

the Olympic Games and the media, and discusses the relations between the Games and its sponsors.

OLYMPIC FINANCES

Capital demands its own reproduction. Money left in a tin is losing the opportunity to gain interest or to accrue profit. The logic of capital is reinvestment. But, as Marx argued, and indeed demonstrated, there is a systematic tendency for the rate of profit to decline (Marx 1981). This has two consequences. First, it produces a considerable pressure to rectify the situation, by forcing wage rates down – by casualisation, unemployment or de-unionisation, sourcing cheaper materials and promoting the product in new markets, or more vigorously in existing markets. The second effect is that capital is constantly seeking new areas to colonise, seeking to monetise areas of human endeavour hitherto not based around profit generation. The development of spectator sport and professional sport can be interpreted in part as instances of capital penetrating and colonising new areas.

The Olympic Games have become an enormous event, not least in terms of their global reach via television, their massive revenues from commercial sources and their huge costs. The Games produce four main sources of revenue – ticket sales; sale of television rights; sponsorship; and licensing and merchandising. The IOC collects television rights payments and international sponsorships and redistributes these funds to the Organising Committee, the National Olympic Committees (NOCs) and the International Federations (IFs). The IOC retains a little under 10 per cent of commercial revenue to cover its own running costs, which include the lavish travel and accommodation expenses available to IOC members. Local sponsorship and merchandising revenue goes to the Organising Committee. The IOC also contributes some of the television and sponsorship revenue to the Organising Committee. The IOC insists on a key distinction in Olympic funding between running costs and infrastructural costs. The costs of running the Games is budgeted to break even – with state support, sponsorship, licensing and ticketing revenue supplemented by IOC funding. The infrastructural costs involved in building new facilities,

	2009–2012	*Percentage*
Broadcast	3,850	47.85
TOP programme	950	11.81
OGOC domestic sponsorship	1,838	22.84
Ticketing	1,238	15.39
Licensing	170	2.11
Total	8,046	

Figure 4.1 Olympic revenues for the quadrennium 2009–2012 (figures in million US dollars).

Source: IOC Marketing Fact File 2015.

Note
The revenue from each consecutive four-year period, or quadrennium, has been rising consistently for the last two decades.

	1993–1996	1997–2000	2001–2004	2005–2008	2009–2012
Broadcast	1,251	1,845	2,232	2,570	3,850
TOP programme	279	579	663	866	950
OGOC domestic sponsorship	534	655	796	1,555	1,838
Ticketing	451	625	411	274	1,238
Licensing	115	66	87	185	170
Total	2,630	3,770	4,189	5,450	8,046

Figure 4.2 Olympic revenues from 1993–2012 (million US dollars).

Source: IOC Marketing Fact File 2015.

and renovating existing ones, transport enhancement and security are met by the host city and nation. In the four-year quadrennium 2009–2012 the total Olympic revenue was over $8 billion, of which 48 per cent came from television rights, 37 per cent from sponsorship and only 15 per cent from ticketing.

Figure 4.2 expresses the sources of revenue for the Olympic Games, and demonstrates a consistent rise in total revenues since 1993. All figures have been rounded to the nearest million US dollars. As with subsequent figures, the source of the statistics is as cited, but the presentation, juxtaposition and calculation based on these statistics to produce extra information, such as percentages, is that of the authors. The one exception is ticketing, where fluctuations are accounted for by local factors; the price of tickets, the numbers available and the percentage sold vary from Games to Games. In the last two Games considerable efforts were made to ensure every seat was filled. The tickets in Beijing were much cheaper, on average, than those in London, although London also deployed a very wide price range with some tickets for many events costing less than £20, while the best tickets for premier events were very expensive.

The number of tickets available fluctuates according to stadium size and organisation of the programme. Organisers can seek to maximise ticket revenue by breaking up the performance day into a number of sessions, by scheduling events over more days, or utilising more venues. For example, the number of tickets available in Atlanta 1996 was much greater than for the other seven Games in Figure 4.3, but they sold a smaller percentage of them than in three of the four Summer Olympic Games since 1996. The average ticket price also varies considerably, partly in relation to the scale of the economy and cost of living in the host country. The average ticket price in London was high, but there was also a great range, with high premium prices for events with major appeal, balanced by £20 tickets for many other events; there was also a wide range of prices within stadia. Despite the rising revenues from ticketing, however, broadcasting continues to provide almost half of the total revenue, with sponsorship producing another 35 per cent. So the majority of Olympic income, typically over 80 per cent, comes from corporate sources – broadcasting and sponsorship.

Despite considerable fluctuations in ticketing revenue, all sources of revenue have grown significantly since 1993. Figure 4.5 shows how each source of revenue grew compared to

82

Olympic Games	Tickets available (millions)	Tickets sold (millions)	Percentage of tickets sold	Average price ($)	Revenue (million $)
1984 Los Angeles	6.9	5.7	82	27	156
1988 Seoul	4.4	3.3	75	11	36
1992 Barcelona	3.9	3.0	77	26	79
1996 Atlanta	11.0	8.3	75	51	425
2000 Sydney	7.6	6.7	88	82	551
2004 Athens	5.3	3.8	71	60	228
2008 Beijing	6.8	6.5	96	28	185
2012 London	8.5	8.2	97	120	988

Figure 4.3 Ticket revenue from the Olympic Games 1984–2012.

Source: adapted from IOC Marketing File 2015.

	1993–1996	1997–2000	2001–2004	2005–2008	2009–2012
Broadcast	48	49	53	47	48
TOP programme	11	15	16	16	12
OGOC domestic sponsorship	20	17	19	29	23
Ticketing	17	17	10	5	15
Licensing	4	2	2	3	2
Total	100	100	100	100	100

Figure 4.4 Olympic revenues as percentage of total for each quadrennium.

Source: adapted from IOC Marketing Fact File 2015.

	1997–2000	2001–2004	2005–2008	2009–2012	1993/1996–2009/2012
Broadcast	47	21	15	50	208
TOP programme	108	15	31	10	241
OGOC domestic sponsorship	23	22	95	18	244
Ticketing	39	–34	–33	352	175
Licensing	–43	32	113	–8	48
Total	43	11	30	48	206

Figure 4.5 Percentage growth in Olympic revenues.

Source: adapted from IOC Marketing Fact File 2015.

the previous quadrennium, with the final column showing the overall percentage growth from 1993/1996 to 2009/2012.

As mentioned in the previous chapter, the IOC distributes 90 per cent of its revenue to organisations throughout the Olympic movement in order to support the staging of the

Olympic Games total ($ millions)		Winter Olympic Games total ($ millions)	
Athens 2004	965	Salt Lake 2002	552
Beijing 2008	1,250	Torino 2006	561
London 2012	1,374	Vancouver 2010	775
		Sochi 2014	833

Figure 4.6 Amounts allocated by the IOC to local Organising Committees.

Olympic Games, and to promote the world-wide development of sport. It retains 10 per cent of Olympic marketing revenue for the operational and administrative costs of governing the Olympic movement (IOC). It makes a contribution to Organising Committees, which is not a fixed amount or percentage, but seems calculated to ensure that the running costs (as distinct from the infrastructural costs) are met. In recent years these amounts have been as specified in Figure 4.6.

The bulk of television revenue has always come from the US, with its large and affluent population and lucrative advertising revenue potential. From the early 1980s, the major US networks lobbied the IOC to raise a greater proportion of the revenue from the rest of the world, one senior executive declaring that Europe was 'getting a free lunch'.[2]

While it is clear that in the last 20 years the percentage of revenue being raised from television rights in the rest of the world has increased, the proportion provided by the US has only dropped by 5 per cent, and the proportion paid by Europe has remained steady at 22–23 per cent. Indeed, it is Latin America and the Caribbean that has provided the most significant growth in revenues.

Despite the growth in sponsorship revenue, television rights payments have continued to provide the dominant share of Olympic revenue, and the bulk of the money has come from the major American networks. Despite the massive growth in the reach and usage of the internet, 'new media' rights payments still account for less than 1 per cent of revenue, although as broadcasters are able to utilise their own internet operations, this figure is misleading.

Ever since the first proper rights payments from US sources, in 1960, the competition between the major American television networks has driven revenues upwards at a rapid rate. Even when, during the mid-1980s, television executives and IOC members alike

	1998–2000	2002–2004	2006–2008	2010–2012
North America	1,124.0	1,397.4	1,579.0	2,154.0
Latin America/Caribbean	14.2	20.8	34.0	106.0
Asia	208.0	232.6	274.0	575.0
Middle East/Africa	11.9	12.9	24.9	41.0
Europe	422.1	514.0	578.4	848
Oceania	64.9	54.3	79.7	126.0
Total	**1,845.1**	**2,232.0**	**2,570.0**	**3,850.0**

Figure 4.7 Revenues from television rights by region ($ million).

Source: IOC Marketing Fact File 2015.

84

	1998–2000	2002–2004	2006–2008	2010–2012
North America	60.92	62.61	61.44	55.95
Latin America/Caribbean	0.77	0.93	1.32	2.75
Asia	11.27	10.42	10.66	14.94
Middle East/Africa	0.64	0.58	0.97	1.06
Europe	22.88	23.03	22.51	22.03
Oceania	3.52	2.43	3.10	3.27
TOTAL	100.00	100.00	100.00	100.00

Figure 4.8 Revenues by region as percentage of total in each quadrennium.

Source: IOC Marketing Fact File 2015.

	2002–2004	2006–2008	2010–2012
North America	24	13	36
Latin America/Caribbean	46	63	212
Asia	12	18	110
Middle East/Africa	8	93	65
Europe	22	13	47
Oceania	–16	47	58
TOTAL	21	15	50

Figure 4.9 Percentage revenue growth by region.

Source: IOC Marketing Fact File 2015.

doubted that the increase could continue, their pessimism was unwarranted. Only in the last decade can signs be detected that they are no longer enormous. The reach of Olympic television is now close to saturation – most people who wish to watch are able to, and television is being challenged by new media for its audiences and hence advertising revenue. However, in an era when broadcast television may be losing a little of its absolute primacy, the Olympic Games are still able to offer live and unpredictable drama, which only sport can provide and hitherto only broadcast television could adequately deliver.

THE GAMES AND THE MEDIA

How did this global spectacle develop? We will chart this emergence and growth in five periods: the pre-television era between 1896 and 1935; the emergence of television as a new technology between 1936 and 1967; the technological perfecting and globalisation of television between 1968 and 1987; the era of digital transformation from 1988 to 2000 and the impact of multi-platform delivery; and the emergence and growth of social media since 2000.

Mediating the Games: 1896–1935

The modern Olympic Games were established in the period of the late nineteenth century in which a modern mass communication system also began to develop. The combination of photography, wireless telegraphy, a reading public and entrepreneurial investment gave birth to the modern popular press. The first cinemas emerged in the closing years of the century, and until television, cinema newsreels were the only way, other than presence at the event, that people could observe sport performance. Not entirely coincidentally, the last decade of the nineteenth century was also a period in which the growth of branded goods and chain stores triggered substantial growth in advertising. By the end of the twentieth century, of course, global corporations would be providing a substantial revenue stream for the Olympic Games in the form of sponsorship. Movie cameras were used to film at the 1896 Games in Athens, although the earliest surviving footage seems to be from 1908. During the early years of the twentieth century, cinema spread rapidly around the world, and in the 1920s the first radio broadcasts were made (see Whannel 2002). Photographs of the 1912 Olympic Games were traded commercially. The 1924 Games were the first to be broadcast by radio. In 1932, newsreel cameras were used to determine the winner of the 100 metres. Despite the emergence of television from the 1930s, radio remained an important medium for the Olympic Games for many years.

In 1932, around 1,500 amateur radio operators offered to help broadcast news of the Games internationally (Yalin 2007). Shen Yalin's work on the historical development of the Press Centre was a valuable resource for this account of Olympic press and radio. Broadcasts of the Berlin Games of 1936 were sent by short wave to over 40 countries, 105 radio reporters from 41 foreign broadcasting companies transmitted 2,328 reports to all parts of the world (*Official Olympic Games Report* 1936). In 1948 the BBC broadcast radio coverage around the world in 40 languages (*Official Olympic Games Report* 1948). Radio continued to be an important means of dissemination during the 1950s, but by the 1960s television was on its way to becoming the dominant medium for the Olympic Games.

The emergence of television technology: 1936–1967

Before the Second World War, only four countries (the US, UK, France and Germany) had developed viable television technologies. For the Olympic Games, the television era began in Berlin in 1936. Pictures were not broadcast direct to the public, but relayed to around 28 local halls, attracting an audience of around 150,000. The image quality was described variously as 'excellent' to 'unsatisfactory'.[3] Three months after the 1936 Games, the BBC introduced the world's first regular television service, in the London area. But the first real broadcasting of an Olympic Games did not occur until the London Olympics of 1948. Pictures could only be received in the London area. There were just 35,000 households with television licences at the start of 1948, but, possibly fuelled by the Olympic Games, this figure tripled during the year. Around 70 hours were broadcast, with one day alone having seven and a half hours of coverage.[4] The audiences were small, but the enormous effort put into covering the Games gave great impetus to the technological development of television.

Despite this, television technology spread much more slowly than did the technologies of film and cinema. Before 1960 fewer than 25 countries had launched regular television services and so the patterns of international sport broadcasting had yet to develop. The 1952 Olympic Games in Helsinki were only televised in two countries. In the build-up to

Year	City	TV rights	Percentage increase	Year	City	TV rights	Percentage increase
1960	Rome	1.2		1960	Squaw Valley	0.05	
1964	Tokyo	1.6	33	1964	Innsbruck	0.93	1,760
1968	Mexico City	10	525	1968	Grenoble	2.6	180
1972	Munich	18	80	1972	Sapporo	8.5	226
1976	Montreal	35	94	1976	Innsbruck	11.6	37
1980	Moscow	88	151	1980	Lake Placid	20.7	78
1984	Los Angeles	287	226	1984	Sarajevo	102.7	396
1988	Seoul	403	40	1988	Calgary	324.9	216
1992	Barcelona	636	58	1992	Albertville	291.9	−10
1996	Atlanta	898	41	1994	Lillehammer	352.9	21
2000	Sydney	1,332	48	1998	Nagano	514	46
2004	Athens	1,494	12	2002	Salt Lake City	738	44
2008	Beijing	1,739	16	2006	Turin	831	13
2012	London	2,569	48	2010	Vancouver	1,280	54

Figure 4.10 Revenue from television rights payments ($ million).

Source: figures derived from IOC Marketing Fact File 2015.

Note
Figures over $10 million rounded up to the nearest million.

the Melbourne Games of 1956, the US networks resisted paying rights for the event, and negotiations with American and European broadcasters were unsuccessful. As a result, only six pre-recorded, half-hour programmes were accessible on a few independent channels in the US. At the 1956 Melbourne Games, television was installed in the Press Centre for the first time, enabling journalists to watch events happening in the stadium. Six television screens linked by closed circuit, with a camera directed on the scoreboard, brought events and results to the Press Centre (Yalin 2007). In 1960, for the first time, significant fees were paid by television companies to acquire the rights to broadcast.

By contrast, the 1960 Olympic Games in Rome were relayed to 12 countries on the Eurovision link. The American network CBS paid around $380,000 for the rights, and daily recordings were flown across the Atlantic for re-transmission. A total of 21 countries saw some Olympic material on television. The audience potential of the Games was clear when CBS reported a 36 per cent audience share, heralding the start of competitive bidding that would push rights payments rapidly up over the next few decades. New communication satellites (e.g. Telstar, Syncom 3) enabled the first intercontinental live broadcasts for 1964 and 1968, and the Olympics were seen in colour for the first time. Television was coming of age, and it was about to transform sport in general and the Olympic Games in particular.

Perfecting the picture: 1968–1987

The rise of television sport was most closely associated with the BBC in the UK and ABC in the US. ABC, in particular, developed a commitment to focusing on the drama, and the stars, epitomised by their two best-known slogans, 'Up close and personal' and 'The thrill of victory, the agony of defeat'. ABC's style featured close-ups, graphics and microphones placed to pick up the sound of the action. In 1968 ABC scheduled 48 hours of coverage (live and recorded), a threefold increase on 1964.[5]

Communication satellites and the spread of television around the world were making the Games a global television event. This, in turn, gave it enormous potential as a platform for symbolic political acts. The Black Power salutes at Mexico 1968, the seizing of Israeli athletes as hostages by a militant Palestinian group at Munich 1972, and the sequence of boycotts that marked the Games between 1976 and 1984 provide three very different instances of exploitation of this opportunity (see Chapter 9). By 1984 the Summer Games were being relayed to 150 countries and the Winter Games to 100. By 2000 the Summer Games became global and universal in reach, being televised in 220 countries, and by 2004 the same was true of the Winter Games. In recent years, the very centrality of television to major sport has made live stadium viewing seem slightly inadequate – with the action a long way away, and no replays. As a result, modern stadia, with their giant screens and hyped up presentation, have begun to adjust. Cairns (2015: 734) makes the interesting argument that the impact of television sport on stadium design is such that 'its architecture has mutated into a semi-real, semi-virtual phenomenon in which the difference between the physical structure and its mediated image has definitively blurred'. In the next chapter we consider the role of stadium architects in constructing the urban spectacle.

Summer Games			Winter Games		
Year	Site	Countries	Year	Site	Countries
1936	Berlin	1			
1948	London	1			
1952	Helsinki	2			
1956	Melbourne	1	1956	Cortina	22
1960	Rome	21	1960	Squaw Valley	27
1964	Tokyo	40	1964	Innsbruck	30
1968	Mexico City	n/a	1968	Grenoble	32
1972	Munich	98	1972	Sapporo	41
1976	Montreal	124	1976	Innsbruck	38
1980	Moscow	111	1980	Lake Placid	40
1984	Los Angeles	156	1984	Sarajevo	100
1988	Seoul	160	1988	Calgary	64
1992	Barcelona	193	1992	Albertville	86
			1994	Lillehammer	120
1996	Atlanta	214	1998	Nagano	160
2000	Sydney	220	2002	Salt Lake City	160
2004	Athens	220	2006	Torino	200
2008	Beijing	220	2010	Vancouver	220
2012	London	220	2014	Sochi	220

Figure 4.11 Countries broadcasting the Summer and Winter Olympic Games, 1936–2014.

Source: IOC Marketing Fact File 2015.

The establishment of the Olympic Games as a global television event made it a site of symbolic importance in the Cold War. As soon as the 1980 Games were awarded to Moscow, lobby groups in Western countries began urging boycotts. However, it was not until 1979, and the Soviet invasion of Afghanistan, that a pretext great enough to cause government action arose. US President Jimmy Carter announced a boycott and went to great lengths to pressure other Western countries into supporting it (see Chapter 9). However, neither this boycott nor the less effective retaliatory one organised by the Eastern bloc in 1984 appeared to diminish the popularity of the Games on television. Indeed, the Olympic Games were well established as a ratings winner, and provided a valuable basis around which the networks could announce and promote their autumn schedules. The pattern of US rights payments from 1960 to 1988 was one of continuing and spectacular growth.

During this period, the Olympic Games became the stake in an intense battle between the US networks. The potential for big audiences, even during the day and late at night, and usually during the slack summer season, helped attract additional advertising revenue. By the 1980s the escalation in rights payments was in danger of outstripping the level of advertising revenue. The 1988 Winter Olympics were scheduled for Calgary, an almost perfect site from the point of view of American television, as a large proportion of events could be transmitted live in either late afternoon or peak time on both coasts – the majority of the American television audience is in the east coast (Eastern) and west coast (Pacific) time zones. Consequently the bidding was especially intense. When ABC's determination to retain their 'Olympic Network' tag led them to bid $309 million for the 1988 Winter Olympics, it was widely felt in the television industry, and not least at ABC, that the payment was too high and could not be recouped in advertising revenue (see Billings *et al.* 1998).

The pessimism was heightened when the American economy slumped in the mid to late 1980s. The American networks began pressuring the IOC to extract higher rights payments from the rest of the world, with top television executives arguing that the European Broadcasting Union (EBU) was getting a free lunch. It is notable that the 1992 Winter Olympics, uniquely, brought in less television revenue than its predecessor. However, in the years since, the US payments have continued their upward trajectory. The ever-growing numbers of countries who wished to have their own broadcasters on site prompted the introduction in 1988 of a separate International Broadcasting Centre, distinct from the

	Summer	Winter	Total
1960	0.39	0.05	0.44
1964	1.50	0.59	2.09
1968	4.50	2.50	7.00
1972	7.50	6.40	13.90
1976	25.00	10.00	35.00
1980	87.00	15.50	102.50
1984	225.00	91.50	316.50
1988	300.00	309.00	609.00

Figure 4.12 US network payments for Olympic television rights ($ million).

Press Centre, with commentary, production and editing facilities (Official Olympic Games Report 1988: 689–706).

The IOC was indeed to embark on an effort to ensure that countries other than the US also paid greater sums for the rights. The bidding wars that had forced the price for the 1988 Winter Olympic Games up to $309 million precipitated a series of changes that led to ABC Television being acquired by Capital Cities, and the imposition of new budgetary restraints on the acquisition of sporting rights. It was the end of an era for ABC, which had dubbed itself the 'Olympic Network', but was now to lose its prime position to rival network NBC. The economic recession of the early 1980s and the declining power of ABC led to IOC fears (misplaced as it turned out) that the income from US rights payments would drop. At the 1986 IOC Session, prompted by ABC, the IOC introduced a new scheduling – the Barcelona Olympics of 1992 would be followed by the Winter Olympics in Lillehammer in 1994, putting Summer and Winter Games in separate years for the first time. This was designed to protect the American networks from the need to cover the cost of two Olympic events in the same year. The global reach of the Olympic Games grew throughout the 1980s. Claims of audiences of between one and two billion were characteristically made, but although the audiences undoubtedly are large, and the reach great, there are some reasons to doubt the accuracy of global audience figures (see Box 4.1).

BOX 4.1 DO WE REALLY KNOW HOW MANY PEOPLE WATCH THE OLYMPIC GAMES?

Television audience figures are gathered by a combination of meters on sets and diaries maintained by households. Typically, a panel of a few thousand sample households will have the meters and complete diaries over a period of months. The meters register when a television is on, and which channel it is tuned to, broken down into three-minute segments. Such methods are not universal but variations on them are utilised in 54 countries. These countries contain 75 per cent of the world's population, and 90 per cent of the world's TV households.

Sport organisations quote audience statistics as part of their case for television rights payments and in order to attract sponsors. The relatively reliable statistics for some countries are augmented by estimates for the rest of the world, for public viewing and new media viewing. There are no accurate means of assessing the numbers who watch in bars and other public places, or watch via computers or mobile phones. Apart from the 54 countries for which verifiable data are available, another 166 provided some television coverage of the 2008 Olympic Games. In some countries diary data alone are used. This is a method which, it has been established, is not accurate. For many countries any attempt to estimate an audience can be little more than guesswork.

Whereas the standard unit of television audience statistics is the *average programme audience* (based on those who watched the whole game/match/event), sport organisations have tended to utilise other means. They will quote the *peak figure* (the maximum size of the audience at some point during the event), which is generally around 1.5 times greater, or they will quote the *reach*, which includes anyone who watched for at least three minutes, generally twice the size of the average audience.

In addition, to provide an audience figure for a whole competition, they will aggregate the reach to obtain a *cumulative audience*, resulting in the claim that, for example, 26.29 billion viewers watched the 2006 World Cup competition. A different form of aggregation is provided in the form of *total viewer hours*. This is derived by multiplying the duration of the programme by the number of viewers in the audience. Such figures, especially where based partly on estimates, are demonstrably of little statistical value or accuracy. An investigation by *The Independent* established a consistent pattern in which the audiences claimed by sport organisations were many times greater than the verifiable portion (which is based on 90 per cent of the available audience). Examples quoted from 2006 included:

Event	Claim	Verifiable
Italy v France (World Cup final)	715.1 million	260 million
American Super Bowl	750m–1 billion	98 million
Winter Olympics Opening Ceremony	2 billion	87 million
Champions League (Arsenal v Barcelona)	120 million	86 million
Formula One: Brazilian Grand Prix	354 million	83 million
Golf: Ryder Cup (final day)	Up to 1 billion	6 million
Commonwealth Games Opening Ceremony	1.5 billion	5 million

There is clear evidence that the claims of audience size made for major sporting events, including the Olympic Games, warrant closer scrutiny. The Olympic Games claimed global audiences as follows:

1988	Seoul	10.4 billion
1992	Barcelona	16.6 billion
1996	Atlanta	19.6 billion

The above figures are based on the 'cumulative audience'. In 2000 the IOC switched to the use of figures based on 'total viewer hours', resulting in the following claimed audiences:

2000	Sydney	36.1 billion
2004	Athens	34.4 billion

From the early 1980s, aware of the danger of dependence on a single revenue stream from television sources, the IOC, in conjunction with Horst Dassler of Adidas, had already begun to develop the blueprint for a globalised sponsorship scheme (detailed below). Since the 1990s, the growth of the internet has come to constitute an opportunity for the

Olympic movement – but also a challenge. It can, potentially, enable live access to all events, 24 hours per day. However, to date there are no indications that it can produce a revenue stream to rival that from broadcast television.

Digital transformations: 1988–2000

Ever since 1988, the digitalised, computerised and globalised internet dissemination of the Games has begun to emerge. However, Olympic-related use of computers has a long history. At the 1964 Tokyo Games an electronic computing system was designed by the organising committee and IBM to report, record and transmit text data of the sports events (*Official Olympic Games Report 1964 Tokyo*, Volume I: 372–374, cited in Yalin 2007). At the 1976 Montreal Games, television was linked to the central computerised results system (*Official Olympic Games Report 1976 Montreal*: 175, cited in Yalin 2007). The growth of the internet and the emergence of the world wide web provided the IOC with both an opportunity and a threat. The net offered a radical new means to promote the Games, the sponsors and Olympism; but also threatened to become a new means of dissemination that could potentially steal television's audience while not replacing its revenues.

By 1988, Eastern communism was falling apart and the IOC was able to move into a boycott-free and image-conscious era. In 1988, Seoul had superb facilities, but the IOC had to prevail on the Organising Committee to bus in large numbers of schoolchildren to provide the full stadiums that television favours. The story illustrates how central the needs of television had become. Between 1984 and 2008 broadcasting revenues were more than $10 billion. But from the end of the 1980s, deregulation, multi-channel television, the internet and digitalisation began to pose new challenges to the cosy relationship between the IOC and television.

US television was struggling to recoup the enormous rights payments. Even after the Summer and Winter Games were separated into different years, it was hard to sell enough advertising to meet the costs. In 1992, NBC tried pay-per-view subscriptions for an enhanced advert-free package on cable, but the scheme failed to appeal to viewers, who of course could still see the bulk of the Games for free. CBS, allied with Ted Turner's TNT, traded 50 hours of their coverage to Turner, who put up $50 million towards the rights.[6]

Just as the IOC had, in the 1980s, assumed greater central control of the negotiation of rights and sponsorship deals, during the 1990s it determined to take greater control of the international feed, the television pictures provided by the host broadcaster to the rest of the world. By 2001 it had established OBS (Olympic Broadcasting Services) to organise the televising of the Games. The OBS is a committee that commissions established broadcasters and production companies from around the world to provide aspects of the coverage. In Beijing 2008, for example, a cooperative joint venture between OBS and the local Organising Committee (BOCOG) created Beijing Olympic Broadcasting (BOB), the on-site host broadcaster for the 2008 Games.[7] After International Sport and Leisure (see below) collapsed in 2001, the IOC assumed more central control of both television and marketing. In 2005 it established a separate company, IOC Television and Marketing Services SA, and following Agenda 2020, it is currently in the process of establishing a year-round, 24 hours per day, Olympic Channel.

92

The rapid growth of the internet has continued to trouble the IOC to this day. In 1996 in Atlanta the first Olympic Games website received 189 million hits. It was introduced in April 1995, and attracted around 10,000 visits per day, growing to 400,000 per day by the time of the Games. In addition, 12–15 per cent of all tickets were purchased online (Yalin 2007). Just two years later, the Nagano website got 634 million hits, while in 2000 the Sydney website got a staggering 11.3 billion hits. For NBC and the IOC, the internet is a threat in that, without tight content controls, it could potentially cause a significant audience migration from television without producing the revenue flows to compensate.

One symptom of these fears was a dramatic shift in the sale of television rights, allowing NBC to acquire the rights to several Games in advance. Michael Payne (2006: 50) attributes this idea to Gary Fenton of Australia's Channel 7. The channel was finding it difficult to offer enough money for the Australian television rights for Atlanta, but were determined to secure the rights for Sydney in 2000. Channel 7 was successful in acquiring both Atlanta and Sydney for $75 million. NBC adopted the strategy. In December 1995, the biggest broadcast deal to date was announced, with NBC paying $2.3 billion for the next three Games. In less than five months, NBC had committed over $3.5 billion in Olympic rights fees. Payne (2006: 50) commented that 'the face of the Olympic TV market had been changed forever. The other networks were left speechless.'

During this period the IOC had constantly flirted with Rupert Murdoch to encourage others, and especially the EBU, to bid higher sums. This policy has recently borne fruit, with the European TV rights for the Olympic Games from 2022 onward sold to the US channel Discovery, which owns Eurosport. The longer contracts, Payne (2006: 55) argued, gave broadcasters a vested interest in building the Olympic brand, meaning they could concentrate on the overall production and promotional style without having to worry about bidding every two years. NBC sport boss Dick Ebersol managed to buttress NBC's huge investment by bringing NBC parent company, General Electric, into the Olympic corporate sponsorship programme (Payne 2006: 62). The long-term link between the IOC, NBC and General Electric meant that NBC were prepared to spend more on promoting the Olympic brand and itself as the network of the Olympics. The willingness of NBC to conclude deals for the 2012 Olympic Games two years in advance of the choice of site would also seem to suggest that the choice of site is no longer seen as a crucial element in determining the value of the rights.[8]

2000–present: the impact of multi-platform delivery and social media

The so-called 'new media' generated by the internet and digitalisation had already begun to make an impact in the last decade of the twentieth century. Email started to become a common feature of working life around 1993. The growth of texting took mobile phone developers by surprise between 1995 and 1998. Amazon was established in 1994 and eBay in 1995, but Google did not appear until 1998 and Wikipedia started in 2001. It was, however, the development of more structured forms of interaction, under the rubric of Web 2.0, which gave rise to social media. MySpace was launched in 2003, Facebook in 2004, YouTube in 2005 and Twitter in 2006. Andy Miah (Miah *et al.* 2008) has referred to Beijing in 2008 as 'the first Web 2.0 Games'.

Given the many uncertainties about the future of television as a medium of delivery, as Wi-Fi and high-speed broadband hasten the convergence of television and the internet, it is not surprising that the major US networks were keen to secure television rights for future Olympic Games; nor that the IOC was keen to arrange such a deal. The *Washington Post* said the bid was a 'risky but potentially rewarding go-for-broke attempt by a network to hold on to mass viewership events in an era when cable broadcasters are eroding network clout' but also pointed out that NBC would utilise its own cable networks – MSNBC, CNBC and Bravo – to broadcast Olympic events, reaching as wide an audience as possible and maximising advertising dollars. After the IOC announced that they were expecting a sponsorship dimension to the deal, it was the commitment of General Electric that helped secure the deal for NBC (*Washington Post* 7 June 2003).

The deals that have been struck underline the enormous commercial value of the Games and the power of the IOC. How many other organisations can successfully sell, for around $1 billion, a product not due to be delivered for nine years, when even the host city is unknown? Indeed, the closing of the deals highlights the manner in which the Games have become a recognisable, routinised and ritualised form of spectacle, in which stars, narratives and national identities are all delivered up for audience identification (see Tomlinson 1996, 1999; Hall and Hodges 1997; Wilson and Sinclair 2000; Roche 2000). Despite the caution over the speed of internet developments, gradual controlled use of the internet and pay-for channels has allowed American viewers a greater range and depth of coverage.

Developments in the technology of digital 'geo-blocking' have made it possible for digital rights management systems to prevent digital streams being accessed from other countries or duplicated on other websites. A joint internet monitoring project run by the Chinese and the IOC discovered over 4,000 cases of illegal broadcasting during the 2008 Games (Marshall *et al.* 2010). Generally these broadcasts were rapidly shut down once detected, but peer-to-peer streaming using BitTorrent proved a bit more problematic. A major torrent website, Pirate Bay, had millions of downloads of the Opening Ceremony, and although the IOC requested Swedish government assistance, Pirate Bay remained defiant and the Swedish were unwilling to enforce IOC demands. The IOC were more successful in preventing unauthorised recycling of Olympic material on YouTube, but did also authorise YouTube to establish an Olympic channel available in countries outside the major regional television contracts (Marshall *et al.* 2010).

NBC had reintroduced extra coverage on cable and satellite channels in 2000, expanded the number of outlets for 2004 to allow coverage of all 28 sports and introduced basketball and soccer channels in 2008. For the Beijing Olympic Games of 2008, for the first time NBC also utilised its own internet site (nbcolympics.com) to stream events. Possibly as a result of this new, more comprehensive coverage, NBC attained its highest ever Olympic Games ratings and largest advertising sales.[9]

In Beijing 2008, 'the first Web 2.0 Games', internet use and video streaming rose dramatically. The NBC website recorded an estimated 1.3 billion page views, 53 million unique users, 75.5 million video streams and ten million hours of video consumption during the Games. The EBU delivered 180 million broadband video streams. In Latin America, Terra's Olympic site reported 29 million video streams and ten million video-on-demand downloads (Hutchins and Mikosza 2010). According to BBC Olympics Director Roger Mosey, there was more video streaming in the first day of the 2008 Beijing Olympics than in the whole of the 2004 Athens Olympics. In total the BBC had 2.6 million video streams in Athens and 38 million video streams in Beijing (Mosey 2010). In China in 2008, live streaming was offered online, with viewing audiences of 53 million watching the Olympics on personal computers (Marshall *et al.* 2010).

This substantial and rapid rise in digital video streaming is a strong indicator that the dominance of the Olympic Games by broadcast television could come under increasing challenge. There are no technological reasons why a centralised internet provider (the IOC itself, for example) could not provide comprehensive coverage. Two factors militate against this. First, television advertising, organised on national lines, is still the most effective business model when it comes to generating income. As long as this is the case, the internet is likely to be used as an adjunct, allowing fuller coverage of those events with less viewer appeal. Marshall *et al.* (2010) point out that the need to ensure primacy of broadcast television meant that NBC's website offered heavily mediated highlights packages rather than live streaming of major events. Second, it may be that audiences tend to prefer Olympics coverage geared to their own national belongingness, focusing on their own favoured sports, competitors and medal prospects, framed within a narrative of national specificity. In 2008, Whannel watched Olympic television coverage in China, France and the UK and the different focuses were striking. In France, for example, the handball (a sport barely visible on the BBC) became more and more prominent as the French team progressed towards triumph.

The UK completed the switchover to digital broadcasting in advance of 2012, and the BBC's coverage of the London Games was the first to be entirely digital. The ability of viewers to watch events they had missed by streaming video via the broadcaster's website became a significant part of the offer, planned by Roger Mosey, Director of the BBC's London 2012 television coverage. The BBC website was central to this process. The digital television red button system is constrained by capacity limits and typically carries six streams. In the 2012 Olympics there were up to 21 events at any one time, and all could be sustained in stream form on the website. While the BBC also used message boards and blogs, interactivity through social networking remained relatively marginal to its core coverage (Mosey 2010)

The London Olympic Games were striking for their expansion of digital services, while the IOC and traditional broadcasters remained in control. Every sport was available online, in real time, for US and British audiences. The LOCOG website received 431 million visits from 109 million unique users. London 2012's social media sites, including Facebook, Twitter and Google+, attracted 4.7 million followers. The IOC's website, olympic.org, attracted more than 16 million unique visitors during the Games, breaking the previous record of 10.6 million during the 2008 Games. The IOC provided live broadcast of the Games via its YouTube channel, which recorded 59.5 million video views in 64 territories in Asia and sub-Saharan Africa. The number of subscribers to the channel increased tenfold during the Games (IOC 2012). The number of media workers, too, has become extraordinary – London 2012 had 20,000 accredited journalists. NBC alone had 2,800 people in London, and the BBC had 765. By way of comparison, there were only 560 athletes in 'Team GB' (Boykoff 2014b: 129).

The growth of social media has caused the IOC to become highly concerned about the maintenance of its positive image. Tight control on athletes is imposed by Rule 40, which effectively prevents athletes from tweeting anything the IOC might be unhappy about, which in effect prevents athletes from posting anything negative at all (Boykoff 2014b: 146).

One of the less visible aspects of the Olympic Games is the complexity of the communications systems. Philip Morris, of BT Japan, commented that 'outside of a war, there really isn't a bigger challenge than putting on an Olympic Games'.[10] The BT network for the 2012 Olympic Games carried up to 6 Gb of information per second, through 1,550 wireless access points. When planning began in 2005, smartphones were less common and the original BT estimate of 400 wireless-access points throughout the Olympic venues had to be quadrupled to 1,600. As in other aspects such as security, the staging of an Olympic Games provides corporations with invaluable research and development opportunities, all funded by the client rather than the provider.

Although the IOC remains committed to the idea that the Games should be available to universal audiences on free-to-air channels, the new complex multi-channel, multi-platform digital environment may in practice facilitate a degree of drift from this position. In 2014 the IOC extended its partnership with NBC, and signed a $7.5 billion contract that runs till 2032, the longest advance deal to date. As we noted above, until 2015 the television rights for Europe have usually been acquired by the EBU on behalf of their members, of whom the BBC are one. In 2015, though, the IOC sold the European rights for the Games from 2022 to the US broadcaster Discovery, which owns Eurosport, for €1.3 billion. There is a link with the proposed IOC-owned Olympic Channel, which Discovery will help gain a Europe-wide reach. In the past the BBC have obtained their rights through the EBU. Discovery has confirmed that they plan to sub-lease some of the rights, which leads the BBC to believe they can acquire some level of access. However, Discovery, through Eurosport, also has their own free-to-air channel in the UK. The IOC currently insists on at least 200 hours of the Summer Games and 100 hours of Winter Games being shown on free-to-air television, so there could be a combination of leasing – some material on pay TV, some free-to-air on Eurosport, some prime events on BBC (*Guardian* 30 June 2015).

GLOBALISATION, SPONSORSHIP AND THE DEVELOPMENT OF 'SPORTSBIZ'

The power of live images of nations competing is that huge television audiences are mobilised, helping to underpin and justify the expensive bidding races to win the right to stage the Games and the ever more exorbitant costs to host cities. It is the convergence of star, narrative, national identity, 'live-ness' and uncertainty that give the Olympic Games this unique power as a cultural event. Television has brought a huge income stream to the Olympic movement, initially dependent on the US, but since 1988 sponsorship and television income from the rest of the world have become significant too.

Yet the very dominance of television has also transformed the Games in other ways. It has brought commercialism, an end to amateurism and a heightened intensity of focus, which has encouraged massive investment to prove and display national prowess – and fostered the use of performance-enhancing drugs. It has made the Games part of the global promotion of cities for industry, trade and tourism. This heightened visibility has forced the Games to be staged inside rings of fortified security. Arguably television has robbed the Games of much of their festive potential.

The explosive growth of television sport from the mid-1960s has inevitably had a transformative impact on the culture of Olympism, in three main forms. First, competitive bidding for the television rights between the major networks of the US moved the IOC from genteel poverty to grand luxury. Second, the heightened visibility of the Olympic Games, the fitness boom of the 1970s and the ruthless competitiveness of the sport and leisure-goods industry combined to make the Olympic Games an attractive proposition for sponsorship. Third, in becoming the global event par excellence, not to say *sans pareil*, the Olympic Games offered one of the first and still one of the few opportunities for global marketing and global visibility.

There is, in fact, a major paradox at the heart of Olympic marketing. Normally, advertisers and sponsors are primarily interested in gaining television exposure. But the Olympic Games allow no arena advertising (apart from the trademarks of equipment suppliers). Ironically, the ban was introduced in 1928 as a response to fears that the Games were becoming too commercial! The only other major event to bar advertising is the Wimbledon Tennis Championships. So sponsors do not get television space, and are instead buying into association with the world's most recognisable symbol, the five rings, a symbol that connotes world excellence. The only way they can gain television exposure is to buy advertising separately. The paradox is that it is the impression of being 'above' commerce produced by a 'clean' stadium that contributes significantly to the aura of uniqueness of the Games and hence enhances their marketability. Indeed, so important is this aura of being above commerce that the legislation a country must introduce if it is hosting the Games specifically prevents any advertising within range of the cameras at the Olympic sites.

The World Cup, the Olympic Games and a few other events had by the 1990s become global television events. As such, they had enormous potential to raise more revenue from advertising and from sponsorship, given the right structures. Until this point the major commercial activity associated with sport was the sports goods business. Two firms, Adidas and Puma, run by two rival members of the Dassler family, had been fighting each other for the Olympic business since 1956. Horst Dassler of Adidas became very adept at making deals, first with individual athletes and then with national teams. He recognised the commercial value of ensuring that whole teams would be seen at the Olympic Games, on television around the world, wearing Adidas kit. So he offered very good deals to poorer nations, ensuring Adidas' dominance. He was also an inveterate networker, keeping track of dozens of rising sports officials around the world and nurturing their friendship, knowing that they would be the decision-makers of tomorrow. In particular, he developed close links with João Havelange, who became head of FIFA in 1974. Two events, the World Cup of 1982 and the Olympic Games of 1984, helped transform the sponsorship business. Working with Patrick Nally, Dassler pursued much greater sums in sponsorship for the 1982 World Cup. The connections established by Dassler during the previous 20 years were beginning to pay off:

> Dassler was no stranger to the workings of large sports organisations. He was closely connected to João Havelange who became president of the Fédération

Internationale de Football Association (FIFA) in 1974. He was also friends with Sepp Blatter who succeeded Havelange in 1998.

(Payne 2006: 14)

Indeed, it was in this period that the basis for corruption in world sport, currently tearing FIFA apart, was first laid down. The IOC, partly as a result of its aristocratic basis, and partly due to its commitment (up until the 1980s) to amateurism, had always been rather cautious about commercialisation. One early attempt to raise money came in Tokyo in 1964. A new 'Olympia' cigarette brand generated more than $1 million in revenue for the OCOG, but the IOC intervened to ban tobacco sponsorship. Until 1985, all sponsorship revenue was raised locally by the organising committees. However, by 1981 the IOC had for some time been concerned at the dangers of being over-dependent on US television money and established a committee to explore new sources of funding. Meanwhile, the organisers of the 1984 Los Angeles Games, forced by a public vote to rely only on private finance, had had to pursue sponsorship more vigorously, developing the principle of limited product categories with a monopoly sponsor in each one (see Ueberroth 1985). As this forced rival companies (Coke and Pepsi, Kodak and Fuji, etc.), into an auction it proved a very successful means of maximising sponsorship revenue (see Reich 1986; Ueberroth 1985). The alliance of Adidas boss Horst Dassler and FIFA President João Havelange had already reshaped the World Cup using similar principles (see Wilson 1988; Aris 1990; Whannel 1992; Sugden and Tomlinson 1998). Meanwhile, Dassler had gone into partnership with the Japanese advertising agency Dentsu to establish International Sport and Leisure (ISL). ISL was set up as a broker to negotiate television and sponsorship deals. It was hired by the IOC, controversially, without public tender, to establish the TOP programme, which involved persuading the NOCs to relinquish their own local rights in the key product areas in order that the IOC could market the Games to sponsors centrally. Thanks to the Dassler link, by 1986 its executives were able to boast, with false modesty, 'we are a small company – we only have three clients – the Olympic Games, the World Cup and the World Athletics Championship'.[11] With Dassler as a major influence, the IOC developed its global Olympic sponsorship system, TOP, first used in 1988.

After the 1988 Olympic Games the IOC also assumed a much greater degree of central control over the key negotiations on television revenue and sponsorship (see Larson and Park 1993). The introduction of limited product categories with sponsor exclusivity meant that by 1992 there were just 12 TOP sponsors, but they brought in $10–20 million each (see Barney et al. 2002). Dassler, who is widely believed to have used his influence to aid the election of both Havelange and Samaranch, was now reaping his reward in power, influence and money. He was the central figure in a web of mutually linked interests, and his power was considerable. He died in 1987, but the transformation he had wrought defined the sporting environment as the 1990s began.

The current TOP sponsors for the 2013–2016 quadrennium are: Coca-Cola, Atos, Dow, General Electric, McDonald's, Omega, Panasonic, Procter and Gamble, Samsung and Visa. Almost half of the total revenue of the Olympic movement still comes from television, but now 35 per cent comes from sponsorship, while a mere 15 per cent comes from ticket sales, giving a clue to the importance of the spectator in the scheme of things. It is worth noting that at the Olympic Games, as at other major events, a large proportion of tickets go to the Olympic 'family' – sponsors, corporate hospitality and the media. For some major

Figure 4.13 Sponsorship: the Visa flag at the torch relay, London 2008. Sponsors do not get their name in the Olympic stadium, but the torch relay provides opportunities to link the brand name with the five rings, the flag of the host country and the visual background of the host city.

Quadrennium	Games	Partners	NOCs	Revenue to IOC ($ million)
1985–1988	Calgary/Seoul	9	159	96
1989–1992	Albertville/Barcelona	12	169	172
1993–1996	Lillehammer/Atlanta	10	197	279
1997–2000	Nagano/Sydney	11	199	579
2001–2004	Salt Lake/Athens	11	202	663
2005–2008	Torino/Beijing	12	205	866
2009–2012	Vancouver/London	11	205	950

Figure 4.14 The TOP sponsorship programme and revenue to the IOC.

sport events less than 60 per cent of tickets have been available to the general public. In general terms, the IOC retains 8 per cent of this revenue, and the rest is shared out between the NOCs, the IFs and the OCOGs.

The TOP programme, established in 1985, has now become a permanent feature, even if it has not grown as dramatically as its promoters might have hoped. Both Adidas and ISL lost their way after Dassler died in 1987, and ISL drastically over-extended itself, partly in the payment of inducements; for example two FIFA executives received around £27m. ISL went into bankruptcy in 2001 with debts of £153 million. In IOC speak, these sponsoring corporations are part of the 'Olympic family' and are referred to as partners – 'Worldwide Partners of the Olympic Games, Partners of the International Olympic Committee, Partners of the Vancouver 2010 and London 2012 Olympic Games, Partners of all National Olympic Committees, and Partners of all Olympic teams competing in Vancouver 2010 and London 2012.' One big happy family. The introduction of limited product categories with exclusivity in each has proved to be a very effective mechanism for increasing revenue. Sponsors are hoping that the expenditure will produce a yield in terms of sales and brand awareness. These benefits are nonetheless notoriously hard to assess with precision.

The TOP sponsors are given a range of privileges, including substantial numbers of tickets. On the Olympic sites in 2012 soft drinks were provided by Coca-Cola and fast food by McDonald's. Ambush marketing laws allowed Olympic stewards to confiscate from spectators the products of their competitors. The TOP programme is global and is organised centrally. Each Organising Committee may also sell local sponsorships, but cannot make deals with competitors of the TOP sponsors and so must generally avoid the main product categories of the TOP programme.

The sponsors also benefit from extraordinary legal protection against their competitors. The IOC insists that a victorious host city signs – immediately after the vote result is announced – a contract which requires the Organising Committee to ensure that its government provides a legislative tool to enforce strict brand protection. The host city, the NOC and the OCOG have to ensure that no unauthorised marketing, advertising or promotion can refer to 'the Games, any Olympic team or the year of the Games or imply any connection with the Games, any Olympic team or the year of the Games (Ewing 2006: 13, quoting the London Host City Contract 2012). In the UK, legislation already existed, in the form of the Olympic Symbol (Protection) Act 1995 which prevented unauthorised use of the Olympic symbol, the word Olympic, and '*Citius Altius Fortius*' or similar words.[12]

After the award of the Games to London, this Act was updated and augmented by the London Olympic Games and Paralympic Games (Protection) Act 2006 which provides the power to combat ambush marketing (Ewing 2006: 14). This Act effectively required anyone, not just Olympic organisers, to do what the IOC wanted them to do. The Act stated that 'Advertising regulations . . . shall aim to secure compliance with obligations imposed on any person by the Host City Contract.'[13]

The draconian powers provided by this Act to prevent unauthorised attempts to suggest an association with the Games by use of words like Olympic, London, Summer and 2012 were of course open to abuse. This Act is part of a broader tendency, more evident in the US, for corporations to seek to control the very language we speak. It is bizarre that the use of the words 'London' and 'Summer' can be subject to legal restriction. The Act used a word-based definition of 'intention to suggest a relationship between a company and the

100

Group 1	Group 2
Games	Gold
Two thousand and twelve	Silver
2012	Bronze
Twenty twelve	London
	Medals
	Sponsor
	Summer

Figure 4.15 Restricted word combinations during London 2012.

Source: Ewing (2006: 15) quoting the London Olympic Games and Paralympics Act 2006, Schedule 4.

Games' (see Figure 4.15). It was forbidden to use a combination of words in group 1 with words in group 2, or a combination of words in group 2.

One legal commentary has even asserted that

> The laws relating to the 2012 Olympics are probably the most restrictive ever in their scope . . . even simple messages of support such as 'X supports the London Olympics' or 'come to our bar and watch the 2012 Games on the big screen' would probably infringe the London Olympic Association Right.

The Act allows existing well-established users (e.g. The Olympic Café) to continue and it makes provisions for news and journalism and 'honest statements of fact'.[14] Common sense prevailing, these heinous powers are restricted to their more appropriate, if debatable, function. However, Ewing states that 'the protection applies not only to commercial sponsorship but to political opposition, and is underpinned in some cases by the criminal rather than the civil law'. People carrying anti-Olympic slogans can be charged with criminal offences. Ewing argues that companies given such privileges and protection by the state should be required to demonstrate a commitment to the highest ethical standards throughout their corporate operations. In particular it ought not to be the business of the state to protect companies that operate – in this country or elsewhere – in breach of international human rights standards (Ewing 2006: 16).

Ewing singles out McDonald's and Coca-Cola as two companies with questionable records. McDonald's 'appears to make no commitment to human rights on its website' and Ewing cites instances of anti-union conduct in Canada, Russia, Germany and Indonesia. Ewing declares that 'there are few human rights activists who will be impressed by the celebration of McDonald's in particular on the IOC website'. Ewing says it is remarkable that these allegations appear not to have been fully investigated by the IOC, and if the allegations are true, 'it is even more remarkable that these companies enjoy extraordinary legal privileges as a result of contractual obligations imposed by the IOC on London and other host cities' (Ewing 2006: 21–31).

Indeed, this policing of commercial rights, and the legislation that host countries are compelled to introduce, is in effect another layer in the cocoon of security within which the Games are protected. The Olympic brand has acquired huge commercial value,

Figure 4.16 Merchandising: the Olympic pins. Official merchandising, in shops and online, provides a valuable additional revenue stream for the organising committee, while customised legislation provides legal protection against 'unauthorised' goods and vendors.

which must be protected from contamination and hence dilution of value, whether in the form of commercial competitors, dissidents and protesters, or terrorists. It is another rampart around the castle of corporate commercial interest that has become embedded within the Olympic movement.

CONCLUSION

The dilemma for the IOC is that it wishes to utilise all the new media resources of the internet and social networking sites to promote the Olympics brand, while remaining in control. But as Hutchins and Mikosza argue, there is a shift in the 'media sport content economy' from the comparative scarcity of television channels to the 'digital plenitude' of the new media environment in which online media challenge both market-driven logic and central control. As they graphically put it, 'the carefully designed and fertile "media garden" tended by the Olympic Movement over the past 25 years was sporadically beset by weeds – uninvited, unpredictable, socially driven, participatory digital media' (Hutchins and Mikosza 2010).

Top sport stars now are the point of intersection between the global spectacle of the Olympic Games and the celebrity-dominated media culture, and star image has become a promotional tool. The issue of sport actuality as intellectual property poses a contradiction – the IOC is selling the images of performance, but the performers receive nothing for this – how long will they be content with this situation? In an era in which top sport stars have agents to oversee their interests, their intellectual property and image rights could become the site of a legal challenge to the current structure of Olympic finance. The great paradox at the heart of the Olympic Games is that this commodified and hugely lucrative global spectacle is owned and run, not by a private corporation with shareholders, but by what is in effect a combination of trust and an eighteenth-century gentlemen's club. So far this situation, combining the archaic and the entrepreneurial, has survived, and arguably thrived, despite – indeed perhaps partly because of – its internal contradictions.

NOTES

1 ONS 2002 Sport and Leisure; results from the sport and leisure module of the 2002 General Household Survey.
2 Personal communication, 1986.
3 Terramedia *The Olympic Media dossier*, www.terramedia.co.uk/media/change/olympic_games_1956.htm (last accessed 23 October 2015).
4 Terramedia *The Olympic Media dossier*.
5 www.museum.tv/eotvsection.php?entrycode=olympicsand (last accessed 23 October 2015).
6 www.museum.tv/eotvsection.php?entrycode=olympicsand (last accessed 23 October 2015)
7 Olympic Broadcasting Services, www.obs.es (last accessed 23 October 2015).
8 For studies of the power of US television networks in relation to the Olympic Games, see Spence (1988), Wilson (1988), McPhail and Jackson (1989), O'Neil (1989) and Real (1989); for studies of sport and the media see Moragas *et al.* (1996b) and Rowe (1996, 1999).
9 http://sportsbiznews.blogspot.com/2008/08/2008-beijing-summer-olympics-credit.html (last accessed 23 October 2015).
10 'BT's lessons learned at London Olympics provide roadmap for Tokyo 2020', posted by Jason Dachman, editor, 9 October 2014, in Headlines.
11 Conversation with ISL executive, 1986.
12 'Intellectual Property and the London 2012 Olympic Games: what businesses need to know', www.ipo.gov.uk/news/newsletters/ipinsight/ipinsight-200911/ipinsight-200911-4.htm (last accessed 10 July 2010).
13 London Olympic Games and Paralympic Games (Protection) Act 2006. This can be found at www.opsi.gov.uk/acts/acts2006/ukpga_20060012_en_1 (last accessed 23 October 2015).
14 'Intellectual Property and the London 2012 Olympic Games'.

103

FURTHER READING

Barney, R.K., Wenn, S.R. and Martyn, S.G. (2002) *Selling the Games: The IOC and the Rise of Olympic Commercialism*, Salt Lake City: University of Utah Press.

Billings, A. (2008) *Olympic Media: Inside the Biggest Show on Television*, London: Routledge.

Payne, M. (2006) *Olympic Turnaround: How the Olympic Games Stepped Back from the Brink of Extinction to Become the World's Best Known Brand*, London: Praeger.

Smit, B. (2006) *Pitch Invasion: Adidas, Puma and the Making of Modern Sport*, London: Allen Lane.

CHAPTER 5

URBAN DEVELOPMENT, CITY BRANDING AND THE ENVIRONMENT

This chapter relates discussions about the use of the Olympics as part of urban regeneration to the broader use of the hosting of mega-events as part of consumption-based social and economic development strategies. It considers the way that cities are spatial manifestations of broader social forces and struggles and that the built environment and architecture play their part as both metric and motor of change.

In the West, for the past 250 years, the urban environment has been created by industrial capitalist modernity. Space has been restructured in line with changes in capitalism. 'Selling places is now a well-known feature of contemporary urban societies' (Philo and Kearns 1993: 18). In the past three decades most of the developed and developing world, including the so-called BRICS emerging economies (Brazil, Russia, India, China and South Africa), have joined in the competitive marketing of places as social and economic opportunities seeking capital investment. Places have become commodities and 'converted into products to be sold in competitive markets' (Philo and Kearns 1993: 19). Related to this is the globalisation of what sociologist John Urry (2002: 115) calls the 'tourist gaze': 'all sorts of places (indeed almost everywhere) have come to construct themselves as objects of the tourist gaze . . . not as centres of production or symbols of power but as sites of pleasure' (see Figure 5.1).

Hence, in central Beijing in 2006, although a Starbucks coffee franchise was forced to close in its Forbidden City (a World Heritage site) location after some tens of thousands of people campaigned against its presence, just around the corner was a more legitimate retail outlet: a Beijing 2008 Olympic Games official store (see Figure 5.2).

The city of Beijing has been transformed enormously since 1989 (Broudehoux 2004; Sudjic 2005: 106ff.). The focus of urban redevelopment gradually shifted from the centre around Tiananmen Square to the north of the city and the site of the 2008 Olympics. Broudehoux shows how the city's development in the past 30 years has been driven by a larger national agenda to consolidate a new political regime and compete in global marketplaces for capital investment and economic influence. During this time Beijing has come under the influence of local governmental boosters and private (mainly foreign) development interests which operate according to the same patterns that 'growth coalitions' have exhibited in cities around the world (see Schimmel 2001). This has led to the trivialising and commercialising of local history, the fragmentation and privatisation of the public realm and catering to business elites and tourists at the expense of local communities and less empowered members of society.

105

Figure 5.1 This photograph was taken in 2005. This franchise was closed down the following year after an internet campaign against its presence in a World Heritage site.

As the expertise advising prospective Olympic hosts has professionalised, the 'growth machine' has become 'selectively transnationalized' (Surborg *et al.* 2008). Local elites acquire specialised knowledge about new urban entrepreneurial strategies from elsewhere, via a 'growth machine diaspora' (Surborg *et al.* 2008: 341). Hence key members of what architectural critic Sudjic (2005: 117) called the 'flying circus of the perpetually jet-lagged' were invited onto the 13-strong jury that judged the architectural competition to design the Olympic (Beijing National) Stadium. The winners, Jacques Herzog and Pierre de Meuron, also designed the Allianz Arena football stadium in Munich before the 2006 Football World Cup, the Tate Modern in London and the Forum Building in Barcelona. Sudjic (2005: 117) considered their proposed Bird's Nest stadium would be the most distinctive Olympic stadium since 'Munich's Teflon-coated tents' of 1972. In addition to the Olympic stadium, nearby was the National Aquatics Centre (the 'Water Cube'), designed by Australian architectural firm PTW, and Digital Beijing, the information control and data centre for the Games. The building of Terminal 3 of Beijing Airport (designed by Lord (Norman) Foster, who also helped design the new Wembley Stadium in London), the National Theatre, and the headquarters of China Central Television (CCTV) designed by Rem Koolhaas, completes a list of some of the most iconic architectural structures that have been built in Beijing since the awarding of the Olympic Games in 2001.

Figure 5.2 Beijing 2008 merchandise in the Forbidden City.

It is clear that sports and other mega-events have long provided opportunities for nations to signal emergence or re-emergence on the international stage. While there are and can only be a few 'global cities' (Sassen 1991), attempts to promote locations are a commonplace of the past 30 years. Whether as new hubs for business and finance or as tourist destinations, cities increasingly build and utilise iconic architecture and urban spaces to flag their presence in the world and thus engage in 'place promotion'. Sports mega-events play their part in this competition for global promotion and branding. But this is only one of their contributions. As Eisinger (2000) notes, the 'politics of bread and circuses' is about building cities for the wealthy 'visitor class'; iconic stadium construction is about flagging transnational places and creating symbolic capital to attract middle- and upper-middle-class visitors.

Sociologists of sport, along with architects, urban geographers and planners, have identified these developments and begun to explore them critically (see, for example, Friedman *et al.* 2004; Gruneau and Horne 2016; Smith 2012). Reviews of the impact of sports mega-events on the urban environment have noted at least three vested interests involved in their production: sport, corporate and urban. With a focus on 'impacts', 'legacy' or, as Hiller (2003) prefers, 'outcomes', studies have considered the different phases (Essex and Chalkley 2003) and patterns (Liao and Pitts 2006) of urban development that have resulted from the Olympic Games. We agree with Hiller (2003) that it is important to consider the

107

Figure 5.3 Bird's Nest interior. The main stadium, or Bird's Nest, in use during the 2008 Summer Olympics.

controversial nature of urban developments related to sports mega-events. 'Legacies' cannot be considered to be simply positive ones, as we have discussed in Chapter 2. As Jonathan Glancey remarked in his review of architecture for 2008 in the *Guardian*, the Beijing National Stadium was 'the architectural star of the Olympics' (Glancey 2008b: 23). Looking back a year later he included the Bird's Nest in his top ten list of buildings of the decade, yet also noted that since the Olympics 'this charismatic structure has been largely redundant' (Glancey 2009: 19). Now that Beijing has hosted the IAAF 2015 World Championships and can look forward to being a centrepiece in the 2022 Winter Olympics, the stadium will be able to be more than just another expensive-to-maintain site on the tourist itinerary of the Chinese capital.

Rather than rehearse various 'knowns' about sports mega-events (Horne 2007a), such as the likely production of 'white elephants' and the over-estimation of benefits and under-estimation of costs, this chapter discusses the Olympic sports mega-event as an active expression of a globalising neo-liberal political economy (Hayes and Horne 2011). We briefly discuss the attempt to redefine this form of political economy as 'celebration capitalism' (Boykoff 2014a) and then consider the role of the designers and builders of the Olympic infrastructure within it.

Figure 5.4 Water Cube interior. Inside the Water Cube swimming pool, one of the other specially built facilities for the 2008 Beijing Olympic Games.

One of the Olympic Games' well-known features is that, for a limited period of time, they create restrictions on certain forms of movement, public (and commercial) expression, and other cultural, artistic and sporting projects. Indeed, critical studies of Olympic developments have typically focused on the displacement of settled populations and the disruption of accepted legal and social norms in order to ensure a beautified, redeveloped and efficient event space. Localised land ownership and use conflicts are an ingrained (and seemingly endemic) feature of the contemporary Olympics story, whose features are: the mass eviction of (often poor or migrant) resident populations and the reform or de facto suspension of established planning procedures in the pre-event phase; the introduction of highly restrictive regulatory and legal instruments to ensure public compliance with the stipulations of local and global organisers during the event itself; and the continued displacement of the previously settled populations through infrastructural transformation and social gentrification in the post-event phase. COHRE (Centre on Housing Rights and Evictions) was a Geneva-based NGO that worked from Seoul (1988) on evictions, producing a series of critical reports (COHRE 2007, 2008), academic studies (Olds 1998; Greene 2003) and interventions with global institutional actors (Rolnik 2009), until it ceased operations in 2012. The non-respect of planning procedures has been highlighted in a series of studies (e.g. Hall 2001 on Sydney; Karamichas 2005 on Athens; Whitson 2012 and Boykoff 2014a on Vancouver). The securitisation and corporatisation of event space at successive Games, and the concomitant suspension of civil liberties, have similarly been highlighted (e.g. Tajima 2004 on Nagano; Cunneen 2000 on Sydney; Schimmel 2006 on Salt Lake City; Klein 2008 on Beijing).

As we noted in Chapter 2, restrictions on the use of certain phrases and words are required to avoid ambush marketing when the IOC and the OCOG rely so heavily on the sponsorship of global corporations through the TOP and other programmes. While the Olympics are meant to be about much more than simply sport, the cultural activities associated with the Games tend to take second place, while other sporting events have to accommodate the event by changing their schedules (on the Cultural Olympiad, see Garcia and Cox 2013).

In several ways, then, the staging or hosting of sports mega-events promotes neo-liberal forms of governance and the neo-liberalisation of space (Peck and Tickell 2002), and thus has clear similarities with the 'shock doctrine' informing public policy in the wake of social, 'natural' and economic disasters (Klein 2007). Although the idea that capitalism advances on the back of disasters, or violent circumstances, is not a new one (Marx (1976 [1867]), Klein's book offers a valuable insight into recent history, arguing that the use of shock is a technique for imposing an ideology (what she calls the free market fundamentalist ideas underpinning neo-liberal economic thought and policy). The shock doctrine is also a philosophy of how political change can happen and be brought about. Charting the rise of free market fundamentalism over the past 40 years reveals that when ideas are unpopular, advocates of free market neo-liberalism have exploited shocks to help push through their policies without popular democratic consent. The product is what Klein calls 'disaster capitalism' – a form of capitalism that uses large-scale disasters in order to push through radical neo-liberal capitalist policies – and its related privatisation agenda for (formerly) public services.

In the first edition of this book we argued that sports mega-events can be viewed as the benign twin of disaster capitalism's 'shock therapy', involving their own shocks and generating their own forms of awe. Boykoff (2014a: 3–5) suggests that this would be better understood as a different form of capitalism – 'celebration capitalism' – that can act in combination with 'disaster capitalism', rather than a form of neo-liberal development itself. Boykoff (2014a: 5) argues that celebration capitalism is composed of six dimensions:

1   a state of exception where normal rules of politics are suspended;
2   the installation of uneven public–private partnerships (PPPs);
3   festive commercialism to inspire wide public support;
4   a boost for the security industry;
5   rhetorical use of social and environmental discourses of sustainability;
6   mass mediation of the spectacle.

We cannot disagree that most of these elements exist – and indeed discuss them in different chapters in this book – but suggest that a more incisive and inclusive formulation may be to consider the two types of capitalism – celebration and disaster – as necessary elements in the 'creative destructiveness' of spectacular capitalism (see Gotham (2016) for further elaboration of this concept).

110

What happens when the Olympics are coming to town is that substantial parts of cities and other areas designated for the events are disturbed for years by the construction projects, debt accumulation, restructuring and other disruptions of space and time. Indeed, despite the IOC's apparent wish under former President Jacques Rogge to move away from favouring gigantism in Games staging (see, for example, the recommendations of the 'good governance' study commission to the 2003 Prague IOC meeting; Pound 2003: 23, 35), recent decisions for Summer Games hosting have consistently chosen the most expensive and extensive project on offer (Beijing, London, Rio de Janeiro), while overlooking relatively compact bids (Paris and, especially, Madrid).

We want to suggest that these decisions reveal a fundamental tension between the requirements of event staging and of legacy creation, between short-term demands and the impact necessary for transformative cultural change and infrastructural development. Affected urban areas accordingly face the imposition of temporary extra-legal forms of governance, which then dissolve after the event, leaving 'legacies' that have to be dealt with. In London, the ODA, charged with building the site and facilities, with the powers of an urban development corporation, acted as its own planning authority within the Olympic precinct area, while LOCOG was a private company established to run the events

Figure 5.5 London Olympic site, looking west. In Stratford, East London, the stadium and the swimming pool for the 2012 Summer Olympics are constructed against a cityscape of other iconic buildings, such as The Gherkin (Swiss Re) office building in the City of London.

111

Development, city branding, environment

until they concluded in September 2012 (Raco 2014). Sports mega-events promote the use of vast amounts of public money for private gain into a civic obligation (and therefore make it difficult to criticise without being portrayed as unpatriotic or a 'naysayer'). With sports mega-events, however, the shock is largely perceived not as trauma but as a festival and global media spectacular (Gaffney 2010). Winning a bid to host a mega-event, putting the fantasy financial figures of a bid document into operation, dealing with the proposed location both before and after the event are just some of the moments where shock and awe are generated by sports mega-events.

The rest of this chapter considers three issues. First, we consider who the agents and institutions are that assemble, build and especially design the material infrastructure, including the stadiums and facilities, for sports mega-events such as the Olympic Games. Adopting a 'production of consumption' approach to the study of sport in consumer culture, related to, but not completely informed by, the critical political economy of sport (to be found, for example, in the work of Belanger 2009, Whannel 2008 and Whitson and Macintosh 1993), we discuss the creators of the emblematic buildings and the leisure and sport spaces constructed to assist in the pursuit or maintenance of 'world class' status. Second, we ask why cities like London and Paris, which do not need the Games to attract tourist visitors, still bid to host them? Ever since Barcelona in 1992, bids to host the Olympic Games have emphasised the marketing of a city as a tourist destination, and urban development and legacy have also become familiar terms in the bidding context. It seems that winning the Games functions to enable a whole range of giant infrastructural projects that would otherwise struggle to win support. The Games stimulate the dreams of architects and mayors, builders and planners, leaders and entrepreneurs, as well as politicians (such as President Lula of Brazil). 'Legacy' has become justification in the rhetoric of 'major event speak'. We consider this development, after the apparent success of Barcelona, in terms of the shift from (inter-)national politics to (inter-)city politics as the rationale for Olympic bid funding. Third, we conclude with a discussion about the function and relevance of the Olympic Games for environmental sustainability and whether the 'greening of the Games' are doing more than simply sustaining the unsustainable.

ARCHITECTS AND THE PRODUCTION OF THE MATERIAL INFRASTRUCTURE OF CITIES

Previous research has identified the stadium as a site for multidisciplinary investigations into the meanings of urban leisure, and the economy and politics of sports spaces (Bale and Moen 1995; Marschik *et al.* 2005; Trumpbour 2007; Gaffney 2008). The focus here is on the builders – especially the project and design architects – responsible for the production and design of the material infrastructure that is increasingly required to be in some way as iconic as the people who are expected to perform in it. In this section we consider the production of the material infrastructure and, particularly, debates about the political economy of architecture and architects. Included here is an outline of the growth of what Leslie Sklair (2001) calls the 'transnational capitalist class' and the place of architects in this class. The leading firms and architects that build sport stadiums, and especially stadiums for sports mega-events, are briefly outlined and their key characteristics

112

identified. The changing profile of architecture and architects in relation to the urban sport spectacle in both the UK and North America is also discussed (see also Horne 2013).

Architecture – and the social role of architects in particular – have not been a significant topic for sociological analysis. Partly this has been supported by the view that architecture is an artistic practice, the creation of individual genius, and therefore cannot be adequately comprehended by sociological theories. Three books usefully demonstrate that it is possible to produce a sound understanding of the social world of architecture, architects and architectural education, utilising contemporary social theories. Garry Stevens (1998) found great value in Pierre Bourdieu's work for understanding the way the architectural 'field' produces cultivated individuals with distinctive styles and tastes, and thus the way in which individual architectural creativity is derived from a social process. Like other artistic practices, contemporary architecture can be examined in Marxist and sociological terms by looking at the social relations of production within which it emerges and operates. These approaches pay attention to the institutions through which architects are educated, how building designs are produced and hence how architecture is socially constructed. Architects may operate today within conditions that are determined by the market for design and iconicity, but also, as Donald McNeill (2009) suggests in his important book, architecture is a *heteronomous* practice – it is reliant on other agents and practices in order to take place. As the managing principal at the world's largest architectural practice in 2008, Chris Johnson of Gensler told *Building Design* magazine 'we don't really do projects, we do relationships' (*Building Design* 2008: 6). Taking this notion of architectural dependency further is the study *Architecture Depends* by Jeremy Till (2009), which demonstrates the *contingency* of architecture and architects via a discussion of the sociological ideas of Zygmunt Bauman, Henri Lefebvre and Bruno Latour, among others.

While Ewen (1988) alludes to the changing celebrity status of architects and architecture during the twentieth century, Till (2009: 42) comments that 'the values and currency of the famous' dominate architectural culture, and the production and marketing of architectural icon buildings and signature architects (Larson 1994: 470), or 'starchitects', has certainly grown since the 1980s. While architecture may have a cultural and aesthetic existence independent of those paying for it, it is unquestionably the case that 'architecture is about power' (Sudjic 2005: 6). As Stevens notes:

> The field of architecture is responsible for producing those parts of the built environment that the dominant classes use to justify their domination of the social order. Buildings of power, buildings of state, buildings of worship, buildings to awe and impress.
>
> (Stevens 1998: 86)

Politically, architecture tells a story about those who determine that something is built. Whether democratic or totalitarian, a regime utilises architecture as a tool of 'statecraft' (Sudjic 2005: 8; see also Marvin 2008 for the role of architecture in Chinese statecraft). One very important economic feature is the growth of the marketplace for building design. The market provides the basic economic structure that encloses and also creates the experiences of architects. The structure makes some aspirations possible, and others inconceivable. A brief consideration of the political economy of architecture would reveal that

113

while architects design buildings, they do not do so under circumstances of their own choosing. As Till (2009: 123) states, 'qualities of hard space that dominate architectural production allow that space to be easily appropriated by the market'. This is exacerbated by the architects' code of conduct, whereby they provide a service for clients (not users) whose own demands are most often driven by market and 'short-term opportunism'. If 'architects can never fully control the actions of users' (Till 2009: 41) they most certainly cannot easily dictate to those for whom they provide a service. This is one of the ways in which the position and role of architects are contingent.

Architects are involved in the construction of 30–50 per cent of the contract value of buildings in the developed world (Stevens 1998: 228 n. 64). Traditionally it has been considered that there are three types of architectural firm: 'strong delivery', 'strong service' and 'strong ideas' firms (Gutman 1988). The first type of firm are highly commercial and rarely win awards, but they build a lot of structures. The second type are organised to deliver experience and reliability on complex assignments, and include architectural practices such as Skidmore, Owings and Merrill, which designed Canary Wharf in London and the One World Trade Center at 'Ground Zero' in Manhattan. The third type of firm contains well-known 'starchitects' such as Frank Gehry, Norman Foster and Robert Venturi, all famous for producing iconic buildings. Gehry's design for the Guggenheim Museum in Bilbao, for example, became the world's most famous new building in the 1990s and led to calls to replicate the 'Bilbao effect' as it appeared to attract a lot of visitors. The building – a titanium-covered museum juxtaposed against central Bilbao's river valley and built on the site of a former steelworks – 'brought together deeply politicized place marketing, the architectural branding of an aspirational art institution, and the worldwide projection of Frank Gehry as a celebrity architect' (McNeill 2009: 81–82). Gehry even featured in an episode of *The Simpsons*.

Despite the symbolic value of such iconic architecture designed by celebrity architects, Sklair (2005: 487) noted that entry level to the *Fortune* Global 500 – the annual list of the world's largest transnational corporations identified by *Fortune* magazine – was $10 billion in 2003, and no leading architectural firm reached anywhere near this figure. Even strong delivery firms, which produce a lot of buildings but few icons, operate in consortia chasing mega-projects (here defined as construction projects estimated to involve expenditures over $1 billion). The two main locations for most mega-projects in the past 15 years have been the US and China. In 2006 the US had an estimated 150 projects that provided the bulk of opportunities for engineering, architectural and construction firms there (RKMA 2006: 46). The restructuring of the financial sector globally has had an impact on these projects, yet economic growth in the Asia-Pacific (especially stimulated by China's building boom since the 1990s, see Olds 1997, 2001) and the Middle East (until recently) has encouraged more celebrity architects to operate globally. These 'starchitects' have taken on an increased role in planning and building in cities in the Asia-Pacific. The so-called 'Global Intelligence Corps', including architectural celebrities, have been used to brand local developments by indigenous developers, politicians and bureaucrats, who thus in turn gain symbolic capital by association (Olds 1997; Larson 1994; Rimmer 1991). As Broudehoux (2004: 21) notes, since the death of Mao Zedong, Beijing has been 'turning itself into a scenographic venue for the hosting of world class media events and the staging of grand urban spectacles'. This works in sport as much as any other form of spectacle.

114

Trumpbour (2007), for example, provided an interesting focus on the stadium construction boom that beset the US from the late 1990s. As cities in the US have competed to retain or gain 'major league' or 'world class' status, association with a professional sports franchise has been seen as a valuable source of symbolic capital.

Production relations in architecture can be understood as 'a field of cultural contestation' (Jones 2006: 550) or, as Ulrich Beck (1998: 115) once put it, 'politics with bricks and mortar', in the midst of global–local processes. In the contemporary globalising world, starchitects producing iconic buildings have increasingly become useful to what Sklair (2010) calls the transnational capitalist class (TCC).

Sklair (2005) argues that the emergence of contemporary 'iconic architecture' is a result of transformations in the production, marketing and reception of architecture, which is itself a consequence of capitalist globalisation. 'Iconic architecture' refers to two things – buildings and spaces that are famous because of the architects who design them, and buildings and spaces with special symbolic/aesthetic significance attached to them. Architects can be iconic in this sense – hence the media label 'starchitect'. Before the 1950s – which in Sklair's formulation is the pre-globalisation era – the interests of the state and/ or religion drove iconic architecture. In the globalisation era he argues that the dominant force driving iconic architecture is 'the transnational capitalist class' (Sklair 2005: 485).

Architecture has been internationalised as its source of patronage and sponsorship has altered (King 2004). Modes of production and associated ideologies increasingly shape architectural design rather than the nation-state (although see Brownell 1995 on stadium building in Beijing). Globalised production, aided by new technologies of communication and design in addition to an already internationalised profession (formalised by the formation of the International Union of Architects in 1948), led to the growth of architecture as a global cultural form. The 1950s and 1960s saw the building of American-style hotels throughout the world, prompting debates about homogenisation and plurality that became familiar in subsequent decades with respect to the notion of socio-cultural globalisation.

According to Sklair, the TCC comprises people with globalising as well as localising agendas, who have a home in more than one place, and who have a cosmopolitan outlook. The TCC seeks to secure the conditions under which its largely capitalist interests are furthered in global and local contexts. The TCC has four fractions: corporate, state, technical and consumerist. The corporate fraction owns and controls major transnational corporations and their local affiliates. In architecture these are the major architectural, architecture–engineering and architecture–developer–real estate firms listed in such magazines as the (now defunct) *World Architecture* and *Building Design's World Architecture 100*. As we have suggested, the revenues of these companies are relatively small compared to firms in the *Fortune* 500, and the number of starchitects with the biggest firms is also small, but they have great significance for the built environment and their cultural importance for cities outweighs their financial muscle. This is one reason why Preuss (2004: 235–236) is mistaken to ignore the symbolic role and value of architectural design in sports mega-events such as the Olympic Games. Nor is it enough, without further investigation, to say that the impacts of sports mega-events on the urban, spatial, architectural and built form of cities (including negative ones such as mass evictions, see COHRE 2007) are 'obvious' (King 2004: 35).

115

Figure 5.6 Sydney Telstra Stadium in 2007. Following the Sydney Summer Olympics in 2000 the main stadium was reconfigured to shorten the north and south wings and hold fewer spectators. It has been renamed twice – Telstra (at the time of this photograph) and now ANZ Stadium after sponsors with naming rights.

Five features are immediately noticeable about sport sector architectural firms, practices and projects. First, as with most other architectural work, as McNeill (2009) and Till (2009) both demonstrate well, is the necessity of working in partnership with other architectural practices and construction and design services – such as service and structural engineers, project managers and building contractors. Both JSK and Cox have worked in collaboration with HOK on projects in Germany (World Arena, Berlin) and Australia (MCG, Melbourne), respectively. Dependence also applies with respect to the necessity of conformity to local building regulations and safety guidelines (e.g. DCMS 2008), which are as much a feature of the sports facilities and stadiums sector as of other areas of architectural practice. Second, the stakeholders'/clients' needs come before those of potential users or citizens of the locations where stadiums or arenas are built. Third, the leading firms tend to be those with a more global presence. Those that seek a global presence will use any successes in design competitions to enhance their reputation and thus sustain their presence in the market sector. Fourth, despite apparent globalisation, there has been a tendency for most sports-related work in North America, Europe and the Pacific

Rim region (including East Asian countries) to be designed by 'local' companies, although the Beijing Olympic Stadium and the associated Water Cube aquatic centre were exceptions to this. Fifth, and finally, high-profile starchitects and well-respected companies, such as Foster & Partners and Herzog & de Meuron, are not part of the sport stadium 'top ten' even though they have been and will be involved in some highly significant developments in the sector (Horne 2013).

Ren (2008: 176) suggests 'social scientists have just begun to explore the linkage between architectural mega-projects and nation-building practices in global or globalising cities'. Next we sketch some examples of how stadium architects contribute to the construction of not only sport stadiums and spectacles, but also urban built environments, and thus help to produce symbolic capital for localities seeking a global profile.

SPORTS MEGA-EVENTS AND URBAN DEVELOPMENT

In the first edition of this book four years ago we wrote 'the allure of sports mega-events has grown greatly in the past 30 years'. Yet since then this would appear to have been challenged. At the beginning of 2015 sports economist and industry consultant Andrew Zimbalist (2015: 6) could state that 'The problem for the IOC and FIFA is that rising popular protests are alerting politicians to the fact that hosting the Olympics and World Cup may not be such a good deal economically or politically'. Some of the scenes in Brazil before the FIFA Football Confederation and World Cups in 2013 and 2014, outlined in Chapter 1, as well as ongoing issues about the impact of sports mega-events on local populations and economies at a time when the politics of economic austerity has been taken up by national governments, would suggest that mega-events are facing great challenges. What has happened with respect to the Olympics, as we saw in Chapter 3, is that the IOC has tinkered with the criteria for hosting in order to reinforce the Games as an attractive proposition in an economy of events and spectacles (Gruneau and Horne 2016). In Zimbalist's terms, as a monopoly seller of hosting rights, the IOC (and FIFA) encounters the 'principal–agent problem' (Zimbalist 2015: 122–123) in which the local organising committee (the 'agent') is controlled by private interests (the IOC or 'principal') that stand to gain most from hosting the event. Nonetheless, for the past 25 years the Olympics have been integrated into a global pursuit of world-class city status through urban regeneration schemes (see, for example, Poynter *et al.* 2016). We examine this next.

When Los Angeles hosted the Summer Olympics in 1984 there were no competitor nations. Nagoya was the only rival to Seoul to host the Summer Games in 1988. Clearly the significant alteration in the global geopolitical landscape – the collapse of the Soviet Union, the highly symbolic but material demolition of the Berlin Wall, and the associated break-up of the East European bloc of nations at the end of the 1980s – has helped the Olympic 'mega' develop into the position it now holds in the global imagination and the global economy of appearances. As noted earlier, journalist and architectural critic Deyan Sudjic (2005: 326) suggests that architecture 'is constantly about . . . power, glory, spectacle, memory, identity', while it always changes in form. That this is as true for the buildings and facilities underpinning sport and sports mega-events as it is for other construction projects can be seen through a brief examination of selected buildings designed for Summer Olympic Games.

117

As we have suggested, the role of architects in the creation of memorable Olympic infra-structures has not been analysed much until relatively recently. This may partly be to do with the fact that while a list of stadiums built prior to 1984 includes the well-received Tokyo (1964) and Munich (1972) projects, it also includes Montreal (1976), which stands out as one of the most negative examples of contemporary architectural ambition. This complex design and ambitious *grand projet* left the city with an enormous debt, only paid off completely 30 years later, in 2006. Use of the Montreal site has largely been restricted to non-sports events and a zoological garden. It is clear that the Olympic Games and other sports mega-events have long provided opportunities for nations to signal emergence or re-emergence on the international stage. While there are – and can only be – a few 'global cities', attempts to promote locations have become a commonplace of the past 25 years. Whether as new hubs for business and finance or as tourist destinations, cities increasingly build and utilise iconic architecture and urban spaces to flag their presence in the world. Sports mega-events play their part in this competition for global promotion and branding.

Researchers have noted that the attraction of hosting sports mega-events has grown since the 1980s because it enables multiple sets of agendas to be addressed. The main ones are place promotion, internal (social, cultural and economic) development and global status. The hosting of a major event enables symbolic as well as material nation-building to take place (Smith 2012). Short (2004: 68ff.) identifies four modalities of global cities: transport hubs and networks; global cultures and cosmopolitanism; global imaginings and place marketing; and global spectacles, signature architects and cosmopolitan urban semiotics. The Summer Olympic Games are 'the mega-event with the ability to create, reinforce and consolidate global city status' (Short 2004: 108) as it condenses these modalities. The Summer Olympics are 'global spectacles, national campaigns and city enterprises' at one and the same time (Short 2004: 86).

Globally, the IOC, prompted by concerns about its environmental impact, wavering public opinion in the light of corruption revelations and interest in the amorphous concepts of 'legacy' and 'sustainability' which developed in the 1990s, has helped shape the environment in which the change in the role of architecture and stadium architects in sport has taken place. Concerns about legacy have been the focus of an IOC conference and transfer of knowledge has become a vital part of the organisation of Olympic events. The related concern with 'sustainability' has existed since 1994 when the IOC adopted the environment as the third pillar of the Olympic movement. Both former IOC Presidents Samaranch and Rogge have written highly positive forewords to books on stadium design (see John and Sheard 2000; John *et al.* 2006).

Sklair argues that starchitects assist the TCC through the construction of transnationally attractive consumption spaces and the production of iconic architectural forms. Since the 1980s, starchitects have been invited to build iconic buildings and consumption spaces and the ideological role of these reflects other processes going on in cities. This includes: the reimagining/imagineering of cities as consumption centres, rather than centres of produc-tion; the building of urban entertainment destinations and other themed environments; and the construction of spaces for the consumption of experiential commodities, such as sports and recreational events, concerts and other commercial gatherings, which include stadiums – or 'tradiums', often increasingly named after a sponsor rather than their

118

location in the city (Rutheiser 1996; Hannigan 1998). Saunders (2005: viii) suggests that '*Spectacle* is the primary manifestation of the commodification or commercialisation of design.' This has involved a simulated de-McDonaldisation in some places and the creation of ballparks as theme parks, especially in the US (Ritzer and Stillman 2001). The end result is 'a heavily themed environment rationally organised to maximise consumption' (Giulianotti 2005: 134). In addition, this process has seen architects become brands in their own right (Frampton 2005), creating 'architainment' for some.

As noted, some sociologists have already responded to these developments critically. In North America journalist Dave Zirin has also identified the building of iconic sports and leisure spaces as a poor 'substitute for anything resembling an urban policy in this country' (Zirin 2009: 262). He described the way that the Louisiana Superdome became a shelter for 30,000 of New Orleans's poorest residents left homeless by the effects of Hurricane Katrina in August 2005. Although it was built from public funds 30 years earlier, it would normally have been beyond their means to enter the arena. The homeless people were then moved on from there to the Houston Astrodome in Texas, not to government housing, public shelters or somewhere nearer to their devastated homes. Zirin (2009: 262) argued, 'stadiums are sporting shrines to the dogma of trickle-down economics'. US public money amounting to $16 billion has been spent on stadium construction and upkeep in the last decade. Despite no evidence that they function as financial cash cows, 'the domes keep coming' (Zirin 2009: 262).

In the UK, Inglis (2000, 2005) identifies two moments when sport stadium architecture underwent fundamental changes – at the end of the nineteenth century and the end of the twentieth century. The 'local' stimulus to the most recent shift in Britain has been the sustained investment in the infrastructure of football stadiums in England, Wales and (to a lesser extent) Scotland since the publication of the Taylor Report (1990) into the Hillsborough Stadium disaster in 1989, which recommended, among other things, the move towards all-seat football stadiums. One of the first fruits of this tragic stimulus was the Alfred McAlpine (now Galpharm) Stadium built in Huddersfield, designed by Rod Sheard, which became the first sports venue to win a Royal Institute of British Architects 'building of the year' award in 1995. As we have seen, following the merger of Sheard's Lobb Partnership and HOK in 1999, Sheard and HOK Sport (and now known as Populous™) have become even more prominent in promoting sports architecture.

Belanger (2009) identified several contradictory and contested features of the urban sport spectacle that architects can become enmeshed in as they produce (trans)national sport spaces. First, the paradox of distinctiveness is that if everywhere has iconic architecture then there is a global sameness to the pursuit of distinction. This can lead to the creation of unspectacular spectacles, or the predictable monotony of the spectacular in commodified space, as geographer David Harvey once argued was the case with respect to postmodernist architecture (see Merrifield 2002: especially 144–155).

Second, there are various urban narratives, imaginaries and themes that can create a division, in architectural as well as other terms, between the spectacular global and the vernacular local. This in turn can lead to spectacular local resistance to and/or negotiation with the global spectacle through novel uses and vernacular appropriation of the built environment (Stevens 2007). With Brazil hosting the two biggest sports events in the world

119

in 2014 and 2016 it was inevitable that various struggles would develop over urban projects planned to transform stadiums, roads and neighbourhoods close to key sports facilities and sites (see Chapter 1; Zirin 2014).

Third, the production of consumption spaces, such as the 'new made to look old' nostalgic baseball parks in the US (such as Camden Yards in Baltimore or PNC Park in Pittsburgh), uses collective memory to reformulate a new consumerised public sphere. Yet, as spaces, sports stadiums are both public and private – both popular and disciplining, intimate as well as commercial. They are shaped by public meanings and form the basis of popular memories, at times of disaster, becoming the forum for cultures of commemoration (Russell 2006). Hence Belanger alerts us to the ever-present gap between capital's intentions and the use-values of spectacular urban sport spaces while the local populations are asked to believe in the promises of urban development associated with hosting sports mega-events such as the Olympic Games (Minton 2012).

Figure 5.7 Diga Não: 'Say no to removals' reads this sign used by residents of Vila Autódromo in Rio de Janeiro in their campaign to prevent eviction from their homes adjacent to the main site being developed for the 2016 Summer Olympic Games.

THE SPATIAL AND POLITICAL IMPACT OF SPORTS ARCHITECTURE AND ARCHITECTS

Individuals, companies, practices and consortia are required to produce sports mega-events and their material infrastructure. Yet in building and designing for sport, firms such as Populous™ have come to dominate international stadium design by 'turning out an interchangeable series of huge spectator machines that can process crowds quickly and efficiently yet entirely lack personality or charisma', according to Sudjic (2005: 117). As some starchitects have taken on an increased role in planning and building in cities in the Asia-Pacific, as well as the rest of the developed world, their global influence can be seen in stadium architecture as much as in any other form of iconic architecture. It is almost a truism that the design of the built environment has been increasingly 'engulfed in and made subservient to the goals of the capitalist economy' in the past 30 years (Saunders 2005: vii). One of the major criticisms of the transformation of the 'sportscapes' of Brazil in recent years, and of Rio de Janeiro specifically, has been this transformation of the sports stadia into 'tradiums'.

As part of the State of Rio de Janeiro's proposals for the 2014 World Cup, the Maracanã Stadium, which had undergone a multi-million dollar reform for the 2007 Pan American Games, received yet more public funding to make the stadium 'FIFA-standard'. This time, though, the stadium would be taken out of the public sphere, being transferred to a private consortium as part of a 30-year concession. The realisation of the reform and privatisation of the Maracanã complex (see Chapter 1) reminded journalist Dave Zirin (2014: 28) of the US, 'whose cities have built mega-stadiums with public funding: the people who pay the taxes that made the new Maracanã now cannot afford tickets to the Maracanã'.

Nonetheless, while architects are caught in the dilemmas of involvement in the market, some seek to imbue their designs with greater public access (Bauman Lyons Architects 2008; McNeill 2009). According to architect Irena Bauman, 'Architects need to become sociologists as well as researchers' (Wainwright 2008: 2). Jones (2006: 550) suggests that architecture may have become an increasingly significant expression of diverse collective identities in recent years. While landmark buildings were once a central way of 'expressing and developing the national code', Jones notes that they are now increasingly sites of symbolic conflict and competition over identities. In what he considers could be a post-national context, architecture can provide a cultural space for new identities to be expressed and contested. The role of architects as cultural intermediaries in all this is to make their buildings meaningful to non-architects. The 'architect's role in translating and disseminating meanings is key' (Jones 2006: 556). They do this by reflexively situating their buildings in terms of identity projects.

We might ask: How can architects align their buildings with various identity discourses? There are three ways in which architects can engage with their designs' meanings – interpreting the buildings they design, conveying the meaning of the buildings and linking the buildings to identities – collective and personal. First, architects have become more active in disseminating their interpretations of their buildings (Jones 2006: 551–553). They appear more on television, give more lectures, write more books and letters to newspapers

121

Figure 5.8 'I believe': 100 metres from the entrance to the Estádio Olímpico João Havelange, to be used for track and field athletics during Rio 2016, graffiti artists offered reflections in 2010 on hosting the Pan American Games in 2007 and their aspirations looking forward to the 2016 Olympic Games.

and generally have a higher media profile. Rod Sheard's recent output is one good example of this. In his books, contributions to collections and articles discussing his work he has even developed a theory of the development of stadiums – 'the five generations of stadiums' theory – that identifies five overlapping phases of sports stadia development from the nineteenth century to the present day (Sheard 2001a, 2001b, 2005: 100ff.; Culf 2005; Inglis 2000). Sheard's theory firmly places the contemporary stadium at the centre of urban regeneration projects – with the potential for inspiring urban change through the building of iconic sports architecture.

A second way architects communicate the meaning of their work is to attempt to create symbolic narrative associations between their work and positive or warm political concepts – such as 'democracy', 'transparency' and 'openness' (for example, this was especially evident in the relationship between architects EMBT headed by Enric Miralles and the

Figure 5.9 The new Wembley Stadium plays host to the Women's Olympic Football Final between the US and Japan in August 2012.

design of the Scottish Parliament building in the 1990s). With respect to stadium architecture, the guided tour of the new Wembley Stadium building given by Lord (Norman) Foster that was broadcast during the FA Cup Final Preview on 19 May 2007 on BBC TV was another example of this. Throughout, Foster referred to the stadium as 'intimate', praised the 'closeness' of the 'fantastic views' (even from the 'cheap seats') and emphasised how much more the new stadium resembled 'a spa', 'a luxury hotel' or 'a cultural building like an opera house or a hotel' than a football stadium. The arch, on the other hand, was 'one of those inspirational things'. This type of language fails to persuade either of us, who have attended several events at the new Wembley Stadium, that the social segmentation of sports stadia is a thing of the past.

The third way architects attempt to make their buildings mean something is to avoid privileging one collective identity over another – focusing instead upon concepts such as 'multiculturalism', 'diversity' and 'accessibility'. In this way the architects create links between buildings and collective identities, even though some are very exclusive and privileged identities. Meanings can change, and values linked to buildings can be detached. Architecture reflects tensions in global and local identity. So how buildings are coupled to collective identities is best understood as a process over time, involving a 'complex web

123

of highly charged discourses about identities' (Jones 2006: 562). Since meanings are not self-evident they have to be identified, translated, interpreted and communicated.

Some architects can also be producers of alternative, protest, hybrid and more locally relevant meanings and identities. Ai Wei Wei, consultant designer on the Beijing Bird's Nest project with Herzog & de Meuron, referred to it as a 'public relations sham' and the 2008 Olympics as 'a pretend smile' (Glancey 2008a). Shortly before the event in August 2008 he clarified his position towards the stadium. 'I don't criticise the stadium. I criticise the government's use of the Olympics for propaganda. I am disappointed that the system is not able to turn this historical event into political reform' (Watts 2008).

In sum, the role of architects in contemporary culture is to act as conveyors of meaningful discourses about the buildings and the cultural spaces they produce. The same can be said for the designers and architects of sports facilities and stadiums. Their ideas do not always meet with final approval, even after being commissioned, as in the case of Zaha Hadid Architects (ZHA), run by the award-winning British-Iraqi architect, whose design for the Tokyo 2020 Olympics main stadium was scrapped by the Japanese government over concerns about rising costs in July 2015 (Gibson 2015b). Yet those that are, through sustaining and perpetuating the global sports mega-event cycle, contribute to and form part of the culture of consumption. While for some, consumption has been seen as a means of overcoming many urban problems, investment in the cultural economy 'cannot single-handedly save the city' (Miles and Miles 2004: 2). As Miles and Miles suggest, 'consumption divides as much as it provides'. Likewise, among writers on the commodification of architecture, it remains a central debate whether it is indeed possible 'for designers to resist, escape or offer substantial alternatives to the dominant commercial culture' (Saunders 2005: viii).

The Olympics: an unsustainable sustainability?

The Summer Olympic Games are a, arguably *the*, mega-event with the 'ability to create, reinforce and consolidate global city status' (Short 2004: 108). Yet, as Broudehoux suggests about urban entrepreneurialism:

> The ready-made identities assigned by city boosters and disseminated through the mass media often reduce several different visions of local culture into a single vision that reflects the aspirations of a powerful elite and the values, lifestyles, and expectations of potential investors and tourists. These practices are thus highly elitist and exclusionary, and often signify to more disadvantaged segments of the population that they have no place in this revitalised and gentrified urban spectacle.
> (Broudehoux 2004: 26)

The conflicts, resistances and negotiations involved in, in this case, the East Asian experience of hosting sports mega-events can be found among the debates about architecture and two issues worthy of future research in the sociology of sport architecture are, first, 'whether and to what extent it is possible for designers to resist, escape, or offer substantial alternatives to the dominant commercial culture' (Saunders 2005: viii) and second, the power relations involved in local and global forces that collide in the production of sport stadiums. As Short (2004) remarks, winners and losers can be identified. Winners include: political regimes seeking to redevelop a city's image; subtle place-specific discourses; and real estate and building companies. The losers are the marginal and weaker social groups – those living in poorer inner-city sites who often face relocation without adequate (or any) compensation. Crilley (1993: 249) has argued that the architecture of redevelopment can perform 'an effective screening role conducive to geographical and social myopia'.

Arguably one of the greatest forms this myopia takes is in terms of the environmental impacts of hosting sports mega-events. All sports mega-events carry a carbon cost and create material environmental impacts – including the production of waste, consumption of energy, development and use of transport, communication and leisure infrastructures, national and international travel and the symbolic promotion of individual mobility and consumption-based lifestyles (Chernushenko 1994). At the same time the Olympics, the men's Football World Cup and other major sports events can potentially create and grow new markets in sustainable goods and services, act as an agent of technology transfer and technical know-how diffusion, extend the use of environmental monitoring and benchmarking and raise expectations that this will be done and in other ways act as a showcase for the wider dissemination of environmental values and norms (Hayes and Karamichas 2012a; Karamichas 2013). For there to be a real, as opposed to tokenistic, 'greening of the games', however, there is a need for initiatives to minimise the negative environmental impacts; one of these in relation to the Football World Cup has been a carbon remediation scheme,[1] introduced for the first time in 2006. The London 2012 Summer Olympic and Paralympic Games did seek to calculate emissions from bid to closing ceremonies and this was estimated at 3.4 million tonnes CO2e. London quietly dropped carbon offsetting in 2009 (Horne 2014b).

Karamichas (2013: 8) argues that academic 'sports studies may be infused with environmental concerns as more and more sporting events subscribe to environmental management systems and attempt to account for their carbon footprint'. Yet there remains incoherence and confusion at the global as well as local level about environmental management with respect to major sports mega-events – since neither the IOC nor FIFA play a regulatory role in terms of defining standards or methods for carbon remediation schemes related to the sports mega-events they bestow on the world. 'Low carbon', 'zero net emissions' and 'carbon neutral' all sound like 'green' initiatives, but there is no general public information about carbon mitigation schemes and it is not possible to compare successive mega-events in the absence of reliable, transferable, reporting and auditing systems (Hayes and Karamichas 2012a: 13; Hollins 2011).

Furthermore, carbon offsetting places a burden on countries in the global South, restricting the scope for developing countries to reduce their own emissions. For example, the 'Green Goal' associated with the 2006 World Cup held in Germany involved investment in two greenhouse gas reduction projects in South Africa. But South Africa could not so easily offset carbon when it acted as World Cup host in 2010. 'Developed countries can offset in the South. Southern countries cannot do the reverse' (Hayes and Karamichas 2012a: 4). As carbon offsetting for non-German competitors in 2006 was voluntary it also raises questions about what is meant by sustainable development and whether people affected

125

are involved in project definition or just implementation? The trade-offs between growth and social justice, civil rights and security and environmental protection and accountability, are some of the central legacy challenges associated with sports mega-events (see also Wilson and Millington 2013).

Arguably, then, profit and event delivery come before environmental sustainability, democracy and social justice (Hayes and Karamichas 2012a: 21), leading to a variety of responses and resistances. One of the unintended legacies of hosting a sports mega-event is that it can lead to social mobilisation – and sometimes confrontations, as was witnessed in Brazil in 2013 and 2014 before the FIFA World Cup (see Chapter 1). Some organisers have attempted the integration and incorporation of NGOs and protest groups into the planning of events. But the mobilisation of people and communities affected remains one of the most unstable and unpredictable of the social legacies of mega-events. We discuss the politics of the Olympics in this light further in Chapter 9.

CONCLUSION

This chapter has discussed the Olympics as an active expression of a globalising neo-liberal political economy. Over two decades ago, David Harvey (1989: 21) suggested that downtown redevelopments could be likened to a 'carnival mask that diverts and entertains, leaving the social problems that lie behind the mask unseen and uncared for'. Future research into the legacies – actual and claimed – for sports mega-events such as the Summer Olympic Games will require us to continue to explore what lies behind this mask.

Both critics and boosters of spectacular sports mega-events now conduct research into the organisation and networks surrounding them and their impacts, legacies and outcomes – see, for example, Cashman (2006, 2011) for a critical yet generally enthusiastic discussion of the IOC-funded Olympic Games Global Impact project and the legacy of the Olympic Park in Sydney, respectively. Research by academics and investigative journalists has also looked at the workings of international sports organisations and international sports federations in examining the background to sports mega-events (e.g. Chappelet and Kubler-Mabbott 2008; Tomlinson 2014; Jennings 1996, 2006). In addition to the IOC and FIFA, media corporations, transnational sponsors, politicians, members of bid teams and national sport organisations have been considered as constituent parts of the networks of power and influence that produce, mediate and transact sports mega-events. Yet as well as their political, economic, cultural and symbolic impacts – through showing off places as global – sports mega-events as spectacles have a spatial impact, in particular upon the built environment, which is generally urban, modernist and consumerist.

There is nothing new about commercial relations and sports and sport mega-events, or about explicit relationships between sport and politics. What has happened is that the way in which sport and sports events are related to both economic and political processes has changed. Sport and sports mega-events, especially the Olympics since the 1980s, have become more commercial and implicated in market relationships. Sport and sports mega-events are experiential commodities and have many attractions for both corporate and governmental agencies seeking a presence in the globalised world. Sports mega-events are also part of the promotional culture of contemporary capitalism. Hence an increased

126

supply of spectacle creates opportunities to attract inward investment and generate consumption spending.

The basic message of this chapter has been that the relationship between sports mega-events and the urban infrastructure may be 'obvious', but it needs examining. Buildings are part of the legacy of sport and sports mega-events – both negative and positive. Architects act as interpreters of the transnational sport spaces they help to design and in so doing they may sustain the work of the TCC and the maintenance of the culture-ideology of consumerism or, on some occasions, challenge it. As Hannigan (1998) suggests, seeing the city as a centre of consumption is not new, but the way we are currently encouraged to consume is.

NOTE

1 www.bloomberg.com/news/2011-08-31/olympics-drops-carbon-offset-plan-to-focus-on-u-k-benefits.html (accessed 7 January 2014).

FURTHER READING

Broudehoux, A.-M. (2004) *The Making and Selling of Post-Mao Beijing*, London: Routledge.
Gold, J. and Gold, M. (eds) (2016) *Olympic Cities*, 3rd edition, London: Routledge.
Smith, A. (2012) *Events and Urban Regeneration: The Strategic Use of Events to Revitalize Cities*, London: Routledge.

PART II
THE HISTORY AND POLITICS OF THE OLYMPICS

CHAPTER 6

REVIVING THE OLYMPICS

The establishment of the modern Olympic Games in 1896 involved a classic instance of the invention of tradition, in which elements of the Ancient Greek Games, English public school education, nineteenth-century sport festivals, emerging cultures of physical education, and a contemporary French perspective were grafted together. This took place in the context of late nineteenth-century European politics, and particularly the attempts of France to cope with the humiliation of its defeat by German forces in 1870, the year before a united Germany became a nation-state.

The ancient Olympic Games were held every four years for more than 1,000 years, between 776 BC and AD 260, in Olympia in the state of Elis. They continued to be held with some interruptions until AD 393, when the Christian Emperor Theodosius banned pagan festivals, including the Games. They were not the only such events in Ancient Greece – there were Pythian, Nemean and Isthmian games, and many smaller-scale events, but the Olympic Games were the most important and longest lasting (Finley and Pleket 1976: 13). All these games were sacred and religious in character, staged to please the gods such as Apollo and Poseidon; the Olympic Games were dedicated to the god Zeus. They were held at the religious shrine of Olympia, the site of a temple to Zeus with a 40-foot-tall gold, silver and ivory statue, which was one of the Wonders of the Ancient World. Competitors, trainers and judges all took an oath before the statue that they would obey the rules. Oxen were sacrificed and victors crowned in front of the statue (Kidd 1984).

The Games were attended by many thousands of spectators. Initially only a single sprint of 190 metres was staged, but the programme gradually expanded to include more foot races, boxing, wrestling, pankration (unarmed combat) and the pentathlon (discus, javelin, jumping, running and wrestling). There were no team events. Contrary to their mythologising in the nineteenth century, the Games were not amateur in character – the Ancient Greeks knew no such concept (see Young 1984, 2004: xi). Rewards for victory could be great. Money, pensions and gifts were common, and an Olympic victory could form a platform to launch a career in politics (Kidd 1984). Experts differ on the issue of material rewards for success at the Games. It is generally agreed that while the immediate rewards were limited to the olive wreath of victory, winners received rich rewards, both in cash and in privileges, when they returned home. Some, such as Young, believe this was always the case; others, such as Pleket, maintain that this only became the case in the later era of the ancient Games. Others again attribute growing professionalism to the Roman influence. Evidence is limited and inconclusive (Hill 1992: 7).

Some of the events would appear extremely violent to us. Combat often continued till death. The events grew out of military training in the context of the warlike and combative culture of Greek life. The Games lasted as long as they did in part because of the principle of the Olympic truce. This required safe passage to be given to all competitors and spectators. It also forbade other states from attacking Elis during the Games, and barred Elis from attacking its neighbouring states. The truce did not prevent wars but it did protect the Olympic Games from disruption by them (Kidd 1984).

The economic and political system of Greek city-states was rooted in slavery and patriarchy. They were ruled by small, elite male groups, whose power and wealth were sustained by a slave-based economy. Women, many of whom were slaves, had no political rights. Even when more elaborate forms of 'democracy' began to evolve, most notably in Athens, the dependency on slave labour remained. In the Games, only free males could enter, and women were barred as spectators (Kidd 1984). There were, though, also female sporting contests, such as those honouring the Goddess Hera.

It is important, of course, to be wary of generalisations about events which lasted over such a long period of time. The most striking and consistent feature which marks the ancient Games as distinct from their modern revival was their pagan religious character, as opposed to the secular ritualised form of the modern Olympic Games. The modern Olympics too, though, do feature elements of reworked neo-pagan ritual, most notably the lighting of the 'sacred' flame from the rays of the sun, the conveying of this flame, by means of a torch relay, to the Olympic site, and the burning of the flame throughout the 15 days of the Games.

REDISCOVERY AND REVIVAL

The collapse of the Roman Empire meant that, in the Western world, knowledge and understanding of the classical world of Greece and Rome declined for many centuries. During the Renaissance there was a period of rediscovery and re-appropriation of Roman and Greek cultures that placed the Latin language and Greek philosophy at the heart of humanist education. Once inscribed at the core of Western education and philosophy, the classical influence remained strong through the Enlightenment and into the nineteenth century. In particular, the reformed English public schools of the mid-nineteenth century placed emphasis on the need to develop mind and body in harmony, inspired by Ancient Greek philosophy. It was out of this that the cult of athleticism developed.

Contrary to myth, the ancient Olympic Games did not disappear from memory until the nineteenth century. Bill Mallon cites a multi-volume book on the Olympic Games, published in 1419, and points out that Shakespeare and Milton both mention the Olympic Games in their work, as do Goethe, Rousseau and Byron.[1] Voltaire referred to the *jeux olympiques* and Flaubert and Gide both used the word *olympique*, although not referring to sport (Mandell 1976: 29; see also Polley 2011). But it was with the emergence and development of organised sport in its modern forms, from the eighteenth century onwards, that the term 'Olympic' began to enter into wider usage. Festivals involving sporting activity had been common across Europe from medieval times. Indeed, multi-sport festivity, far from dying out in the fourth century, had continued to thrive in medieval fairs and festivals

The history and politics of the Olympics

Figure 6.1 The start line at the ancient stadium in Olympia, Greece. Since the excavations of the site of the ancient Games at Olympia during the nineteenth and twentieth centuries, the ancient stadium has become a site of 'pilgrimage', an appropriate term for a movement so committed to ritual and religiosity. Photograph courtesy of Annette Hofmann.

(see Brailsford 1969; Malcolmson 1973). Only from the late eighteenth century, with the onset of the industrial revolution, did the rather informal popular sporting cultures of the fair and festival begin to die out, to be replaced by the second half of the nineteenth century by the more organised and regulated games of the reformed public schools (see Bailey 1978; Cunningham 1980).

In the seventeenth century, Robert Dover established the Cotswold 'Olympick Games', which occurred, with some gaps, for the next 250 years. Robert Dover staged the events, in part, in order to combat the 'joyless moralism of the Puritans, whom he loathed' (Kidd 1984). Robert Dover was born in Norfolk, sometime between 1575 and 1582, and died in c.1652. He was a barrister, and may have been Catholic, but there appear to be few firm facts about his life. It is not clear whether Robert Dover founded or revived the Cotswold Games, but his involvement dates from 1612. The games owed more to the festive traditions of medieval England than they did to any knowledge of the Greek Games. They included singlestick combat, wrestling, cudgelling, dancing, jumping in sacks and shin-kicking (Williams 2009).

In staging such an annual event, Dover was provoking a puritan backlash, but was able to draw on the support of *The Book of Sports*, an official proclamation, which defended the right of respectable leisure after worship. It was first issued in May 1618 by James I, and reaffirmed in 1633 by Charles I (Williams 2009). The games were terminated during the civil war, but reinstated after the Restoration. They were certainly staged in 1725, and carried on into the nineteenth century. In later years they apparently became quite rowdy and were again terminated, this time by Act of Parliament in 1851. They were revived once more in 1951 in conjunction with the Festival of Britain, and by 1972 were being invoked in discussion as part of a case for the importance of England in reviving the concept of the Olympic Games (Williams 2009: 150–170).

However successful Coubertin's establishment of the IOC and the modern Olympic Games at the end of the nineteenth century was, it has to be considered in context. From the late eighteenth century and throughout the nineteenth century, various forms of multi-sport festival were developed – in Greece, Scandinavia, North America and not least in the UK. The Highland game tradition of Scotland was revived during the 1820s and spread to North America by the 1850s. Circus-style entertainment incorporating elements of the Roman circus were developed in Paris from the 1820s and in New York in the 1850s. Use of the terms 'Olympic' and 'Olympian' occurred in Scandinavia in the 1830s, and in Liverpool in the 1860s. More significantly, the Much Wenlock Games were established in Shropshire in 1849 by Dr William Penny Brookes, a significant influence on Coubertin. The Greeks made several attempts to revive Olympic Games from 1859 onwards. So Coubertin's own project did not develop in a vacuum.

European sporting cultures

The process by which sport took on organisational forms only developed through struggle and contestation between competing notions of 'sport'. In eighteenth-century English dictionaries, 'sport' meant the field sports of hunting, shooting and fishing. By 1900, in Europe the term typically denoted organised sporting contests, with the team games of football, rugby and cricket prominent. Yet in Asia, Africa and Latin America, the term would either have had no social currency or very different connotations. In the twentieth century, international sport governing bodies, including the IOC, would play a key role in establishing a new dominant understanding of 'sport'.

Two of the most influential sporting cultures, based partly on different conceptions of gymnastic exercise, were to emerge in Germany and Sweden during the nineteenth century. In Germany, this occurred around the Turnen Societies, and their pioneering figure Friedrich Jahn, and involved apparatus-based exercises. Johannes C.F. Guts-Muths, the father of German gymnastics, who was a formative influence on Friedrich Jahn, wrote about the ancient Games in his *Gymnastik für Jugend* (1793). In Sweden, the key figure, Ling, favoured free-standing exercise performed in disciplined unison. These two variants of gymnastics, along with the culture of athleticism and team games developed in English public schools from the 1840s, constituted, by the mid-century, three major European traditions of sporting exercise. When Coubertin began his own investigations into the subject of physical education, deeply influenced by his childhood reading of *Tom Brown's Schooldays*, he favoured, right from the start, the English model.

134

One of the earliest instances of the explicit use of an imagined and idealised ancient Olympism as a model was in Drehberg, outside Wörlitz in eastern Germany. Between 1777 and 1799, Prince Franz staged a festive competition supposedly based on the Olympic Games of antiquity. The games included horse races and gymnastic contests. The contestants were boys and girls from the surrounding schools, which were based on a model of progressive, child-oriented education, Das Philanthropin, devised by the prince. The event was not restricted to athletics, and also included celebration of Saturnalia, the Roman festival of wild joy, even debauchery. It was a day when class differences were ignored and rulers could fraternise, as Franz did, with their subjects. Marriageable girls were encouraged to dance with potential mates until deep into the night.[2] According to Gary Schwartz, the games were part of a pedagogic and social ideal, played by schoolchildren to give 'a competitive edge to the physical training that was part of their humanistic education'. Schwartz says that the Drehberg fair became famous, drawing thousands of visitors and serving as propaganda for Wörlitz as a model for the world. Goethe attended and recommended it to the entire court of Weimar.[3]

In France in 1796, during the Revolution, 'Jeux Olympiques' were staged on the Champ de Mars in Paris (Kidd 1984). 'Olympic' games were organised for the students of a Dominican seminary near Grenoble in 1832, and continued to be held every two years until the twentieth century. An early winner, in 1846, was Henri Didon, who subsequently became a priest and, many years later, gave Coubertin the Olympic Motto 'Citius, Altius, Fortius – Faster, Higher, Stronger' (Durry, undated). In Sweden, in 1834 and 1836, Gustav Johan Schartau organised sporting events, which he referred to as 'Olympic Games', in Ramlosa. Schartau was a disciple of the Swedish gymnastics pioneer Ling and was Professor at the Royal Charles Academy in Lund. There was also an 'Olympic'-styled event in Hungary. Vermes Lajos from Subotica, a landowner, sport enthusiast and athlete, organised sports competitions in which the best sportsmen took part at Lake Palić between 1880 and 1914, and several sports grounds were specially built.[4]

In popular entertainment, as well as in education, the term Olympic was in circulation. In the early nineteenth century, the Cirque des Champs-Élysées, also known as the Cirque Olympique, was an enclosed hippodrome off the Champs-Élysées. The Cirque Olympique subsequently established itself in a building near Temple in 1827. The manager, Louis Dejean (1797–1879), then acquired a new permanent building, the Cirque d'Hiver, to provide a winter base for his touring circus, selling the old Cirque Olympique building in 1847. Located near the Place de la République, the Cirque d'Hiver is the world's oldest functioning extant circus building, and the company is also the world's oldest circus still active.[5]

Franconi's Hippodrome, established in New York in 1853, staged Roman chariot races and Roman circus events. The arena, which held 6,000, was built by American showmen and named after the Italian horseman Antonio Franconi, who, with family members, performed in the Cirque Olympique in Paris. It included an indoor auditorium and an open-air course, around 300 metres long. As well as horse and chariot races, it featured gymnastics, ostrich races and monkeys, deer, camels and elephants. Although quite successful, it was demolished in 1859 to make way for the Fifth Avenue Hotel.[6] An Olympic Club was created in Montreal in 1842. It staged a two-day 'Olympic' Games in

1844, which included the first public lacrosse match, featuring aboriginals versus non-aboriginals. However, during the nineteenth century the Scottish 'Highland Games' and 'pedestrianism' (professional athletics) may have been more influential and popular forms of multi-sport festivity.[7]

In Ireland and Scotland there was a long history of staging multi-sport festivities, which still exists today in the form of the Highland Games (see Jarvie 1991). These were based on earlier Irish festivals, the Tailteann Games, which are known to date back to the twelfth century. After the years of oppression following the final defeat of the Jacobite rebellion in 1745, in which manifestations of 'Scottishness' such as the wearing of the plaid and the speaking of Gaelic were outlawed, the Victorian aristocracy embarked on a reinvention of Scottish tradition, in tartan-drenched form. This was given great impetus by the enthusiasm of Queen Victoria for Scotland, her acquisition of Balmoral and the subsequent emergence of a culture Jarvie calls 'Balmorality'. However, the reinvention and re-emergence of Gaelic traditions was already under way when the Celtic Highland Games were revived in the early nineteenth century. The thousands of Irish and Scots who emigrated to North America took these traditions with them, as marked by the staging of 'Caledonian Games' in Boston (1853) and New York (1856).

The Much Wenlock Games and the National Olympian Association

By the mid-nineteenth century, then, there are plenty of examples of the use of the terms Olympic or Olympian. At this point, three social themes begin to converge in the work of a few sporting pioneers. The first is the revival of interest in ancient Greek culture and in particular the concept of the development of mind and body in harmony. The second is the resultant cult of athleticism developed in the English public schools. The third is the growing concern within the Victorian bourgeoisie with social reform and rational recreation. The Much Wenlock Games, established in 1850 by William Penny Brookes, constituted a more organised and concerted attempt to establish a regular event. Brookes

Figure 6.2 Memorial to Dr William Penny Brookes in Much Wenlock, Shropshire. The inscription reads 'his imagination, a worldwide inspiration'.

was probably the first person in this period to bring together the idea of the sport-based festivity, the term Olympic and a revival of Greek philosophical principles. Historian David Young argues that he, rather than Coubertin, might be seen as the founder of the modern Olympics, although it is true, as MacAloon reminds us, that only Coubertin had the international breadth of vision crucial to the project (Young 1996: 12; MacAloon 1981). Hill, more cautiously, regards him as an 'intriguing footnote to world sports history in his own brand of rational recreationist intervention' (Hill 1992: 9–15).

Brookes, born in Much Wenlock in 1809, was the son of a doctor, became a doctor himself, and also, in 1841, became a Justice of the Peace. Like many middle-class gentlemen in this period, he became concerned with social reform and with encouraging rational recreation among the working classes. He founded the Agricultural Reading Society to promote 'useful information' and the 'Olympian Class' (renamed in 1860 the 'Wenlock Olympian Society') to 'promote the moral, physical and intellectual improvement of the inhabitants of the Town and neighbourhood of Wenlock'. Brookes set up the Agricultural Reading Society to encourage people to read as a way of informing their voting, after the 1832 Reform Act extended the franchise. He also wanted to discourage the local population from drinking (Hill 1992: 9). In 1850, he organised the first Much Wenlock Olympic Games. They included athletics, quoits, football and cricket. Brookes had an interest in Greek culture, but was also possibly aware of and influenced by the Cotswold Games of Robert Dover (see Williams 2009). A classics scholar, Gilbert West, had, in the eighteenth century, written extensively about Pindar's Odes and in the course of this also wrote about Olympism. As Lee (2012) suggests, in terms of the British tradition, he comes between the seventeenth-century establishment of the Cotswold Games by Robert Dover, and the nineteenth-century establishment of the Much Wenlock Games by Dr Penny Brookes. While there are some thematic consistencies between the understanding of Olympism in the writing of Gilbert West and the understanding of Olympism by Penny Brookes, Lee is not able to establish that Penny Brookes read West – although clearly he may well have done so (Lee 2012).

The Olympian Society organised annual games, which gradually came to be more athleticist and national in profile. Brookes, as a doctor, sports enthusiast and rational recreationist, had strong views on the necessity of providing physical education in state schools, and welcomed the 1871 Act in which instruction in drill for up to two hours per week and no more than 20 weeks per year could count as part of school attendance. In the late 1870s Brookes argued for the introduction of Swiss-style gymnastics in schools, and was a vigorous advocate of the values of athletics for the masses:

> The encouragement of outdoor exercise contributes to manliness of character. I say contributes, for true manliness shows itself not merely in skill in athletic and field sports, but in the exercise of those moral virtues which it is one of the objects of religion to inculcate.
>
> (Cited in Hill 1992: 10)

In 1862, a Liverpool Olympic Festival had been held on the military parade ground, Mount Vernon, the first of six such annual events. The festival was promoted by John Hulley (1832–1875), a gymnasium owner and physical fitness expert, and Charles Melly

(1829–1888), a Victorian philanthropist (and an ancestor of jazz singer George Melly). Hulley had been co-founder of the Liverpool Athletic Club. Melly was involved in the National Association for the Promotion of Social Science, the Working Men's Improvement Society, 'ragged schools', the Unitarian Mission, and the provision of infirmaries, public parks, playgrounds and drinking fountains for all.[8] Melly, as an ex-pupil of Rugby School, was a product of the muscular Christianity ethos. Hulley and Melly proposed to revive ideas of physical perfection, drawing on what they knew of the ancient Olympic Games, and, it was claimed, the Liverpool Olympic Festivals 'were organised on the lines of the ancient Greek ones'. According to Ray Physick (2007) around 10,000 people turned up to watch running (120 yards and 300 yards), walking (1.5 miles and four miles), high jump, long jump, pole leap, throwing the disc (discus) and the cricket ball, boxing, wrestling and gymnastics. The following year the crowds grew to 15,000. A third event, in 1864, was marred by gambling and prostitution, prompting the organisers to move the 1865 event to Llandudno. That same year they were involved in establishing the National Olympian Association. After one more year at Llandudno the Olympic Festival returned to Liverpool for a final year in 1867, which featured over 300 competitors. After this point financial

Figure 6.3 The German Gymnasium. Built by the German Gymnastic Society in 1864, this was the first purpose-built gymnasium in the United Kingdom. Ernst Revenstein, an organiser of the first National Olympian Games in London in 1866, was a president of the society.

138

problems meant that no more were staged.[9] Meanwhile, Brookes had organised the third Shropshire Olympics that were combined with the thirteenth Much Wenlock Games (Matthews 2005: 56).

Brookes and the National Olympian Association were able to stage the First National Olympian Festival in London in 1866. The first National Olympian Games were organised by William Penny Brookes, John Hulley and Ernest Ravenstein of the German Gymnastic Society (GGS) in London. Ravenstein managed the Games, and many of the several nationals belonging to the GGS took part in the Games, as did cricketer W.G. Grace (Anthony 1986). A second National Olympian Games were held in Birmingham in 1867, with a third in Wellington, Shropshire the following year. But the embryonic Olympic movement in Britain was crushed by the rise of the Amateur Athletic Club (AAC), which, concerned to exclude the lower orders, introduced the famous clause excluding 'mechanics, artisans and labourers'. The AAC opposed the National Olympics and after 1868 only the Wenlock Olympic Games continued in England (Matthews 2005: 58). After a long, drawn-out struggle between various aspirants to control and define both athletics and amateurism, a compromise was engineered by a group from Oxford and Cambridge who persuaded the supporters of the AAC to drop the commitment to the exclusion of the working class, but to retain the concept of amateur sportsmen, excluding any form of professionalism (see Lovesey 1979). The resultant formation of the Amateur Athletic Association (AAA) produced a template for the distinction between amateur and professionalism that was copied by many other sports, and came to constitute a taken-for-granted reality among the bourgeois gentlemen who formed subsequent organisations. Brookes worked hard to promote the Olympic idea from 1850 until his death, which was, ironically enough, in 1895, one year before the first modern Olympic Games were staged (Matthews 2005: 57). A fourth National Olympian Games took place in 1874 in Much Wenlock, followed by a fifth in 1877 in Shrewsbury, and a final one in Hadley in 1883.

Morpeth also appropriated the Olympic name in 1883 for its annual Morpeth Games. The Morpeth Olympic Games involved Cumberland and Westmorland and featured wrestling and professional athletics. They took place regularly between 1881 and 1959, originally as a one-day event, but by 1912 popularity prompted their extension to a second day (McCusker 2008). The area in which they were staged has been marked by street names – Olympia Hill and Olympia Gardens – and a local shop called Olympia Stores (which was recently closed and converted into flats).[10] Unlike the Olympic festivals in which Brookes was involved, this cannot be regarded as a significant forerunner of the Olympic Games. It does, however, contribute to the accumulating instances from the late eighteenth to late nineteenth centuries of the common use of the term Olympic to denote a multi-sport festival.

Greece, Soutsos and Zappas

The politics of the soil alone would seem to give the Greeks a privileged claim to 'ownership' of the concept of the Olympic Games. Coubertin was alert enough to this to recognise the symbolic importance of staging the first Games in Greece, but the relationship of Coubertin and the IOC to Graecian proprietorial claims was always an uncomfortable one. Coubertin, who in the end wished to be the father of the event, paid more credit to Dr Brookes than to Zappas and the other Greek pioneers. Later, when the second and third Olympic Games were shambolic, Coubertin was grateful to the Greeks for staging an interim or 'intercalated' games, but had no desire to encourage a regular Greece-based event. For the hundredth anniversary year in 1996, the IOC, in the view of many, chose mammon over tradition in awarding the Games to Atlanta; subsequent guilt, Greek righteous anger and strong lobbying prompted them to make amends by awarding the 2004 Games to Athens. The Greek attempts at revival during the nineteenth century have been the subject of contestation and debate by historians ever since.

The growing interest in Ancient Greece in general, and the Olympic Games in particular, was fuelled by archaeology and excavation of some of the key sites, including Troy, Mycenae and Olympia. The idea of excavating to unearth the site of the ancient Olympics was mooted in the eighteenth century, and the site was discovered by excavations in 1766, with additional early excavations in 1787. There were further excavations by the French in 1829, and a real breakthrough by German archaeologists in 1852. The first excavations on a major scale, though, did not take place until 1875 and, after a decade of extensive work, an Archaeological Museum was opened on the site in 1886. The 1889 'Exposition Universelle' in Paris included models of the excavations.

Young considers the idea of a Greek revival to have been commenced by Panagiotis Soutsos, a poet, publisher and patriot. From 1833 onward, his poems alluded to the Olympic Games. In 1835 he contacted the government to propose that 25 March be made a national holiday in celebration of the War of Independence, and that the celebration should include a revival of the Olympic Games. His proposal envisaged a four-year cycle, with the Games staged in four Greek cities. There was no immediate response, but in 1838 the town of Letrini established a committee to revive the Olympics, although no such event took place. Soutsos continued his campaign through the 1840s, but further developments were due to the work of Evangelos Zappas (see Young 1996).

Evangelos Zappas (1800–1865) was a wealthy landowner and businessman of Greek ancestry. In early 1856, he proposed a permanent revival of the Olympic Games, and offered to finance the project. The first of the Zappas Olympic Games was held in 1859. He also provided funds for the eventual restoration of the ancient Panathenaic Stadium, although this was not completed until after his death. Zappas-inspired Olympic Games were staged in Athens in 1859, 1870, 1875 and 1889, with varying degrees of success. In 1859 Dr William Penny Brookes was in contact with Greece, sending £10 to be presented to the winner of an event in the Olympian Games. Brookes, corresponding via the British Ambassador, also urged the Greek government to revive the ancient Games.

The 1870 Games in the restored stadium were the most successful of the Zappas Olympics, with over 30,000 spectators, and enthusiastic reviews in the newspapers. Members of Athens' elite then suggested that the Games should be restricted only to athletes from the upper class and that the general public be banned. This social exclusion damaged the 1875 Games, which attracted only 24 athletes and small crowds. Young (1996) called the 1875 Zappas Olympics a 'disaster'. The next event in 1889 was a badly run event in a gymnasium, and in 1891 and 1893 the Panhellenic Gymnastic Society took up the baton. The Zappas Olympic Games and the Much Wenlock Olympian Games were more important staging posts on the road to full revival than many of the other events, which merely utilised the Olympic word.

COUBERTIN, THE FRENCH AND THE ENGLISH

So, during the nineteenth century, the term 'Olympic' was coming into more common usage, and multi-sport events were being staged, not least in the UK and Greece. That Coubertin's model was ultimately the one that became dominant was due to a combination of circumstances. Coubertin's own determination, his organisational and diplomatic skills and his social contacts were central. His early exposure to and romantic obsession with the world of English school sport, as portrayed by Thomas Hughes in *Tom Brown's Schooldays* – which Coubertin first read in 1875, when he was 12 – was significant. All this, though, must be set in the context of social and political factors. The Olympic Games were only one manifestation of the emergence of modern organised spectator sport that had been growing for 100 years, but was by the late nineteenth century becoming a more significant form of leisure activity. Sport and the modern media began their fateful interaction around the time that the first modern Olympic Games were staged. In this sense the emergence and success of the modern Olympic Games were in part the outcome of social processes beyond the ability even of as striking a figure as Coubertin to manage. Sport acquired national and then international governance between 1860 and 1920. Regular international competitions (such as the Football World Cup) were established. It seems inevitable that some form of international multi-sport event would have evolved. Coubertin's distinctive contribution consists of the construction of this in the form of Olympism, which combined ritual, festival and spectacle, ethical principles and a particular, if not peculiar, organisational form (see Chatziefstathiou and Henry 2012).

BOX 6.1 BARON PIERRE DE COUBERTIN

Pierre de Coubertin (1863–1937) was born in Paris in 1863, the fourth child of an aristocratic Catholic family. Educated at Jesuit schools and colleges, he completed a Bachelor of Science degree in 1881. His interest in education and sport led him to his life's project, reviving the Olympic Games. He was married in 1895 to Marie Rothan, from a Protestant family (who lived until 1963, when she was 102). In later years Coubertin suffered financial problems and the family home had to be sold. He died in 1937 at the age of 74.

One needs to understand the emergence of sport in relation to modernity and capitalism, and particularly in relation to the period from 1880 to 1914. What was going on during this time? It marked the pinnacle and final moment of grandeur for the British Empire, before its challenge by new rising powers such as Germany and the US, and its ultimate eclipse and demise. It marked the rise of Germany, formed in 1871, and the rise of German power, provoking new alliances and rivalries in Europe. It marked the rise of American power towards its dominance of the world economy. The British historian Asa Briggs (1991) identified it as the period of the birth of mass entertainment. The spread of literacy, wireless telegraphy, development of a mass circulation popular press and the emergence of cinema from the mid-1890s were all factors. Branded goods had become more common, distributed more effectively by the new chain stores. A revolution in advertising was bringing brand names to the domestic vocabulary.

This period fostered the birth of modern sport – the establishment of governing bodies, agreed rules, competitions, stadiums and spectatorship. To an extent this can be seen as a process of a rationalising modernity – bureaucratised, systematised, institutionalised, rule-governed and subject to quantification (Guttmann 1978). In its routine separation of performer and spectator, it also established the structural bases for the commercialisation and commodification of sport that become such a central part of the Olympic story from the 1970s onwards. From the late nineteenth century, sport was also in the forefront of globalising processes – some of the first international bodies were sport-related ones such as the IOC, the IAAF and the ILTF. National and international competitions grew in scope and ambition, most notably with the establishment of the modern Olympic Games in 1896.

But if it was a world that was becoming more globalised, it was certainly not a flat world, and this process was not a neutral one. The very technologies and infrastructures of communication inscribed the dominance of the major imperial powers. Telegraph lines linked the peripheries of empires to their core centres in Paris and London – so it was, for example, easier for Ghana to contact London than neighbouring Upper Volta (now Burkina Faso).

Sport diffusion was strongly linked to the structure of empires (cricket and rugby spread to British Empire countries and almost nowhere else). By comparison, soccer – increasingly rejected by the British bourgeoisie in favour of rugby – was spread by skilled tradesmen, engineers, etc. to South America and elsewhere but not to the British Empire countries. The old imperial rivalries between Britain and France were replayed in sport as each country sought to be a dominant organising force, with greater success going to the French. Despite American economic power, its own sports, lacking the support of an established imperial network, did not export successfully. Indeed, the cultures of sport in the US were characterised by the establishment of a distance from Europe, and the construction of a distinctive American-ness. The myths of origin around baseball and American football minimised and marginalised their European sources. International sporting organisation was largely forged by English and French elites. So it was in this period that the modern world – the world of the twentieth century – was largely forged and, with it, modern spectator sport and the roots of media sport.

Coubertin's own youthful world was one in which a mood of national shame prevailed. The impact of the defeat of France on 1 September 1870 at the battle of Sedan, less than eight weeks after Napoleon III had declared war on Prussia, was considerable. On 4 September 1870 France became a republic again, and the following year France lost Alsace and Lorraine as Germany became a united nation and a threat of growing significance to France. Coubertin was greatly concerned at what he regarded as the physical degeneracy of French youth, especially when compared to the well-trained and disciplined

German youth. His lifelong concern for education, and in particular physical education, was shaped by this formative moment.

The novel *Tom Brown's Schooldays* was to have a great influence on the growing cult of athleticism, and on the thinking of Coubertin, who read it as a boy and re-read it as an adult. According to Mangan, Coubertin was inspired not so much by the actual headmaster, Dr Arnold, as by the version of him that existed only in the imagination of Thomas Hughes. In *L'Education en Angleterre* (1888), Coubertin testified to an absolute belief in the English boarding school system (Mangan 1981: 130). The association of sport and moral education became a significant element in Coubertin's re-articulation of Olympism. It was not just an obsessive admiration for the Hughes version of Arnold, though – more generally, Coubertin was something of an Anglophile, who was also heavily influenced by Hippolyte Taine's *Notes sur Angleterre* (1872).

BOX 6.2 *TOM BROWN'S SCHOOLDAYS*, BY THOMAS HUGHES

The novel *Tom Brown's Schooldays*, by Thomas Hughes, is identified in many British sport histories as an emblematic text, representing the emergence of the cult of athleticism and the ethos of muscular Christianity. The popularity of the book led to an over-emphasis on the importance of Rugby School and of its headmaster, Thomas Arnold. The new Victorian bourgeoisie were preoccupied by the ever-present danger of lower-class unrest. Arnold was haunted by visions of mob violence, chaos and revolution, and lay awake at night contemplating the ever-growing crowds of workers demanding parliamentary reform (Gathorne-Hardy 1977: 80–81).

Thomas Hughes (1822–1896) was the son of a paternalistic Tory who sent him to Rugby School. He became an active Christian Socialist and muscular Christian, organising gymnastics, boxing, rowing and cricket at the Working Men's College (Lowerson 1993: 158). His one successful novel, *Tom Brown's Schooldays*, was hugely popular with the middle-class families who were being attracted by the new reformed public schools and it had a significant influence on the subsequent growth of the cult of athleticism. In the book, Tom, reduced on his first day to a 'motionless body' by a rugby scrum, is nonetheless transformed by the end of the tale into an active and rounded person – thus boys were turned into men through the process of schooling.

Hughes' fictionalised version of Dr Arnold differs significantly from Arnold himself. There is little evidence that Arnold directly and deliberately promoted cricket and football for their educational value (McIntosh 1952: 30). He had only a mild interest in the games themselves, but encouraged them as part of his new regime of power, based on a reformed prefect and fagging system, with Christian morality and social responsibility at its core. Hughes' rather humanised and jolly portrayal of Arnold's regime was 'made rosy by nostalgia' (Birley 1993: 209–210). However, the masters and prefects under his influence took to athleticism with a growing enthusiasm (Holt 1989: 80), although Mangan establishes clearly that the real seed-bed of athleticism

---

was at other public schools, such as Uppingham (Mangan 1981). By the 1860s, Birley suggests, sport was seen as 'the great character-builder on which the nation depended to train its leaders' (Birley 1993: 286). The 1860s saw the introduction of games masters, professional coaches and inter-house and inter-school competitions. Mangan suggests that parents and masters alike subscribed to the ethical value of games as a source of good sense, noble traits, manly feelings, generous dispositions, gentlemanly deportment and comradely loyalty (Mangan 1981: 132).

Many accounts of the period emphasise the commitment to developing sound minds and healthy bodies, and its roots in classical Greece. Yet in Tom Brown we also see the traces of an English philistinism – a lack of interest in the cultivation of the intellect. Social Darwinism – in which life is conflict, strength comes through struggle, and success is the prerogative of the strong – became more influential in the second half of the nineteenth century. There was a gulf between the constructed image of the schools and the brutality of existence within them (Mangan 1987: 139–142).

(Adapted from Whannel, 1999)

Coubertin combined, sometimes uneasily, a very real commitment to internationalism with a deep concern for France and its education system. He also had pacifist sympathies (see Quanz 1993). He was influenced by the work of social theorist Frédéric LePlay, who, concerned at the impact of class division, sought means to restore peace and harmony (see Guttmann 1992: 7). He believed that sporting competition between all the nations of the world could lead to mutual understanding and respect between individuals of different nations, races and social positions (Charpentier and Boissonnade 1999: 32). John Macaloon, in a preface to a new edition of *This Great Symbol*, acknowledges that Dietrich Quanz demonstrates close ties between the Olympic movement and the international peace movement. He agrees with Quanz's speculation that the organisational design of the new IOC owed something to the International Peace Bureau. Macaloon (2006a) comments that

At a time of worry that the new IOC regime in Lausanne is turning away from formal relations with peace organizations and with universities under the pressure of or in preference to its sports business responsibilities, it is important to be reminded of how inseparable educational sport, international understanding and peace activism were at the outset for the modern Olympic Games.

Coubertin believed that the classic gymnasia of Ancient Greece (basically sports fields rather than modern enclosed buildings) enabled a triple unity: between different sporting disciplines, between young and old, and between practical and theoretical approaches (Hill 1992: 6). In turn, this last point relates to the Greek notion of developing mind and body in harmony, which also underpinned the development of athleticism in the English public schools of the nineteenth century. For Coubertin, this did not involve a unity of men and women; while in favour of greater social equality, Coubertin did not extend this to gender, and to the end he was hostile to the involvement of women as competitors.

144

Coubertin visited England several times during the 1880s to study the educational system. In 1883 he visited Oxford and Cambridge and also the public schools of Rugby, Harrow and Eton. Confusingly, in England the term 'public school' refers to a fee-paying school, although in practice the term is reserved for the elite schools that first flourished during the nineteenth century as the means of educating the sons of the social elite. They were 'public' in contrast to the earlier aristocratic tradition of educating children at home. The public schools were originally largely aristocratic, but, following the reforms of the 1840s, became increasingly popular with the new Victorian bourgeoisie. Other fee-paying schools of lesser status are generally referred to as private schools. The schools that in other societies would be known as public schools are called in the UK 'state schools'. Free state education began to develop in the 1870s following the 1870 Education Act.

Throughout the twentieth century the dominant proportion of the political class in the UK were educated at public schools. After a more egalitarian shift – with the Prime Ministers Heath, Callaghan, Thatcher and Major all products of state schools – the UK appears to have reverted to tradition with Tony Blair and the current Prime Minister David Cameron both educated in public schools.

By 1887 Coubertin had also gained knowledge of Winchester, Wellington, Marlborough, Charterhouse, Coopers Hill, Westminster and Christ's Hospital. He contrasted the lack of physical education in French schools with active physical activity in English schools. He became an ardent campaigner and lobbyist, visiting the UK and US to produce reports for the French government on physical education. His report on the US represented America as a place where the gymnastic systems of Jahn and Ling were being rejected in favour of British team games (see Coubertin 1890 for an account of Coubertin's trip to the US, and American education). In the light of his passionate advocacy of the British system, this perspective cannot be taken as neutral, balanced or dispassionate (see also Coubertin 1917, which contains material on English education, Arnold and sport).

Coubertin knew and understood diplomacy, and made elaborate manoeuvres to build political allies. A keen rower, Coubertin visited Henley Royal Regatta. He was impressed by the Henley organisation, which he described as 'three concentric circles' – the nucleus, the nursery and the façade. This distinguished those who were deeply committed, those who could be educated to the cause and those whose position and influence could be useful. This model was used as the basis of the IOC constitution (Anthony 1997) and indeed still serves as a characterisation of the way the IOC operates today. When planning the Paris Congress that established the IOC, Coubertin was politically astute enough to include dignitaries from Scotland, Wales and Ireland as well as England.

In 1881 Brookes visited France and was so taken aback by the physical degeneracy of the population that he wrote to the French government on the subject (Hill 1992: 11). In January 1890 Brookes wrote to Coubertin, they commenced a correspondence and in October Coubertin visited Brookes in Much Wenlock (Hill 1992: 11–13). Brookes was then aged 80, while Coubertin was only 26. Brookes and Coubertin continued to correspond, Brookes lending his support to the Olympic project. In 1890, Coubertin wrote in *La Revue Athlétique* that 'If the Olympic Games that Modern Greece has not yet been able to revive still survives today, it is due, not to a Greek, but to Dr W. P. Brookes.'[11]

Coubertin invited Brookes to the 1894 Congress but he was too ill to attend and died the following year, missing his dreamed-of Olympic revival by just one year. It is also clear that Coubertin knew of the work of Zappas. According to some assessments, Coubertin subsequently tended to gloss over and minimise the role of his predecessors, Zappas and Brookes. He did, though, write an obituary of Brookes for the *New York Review of Books*, in which Brookes is described as his 'oldest friend' (Anthony 1986).

In England, the fears of the bourgeoisie of the threat from the 'lower orders' and their desire to maintain social distinction had led to the development of a sharp division between amateur and professional sport. In governing bodies for sport, professionals were either excluded altogether, as was the case with athletics, rowing and tennis, or had their inferiority marked, as was the case with golf and cricket. Only the Football Association, faced with the huge popularity of professional football and the threat of a breakaway, had been forced to compromise and admit professionalism. Rugby, by contrast, ended by splitting into two distinct sports, one professional and one amateur. Coubertin was certainly concerned about the commercialisation of sport, which he saw as a threat, and he shared the values and orientations of the world of aristocratic links and gentlemen's clubs in which amateurism was a taken-for-granted feature of sporting contestation. However, he never regarded amateurism as the most vital issue. Nevertheless, the modern Olympic Games inherited and enshrined for the next 90 years a concept of 'amateur' born of class discrimination. It was during the presidency (1952–1972) of Avery Brundage that the issue came to a head, and only in the 1980s, when the widespread payment of athletes could no longer be ignored, did the IOC move to neutralise the issue by making it a concern of the individual sport federations rather than of the IOC.

At the same time that Coubertin's plans for the IOC and the first Olympic Games were beginning to crystallise, so were plans for a multi-sport event linking British Empire countries. This scheme, with roots in imperial power and racism, was developed by John Astley Cooper, who began proposing a Pan-Britannic Festival in print in 1891. This idea was overtaken by the modern Olympic Games, but it sowed the seeds of the idea that resurfaced as the 'Empire Games' (see below). Indeed, Cooper and Coubertin met in the early 1890s to discuss these matters, but Cooper's essentially racist and imperialist vision cannot have appealed to Coubertin. Cooper's ideas combined

> several important aspects of life – culture, industry and athletics in a grandiose festival celebrating the British race. The concept implied, but did not explicitly state, that the race was superior; Cooper asked if Britons were ready to undertake 'actions for the benefit of mankind which may make the name of England to be sung for all time as an example to races yet to come'.
>
> (Moore 1987: 146)

It is clear, according to Moore, that Cooper's idea was intended to include 'only adult males from the so-called white Dominions – Australia, New Zealand, Canada and South Africa as well as those subjects eligible in Great Britain' (Moore 1987: 148). In the event, the Empire Games were first staged in 1930 in Hamilton, Ontario, at a moment when the relationship between the UK and the old 'white' empire countries was being reshaped. Historian Richard Holt commented that 'the loosening bonds of Empire came at the same

146

time as new economic pressures were being placed upon the relationships between the Dominions and Britain' (quoted in Phillips 2000: 5).

The subsequent trajectory of the Empire Games makes an interesting contrast with the Olympic Games – the very title of the event, unlike that of the World Cup or the Olympic Games, had to keep changing to match contemporary political realities. Until 1950 it was the 'British Empire Games', after which it became the 'British Empire and Commonwealth Games'. In 1970 the embarrassment of 'empire' was dropped, and the games became the 'British Commonwealth Games'. Four years later, in a symbolic deterritorialisation, 'British' was dropped and the event became the 'Commonwealth Games' (see Moore 1986, 1987, 1989, 1991). The huge success of the Olympic Games and subsequently both the World Cup and football's continental championships has reduced the status of the Commonwealth Games immensely – but none of this could be foreseen in 1890.

THE 1894 CONGRESS AND THE 1896 GAMES

During the 1880s, Coubertin's commitment to educational reform, his research into physical education and his interest in the concept of reviving the Olympic Games were converging. At the Exposition Universelle in 1889, he organised the first Congress of Physical Exercise and school competitions. In the last decade of the nineteenth century the long gestation of Coubertin's thinking came to fruition. At a conference at the Sorbonne in 1892, he spoke with eloquence about the project of re-establishing the Olympic Games (Charpentier and Boissonnade 1999: 29–33). Coubertin utilised the fifth anniversary of the Union des Sociétés Françaises de Sports Athlétiques (USFSA) in 1892 to propose the project of reviving the Games. He ensured that at the 1893 General Assembly, the Society would stage a Congress to discuss the project further (Hill 1992: 18). He then discovered a general lack of enthusiasm for the revival of the Games and was forced to recast the proposed Congress as being primarily about amateurism, with the Olympics as a side issue. He was, however, able to recruit two strong supporters, Charles Herbert, the secretary of the English AAA, and Professor William Sloane of Princeton University (Hill 1992: 19–20). In the event, the 1894 Congress established the IOC and instigated the planning of the first modern Olympic Games, to be staged in Athens in 1896. The choice of Athens is the subject of considerable confusion. Evidence from the minutes suggests that delegates favoured London. Young suggests that Coubertin, having himself determined in advance upon Athens, manoeuvred to ensure this outcome (Young 1996: 100–105).

The 1894 Congress was attended by 79 delegates, representing 49 organisations from 12 countries (Mandell 1976: 86). The meeting was, not surprisingly, heavily European, with Australia and the US the only non-European countries represented. In the event, the first IOC had 13 members, all male. There were two each from Great Britain and France, and one each from Italy, Greece, the Russian Empire, Austria-Hungary, Norway–Sweden and Bohemia. There were three non-European members, from the US, New Zealand and Argentina. The IOC was established as a body whose members did not represent any external body, nor were they answerable to any external institution. The IOC alone was the owner of the Olympic Games, and the custodian of 'Olympism'. It determined to have regular Congresses every few years, along with annual meetings referred to as 'Sessions'.

Figure 6.4
The de Coubertin monument. The heart of de Coubertin was entombed in this monument in Olympia, which has become another site of Olympic pilgrimage. Students and their professors from all over the world attend the annual International Olympic Academy, and a visit to the de Coubertin memorial is obligatory. Photograph courtesy of Annette Hofmann.

The IOC's rules call on it to guide modern sport into desirable channels and promote the development of those fine physical and moral qualities which are the basis of sports.

CONCLUSION

In the establishment of a new regular event, symbols, myths, narratives and an imagined history are all important. From the start, certain traditions were invented. There was an Opening Ceremony, with a key ritualised opening phrase. Winners got a silver medal and an olive wreath, and runners up a copper medal and a laurel wreath. National flags were hoisted at victory ceremonies. Coubertin derived the 'Faster, Higher, Stronger' motto from an 1891 speech by the Dominican priest Father Henri Didon. The Olympic Oath taken by competitors was first written by Coubertin in 1906, but was not utilised until 1920.

Figure 6.5 The stadium built for the Inaugural Modern Olympics (1896) in Athens.

The Olympic Village, the Olympic flame and the Olympic torch relay did not appear until much later.

That there was a substantial mythologising of the Ancient Greek Games has long been clear. Where blemishes in Olympic 'purity' are acknowledged this is often ascribed to the malign and decadent influence of the Romans in the later period of the ancient Games. An English Olympian, Theodore Cook, manages, with patrician grandeur, to link the supposed commercialism of the Romans with late nineteenth-century sporting professionalism:

> But we may at least remember that the ancient Games of Greece were only ruined by the professionals of the late Roman Empire, that there was once a time when athletic energy did not imply limited liability companies, when first-rate games did not depend on gate money for their existence.
>
> (Cook 1908: x)

In Athens in 1896 there were 81 athletes from 12 countries, and another 230 athletes from Greece, in nine disciplines and 43 events. The Games also included the marathon, devised by the French philosopher Michel Breal shortly after the Congress of 1894

(Durry, undated). There were nine sports: cycling, fencing, gymnastics, lawn tennis, shooting, swimming, athletics, weightlifting and wrestling. So both the organisation and the Games were almost entirely European, but Coubertin was keen to get his show on the road. Coubertin did not expect the Greeks to be capable of staging the Games but was convinced by Dimetrias Bikelas that it could be done. In the event, once the Greeks secured the Games, they tended to sideline Coubertin, who was upset not to be more involved. He was further put out when the official account only mentioned him once, although he retaliated by proclaiming of the Olympics, in his own introduction to the report: 'I claim its paternity with raised voice.' The king of Greece wanted to have the Games permanently sited in Greece and Coubertin had to utilise his diplomatic skills in proposing a separate Pan-Hellenic Games, spaced between the Olympics. In the event this only happened in 1906 (Hill 1992: 20–25). By the 1920s Coubertin had come to believe that his project to promote moral education through sport had not been successful: in a 1928 speech to the International Bureau of Sports Pedagogy at the University of Lausanne he blamed educators for failing to use sport to create a moral culture (Brown 2012: 160).

The question of whether Coubertin, Brookes, Zappas or indeed others have the best claim to be the key figure is in the end not crucial, although clearly Coubertin has by far the strongest claim to have formed and shaped modern Olympism. The modern Olympics came into being because of the energetic work of all these figures, but the project was successful because the combination of circumstances was favourable. Indeed, it seems inevitable that some form of international sporting event would have been created. What is of greater interest is the particular manner in which this happened, allowing the IOC, itself a very peculiar organisational form, ownership over such a powerful symbolic cultural event.

NOTES

1 Bill Mallon, *Track and Field News*, http://mb.trackandfieldnews.com/discussion/viewtopic.php?p=412657 (last accessed 25 October 2015).
2 http://industrielles-gartenreich.com/english/03_projekte/311_drehberg.htm (last accessed 23 October 2015).
3 The Olympics of 1777, www.garyschwartzarthistorian.nl/schwartzlist/?id=65 (last accessed 23 October 2015). See also www.gartenreich.com.
4 See www.shd.org.rs/ESSEE4/AboutPalic.html (last accessed 23 October 2015).
5 See Cirque Olympique, www.hberlioz.com/Paris/BPOlympique.html and www.circopedia.org/index.php/Cirque_d'Hiver (last accessed 23 October 2015).
6 Franconi's Hippodrome: New York's Roman Coliseum, http://thevirtualdimemuseum.blogspot.com/2010/01/franconis-hippodrome-new-yorks-roman.html (last accessed 30 June 2010).
7 Sports from 1840–1945, www.mccord-museum.qc.ca/scripts/explore.php?Lang=1&tableid=11&tablename=theme&elementid=26__true&contentlong (last accessed 25 October 2015). www.thecanadianencyclopedia.com/index.cfm?PgNm=TCE&Params=A1ARTA0008078 (last accessed 25 October 2015).
8 www.liverpooldailypost.co.uk/liverpool-life-features/liverpool-special-features/2008/08/08/how-we-lit-the-olympic-flame-64375-21490142 (last accessed 25 October 2015).

150

9 www.liverpooldailypost.co.uk/liverpool-life-features/liverpool-special-features/ 2008/08/08/how-we-lit-the-olympic-flame-64375-21490142 (last accessed 25 October 2015).

10 *Morpeth Herald*, 10 July 2010, www.morpethherald.co.uk/CustomPages/CustomPage. aspx?PageID=40295 (last accessed 25 October 2015). See also Thielgen (n.d.) and Ruhl (1999).

11 www.wenlock-olympian-society.org.uk/william-penny-brookes/wpb-book.shtml (last accessed 12 August 2010).

FURTHER READING

Coubertin, P. de (2000) *Olympism: Selected Writings*, Lausanne: International Olympic Committee.

Finley, M.I. and Pleket, H.W. (1976) *The Olympic Games: The First Thousand Years*, London: Chatto & Windus.

MacAloon, John (1981) *This Great Symbol: Pierre de Coubertin and the Origins of the Modern Olympic Games*, Chicago: University of Chicago Press (2nd edition, 2006).

Mandell, R. (1976) *The First Modern Olympics*, Berkeley: University of California Press.

Young, D.C. (1996) *The Modern Olympics: A Struggle for Revival*, Baltimore: Johns Hopkins University Press.

CHAPTER 7

FROM WORLD'S FAIRS TO MEGA-EVENTS

While this book is concerned with the Olympic Games, we consider it essential that the modern Olympics are understood in relation to other developments of their time. The early (modern) Olympic Games as a cultural form were closely linked to international or universal expositions (expos) or world's fairs. Although they achieved some independence from 1912 onwards, it was only in the post-Second World War television era that the Olympics were able to become a full-fledged, stand-alone, sports 'mega-event'. This chapter traces that development, examining how the Olympic Games retained elements of its origins while it altered in relation to other significant political, economic and cultural processes. Historically the sport genre of mega-event can be seen as the cuckoo's egg in the world's fairs' nest. While world's fairs drew, and continue to draw, many more people to their locations and last much longer temporally than an Olympic Games or Football World Cup, they are nowhere near as highly mediated or as TV-dependent as sports mega-events. The Olympic Games, however, became the 'world championship of world championships' (Donnelly 1996: 35) and a mass-mediated global spectacle (as we have seen in Chapter 4). This potentially vast global audience is one of the major dimensions in any claims to be a mega-event.

In this chapter we look first at alternative views of the growth of the Olympic Games, in the context of empire and capitalist modernity. Next we briefly describe the development of the first three Olympic Games (1896, 1900 and 1904) in relation to world's fairs and expos. Then we shed particular light on London's experience of hosting the 1908 and 1948 Olympics and, finally, we consider alternative sports and physical culture events and the growth of the reach of the Olympics in the twentieth century.

WORLD'S FAIRS, EMPIRE AND TECHNOLOGY

In this section we contrast two theoretical approaches to the Olympics – what might be called the structural and the phenomenological. Maurice Roche (2000, 2003) suggests that the transition from world's fairs to sports mega-events reflects a broader differentiation in stages of modernity – from early, through mature to late periods of modernity. From the mid-nineteenth century (and the 'Great Exhibition' held in London in 1851) until 1914 and the start of the First World War these mega-events reflected an ambitious and optimistic view of progress. From the end of that war in 1918 until the early 1970s, despite the major wars, economic and political crises and other social and cultural events of the twentieth century, there was an assumption of qualified progress underpinning the expos. From the mid-1970s onward there has been greater uncertainty about the future attached to the mega-events. Over this period mega-events have moved from being 'timekeepers of progress' to 'media events'. In fact Roche (2003: 107) contends that late modernity is an 'event-oriented culture' providing people with 'important cultural resources for the organization of time and identity at both a personal and a societal level'. In this culture, sports mega-events:

> provide people with enduring motivations and special opportunities to participate in collective projects which have the characteristics of, among other things, structuring social space and time, displaying the dramatic and symbolic possibilities of organized and effective social action, and reaffirming the embodied agency of people as individual actors, even if the latter is only displayed in the activity of spectatorship.
>
> (Roche 2003: 109)

To unpick this statement a little it is worth considering the extent to which world's fairs in the nineteenth and early twentieth centuries were linked to the emergence of 'a system of international politics undergirded by a liberal capitalist world order' (Keys 2006: 184). In these emerging conditions technology, trade and imperialism played a part in the struggles between the French and British empires and the rising new US power. The international, and increasingly global, sport 'system' that developed in the first half of the twentieth century (discussed in Chapter 3) with the IOC, NOCs and IFs 'run primarily by men in Western democracies' (Keys 2006: 185) can be seen to be dependent on this context (on the notion of a 'global sport system', see Bale and Sang 1996).

The first significant 'expo' was held in the 'Crystal Palace' in Hyde Park, London, in 1851 under the title 'The Great Exhibition of the Works of Industry of All Nations'. This British exhibition was an attempt to make clear to the world its role as the industrial leader. As the 'Great Exhibition' was the first international exhibition of manufactured products, it influenced the development of several aspects of society, including art and design education and international trade and relations, and it set the precedent for many subsequent international exhibitions, also referred to as 'world's fairs', which have been staged to the present day. Such exhibitions constitute a link between pleasure gardens and theme parks (Philips 2012: 7–30).

The main attractions at expos are the national pavilions, created by participating countries, at which innovations in science, technology, manufacturing and the arts can be displayed. This remains the case today even if the emphasis is now on the potentially contradictory themes of consumption and sustainability. In 2010, at the expo in Shanghai, millions of visitors came to marvel at new designs and technologies. A particular attraction for the burgeoning Chinese middle class was the Japan Pavilion, featuring the latest in toilet technology with high-efficiency flushing systems, heated seats and built-in bidets (Pierson 2010). The current (2015) expo in Milan ('Expo Milano') has attracted over 140 countries to exhibit with a focus on 'Feeding the Planet. Energy for Life' (Nordin 2015).[1] The official website states that it expects the expo 'to attract over 20 million visitors to its 1.1 million square meters of exhibition area' between May and October 2015. The five-year cycle will continue with Dubai Expo in 2020,[2] which promises the creation of 277,000 jobs and to attract 25 million visitors to the first expo to be staged in the Middle East, North Africa and South Asia (MENASA) region.

As Figure 7.1 illustrates, between 1851 and 1970 expos or world's fairs presented various novel types of industrial machinery, manufacturing processes (steel making), materials and energy sources (petroleum, gasoline engine, the peaceful use of atomic energy), modes of transport (the elevator, monorail, moving sidewalk, mass-production cars and aeroplanes), media and communication (mechanical typesetting, which underpinned the newspaper industry, the telephone, telegraph, cinematography and television) and buildings (Eiffel Tower).

Since the signing of the 1928 Convention on International Exhibitions, the Bureau International des Expositions (BIE) has served as the international sanctioning body for expos. BIE-approved fairs are divided into a number of types: universal, international or

Year	City	Visitors (millions)	Technology
1851	London	6.0	Industrial machinery
1853	New York		Elevator
1862	London	6.2	Steel making, mechanical typesetting
1867	Paris	6.8	Aluminium, petroleum, gasoline engine
1873	Vienna	7.2	
1876	Philadelphia	9.9	Monorail, large steam engine, telephone, telegraph, typewriter
1878	Paris	6.0	Internal combustion engine, rubber tyres, refrigeration, phonograph
1889	Paris	32.0	Electric light, Eiffel Tower
1893	Chicago	27.5	Alternating electric current, electric light bulb, electric train, kinetoscope
1900	Paris (including second Olympic Games)	48.0	Moving sidewalk, military technology, large-screen cinematography
1904	St. Louis (including third Olympic Games)	19.7	Flying machines, long-distance wireless telegraph, radio tube
1908	London (including fourth Olympic Games)	8.4	
1911	Glasgow	11.5	
1915	San Francisco	18.8	Mass-production cars
1924/5	London	27.0	
1933/4	Chicago	48.7	Deco architecture and design, experimental television
1939/40	New York	45.0	Rocketry, nylon, plastics, domestic air conditioning, mass television
1958	Brussels	41.5	Nuclear reactor, atomic clock, atomic energy
1967	Montreal	51.0	Lasers, split-screen film technology
1970	Osaka	64.2	

Figure 7.1 Selected world's fairs and expos and new technologies, 1851–1970.

Source: adapted from Roche (2000: 43, 46, 160).

154

specialised. They usually last between three and six months. Unlike the Olympic Games, however, they do not follow a regular four-year cycle. The Olympic Games have been associated with breakthroughs in new technology, but this is more tangential to their main purpose. New developments in design and the use of materials for constructing venues and facilities have been a feature of the Olympic Games since at least the Tokyo Summer Games in 1964. Arguably, as we have suggested elsewhere in this book, in recent years the Olympics have also served as a test-bed for new technologies in the media and in terms of security and surveillance.

As we noted in Chapter 3, John Hoberman (1995: 6 ff.) argues that the IOC formed in 1894 bears comparison with other idealist international organisations developed at the end of the nineteenth century and beginning of the twentieth century, such as the Red Cross (1863), Esperanto (1887) and the Scouting Movement (1908). He argues that such groups 'belong to a genre of international organizations' based on anxieties about war and peace, and comprising bourgeois and socialist factions (Hoberman 1995: 11). All four organisations were ideologically distinct from Marxist internationalism and the First International founded in 1864. They share elements in common with cultural movements such as Wagnerism (developing from 1872) and the Salzburg music festival that began in 1920. Hoberman (1995: 15–17) suggests that a comparison between Coubertin and Baden-Powell (founder of the Scouts) and the approach of the IOC to nobility reveals the autocratic politics of the founder of the modern Olympics. As we have seen, the IOC was not founded as an 'association' of democratically elected members, but as a 'club' derived from the model of the Henley Royal Regatta, in England.

In contrast with this view of the growth of the Olympics, tied very much into the development of international political systems and capitalist modernity, anthropologist John MacAloon (1984, 2006a) argues that the event or international exposition genre – of which world's fairs and the Olympics were a part – derived from a cultural movement that shared affinities with the spirit of modern sport. The 'MacAloon thesis', as Roche (2000: 91–94) calls it, is expounded in several other places (MacAloon 1981, 1996, 1999) and discussed more fully in Chapter 10. He essentially sees the Olympic Games as a 'modern secular ritual' (MacAloon 1999) and (referring to the Barcelona Games in 1992) a highly complex operation (MacAloon 1996: 75–76). For MacAloon, spectacle as a distinct genre is 'neither good nor bad, neither liberating nor alienating' (1996: 272). Hence there is a need to evaluate 'particular spectacles' because spectacle is a new genre of cultural performance which offers the chance to gain control over the difference between image and reality (as discussed by Boorstin (1961) and Debord (1967/1970), among others). He argues that 'the Olympic Games create a sort of *hyper-structure* in which categories and stereotypes are condensed, exaggerated and dramatized, rescued from the "taken for granted" and made objects of explicit and lively awareness for a brief period every four years' (1996: 274–275). He concludes that the Games have become a 'sort of collective divination about the fate and condition of the world . . . a nervous dramatization of our hopes that the ensuing divination will be reassuring and that the Games will go on forever' (1996: 280 n. 71). In the next section we comment briefly on the 1896, 1900 and 1904 Olympic Games in the light of this discussion. In particular, we identify the lack of prominence of the Olympics and sport in general among the public at this time.

THE EARLY MODERN OLYMPIC GAMES: 1896–1904

MacAloon (1981: 198–203, 244–247) notes how the first modern Olympic Games held in 1896 in Athens can best be described as haphazard and unremarkable. They were poorly advertised, attracted few athletes and gained little coverage in the European press. Representatives of 13 nations attended the inaugural Olympic Congress in 1894 and another 21 sent their written support, but only 12 nations were represented in Athens (the US, UK, Germany, Australia, France, Denmark, Greece, Sweden, Switzerland, Bulgaria, Hungary and Chile). There were nine sports: cycling, fencing, gymnastics, lawn tennis, shooting, swimming, athletics, weightlifting and wrestling. The athletes were almost entirely European, but Coubertin was keen to get the Olympic show on the road.

In 1900 in Paris the Olympic Games were overshadowed by the world's fair. Originally the Games were advertised as the 'Competition of the Exhibition', as a sideshow. It is impossible to find traces of the main stadium because there was no main stadium – the track and field events appear to have been held mostly in fields in the Bois de Boulogne, and the swimming in the Seine. Young (2004: 154) says that athletes did compete sporadically on the outskirts of Paris, but 'there were no crowds of spectators and apparently most athletes did not even know they were in the Olympics. It was a total failure.' Coubertin called the 1900 Olympics a 'humiliated vassal' to the world's fair (Keys 2006: 207 n. 22). Nonetheless the Paris 1900 poster features a woman holding fencing épées and a helmet, and French Olympic historians Charpentier and Boissonnade (1999: 54) write 'this intrusion of women in the sporting domain, till now reserved for men, provoked arguments involving some talented writers'. French intellectuals such as Emile Zola, Sully Prudhomme and Léon Bloy were disdainful of sport, Bloy commenting that sport was the best way to produce 'a generation of cripples and dangerous cretins'.

If Paris was a humiliation for Coubertin in his own backyard, although somewhat understandable in the context of the French disdain for team games at the beginning of the twentieth century, he must have been very demoralised by the 1904 edition of the Olympics, held in St. Louis. In fact, he did not attend, stating that it was 'completely lacking in attraction' (cited in Keys 2006: 207 n. 22). Originally awarded to Chicago in 1901, the Third Olympics was staged as part of the 1904 World's Fair in St. Louis, which is also known as the Louisiana Purchase Exhibition. It was scheduled to commemorate the acquisition by the US of 828,800 square miles of France's claim to the territory of Louisiana in 1803, but was delayed by a year. The Louisiana Purchase doubled the size of the US at the time and comprises 23 per cent of the US landmass today. The St. Louis World's Fair therefore staged the third modern Olympic Games, although very much as a sideshow. In addition, various 'Anthropology Days' were scheduled as part of the Olympic Games – with the scientific goal of measuring the performances of 'savages' against 'civilised' men. As John Bale puts it:

> members of ethnic groups from the 'living displays' on the grounds of the Louisiana Purchase Exposition . . . were presented to the public as athletes and put through tests (i.e., modern sports events) designed for the trained athletes of Europe and North America.
>
> (Bale 2008: 325)

156

Needless to say, the performances of the 'natives' were rated as inferior.

In a collection of essays, Susan Brownell (2008) and contributors – including Gems (2008) and Knott (2008) – consider these events and the ideas of 'race', imperialism and the West that underpinned them, and their continuing ramifications over 100 years later. Brownell poses the questions: 'Why do Olympic Games now attract much greater global attention than world's fairs, when a century ago they were only a minor side event? and what does this tell us about the world in which we now live?' (2008: 1). We have explored some answers to these questions in connection with the globally mediated nature of the Olympic Games in Chapter 4. As Brownell and her contributors underline, the disciplinary impact on anthropology of the associated International Congress of Art and Science held in conjunction with the world's fair was highly significant as evolutionary racial models started to give way to the cultural relativist paradigm (associated with Franz Boas). Held in 1904, the Scientific Congress was actually more international than the Olympic Games, with 96 foreign participants – including sociologists Max Weber and Ferdinand Tonnies, Henri Poincaré and many others – and it also helped to consolidate physical education as a discipline.

As Brownell (2008: 29) notes, the association of the Olympic Games with world's fairs made sense at the time. It continued the association of sports with market fairs and linked the demonstration of (physical) progress to that of technological development. Modern sport was clearly a subservient cultural form. Nonetheless, official sports events during the 1904 World's Fair actually took place between 14 May and 19 November, and 9,000 athletes competed in 400 events. The Olympic Games, however, only lasted from 29 August to 3 September, with 80 competitions and 687 entrants who were mostly American – and all were men, apart from six women in the archery competition. There were only eight nations involved, four of them European, and some confusion about the true nationality of the athletes remains to this day. Typically, crowds were no more than 4,000–5,000. As Knott states (2008: 297 n. 5), 'In 1904 the Olympics did not yet represent the pinnacle of sporting events: to many, they were still considered an oddity.' The chaos of the Olympics in St. Louis can be illustrated with reference to the experiences of the 'German' delegation which German Olympic historian Karl Lennartz (1983) has noted. First, although it was hoped to send more, 20 athletes travelled, but only 17 participated – '10 Turnern, 2 Leichathleten, 7 Schwimmern, und einem Fechter' ('10 gymnasts, 2 track and field athletes, 7 swimmers and one fencer') (Lennartz 1983: 131). Second, the absence of any accommodation specifically for athletes attending the St. Louis Olympic Games meant that the wealthy brewer Adolphus Busch of the Anheuser-Busch company provided German gymnasts housing. Third, not all of the athletes in the German delegation were German. Adolf Spinnler, from Switzerland, competed for the Germans because he was a member of the Esslinger Turnverein (gymnastic club) near Stuttgart in Germany. Another athlete, Otto Wahle, a member of the Austria Wien Club in Vienna, emigrated to the US in 1900 and retained his Austrian citizenship, but also competed as part of the German delegation in 1904 (Knott 2008: 281–282). Yet another athlete, Julius Lenhart, who won a gold medal, this time representing the US, was also Austrian. Olympic historians from his country have since tried to claim Lenhart as an Austrian Olympic champion (Lennartz 1983: 116). As Knott (2008: 281–282) suggests, this imprecision about nationality and representativeness at the Olympics illustrates well the shift in meaning that sport and the Olympics have undergone since 1904.

157

St. Louis was marked by another distinctive attraction. World's fairs had begun to display peoples of the world from 1889 as a central feature of ethnological displays. At the 1904 World's Fair and Olympic Games, 3,000 'native peoples' were on display. While the Anthropology Days section can be perceived as an odd, naive and racist practice today, in this way sport has played an important role in the encounters of the West with its Others. International expos had operated according to various cultural themes since the 1870s – peace, brotherly love and understanding among nations. Before the Olympics, games events had been developed to promote national unity; Pierre de Coubertin sought to promote peace through internationalism. As Brownell states, his was 'the idea of combining in the medium of sport the lofty aspirations and educational goals of the world's fairs with popular ethnography and the neoclassical revival' (2008: 50). From the first London Olympics of 1908 onward, when the Parade of Athletes was established as a part of the opening ceremony, nation-states were recognised as the only legitimate global units in the Olympic Games. It was on the basis of cultural rather than 'racial' differences that Otherness would be represented. 'World's Fairs . . . are still important global events, but are not the important purveyors of novel intercultural experiences that they once were' (Brownell 2008: 51). They have been eclipsed by the Olympic Games, which allow 'records', seemingly objective quantifications of national difference, to be kept. As Charpentier and Boissonnade note:

> At St Louis, where the aftermath of the Civil War is still visible, although equality between blacks and whites is proclaimed, racial discrimination still persists. The Organisers mounted shameful 'Anthropological Days', special competitions reserved for those who the Americans considered to be sub-human.
>
> (Charpentier and Boissonnade 1999: 64).

BOX 7.1 THE 1904 ANTHROPOLOGY DAYS

St. Louis was an opportunity for the Anglo-American to claim superiority over the 'primitive' nature of others. These included Ainus from Japan, Yehuelche Indians from Patagonia, pygmies from Central Africa, a variety of ethnic groups originating in the Philippines and many others representing tribes of indigenous Americans. To publicise these days, anthropologists persuaded the legendary Apache chief Geronimo to put in an appearance (Charpentier and Boissonnade 1999: 64). These 'natives' competed in standard running events and also in novelty events like mud wrestling and climbing the greasy pole. Len Tau and Jan Mashiani, two black students at Orange Free State University, were South Africa's first Olympians. However, they were billed as 'Zulu savages' and were participants only in the Anthropology Days segment of the competition. (www.historyhouse.com/in_history/olympics; accessed 19 October 2010). The World's Fair village from which participants were taken was organised with what popular prejudice regarded as the most advanced tribes at the centre, where there stood a 'model Indian school'. In this human zoo, the so-called least civilised peoples were exhibited at the fringes. W.J. McGee, head of the Anthropology Department at the World's Fair, stated: 'the aim of the Department of Anthropology at the World's Fair will be to represent human progress from the dark prime to the human enlightenment, from savagery to civic organization, from egoism to altruism' (quoted in Gems 2008: 200). The crown jewel was a 47-acre site organised by the US government to display the conquered peoples of the Philippines, the newest American possession acquired during the recently concluded Spanish–American War. A homage to imperialism, the exhibit was designed to show how America would bring progress to savage peoples. The participants in the Anthropology Days events included Crow, Sioux, Pawnee, Navajo and Chippewa people from the United States; Ainu from Japan; Cocopa from Baja California in Mexico; two 'Syrians from Beyrout', Patagonians from South America, Zulus and pygmies from Africa and, from the Philippines, Moros, Negritos and Igorots. Teobang, another African, was described simply as a cannibal.

(Source: www.antropologi.info/anthropology/copy/
anthropological_days.html; last accessed 22 October 2015)

Matthews (2005) offers an attempt to defend the Games as more successful than other accounts recall, blaming Coubertin's own 1933 memoir for elevating the Anthropological Days to greater significance than they warrant. Matthews himself, in contrast to other historians, seems curiously reluctant to acknowledge the Anthropological Days, not mentioning them until late in his book and then only in the context of criticising Coubertin for offering a misleading account of the events. Matthews claims the 1904 Games were seen as a success at the time and blames Coubertin's memoirs for changing the climate of assessment. He says Coubertin also misrepresented developments in claiming it was Roosevelt who decided that the Games should be moved to St. Louis from Chicago, and not the IOC or Coubertin. Matthews charges that Bill Henry's *An Approved History of the Olympic Games*, published in 1948, drawing on Coubertin, was even more condemnatory. Matthews accuses Henry of fabrication, but frustratingly does not cite clear sources supporting his alternative versions of events (Matthews 2005: 209–210). In contrast, Young's curt summary (2004: 154) is that the 'games were not truly international; almost all the athletes were North American. Attendance was poor, organization abysmal, and sometimes even perverse.'

Analytically, the focus of the 2008 Brownell collection is on the 'framing' of behaviour that leads to a plurality of interpretations of experiences. Frames of spectacle, festival, ritual and game are the main interpretative frameworks for understanding the 'performance system' of the Olympic Games (using MacAloon's development of Erving Goffman's 'frame' concept; Goffman 1974; MacAloon 1981, 1984). The general 'MacAloon thesis', that the exposition genre of mega-event was crucial to the genesis of the Olympic movement, and thus that a cultural movement had a shared affinity with the spirit of modern sport, is generally sustained rather than subjected to a critique by most of the contributors. A few, including Brownell, indicate they have some differences with MacAloon's thesis, but all are interested in the Olympic Games and world's fairs as performances in process.

The relative insignificance of the early Olympic Games was a reflection of the marginal status of sport in much of Europe, where according to Keys (2006: 48) it was still often regarded 'with suspicion as the "English disease"'. Additionally at this time, as Brownell notes, 'With the exception of the special situation in Greece, the Olympic Games were simply not strong enough to stand on their own financially' (2008: 30). This continued even after the 1914–1918 war, and the organisers of the 1920 Olympics in Antwerp were declared bankrupt and unable to complete an official report (see Box 7.2 and Figure 7.2).

BOX 7.2 THE VIITH OLYMPIC GAMES (ANTWERP 1920):
A FORGOTTEN OLYMPICS?

Given final approval to stage them just over a year before they were due to start, and in the immediate aftermath of the Great War (1914–1918), the local Antwerp Olympic Organising Committee went bankrupt during the 1920 Games and so no official report of the Games was ever produced. The documents of the Games were archived at the Belgium Olympic Committee (BOC) headquarters in Brussels, however, and a report written in French was produced in 1957 by the BOC from the original data (available online at: library.la84.org/6oic/OfficialReports/1920/1920. pdf). A more detailed account, with photographs, of the Antwerp Games (which included some winter sports including ice skating in April 1920) can be found in the *Official Report of the United States Team at the Antwerp 1920 Games*, published in 1921 by the American Olympic Committee (available at http://babel.hathitrust.org/ cgi/pt?id=coo.31924029945650;view=1up;seq=41; last accessed 10 October 2015).

For the first time an Olympic oath was taken, doves were released to symbolise peace and the Olympic flag was flown at the formal start of the Games in August 1920. The Antwerp Games are not forgotten in certain parts of the world either. It was in Antwerp that Brazil won its first gold medal (at shooting), ice hockey made its Olympic debut and the final events in the sailing competition were held in the Netherlands as the two final contenders were from there.

The Olympisch Stadion, nicknamed "t Kiel', or Kielstadion, where the opening ceremony took place, was located in the south of the city of Antwerp in what is now the district of Wilrijk, about 4 km from the city centre. Specially built for the 1920 Summer Olympics, construction started in July 1919, and was completed in less than one year, as the stadium was officially opened in May 1920. The stadium had a capacity of 30,000 spectators, 20,000 of them standing. It was bowl-shaped, and had an athletics track that circled the pitch. Over the years, capacity gradually reduced to about 25,000, and parts of the stadium were demolished. In 2000 a redevelopment programme resulted in an even smaller, all-seater, stadium – holding around 12,700 – with four separate stands, no running track and with little resemblance to the original Olympic Stadium. The teams playing football in the stadium have undergone a number of transformations, mergers and name changes, but have never reached the highest levels of professional football in Belgium. In the 2015–2016 season it was the home of third division Football Club Olympia (FCO) Beerschot Wilrijk. Hence although an 'O' remains in the abbreviated title it is not immediately evident that Beerschot play in the Olympic Stadium.

160

Although one of the tram stops en route to the stadium from Antwerp city centre is called 'Olympiade', the closest stop is further out at the small community of Schijfwerper. There is no sign or plaque commemorating the Olympics anywhere in the approach to the stadium, although the name over the main gate is 'Olympisch Stadion – Kiel'. The only other visible sign of the Olympic heritage of the site today are copies of a small black-and-white photograph of the stadium staging the Olympics in 1920 that feature at the 'Friends of the Olympic Stadium' entrance to one of the stands. Simon Inglis (2006: 190) suggests that Archibald Leitch, the Scottish engineer and factory architect responsible for the design of stadiums for the most famous football clubs in England and Scotland in the nineteenth and early twentieth centuries, may have been involved in the design of the original Kielstadion, having made several visits to Antwerp prior to the Games.

(Sources: www.stadiumguide.com/kiel; last accessed 10 October 2015; JH interview with ground staff at Kielstadion in October 2015)

As we have shown, for the first three editions of the twentieth century (1900, 1904 and 1908) the Olympic Games were a sideshow to world's fairs and international expositions.

Figure 7.2 Kiel stadion – the Olympic Stadium – Antwerp, in 2015.

However, in 1908 in London the Games began to be taken more seriously in their own right. In the next section we turn to London and the 1908 Olympics where, although held in conjunction with an exhibition, the Games were not upstaged by it (Keys 2006: 207 n. 22). The next section offers a more detailed account of the First and Second London Olympic Games that seeks to illustrate the relationships and agencies involved in their construction.

LONDON, EXHIBITIONS AND THE OLYMPIC GAMES

We want to commence this section by highlighting two themes in Roche (2000). First, he is concerned with the ways in which expos reflect the development of capitalism, nationalism and imperialism. Second, he regards them as important focal points in the emergence of an international dimension in modern public culture. Clearly there is a potential contradiction here, indeed a contradiction manifest in the person of Baron Pierre de Coubertin, whose life project was the establishment of the modern Olympic Games. As we discuss in more detail in the next chapter, Coubertin was a committed internationalist who inscribed internationalism into the founding documents, practices and rituals of the Olympic Games. But he was also a patriot who was concerned about the poor physical state and discipline of French youth, and worried about the decline of his country and its eclipse by the rising power of Germany. The tension between nationalism and internationalism continues to be a significant feature of the Olympic Games.

Whatever Coubertin was, he was no economist, and the lack of a clear financial strategy for supporting the nascent Olympic Games, as we have seen, forced Coubertin to attach the Games of 1900 and 1904 to the world's fairs in, respectively, Paris and St. Louis. Such events tended to draw on a combination of public and private organisation and finance, had to balance short-term intentions with the question of legacy, and have been caught between idealism and pragmatism. Mega-events are rarely simply the realisation of a clear blueprint from a commanding designer; rather they are the outcome of competing intentions, interests, preoccupations and strategies. Where mega-events are concerned, a study of the relationships between national politicians, local politicians, sports administrators, builders, architects and urban planners is often instructive.

We focus in this section therefore on aspects of the three London Olympic Games of 1908, 1948 and 2012, but we have also included the 1924/1925 British Empire Exhibition, the stadium of which at Wembley in north-west London was subsequently used for the 1948 Olympic Games. One of the most striking features of mega-events is how rarely they utilise the sites of previous events, almost as if they wanted to avoid taking on the ideological detritus of a former conjuncture. In 1908 the London Olympics had close links – and shared a site (the 'White City') – with the Franco-British Exhibition near Shepherd's Bush. The 1924/1925 British Empire Exhibition shunned the option of the White City site from 1908, and established itself at Wembley Park. In 1934 the Empire Games used the newly constructed Empire Pool at Wembley, yet used White City for the athletics. In 1948 the hastily arranged and financially pressed London Olympic Games did utilise the Wembley site originally constructed for the Empire Exhibition of 1924/1925, but just three years later, in 1951, the Festival of Britain rejected both Wembley and White City and based its major attractions in Battersea Park and on the South Bank in Central London.

The Millennium Dome, rejecting all other available options, was built to celebrate the year 2000 on a derelict industrial site in North Greenwich. In many cases the sites subsequently suffered years of decline, neglect and decay. The White City stadium was demolished in 1985 and there is no easily visible memorial proclaiming its moment of glory as the 'Great Stadium' of the 1908 Olympics.

Wembley stadium has been demolished but reborn in rebuilt form, and the Empire Pool survives, renamed the 'Wembley Arena' and recently renovated. The rest of the site has been crumbling for years, and is only now undergoing substantial redevelopment. Very few traces of the Festival of Britain remain, aside from the Festival Hall. But after the 2012 Olympic Games, a vast privately owned shopping mall at Stratford in East London will become the beneficiary of the massive public investment in infrastructure that has seen the creation of the Queen Elizabeth Olympic Park.[3] This section therefore explores the significance that we can read into these events, crossing as they do concepts of nation and internationalism; past and future, heritage and tradition, public and private, production and consumption, festival and spectacle.

The Franco-British Exhibition of 1908

The Franco-British Exhibition had its roots in late nineteenth-century diplomacy. The decline of France after Napoleon, the end of the period of Franco-British wars, the French defeat by the Prussians in 1870, the formation of Germany in 1871, and the growing power and ambition of Germany meant that France had to forge alliances with Britain. The Entente Cordiale was signed in 1904, and the Franco-British Exhibition in 1908 was planned to celebrate it. It attracted eight million visitors, and only included goods and produce of Britain, France and their respective colonies. The British Empire at this point still commanded one-quarter of the world's land, and one-quarter of the world's population. The British Navy was twice the size of the next largest (Mallon and Buchanan 2000). Founded on the imperatives of trade and diplomacy, the Franco-British Exhibition was structured around an imperial ideology of civilisation, brought to savage peoples, for their betterment. Like previous such events, it combined displays of technological mastery, educative rational recreation and popular amusement.

London only acquired the Olympic Games of 1908 after Rome pulled out. The 1904 IOC Session in London awarded the Games of 1908 to Rome. In 1906 Rome withdrew (Llewellyn 2012: 45–46). This was attributed to the impact of the Vesuvius eruption, but in fact the Italian prime minister was opposed to the project and prevented funding, which he wanted to spend on other projects like the Simplon tunnel (Mallon and Buchanan 2000). It was clear that no government funding would be available for building a main stadium, but the Franco-British Exhibition organisers agreed to build the stadium complete with running and cycling tracks and a swimming pool, in return for 75 per cent of the gate receipts. The stadium was projected to cost £44,000, but some estimates suggest it may have been a lot higher (e.g. Zarnowski 1992). The Exhibition organisers also agreed to give £2,000 to the BOA, but this was later increased to £20,000 (Mallon and Buchanan 2000: 4). It appears that the Exhibition organisers were prepared to accept a loss on the stadium in return for the benefits of bringing extra visitors to the Exhibition, and of course they retained the use of the stadium after the Games. The BOA made £6,000 and the

Franco-British Exhibition £18,000 from gate receipts (Mallon and Buchanan 2000: 5). Although the Exhibition was prompted by diplomacy, its key organising figure was a showman and promoter, Imre Kiralfy.

BOX 7.3 IMRE KIRALFY

Hungarian and Jewish, Imre Kiralfy was born in 1845, and soon showed a precocious talent for music, art and especially dance. He toured Europe, performing with his siblings, and saw the 1867 International Exhibition. In the US the Kiralfy brothers became producers of spectacles such as Jules Verne's 'Around the World in 80 Days'. Kiralfy also worked with and no doubt learned from Barnum and Bailey. Returning to London, he rebuilt the Earl's Court exhibition grounds as a small-scale version of Chicago's White City in 1893, complete with Ferris wheel, amusement park and exhibition halls in an Indian style. At night the grounds were electrically illuminated. As a member of the British Empire League and a senior Freemason, Kiralfy was undoubtedly well connected.

The first initiative towards the Exhibition came from the French Chamber of Commerce and the Lord Mayor of London, the objective being for France and England to display their industrial achievements. Kiralfy was commissioned to create it. Initial costs were covered through donations, and any profits were intended to go to 'some public purpose' (Knight 1978: 1). The 140-acre site was eight times larger than the Great Exhibition of 1851. In the event 123,000 people visited on the opening day and the caterers, J. Lyons & Co., planned for 100,000 per day (Knight 1978: 4).

Before work started, a company called the International and Colonial Commercial Co. Ltd was established. Subsequently eight directors resigned, and this appeared to leave the Kiralfy brothers in effective control. The name of the company was changed to Shepherd's Bush Exhibitions Ltd, and I. and C. Kiralfy and associates took up over 16,000 shares. A public company, the 'Great White City Ltd' was established and acquired significant shares in Shepherd's Bush Exhibitions Ltd (Knight 1978: 5).

The site benefited from investment in transport infrastructure. The Central London Railway was extended from Shepherd's Bush to Wood Lane Station in 1908 to serve the Franco-British Exhibition. There was also a separate station on the Metropolitan Line, also called Wood Lane. Following the success of the Exhibition, the temporary station became a permanent fixture, with passenger demand buoyed by the creation of a number of new entertainment venues in the area, notably the White City Stadium.

The site featured elaborate white-walled palaces and waterways. The central court had a lake and illuminated fountains. There were 20 palaces and 120 exhibition halls.[4] Orientalism was a dominant stylistic motif. Rickshaw drivers were brought to London from Asia to work on the site.[5] There was a distinct contrast between the elements of rational recreation and hedonism. At one pole was the London County Council exhibit of municipal works and at the other the showmanship of Kiralfy. The latter is illustrated by the general attractions on the site, which by the time of the Japan–British Exhibition

164

	Passengers	Revenue (£)
The Lake in the Court of Honour	1,108,700	27,000
The Flip Flap	1,110,800	27,000
The Mountain Scenic railway	2,800,000	70,000
The Spiral	653,600	16,340
Canadian toboggan	807,000	20,175
Old London	500,000	12,500
Mountain Slide	250,000	6,250
The Johnstown Flood	715,000	17,875
The Stereomatos	425,000	17,875

Figure 7.3 Selected attendances at the 1908 Franco-British Exhibition.

Source: Knight (1978: 38–42).

held two years later included: Brennan's Monorail, the Flip Flap, the Great Mountain Railway, the Wiggle Woggle (a form of slide), Witching Waves, the Motor Racing Track, the Submarine, Webb's Glassworks, Whirling Waters, the Canadian Toboggan, the Spiral Railway and the Hall of Laughter.[6] In 1908 the stadium contained running and cycling tracks, an open-air swimming pool and a pitch for football, hockey, rugby and lacrosse, and held 93,000 spectators.[7] It is clear that, despite the large investment in the site, it must have been lucrative. The attractions alone generated much revenue, as Figure 7.3 illustrates. Combined, these attractions brought in around £200,000 – close to £20 million in 2015 terms.[8]

The site continued to be a viable exhibition venue for some years. In 1909, the Imperial International exhibited the imperial achievements of the Triple Entente powers: France, Russia and Britain. In 1910 the Japan–British Exhibition emphasised the suitability of Japan as a worthy ally of Britain. The 1911 Coronation Exhibition, the 1912 Latin–British Exhibition and the 1914 Anglo-American Exhibition followed these. During the First World War, the army used the site. From 1921 to 1929, it became the venue for the British Industries Fair.[9] In 1927 the Greyhound Racing Association leased the stadium for greyhound racing. The Amateur Athletic Association (AAA) Championships were first held there in 1932. The BBC bought part of the site in 1949 and built the Television Centre, which opened in 1960. Athletics moved to Crystal Place in 1971, the last greyhound racing took place in 1984 and the Great Stadium was demolished a year later (Mallon and Buchanan 2000: 6).

As for the owners, one resigned as director of Shepherd's Bush Exhibitions Ltd in 1918, while Imre Kiralfy died in 1919. Bits of the site were sold off during the 1920s and 1930s (to the BBC, and to Hammersmith Council for the White City housing estate). The stadium was leased to the Greyhound Racing Association. Shepherd's Bush Exhibitions Ltd began its voluntary wind-up in 1950, but was not dissolved until the 1960s, its assets of £550,000 being used to pay surtax, solicitors' fees and liquidators' fees, with the remainder being divided among shareholders (Knight 1978: 6). It is not clear what happened to the 'public purpose' referred to by the organisers. The stadium disappeared with no trace and no proper commemoration of its historic role. The White City was not simply demolished, but virtually obliterated from history. With the exception of a plaque hidden away inside the courtyard of the BBC building occupying the site, there is no proper memorial to the 'Great Stadium' or to the 1908 Olympic Games.[10]

Exhibitions and Empire Games: 1924/1925 and 1934

The idea of a great exhibition to celebrate Empire trade had been discussed in 1913, when it was planned to stage it at White City. By the 1920s the British economy, damaged by the impact of the First World War, was already beginning to feel the impact of the rise to dominance of the US. The idea of a British Empire Exhibition was revived, and Lloyd George and the Prince of Wales actively supported the project (Roche 2000: 61). The government committed half the £2.2 million needed, the rest coming from pubic subscriptions. The government acted as co-guarantor of the expo and it intervened to have its appointees on the organising committee. Parliament supported the project in 1920 on the grounds that the expo would 'benefit trade, provide employment and be a token of goodwill towards the dominions' (Roche, quoting Stallard 1996: 7). In 1922, the government provided the funding for it to go ahead. The White City site was still intact but was rejected as a suitable location, in favour of Wembley Park in north-west London.

BOX 7.4 WEMBLEY PARK

The Wembley site itself has an interesting history. Wembley Park had belonged to the Page family since the sixteenth century. In the 1870s the estate was landscaped and at the end of the nineteenth century it was purchased by the Metropolitan Railway to create a pleasure grounds. The Park opened in 1894 and it was only 12 minutes from Baker Street, thanks to the Metropolitan Railway station at Wembley Park (Brent Heritage 2002). In 1895 Metropolitan's Chairman, Sir Edward Watkin, seeing the need to attract people to the railway, decided to construct a major tourist attraction close to the station. During a visit to Paris in 1889, Watkin had seen the newly constructed Eiffel Tower, and set up the Metropolitan Tower Construction Company. The tower was going to be 1,200 feet high (compared to the 849 feet of the Eiffel Tower), but building difficulties, marshy ground and financial problems curtailed full completion. The first stage of the tower was eventually opened to members of the public in 1896, by which time pleasure gardens had been created around it. In 1899 the Tower Construction Company went into liquidation, and in 1904 'Watkin's Folly' was demolished.

(Source: www.ianvisits.co.uk/blog/2007/10/24/the-tale-of-londons-attempt-to-build-an-eiffel-tower; last accessed 7 September 2015)

Construction of the site began in January 1922, with Wembley Stadium finished in time for the 1923 FA Cup Final. When it took office in 1924, the Labour Party actively supported the expo project (Roche 2000: 61). The project was framed by imperialism throughout – made explicit on the first page of the *British Empire Exhibition Handbook*:

> I welcome the opportunity that will be afforded by the British Empire Exhibition to increase the knowledge of the varied resources of my empire and to stimulate inter-imperial trade.
>
> (HM the King, quoted in *The British Empire Exhibition: Handbook of General Information* 1924)

> we must unite to make the British Empire Exhibition a success worthy of our race.
>
> (HRH the Prince of Wales, quoted in *The British Empire Exhibition: Handbook of General Information* 1924)

Apparently, contractors made 'huge profits', while the government made a loss. The Board of Trade produced a report suggesting the government 'might minimise involvement in future world's fairs and suggesting some form of international regulation minimising the frequency with which fairs could occur' (Stallard 1996: 10).

At the exhibition's heart were 16 buildings representing the Empire countries. These ranged in size from the Australian 'palace' to the smaller West Indies/British Guiana pavilion, which sold cocktails and displayed exhibits on sugar. The West African building was a miniature reproduction of the walled city of Zaria in Nigeria; Ceylon's was modelled on the Temple of the Tooth in Kandy; Burma reproduced in Burmese teak one of the gates of a famous pagoda at Mandalay. A street of Chinese shops represented Hong Kong, and East Africa was represented by a white-walled Arab building. Inside, the countries themselves had organised displays of their goods and products. The Australian pavilion sold seven million apples. The Canadian pavilion promoted butter with a life-size sculpture of Edward, the Prince of Wales, in the setting of his cattle ranch at Pekisko, Alberta. The 1924 tableau included the prince, a horse and several outbuildings set against the distant foothills of the Rocky Mountains, all carved entirely out of Canadian butter – 3,000 pounds of it (Clendinning 2006). The butter tableau was an advertisement for Canada's dairy industry, the Department of Agriculture and the wonders of modern refrigeration, since the entire scene was preserved behind glass and kept at a cold storage temperature a few degrees below freezing. The following year, and possibly to reuse the enormous cold storage display case, a refrigerated butter sculpture of the Prince of Wales in the costume of a First Nations chief (Chief Morning Star) alongside several Native women, a tepee, a dog and a small child, was produced. According to the British newspapers, Edward in 'full feathers as an Indian chief' was one of the new wonders of Wembley (Clendinning 2006). As well as several train stations, the exhibition benefited from what it claimed was 'the world's first bus station'. Car transport was only just beginning to impact. No new roads were constructed specifically for the Exhibition, but the origins of London's North Circular Road (the A406) are contemporary with it.

The 1908 Franco-British Exhibition – extravagant, a visual feast, exotic – had shown the flair of a promoter who had worked with Barnum. The 1924 British Empire Exhibition, by contrast, seemed more official, pompous, worthy – and dull. Ulick Wintour, an ex-civil servant who had worked at the Ministry of Food and the Stationery Office was picked as a man who could get things done – he introduced his engineer friend Owen Williams to Maxwell Ayrton, who was to be the architect of the Exhibition's main buildings – but he did not seem to have the P.T. Barnum spirit.[11]

The rational educative impulse of the Exhibition was clear. The official guide said of the potential visitor, 'In a single day he [sic] will learn more geography than a year of hard study would teach him' (quoted in Roche 2000: 63). And not just geography – the General Post Office exhibited a working model of an automatic telephone exchange, and the Ministry of Health had a model of sewage disposal. But, as Maurice Roche argues, whatever messages about empire were intended would have been filtered through the strong entertainment, fairground and leisure character of the expo (Roche 2000: 63). There is an apologetic note sounded for 'amusement' in the handbook:

> No matter how attractive or interesting an exhibition may be, a certain degree of fatigue is always involved. In order to obviate this, Wembley will be equipped with what will certainly be the finest Amusements Park in the world.
>
> (*The British Empire Exhibition: Handbook of General Information* 1924: 35)

The site staged a daily 'Pageant of Empire' featuring 15,000 performers and hundreds of animals. There was an amusement park and fairground rides – dodgems, river caves, water chutes and a rollercoaster and a number of dance halls. Roche says that 'dancing and popular music were strongly associated with the experience of visiting the expo' (Roche 2000: 63).

After the Exhibition, the buildings were sold and many demolished. The stadium was saved. Before the Second World War some large engineering and luxury goods manufacturers took over the empty buildings of the Empire Exhibition. Unlike most previous expos, which used temporary architecture, many of the buildings at Wembley were built as permanent structures, with 'after use' in mind (Roche 2000: 63). Despite this, they didn't seem to get much significant after use. Just as the 1924/1925 Empire Exhibition had eschewed the earlier White City site, so the 1951 Festival of Britain did not utilise Wembley. Newness and novelty constantly win out over economy and legacy!

In 1934, the second Empire Games (since 1978 renamed the Commonwealth Games) came to London. The original idea for a multi-sport event linking countries of the British Empire had its origins in imperial power and racism. As noted in the previous chapter, John Astley Cooper began proposing a Pan-Britannic Festival in print in 1891. This idea was overtaken by the modern Olympic Games, first held in 1896, but it sowed the seeds of the idea that resurfaced as the Empire Games. As we have noted, Cooper asked if Britons were ready to undertake 'actions for the benefit of mankind which may make the name of England to be sung for all time as an example to races yet to come' (Moore 1987: 146).

It is clear, according to Moore, that Cooper's idea was intended to include 'only adult males from the so-called white Dominions – Australia, New Zealand, Canada and South Africa as well as those subjects eligible in Great Britain' (Moore 1987: 148). The Empire Games were first staged in 1930 in Hamilton, Ontario, at a moment when the relationship between the UK and the old 'white' empire countries was being reshaped.

The Empire Pool (now known as Wembley Arena) was built for the Empire Games of 1934. The building was built by private enterprise as a commercial project and is still owned by a private company. It is a unique building, not only for its structural form, with long cantilevers meeting in the middle as a three-pinned arch, but also because it was designed entirely by an engineer, with no involvement by an architect. This fact is clearly demonstrated in the style.[12] It was built on part of the site of the lakes which had been laid out for the British Empire Exhibition ten years earlier. The design did not attempt to blend with the adjacent Palaces of Art and of Industry that had survived from the Empire Exhibition. It was designed as an adaptable, all-purpose performance space. The swimming pool was closed at the outbreak of war (1939) and was subsequently only used as a pool for the Olympic Games (1948). The Wembley Arena building was listed Grade II in 1976.

Two years after the Empire Games of 1934, one of London's earliest exhibition buildings – the Crystal Palace – burned down. The building, built for the Great Exhibition of 1851, had been moved in 1854 from Hyde Park to Sydenham Hill, forming the dominant feature of what became known as Crystal Palace Park. The site has remained largely derelict ever since, with only the brick arches of the lower level still visible. [13]

The 1948 Olympics

If 1908 was a time when the Empire was still just dominant, and 1924 a time when it was under threat, the 1948 Olympic Games were staged by a country whose Empire was being dismantled. The US was now becoming a global hegemonic force. The old Empire Exhibition site at Wembley had already fallen into decline, and must have served as a poignant visual metaphor for Britain's economy, seriously weakened by the impact of the war. Post-war reconstruction was only just beginning to make an impact. The relaunch of television after the war, however, enabled the 1948 Games to be the first ones to be broadcast live by television.

As was the case with the 1908 Games, the 1948 Games had to be organised very rapidly, in less than two years. But, unlike the 1908 Games, this had to be done in a context of a country still recovering from the impact of the war, with shortages, rationing and a severe fuel crisis in the run-up to the Games. There is a striking emphasis on economy in the Olympic report, the authors pointing out ways in which they attempted to control costs – no new facilities were built, for example. So the Games were not, unlike Games of more recent years, to produce any architectural symbols of modernity, although they did utilise the rather hefty-looking halls of the Empire Exhibition constructed in the era of Art Deco.

A concern with how to mark Britishness drew on the past, tradition and heritage in its use of Big Ben and Kipling. The arts competitions, added as official events at the 1912 Stockholm Olympics, by contrast, being restricted to works in architecture, sculpture, painting, literature and music and inspired by sport and produced during the Olympiad (a four-year period beginning 1 January of the year in which a Summer Olympics are due to occur; hence the XXX Olympiad began in January 2012 and ended in December 2015), were predominantly modernist in tone and style. The organising committee chose as a symbol the clock tower of the Houses of Parliament, with the hands of Big Ben pointing to 4:00 p.m., the hour at which the Games were declared open (Official Olympic Games Report 1948: 22).

Pragmatic concerns seem to have marked the organisation of the torch relay and the opening ceremony. There is a map of the route in the 'Illustrations from the XIVth

Olympiad Sport in Art Exhibition'. To keep the cost down, the route was almost as direct as could be – from Olympia across the sea to Italy, straight up the east coast and across the Alps, north through France, along the Rhine valley, and then by ferry to Dover. According to the Official Report, 'the Committee decided after careful consideration, that the torch relay, first held in 1936, had a great symbolic value to the Olympic Games and that, although considerable expense would be involved, it should be included in the plans for the Games' (Official Olympic Games Report 1948: 22).

Led by bastions of the establishment, the organising committee was clearly concerned to do things properly and not to tamper unduly with tradition – there was little innovation in the staging of the Games. There was, however, an excitement around the engagement with emergent technologies – particularly television, still only two years into its post-war relaunch. If post-war austerity made for a pragmatic approach, the Olympic movement itself would seem ill-equipped for both modernity and austerity. The IOC was then – and to a degree remains – dominated by European aristocracy. In 1948 only 41 countries were represented on the IOC, 24 of them European. The 66 members, all male, included three princes, five counts, two barons, a marquis, a duke, two his excellencies, two lords, two generals and a colonel. As for the London Organising Committee, the President of the Games was the Rt Hon. The Viscount Portal, DSO, MVG; and the chairman of the organising committee was the Rt Hon. The Lord Burghley, KCMG.

By the early 1980s, this aristocratic IOC body had become firmly wedded to commerciali-sation, but in 1948 the Official Report stated that because the IOC had to ensure that the Games were promoted 'not so much as a commercial venture but in the best interests of sport', many means of raising money were not permissible, such as the inclusion of advertisements in the brochures and programmes. In the balance sheet, receipts were £761,688 and expenditure was slightly less, leaving a small surplus (£29,420) which presumably went to the BOA. The IOC received £5,000. Wembley Stadium was paid £92,500, around 12 per cent of the total revenue of the Games, so also was one of the beneficiaries. In some ways this Olympic Games was on the cusp of the transformation from a pre-media event to a global spectacle. From today's perspective, the media-management strategy has a fascinating quaintness about it. The Press Department policy in the build-up to the Games was as follows:

> The Press Officer decided to tackle every individual critic and follower on his own ground and persuade him by specialist treatment, of the rightness of the course. Those with influence on the sports side of the newspapers were encouraged and those hoping to intrude with political opinions avoided or completely ignored.
> (Official Olympic Games Report 1948: 105)

The arts competitions, on which Coubertin was so keen, were staged for the last time in 1948 (Girginov and Parry 2005: 206). Since 1948 there have been art *exhibitions* linked to the Games, but not competitions.

As far as legacy was concerned, £1,000 was to be allocated for the establishment of a permanent record of winners at the main stadium (Official Olympic Games Report 1948: 29). There is a picture of two plaques on the external wall of the stadium – they seemed to be either side of the circular entrance gate between the two towers. Wembley subsequently established itself as the home of English international football, the twin towers were mythicised and the stadium was the venue for the 1966 World Cup Final. The Olympics appeared to retreat from view. The lack of any real commemoration at either the White City or Wembley Stadiums was striking up to 2012, and the London 2012 bid chose not to make a lot of the 1908 and 1948 Games.

The shopping mall: 2012

Considering the 2012 bid, and the possibilities of drawing on England's traditions and heritage, especially in terms of sport, the inspiration of Coubertin, Penny Brookes, Robert Dover and all of that, it is somewhat surprising that there is such an absence of memorial to 1908 and to 1948. As we have discussed already in Chapter 2, the organisational separation between a delivery authority (which organised venues and facilities) and the organising committee (which organised and marketed the Games), adopted by London in 2012, was also utilised by Sydney in 2000 (see Preuss 2004: 17). The great merit of this separation, as we have noted already, is that it removes infrastructural expenditure from the official budget. Although, combined, the official cost of London 2012 was over £11 billion, because of a distinction between 'Games-related' and 'non-Games-related' costs it is possible to suggest that the organising committee actually cover their costs from revenue and make a surplus, while the 'non-Games-related costs', in our terms the hidden subsidy, means the host city still picks up a large tab.[14]

As we have argued, the Australian property development company Westfield, the key developer of the Stratford site, is one of the main beneficiaries of the 2012 Olympic Games. Westfield have established around 124 shopping centres in Australia, New Zealand, the UK and the US, and with around £14.3 billion of assets, can lay claim to being the, or at least one of the, world's largest retail property groups. At the time the Stratford City development was one of the largest regeneration projects in Europe. It included homes and shops as well as accommodation for athletes competing in the 2012 Olympics. In the media narration of the major controversy surrounding the soaring cost of the 2012 Olympic Games, there was virtually no reference to the Stratford City development, although it is certainly one of the most tangible, long-lasting and profitable legacies of the Olympic Games.

ALTERNATIVE SPORTS EVENTS AND THE OLYMPIC GAMES

As Barbara Keys (2006: 49) writes, by the 1920s a division of labour had been established in international sport that has persisted more or less until today. The IOC – an undemocratic as well as Eurocentric 'club' dominated by rich European men – determined the programme, location and general philosophy governing the Olympic Games, while the National Olympic Committees (NOCs) oversaw participation and the International Federations (IFs) set the technical regulations and made final judgements on the eligibility of athletes to take part. Along with other international sports organisations – such as FIFA – the IOC helped to establish sport as an international and now global regime – a form of governance without government, based on the rules and norms not of localities but of sport. Sport developed increasingly popular festivals that provided a physical and temporal locus for the sporting 'imagined world' (Keys 2006: 184). Rites and symbols have been constructed which in turn provide a sense of sport as a global force. It is this that has given sport a feeling of autonomy from 'ordinary' life and social contexts. That this had been accomplished is one of the major contributions of the Olympic movement to world history.

Of course, as we have shown in this book, sport is not really so distinct from its social, political, economic and cultural contexts. The development of the Olympics as a major, if not the premier, sports mega-event was accomplished through accommodations and struggles. Before the Second World War, Olympic or 'bourgeois' sport had powerful rivals – in Europe, workers' sport and gymnastics; in the rest of the world, traditional games and contests, as Eichberg (1998), among others, has shown. Workers' Olympics, women's sports events and the professional Football World Cup all developed and waned in particular socio-historical conditions. Sport's central position in contemporary conceptions of 'physical culture' is a historically contingent outcome, not the product of some natural evolution. We look at this in more detail in the next chapter.

Before the Second World War, the Left critiqued sport on the grounds that it was 'bourgeois sport'. From this perspective, it was seen as a form of bread and circuses, devised to distract workers from their real interests. Workers' sport promoted instead collectivism, mass participation, gender equality and internationalism. Strongest in Germany, workers' sports organisations existed in most European countries. Tens of thousands of participants and hundreds of thousands of spectators were involved in the events in Vienna in 1931, for example (Riordan 1984). In addition to workers' events there were the Soviet Games and women's Olympics (Hoberman 1995: 7; Harvey *et al.* 2014: 27–41). Figure 7.4 outlines a few of the alternative events in existence between 1920 and 1938.

Year	Olympic Games	Worker's Olympics	Women's Olympics	Football World Cup	Empire Games	Soviet Games
1920	Antwerp					
1921		Prague				
1922			Paris			
1924	Paris					
1925		Frankfurt				
1926			Gothenburg			
1927		Prague				
1928	Amsterdam					Moscow
1930			Prague	Uruguay	Hamilton	
1931		Vienna				
1932	Los Angeles					Moscow
1934			Prague	Italy	London	
1936	Berlin	(Barcelona)				
1938			(Vienna)	France	Sydney	

Figure 7.4 Selected major international sports events, 1920–1938.

Source: adapted from Roche (2000: 101).

172

The history and politics of the Olympics

Gradually, however, policy changed in the Soviet Union. Engagement with, rather than the establishment of alternatives to, bourgeois sport became the means by which it was thought internal and external legitimacy could be secured for the alternative economic system. In the same manner, although alternatives to sport existed – such as the Turnen movement in Germany, which highlighted processes rather than products or results – they gradually became co-opted by sport. From being an alternative to sport they became an alternative sport among many (Keys 2006: 182–183). International competitive sport became the playing field – and the surrogate battlefield between ideological systems – as we discuss in the next chapter.

From the 1904 Olympics – which were small and feeble, piggy-backed onto the St. Louis exhibition, and included athletes who did not know they were in the Olympics (just as in Paris four years earlier) – to 2008 and the Beijing Summer Olympic Games (with over 10,000 athletes competing from 204 NOCs, watched by 24,562 accredited media personnel representing 159 countries) there has been a major change in the social and global significance of sport, and Olympic sport especially. Sport as an exciting, entertaining and economically and politically exploitable resource has become the cultural form that can create the mega-events which unite the globe through televised coverage (see Chapter 4). The growth in television coverage is echoed by the growth in numbers of nations, NOCs and athletes (including women) involved in the Olympic Games.

In 1908 the Olympic Games in London were subordinate to a trade exhibition, and simply one part of a celebration of imperial might and power. The UK grasp of science and technology had yet to be seriously challenged. By 1948 the Empire was in its final decline. Britain was just starting to get to grips with its post-war subordinate political role. The 1948 Games were in part a heroic gesture, born out of the wartime 'make do and mend', 'Britain can take it', working together, collectivist spirit. The 1948 Games were on the cusp of the television era, although it was to be another 20 years before the Games began to be transformed culturally and economically by television. Developments in TV from 1936 onward have made major sports mega-events such as the Olympic Games and the FIFA men's Football World Cup more important than world's fairs and expositions because they are more likely to be widely – and, since the 1960s, globally – mediated. The growth in participation at them is another indication of the growth in their scale (see Figure 7.5).

As interest in architectural design and the construction of forms suitable for Olympic cities developed (Munoz 2006), there has been a fascinating and consistent denial of the past. The British Empire Exhibition of 1924 did not use the White City site; the 1934 Empire Games did not use Wembley as its main stadium; the 1948 London Olympics did not utilise the 1908 site; the Festival of Britain did not use Wembley Park either; the legacy of the Festival of Britain was ignored or marginalised by the Millennium presentations in the Dome; the 2012 Olympic bid made little of tradition, choosing not to foreground the two previous occasions when London staged the Olympics. Indeed, in the past when the circus has left town, there has rarely been a viable economic strategy for the abandoned buildings – which decay until eventually they are obliterated. It is as if all these iconic buildings and sites are so firmly attached to the configuration which gave birth to them that there is a form of ideological contamination in which they cannot be used or even referred to until they have been razed, purged or otherwise sanitised, and rendered ideologically neutral again.

Olympics	Year	City	Nations/National Olympic Committees (NOCs)	Female athletes	Total athletes
I	1896	Athens	13	0	311
II	1900	Paris	22	12	1,330
III	1904	St. Louis	13	6	687
*	1906	Athens	20	7	884
IV	1908	London	22	36	2,035
VIII**	1924	Paris	44	136	3,092
IX	1928	Amsterdam	46	290	3,014
X	1932	Los Angeles	37	127	1,408
XI	1936	Berlin	49	328	4,066
XIV***	1948	London	59	385	4,099
XV	1952	Helsinki	69	518	4,925
XVIII	1964	Tokyo	93	683	5,140
XXIII	1984	Los Angeles	140	1,567	7,078
XXVII	2000	Sydney	199	4,069	10,651
XXIX	2008	Beijing	204	4,637	10,942§
XXX	2012	London	204	4,676	10,568

Figure 7.5 Growth in participation at selected Summer Olympic Games.

Source: adapted from Toohey and Veal (2007: 199); Greenberg (1987: 9); IOC (2010); www.olympic.org/en/content/Olympic-Games/All-Past-Olympic-Games/Summer/Beijing-2008 (last accessed 19 August 2010); and www.olympic.org/. . ./London_2012_Facts_and_Figures-eng.pdf (last accessed 7 September 2015).

Notes
* This event celebrated the tenth anniversary of the first modern Games; while officially intercalated by the IOC it is not numbered as an Olympic Games.
** The VI Games (scheduled for Berlin) were not held due to the First World War, but it is officially counted by the IOC.
***The XII and XIII Games (scheduled respectively for Tokyo, then Helsinki and London) were not held due to the Second World War, but are officially counted by the IOC.
§ The IOC also recorded 24,562 accredited media representing 159 countries.

CONCLUSION

Today, not only are the Olympic Games an enormous lever for moving public policy and uncorking infrastructural investment – some would argue public investment for private gain – they are also a major contributor to the conception of the world as one place. Sports mega-events, especially (but not only) in their mediated form, provide one of the means by which identity is constituted and reconstituted in the modern world. They enable 'temporal and spatial distance to be reconstructed and re-experienced, in memory and anticipation, in the telemediated lifeworld that characterizes the contemporary period' (Roche 2003: 109). In this chapter we considered the development of the Olympics as a stand-alone sports event. We also considered alternative sports and physical culture events and the growth of the reach of the Olympics in the twentieth century.

The key economic dynamics of the Olympic Games today are associated with globalising processes, transnational corporations, urban renewal, consumption and the new urbanism. Just as one of the legacies of the 2012 Olympic Games arguably has been the construction of Stratford City, a major development with a shopping mall at its heart, so a shopping mall opened in White City/Shepherd's Bush in West London in 2008, built on the site of, and obliterating the last traces of, the series of eight glass palaces that constituted the main entrance to the Franco-British Exhibition of 1908. The White City shopping mall and Stratford City have one other thing in common: they are both owned by Westfield, an Australian company that was also associated for a while with Multiplex, which built the new Wembley Stadium on the site of the 1948 Olympic Games. If in London in 1908, in the early days of the modern Olympic Games, the focus was on trade and production, now the focus is very much on spectacle and consumption – courtesy of the shopping mall.

NOTES

1 www.expo2015.org/en/learn-more (last accessed 7 September 2015).
2 https://expo2020dubai.ae/en (last accessed 7 September 2015).
3 http://queenelizabetholympicpark.co.uk (last accessed 7 September 2015).
4 'Abandoned lines and railways', www.urban75.org/railway/wood-lane-station.html (last accessed 7 September 2015).
5 'Exploring 20th century London', Museum of London, www.20thcenturylondon.org.uk/mol-82-232-138o (last accessed 7 September 2015).
6 http://sequinsandcherryblossom.com/2014/01/05/1910-japan-british-exhibition (last accessed 7 September 2015).
7 'Exploring 20th Century London'.
8 'Five ways to compute the relative value of a UK pound amount, 1270 to present', available online at www.measuringworth.com/ukcompare (last accessed 7 September 2015).
9 'British Industries Fair, 1921', *The Register* (Adelaide SA) 1920, http://trove.nla.gov.au/ndp/del/article/63027185 (last accessed 7 September 2015).
10 Martin Polley (2015: 63) notes that a small street behind the remaining BBC Media Village, named Dorando Close, after the Italian marathon runner Dorando Pietri, is one of the few signs that the 1908 Olympic Games ever took place here.
11 'British Empire Exhibition site, 1921–1924', www.engineering-timelines.com/scripts/engineeringItem.asp?id=395 (last accessed 7 September 2015).
12 Hurst Peirce + Malcolm, available at http://hurstpm.net/con-the-empire-pool-wembley (last accessed 7 September 2015).
13 www.dailymail.co.uk/news/article-2382079/Crystal-Palace-replica-planned-Chinese-billionaire.html (last accessed 7 September 2015).
14 www.bbc.co.uk/sport/0/olympics/20041426 (last accessed 13 October 2015).

FURTHER READING

Brownell, S. (ed.) (2008) *The 1904 Anthropology Days and Olympic Games: Sport, Race, and American Imperialism*, Lincoln, NE and London: University of Nebraska Press.
Keys, B. (2006) *Globalizing Sport: National Rivalry and International Community in the 1930s*, Cambridge, MA and London: Harvard University Press.
Roche, M. (2000) *Mega-Events and Modernity: Olympics and Expos in the Growth of Global Culture*, London: Routledge.

CHAPTER 8

THE INTERNATIONALIST SPIRIT
AND NATIONAL CONTESTATION

The Olympic Games were conceived partly as an international meeting ground, and the first International Olympic Committee (IOC) contained several figures who also played an active role in international peace organisations. Yet, from the start, tensions and rivalries between nations disrupted the internationalist aspirations of Olympism. Indeed, from the earliest years, for a combination of pragmatic, political and cultural reasons, national-based structures, practices and rituals began to develop. National flags, teams, uniforms, anthems at the victory ceremonies and the 'unofficial' medal tables in the media – all contributed to an image of the Olympic Games as a symbolic contest between nations. A good example is a page from the *Daily Mirror* (27 July 1908) published at the end of the first 'Summer Olympics' held in London that contained an image of 'The Olympic Ladder' and the caption:

> How the nations stand in the Olympic contests which have taken place both at the Stadium and elsewhere may be seen at a glance from the above ladder. The hands of the athletes are grasping the rungs corresponding with the number of events in which their countries have been victorious. Thus the United Kingdom leads with 38 wins, followed by the United States with 22.
> (Reference courtesy of The British Library, London)

Hanging on in third place with '7 wins' was Sweden. In fact, during the 1908 Games there were several acrimonious disputes between British and American officials. The 1936 Games became notorious as the 'Nazi Olympics', and in the Cold War era the Games became a symbolic battleground between East and West, communism and capitalism. The IOC also had to manage divided societies in Germany, Korea and China; Middle East tensions associated with the establishment of Israel and displacement of the Palestinians; the impact of decolonisation and establishment of emergent independent nations; and the demands for the isolation of South Africa over apartheid. This chapter examines the inherent contradictions between internationalism and national organi-sation, outlining the development and management of political tensions by the Olympic movement.

Since the end of the Second World War, being a *nation* in the modern world has come to be signified by two things: belonging to the United Nations and marching in the Opening Ceremony of the Olympic Games. However, it is clear around the world that the status of nations and states is subject to contestation. Ireland, Catalonia, the Basque country,

Taiwan, Hong Kong, the two Koreas, Palestine and Belgium provide diverse examples of the disputed nature of national boundaries and state authority.

What constitutes a 'nation'? In different contexts (the League of Nations, the UN, the IOC) different criteria and definitions of nation have been applied. Interestingly, the IOC has a longer list than the UN: 12 'nations' are included in the IOC but not the UN. Many of these can be seen as unresolved issues in decolonisation. The 12 include three British territories (Bermuda, British Virgin Islands, the Cayman Islands); four US territories (American Samoa, Puerto Rico, Guam, American Virgin Islands); and two Dutch territories (Aruba, Netherlands Antilles). Of the remaining, two are linked to China (Chinese Taipei, Hong Kong) and the other one is Palestine. A nation, Benedict Anderson famously argued, is an imagined community – not a natural product of geographical boundary, or linguistic unity, but a construction by practices of mapping, naming, identifying and narrativising (Anderson 1983). Although the nation-state is now generally taken for granted as the primary legal entity into which the world is divided, the primacy of the nation-state is a comparatively recent phenomenon. Over the last few centuries, empires controlling multiple nations have been a significant element in geopolitical organisation and before that city-states had considerable power in many parts of the world. The rise of the nation-state took place during the nineteenth century and is neither permanent nor unchallenged.

The apparent fixity of nation-states is an illusion. Many nations that now exist did not have national status in 1896, and some that existed then, do not now. Even in supposedly stable Europe the pace of change has been dramatic. Germany and Italy are less than 150 years old, and Germany was a divided nation between 1945 and 1990. The Soviet Union welded a set of diverse nations together between 1922 and 1991. After both world wars in the twentieth century the boundaries of Europe and the Middle East were redrawn by the victorious powers. Some nations disappeared, others came into being. The collapse of empires (the Austro-Hungarian, the Ottoman and the British) produced new independent nations. Some nations (Czechoslovakia, Yugoslavia) have been created *and* ceased to exist since 1918. The re-Balkanisation of the last two decades has seen the return to statehood of Croatia, Bosnia and Serbia. Around the world, national boundaries are under challenge, from regional and local forces, from competing national, linguistic, ethnic or religious forces. In countries such as South and North Korea, Ireland and Belgium, separate and competing visions of nation remain unreconciled. By contrast, some nations once divided by war (North and South Vietnam) have become reunified. In some countries, regional demands for independence are strongly asserted, such as in Spain (Catalonia, Basque) and China (Tibet). In some countries there are strong antagonisms between the main nation-state and a former part of it that has become independent (China and Taiwan). Some 'nations', such as Kosovo, have declared their status as nation-states, but have yet to achieve wider recognition or legitimacy.

It could be argued that the IOC has been not simply reflecting this process, but playing an active role as constructor – not least because appearance as a nation on the Olympic stage helps advertise an identity and confer a legitimacy. The German Democratic Republic and Cuba, for example, had explicit policies to utilise the Olympic Games to buttress their visibility and legitimacy on the world stage. The battle to isolate South Africa focused on the Olympic Games because of the event's global prominence and symbolic power.

177

The presence of Palestine as an Olympic 'nation' carries a powerful message to the world. The IOC, however, has from the start been caught within tensions of its own making, between its internationalist aspirations and its nation-based structures and rituals. Indeed, despite his internationalism, Coubertin's own ambitions were also shaped by the humiliation inflicted on France by Germany in 1870–1871, when Alsace Lorraine was annexed. Coubertin's interest in physical education was not unconnected to the need to rebuild French power. Yet Coubertin's vision was also internationalist. The IOC was one of the earlier organisations with global aspirations. Once the IOC was established, many other sports acquired governing bodies during the subsequent two decades (for example IAAF, FIFA, ILTF). The IOC has always been opposed to, and has never endorsed, the concept of medal tables, ranking nations by success. However, the media have always offered such tables and seek to dramatise the Games as a contest of prowess between nations. Indeed, national belongingness and national identity constitute prime means by which audiences around the world engage with the Games.

Conceptions of the world do not exist independently of power relations. From the fifteenth century, voyages of exploration by the dominant nations of Europe enabled a Eurocentric mapping of the world, which contributed to Western constructions of their global imaginary. The aspiring colonial powers conceived of the rest of the world as territory to plunder, and peoples to exploit and enslave. Closely linked to the expansion of territory through empire-building, the religions – especially Christianity and Islam – had always sought to expand their base of adherents, and developed visions of a global reach, built through evangelical activity. During the eighteenth century, new and challenging ideas developed: about the rights of man and rights of woman, universal brotherhood and republicanism, symbolised in the French revolutionary slogan 'Liberty, Equality and Fraternity'. So while trade and colonisation had already recognised and demarcated the world, it is not altogether surprising that some of the first impulses to develop internationalist links were associated with the development of socialism. The International Workingmen's Association, founded in 1864, became known as the 'First International'. Its founders, recognising that capitalism was an international system, sought to build international links between trade unionists and other organised workers around the world.

During the second half of the nineteenth century, other early international organisations were those associated with the establishment of conventions and practices that might assist trade, such as the Universal Postal Union, the International Bureau of Weights and Measures and the International Sanitary Conference. In 1851, as we discussed in the previous chapter, the Great Exhibition in the UK preceded a whole series of international exhibitions, later dubbed 'world's fairs' – one of the first cultural forms to specifically name the 'world' as its scope. The rise of the nation-state in the nineteenth century had in turn produced new forms of contestation, in which the great empires of Europe negotiated a complex set of secret treaties, while fighting for colonial dominance of the rest of the world. The culmination of this process in the First World War persuaded powerful nations of the need to impose some international order by means of an international organisation – the League of Nations was established in 1919, and, following its collapse and the Second World War, the United Nations was formed in 1945.

So the establishment of the IOC needs to be seen in the context of the emergence of a diverse set of international organisational forms between 1850 and 1950. We have become

178

familiar with a range of global organisations – the Boy Scouts, the Red Cross, Médecins Sans Frontières, the World Bank, UNESCO, the International Monetary Fund. Many are not really global but have global aspirations. In this context, four features of the IOC are striking: first, that it was founded relatively early in the context of international organisations; second, that it was almost the first real sporting international body; third, that it has succeeded, perhaps more than any other organisation, in being genuinely global in its reach; and fourth, that it has survived for over 100 years without significant split, schism or challenge to its authority.

It is salutary to remember that in 1896, Germany was only 25 years old as a nation-state, and Italy only 35. Given the extent to which the IOC was a club dominated by European aristocracy and nobility, and the relative difficulty of international travel, it was predictable that the first Olympic Games were a largely European affair – only a dozen nations were represented, all but three European (they were the US, UK, Germany, Australia, France, Denmark, Greece, Sweden, Switzerland, Bulgaria, Hungary, Chile). From the start, the Games featured the symbols and rituals of nation – national flags were hoisted during the victory ceremonies. The first Games could not be said to be a genuine competition between nations as many of the teams had an ad hoc character – being made up of friends and acquaintances of the organisers, tourists who happened to be in Athens (see McFee 1990) and, in one case, students of a member of the NOC. While the first Games were neither national nor international, the stage was set for this key tension around which the Games developed. During the next 12 years the Games struggled to survive, being staged as a sideshow to international trade fairs (the Exposition Universelle in Paris in 1900, the World's Fair in St. Louis in 1904 and the Franco-British Exhibition in 1908). In one contemporary description, the Franco-British Exhibition was at Shepherd's Bush and the Olympics 'took place alongside the enormous site' (Cook 1908: 14).

	General organisations	Sport organisations
1815	Central Commission for Navigation on the Rhine	
1838	Conseil supérieur de santé	
1840	World Anti-Slavery Convention	
1844	Young Men's Christian Association	
1851	International Sanitary Conference	
1861		First English cricket side to tour Australia
1863	International Committee of the Red Cross	
1864	First Geneva Convention	
1864	International Workingmen's Association	
1872		First international football match
1865	International Telegraph Office	
1874	Universal Postal Union	
1875	International Bureau of Weights and Measures	
1881		International Federation of Gymnastics
1886		International Rugby Football Board
1892		International Rowing Federation

(continued)

	General organisations	Sport organisations
1894		International Olympic Committee
1896		First modern Olympic Games
1899	First Hague Convention	
1900		Union Cycliste Internationale formed
1904		FIFA, world governing body of football
1906		FINA: International Swimming Federation
1912		IAAF (athletics)
1913		ITLF (tennis)
1919	League of Nations	
1919	International Federation of Red Cross and Red Crescent Societies	
1920	World Organisation of the Scout Movement	
1930		First Football World Cup staged
1945	World Bank	
1945	International Monetary Fund	
1945	United Nations	

Figure 8.1 Year of formation of selected international organisations.

There were significant tensions in 1908 between the US and the UK. The cause of Irish Home Rule was important to many Irish Americans, including those in the American Olympic squad, and the American team refused to dip their flag as they passed the Royal Box at the Opening Ceremony. The officials were all British, and after they had disqualified an American runner, the Americans were quick to accuse them of bias. The ensuing bitterness continued after the Games, and before the 1912 Games the IOC decided that in future there would be an international team of officials and judges.

It was already becoming abundantly clear that the spectacle of the Games constituted a site for symbolic contestation around concepts of national belongingness. In 1912 Finland was under the control of Russia, but the Finnish team refused to march under the Russian flag and the IOC allowed them to march behind the Finnish flag, to the huge delight of the crowd. At first the growth pattern of the Games appears erratic, with an especially low turnout in St. Louis in 1904, largely for geographic reasons, but by 1912 it was clear that the Olympic Games had become established as a recurrent ritual practice of growing significance.

Year	Number of nations
1896	12
1900	22
1904	9
1908	26
1912	28

Figure 8.2 Nations competing in the Olympic Games, 1896–1912.

180

BETWEEN THE WARS: COMMUNISM AND FASCISM

The growing tension between Germany, Russia, Britain and France during the build-up to 1914 had its impact on the IOC, especially as Berlin was awarded the 1916 Games. When the First World War broke out, Theodore Cook, a British IOC member, demanded the expulsion of German members, and when this was rejected, he resigned. By contrast, Coubertin opted to protect the IOC by moving its headquarters to neutral Switzerland, where it has remained ever since (Guttmann 1992: 37). The 1920 Games were awarded, rather pointedly, given that Belgium was the first victim of the war, to Antwerp. The IOC maintained its own policy of inclusion by leaving the invitations to the organising committee, and Germany was not invited to the Games of 1920 or 1924.

The first multi-sport festival of winter sports, which subsequently became regarded as the first Winter Olympics, was held in 1924 in Chamonix in France. Before the Winter Olympics, there was figure skating in London Olympic Games in 1908 but not in 1912. Figure skating and ice hockey were both included in the 1920 Olympic Games in Antwerp. The year 1924 was what Arnold Lunn called the 'annus mirabilis' of modern skiing. As part of his drive to establish the new forms of skiing, he helped to set up the Kandahar Ski Club at Murren in January 1924; that same month the Federation Internationale du Ski was founded in Oslo and that year, too, Nordic skiing was included in the first Winter Olympics held at Chamonix (Holt 1992: 427–428). The Chamber of Commerce were alert to the economic advantages of staging the Games (Essex 2011: 57). Winter sport, the Winter Olympics, the hotel trade and the travel industry became bound up in a synergistic relationship, each feeding off the growth of the other components. St. Moritz, one of the earliest winter sport resorts, was to host the Winter Olympic Games in 1928 and 1948. 'In 1928 the Games in the Swiss resort of St Moritz were led by the local authority and assisted the consolidation of the resort as an international winter sports destination' (Essex 2011: 58). The construction of a ratcheted railway, conveying people to the higher snowfields, enabled a growth of downhill skiing in time for the 1928 Winter Olympics, held at St. Moritz (Flower 1982: 97).

Its finely tuned sense of international diplomacy meant that the IOC was prone to mark the claims of rising powers by awarding them Games. The cancelled 1940 Games would have been in Tokyo; China's economic dynamism and growing political significance was finally rewarded with a Games in 2008; the Olympics are in Rio in 2016; and one could reasonably expect a South African and an Indian Olympics in the next 30 years. It is also worth noting that neither Berlin 1916 nor Tokyo 1940 happened, due to world conflicts in which the proposed host nations were deeply involved. After both major wars, organising committees responded to anger and political sensitivities by withholding invitations to the defeated nations.

The early years of the Olympic Games constitute an interesting case study in the invention of tradition, in which both the internationalist and nationalist aspects of the Games were buttressed by ritual. The gold medal was first bestowed in 1904. The Olympic Charter and the march of competitors in the Opening Ceremony were introduced in 1908. The Olympic oath-taking ceremony and the Olympic flag were introduced in 1920. An Olympic hymn, different each time, was used until the Rome Olympics, after which the 1960 version became the permanent Olympic Hymn. White doves were first released during the Opening

181

Ceremony in Paris in 1924, and the first Olympic Village was constructed. When Paris was awarded the 1924 Games, the architect imagined 'the most beautiful stadium in the world' (Gravelaine 1997: 13). The village was conceptualised as an innovative construction that would be built to last and used after the Games, and one commentator at the time described it as 'a beautiful village, with all modern comforts installed' (see Charpentier and Boissonnade 1999: 118). On a research visit to the area in 2001, we could find no remaining traces of the village.

The Olympic flame was first lit in the stadium in 1928, national anthems were first used in victory ceremonies in 1932, and the torch relay was introduced in 1936. The Olympic oath illustrates the tensions neatly – taken on behalf of all the competitors as an international group, it nevertheless commits them to competing 'for the honour of our country and the glory of sport'. The nationalist dimension was ritualised by the establishment of medal ceremonies, the raising of national flags, the playing of national anthems and the parading in national teams in the Opening Ceremony.

The impulse to internationalism has led to a continuous recruitment of new nations, yet national rivalries and political tensions have also meant exclusion for some nations. The newly communist Russia was not invited to the 1920 Games. Countries held responsible for the 'Great War' were excluded from participating, so athletes from Germany, Austria, Bulgaria, Hungary and Turkey were relegated to bystander status. Indeed, Germany was not re-admitted until 1928. The scope of the Games continued to grow in the inter-war era, despite a dip in numbers of nations for Los Angeles in 1932.

The inter-war years in Europe were characterised by political instability, stemming from the poorly conceived settlements imposed by the victors of the First World War, the rise of fascism, and the establishment of Soviet communism. Financial crises contributed to instability, from the rampant inflation that wrecked the Weimar Republic, through the Wall Street Crash of 1929 into the Depression of the 1930s. There was a social revolution in manners and morality, less deference to the aristocracy and greater emancipation of women. During this period, the Olympic movement faced its most significant challenge to date, in the workers' sport movement, and the first real tarnishing of its image in the 1936 Games.

The workers' sport movements

In the aftermath of the First World War (1914–1918) and the Russian Revolution (1917) the workers' sports movement developed rapidly, and a whole series of workers' sports

Year	Number of nations
1920	29
1924	44
1928	46
1932	37
1936	49

Figure 8.3 Nations competing in the Olympic Games, 1920–1936.

182

events or 'workers' Olympics' were staged during the 1920s and 1930s as an alternative to the official 'nationalistic' and 'bourgeois' Olympics (Krüger and Riordan 1996; Kuhn 2015: 21–49). The workers' sports movement grew out of the foundation, in Germany in the 1890s, of the Workers' Gymnastic Association. This was established to provide an alternative, and opposition, to the German Gymnastic Society, which had become an intensely nationalistic organisation. Similar groups developed all over Europe, varying in type, but with a shared intention to provide working-class people with healthy exercise in a socialist context (Riordan 1984: 99). At first the focus was on less competitive, exercise-based activity, but after the First World War the orientation shifted towards competitive sports. The movement was split by the divergence, following the successful Russian Revolution, between socialist and communist organisations. The socialists remained with the Lucerne Sports International (LSI), while communists broke away to associate with the Red Sports International (RSI), sponsored by Russia.

Riordan singles out four ways in which these movements challenged the IOC Olympics. First, while the bourgeois Olympics encouraged participation in national teams, the

Year	Venue	Event	Organisers	Participants	Spectators	Countries
1921	Prague	Unofficial 'Workers' Olympics'	Czechoslovak Workers Gymnastic Association			13
1925	Frankfurt	First Workers' Olympics	Lucerne Sports International		150,000	19
1928	Moscow	First Workers' Spartakiad	Communist Sports Organisation	4,000		14
1931	Vienna	Second Workers' Olympics	Lucerne Sports International	80,000	100,000	23
1932	Berlin	Second Workers' Spartakiad	Communist workers	Banned by German authorities		
1936	Barcelona	Third Workers' Olympics	Joint socialist and communist organisers	Spanish fascists stage putsch on morning of Opening Ceremony	Many would-be competitors remain to fight in International Brigade	
1937	Antwerp	Rescheduled Third Workers' Olympics	As above	27,000	50,000	17
1943	Helsinki	Planned Fourth Workers' Olympics	As above	Not staged due to outbreak of war in 1939		

Figure 8.4 Mass-participation workers' sports events, 1918–1939.

Source: Riordan (1984: 98–112); information included about numbers where available.

workers' Olympics stressed internationalism. Second, unlike the IOC Olympics, which imposed minimum standards of performance and limits on numbers per event, the workers' games emphasised mass participation. Third, the IOC Games were seen as largely confined to the sons of the rich and privileged (amateurs, almost entirely male) and the IOC itself was seen as an aristocratic body while the workers' games opposed chauvinism, elitism, racism and discrimination. Fourth, the workers' movement did not believe the Olympic spirit of true amateurism and international understanding could be achieved in a bourgeois-dominated movement (Riordan 1984: 103). The opening ceremonies at the workers' games dispensed with 'nationalist' flags and anthems, and competitors and spectators sang revolutionary hymns such as 'The Internationale'. The movement climaxed in 1936, when, with thousands of would-be participants already in Barcelona, the Spanish fascists staged a putsch, triggering the start of the Civil War. Many of those who had come to compete ended up enlisting in the International Brigade (see Murray 1987; Steinberg 1978; Wheeler 1978).

The period of the Popular Front, uniting communist and socialist parties across Europe during the late 1930s, was unable to halt the rise of fascism and Nazism, and just a year after the Antwerp Workers' Olympics of 1937, Hitler's German troops marched into Austria. The staging of the official Olympic Games in Germany had already provided Hitler with a huge public canvas on which to paint a disturbing image of Nazi power. The 1936 Games proved to be the last for 12 years.

Berlin 1936: the 'Nazi Games'

Although nationalism was already written into Olympic ritual, the 1936 Games, which became notorious as the 'Nazi Olympics', elevated the foregrounding of national power to a dramatic new level (Kruger and Murray 2003). The 1936 Games constituted the moment when the aspirations of Olympism for internationalism and peace were forced, dramatically, to confront the realities of national power and its associated symbolism. The rise to power of the Nazis came amidst growing concern around the world over the treatment of German Jews. Hart-Davis (1986) argues that Germany attempted to produce the appearance of a normal society during the Games, although the concentration camps established from 1933 were known about, and US and British ambassadors relayed critical information back to their governments but it was not taken seriously enough. He outlines the ways in which, from 1933, Jews were gradually excluded from organised sport. The IOC endeavoured to extract a promise that this would not be so, and the Germans agreed to a statement that they would abide by Olympic principles, but had no intention of reversing the anti-Jewish sport policies.

During the three years before the 1936 Games there were extensive efforts to promote a boycott, especially in the UK, US and France. In 1934 in New York, there was a mock trial of Hitler that attracted 20,000 people to Madison Square Gardens (Hart-Davis 1986). In 1935, Supreme Court Judge Jeremiah T. Mahoney published a pamphlet entitled 'Germany has Violated the Olympic Code', which contained specific and detailed instances of discrimination against German Jews in the context of sport. By 1935, according to one opinion poll, 43 per cent of Americans were in favour of a boycott (Guttmann 1984: 72).

IOC leaders, however, were inclined to accept reassurances from the German organisers at face value, and showed little willingness to investigate more carefully. There was also, demonstrably, a degree of anti-Semitism within Olympic circles.

Avery Brundage (President of the United States Olympic Committee, Vice-President of the IAAF and a future President of the IOC) privately referred to the 'Jewish proposal' to boycott the Games, and claimed that every boycott call was 'obviously written by a Jew or someone who has succumbed to Jewish propaganda'. In fact, Guttmann suggests, although many American Jews did play an active role, Catholic organisations and individuals were prominent in leading the boycott campaign (Guttmann 2006). Sigfrid Edstrom (President of the IAAF and Vice-President and future President of the IOC) wrote, in a letter to Avery Brundage, 'they [Jews] are intelligent and unscrupulous. Many of my friends are Jews, so you must not think that I am against them, but they must be kept within certain limits'; and Baillet-Latour (IOC President 1925–1942), also in a letter to Brundage, wrote that he was not personally fond of Jews. But Baillet-Latour at least made some attempts to get the Germans to honour their pre-Games pledges of no discrimination against Jewish athletes in German team selection (Guttmann 1992: 53–71). Brundage, by contrast, for the rest of his life insisted, against all the evidence, that there had been no such discrimination. Guttmann argues that it was his fight against the boycott that turned him anti-Semitic (see Guttmann 1984: 72–73). Brundage, like other right-wing Americans of the period, came to blame many of the problems of the world on Jews and communists, who were, in some ill-defined way, in league. He was an active isolationist during the early 1940s, associating with aviator Charles Lindbergh, who was suspected of pro-Nazi views. After the war he corresponded with Swedish IOC member Count von Rosen, one of whose letters to Brundage proclaimed that Jews were responsible for all the world's troubles, and that communism was the political form of Judaism (see Guttmann 1984: 92).

The one IOC member who opposed the Games and supported the boycott, American Ernest Lee Jahncke, was expelled from the IOC to be replaced by Brundage (Guttmann 1992: 53–71). Baillet-Latour, IOC President from 1925 to 1942, was succeeded by Edstrom (1946–1952), after which Brundage became President and served from 1952 to 1972. Samaranch, who became President of the IOC in 1980, serving till 2001, was an active supporter of Spanish fascism and served as Spanish Ambassador to the Soviet Union under Franco. The fact that four of five presidents, between 1925 and 2001, had either anti-Semitic or fascist tendencies should prompt speculation about, and enquiry into, the cultural climate within the IOC during most of the twentieth century.[1]

The Berlin Games were not simply used as a propaganda platform, as is sometimes asserted; indeed, the Nazi authorities went to some lengths during the Games to mask the true nature of the ideological transformation they had brought about. Nevertheless, the general desire to celebrate Aryan might inflected the presentation of the Games, not least in the innovation of the torch relay. Berlin Olympic organiser Carl Diem had a scholarly interest in Ancient Greece and found support from Hitler, who admired Doric architecture (Hart-Davis 1986: 52). The torch relay, mythologised as a return to Ancient Greek roots, was utilised by the Nazis as a symbol of Aryan power. The Ancient Greeks did have relays carrying torches, but there is no evidence that they ever did so in connection with the Olympic Games. Diem suggested a relay, referring to ancient vases for authority.

185

Hitler was persuaded that the Third Reich ought to sponsor the current excavations at Olympia. Coubertin supported the idea, as it seemed to help legitimate the link between the ancient and modern Games. Krupp, the German arms producer, created and sponsored the torches. The Nazi anthem, the 'Horst Wessel Lied', was played in ancient Olympia when the flame was lit. The song contains the line 'Already millions are looking to the swastika, full of hope'. It was also sung at the Opening Ceremony. 'Altars were set up along the way for semi-religious ceremonies in the tradition of the ancient fire cults, which had been prevalent in ancient Greece as in ancient Germany' (Krüger and Murray 2003). Arguably, this was the point at which the embryonic neo-paganism underpinning some Olympic rituals was consolidated.

In Vienna, 10,000 Austrian Nazis greeted the torch with cries of 'Heil Hitler' and demonstrated against the Jewish members of the Austrian Olympic team, shouting 'Perish Judah'. Five hundred had to be arrested (Walters 2006: 193). The ceremony in Vienna was used by the Austrian Nazis as a demonstration of their power, whereas the one in Prague resulted in street fighting between Sudeten Germans and Czechs. Hart-Davis says of the events in Vienna surrounding the torch relay, 'The message of the evening was clear. In a place as politically volatile as Vienna, the Olympic Games were an explosive subject' (Hart-Davis 1986: 137). As the torch relay was under German jurisdiction rather than that of the IOC, it could be used for unabashed Nazi ceremonies (Krüger 2003: 32–33). The ritual of the relay, and its version in the Leni Riefenstahl film of the Games, was to make explicit the supposed link between Germany and Ancient Greece. The Reich was portrayed as the repository for Ancient Greek virtues. The president of the organising committee, Lewald, said that the Olympic torch created 'a real and spiritual bond between our German fatherland and the sacred places of Greece founded nearly 4,000 years ago by Nordic immigrants' (Walters 2006: 193). The whole ceremony in Olympia was, of course, an invention, but the version in the Riefenstahl film was a further reconstruction of an invented tradition – she worked on it in take after take, eventually insisting on a naked male runner (with whom she subsequently had an affair) rather than the man in modern gym shorts who was the original choice (Graham 1986: 61). Ironically, of course, the nakedness was a more historically accurate rendition of the Ancient Greek customs. When the flame was finally lit in the stadium, the BBC commentator gasped in shock before pronouncing 'I don't think anyone expected such a big flame', inadvertently producing in the process a rather chilling metaphor for the rise of the Nazis (BBC Sound Archives, 1936, Berlin Olympics live broadcast of the Opening Ceremony).

Hart-Davis says that in the lighting ceremony in Olympia in 1936, a 'ridiculously long' message from Coubertin was read out (Hart-Davis 1986: 133). Walters (2006) suggests that Coubertin was, in effect, blackmailed by the Nazis after he stupidly accepted a secret donation from them. The last public statement from the ageing Coubertin praised the 'grandiose games' that, he asserted, magnificently served the Olympic ideal (Guttmann 1992: 70). Although the Games were, on a technical level, a great success, it was not a proud moment for the Olympic movement, with its aspirations for peaceful internationalism. Having been established as a routinised and cyclical ritual by this time, the cancellation of any Olympic Games marks the dramatic disruption of diplomatic relations by global conflict. The 1940 Olympic Games, scheduled for Tokyo, and the 1944 Games, scheduled for Helsinki, did not take place.

THE NEW WORLD AND THE COLD WAR

After the Second World War the Olympic Games resumed their growth trajectory, despite a small drop for the Melbourne Games of 1956, which were affected by boycotts. However, the end of the war did not mean a return to peace or to the world of the 1930s. Rather, a profound new geopolitical environment came into being as the European map was redrawn by the US and the Soviet Union. The next few decades were dominated by the economic, political and cultural contestations between capitalist America and communist Russia. While the possession by both of nuclear weapons prevented direct military confrontation, nevertheless, around the world the struggles of peoples and nations were strongly influenced by the respective regional influences of the dominant superpowers.

In 1979, Richard Espy (1979: vii) wrote 'The Modern Olympic Games symbolize the struggle between man's ideals and the reality within which he must live'. The notion is suggestive of the era of the Cold War and the symbolic contestation that framed the Olympic movement from 1945 to 1989. In the first Olympic Games after the war, the defeated nations Germany and Japan were not invited, although Italy was, and the Soviet Union did not compete. During the 1930s the Soviet Union, after the Revolution, had largely abstained from international sport, not being part of IFs or the IOC, and instead fostered the development of the RSI (see Riordan 1984). After the Second World War, however, they adopted the strategy of entering international competitions in order to demonstrate the superiority of the communist system. In 1948, though, the USSR had not sought recognition from the IOC and did not have an NOC. The American Vice-President of the IOC, Avery Brundage, a strong anti-communist, was opposed to accepting communist individuals as members of the IOC, but did not favour excluding countries from the Olympic movement on the grounds of their political system (Espy 1979: 28). China had intended to compete, but the successful culmination of the communist revolution in 1947 put an end to the plans. In 1948, the Opening Ceremony in London took little more than an hour and consisted of presentation of VIPs and the teams marching in. The elaborate spectacle of the ceremony, as we now know it, has evolved since, largely for television.

Germany, East and West

In 1952 the Soviet Union entered the Games for the first time since Russia competed in 1912. Developments in post-war reconciliation allowed Germany and Japan to compete.

Year	Number of nations
1948	59
1952	69
1956	67
1960	84
1964	94
1968	113

Figure 8.5 Nations competing in the Olympic Games, 1948–1968.

After the conclusion of the Second World War, Europe was, effectively, divided into two spheres of influence, the western half dominated by the US, and the eastern half by the Soviet Union. Germany was divided into Soviet, American, British and French zones, and Berlin itself, lying in the eastern (Soviet) part of Germany, was also divided. The continued Western occupation of half of Berlin was to prove a provocation to the Soviet Union for the next 35 years. A Soviet-inspired blockade of Berlin during the late 1940s was broken by a massive airlift of goods from the West. In 1961, the East Germans constructed the Berlin Wall, which succeeded as a physical barrier, but provided the West with an enormous symbolic victory in propaganda terms.

In 1950 the IOC gave provisional recognition to the West German Olympic Committee. However, a parallel East German NOC began seeking affiliation to international sport federations. An intense debate developed within the IOC, commencing at the Vienna session of 1951. Some members argued that an NOC had to be part of a legitimate state (and East Germany was yet to seek or gain recognition). Some members wanted to emphasise the remit in the charter to bring the youth of the world together, recognise both NOCs and hope for future reunification, while others believed this would merely emphasise the division. The IOC tried without initial success to promote the idea of two NOCs but a joint German team (see Hill 1992: 34). In 1952 a German team comprising only West German competitors featured in the Games, with the East Germans withdrawing (see Espy 1979: 35–36). Deteriorating relations between the IOC and the East German NOC led to a vote against recognition. In 1955 the Soviet Union released East Germany from its status as the 'Soviet zone' of Germany, and recognised it as an independent state. The East German NOC was then formally recognised but only on condition that it cooperated in forming a single team (see Hill 1992: 34–37).

While the IOC was, as so often, driven by pragmatism, many of the European aristocrats were hostile to the communist cause, as was the American millionaire Avery Brundage (IOC President 1952–1972). Despite West German opposition to the recognition of East Germany, the two NOCs were able to enter a joint team in the Games between 1956 and 1964. The competitors shared a flag, emblem, uniform and lodgings (see Hill 1992: 38). Such rapport was remarkable, given that this was the period of heightened Cold War tension. In the 1960 Games in Rome, as in Melbourne, the two Germanys competed as one team, with victories being marked by Beethoven's 'Ode to Joy' from the Ninth Symphony, rather than the national anthem of either (Charpentier and Boissonnade 1999: 293). In August 1961 the Berlin Wall was constructed and, in retaliation, the Western countries began denying visas to East German sportsmen and women for skiing and hockey tournaments (Espy 1979: 77).

During the 1960s it became clear that the existence of East Germany was an established fact that warranted international recognition. The majority of IFs were accepting East Germany as a separate nation and the IAAF allowed separate East and West German teams in the European Championships of 1966. The IOC agreed to recognise two NOCs, although, in the case of the eastern one, the resolution referred to 'the geographical area of East Germany'. In Mexico City in 1968, two Germanys competed for the first time, and the IOC agreed to accept the name 'German Democratic Republic (GDR)' (Hill 1992: 39). By the 1970s the West German government developed its Ostpolitik, which aimed at

188

peaceful coexistence, with the hope of eventual reunification. The GDR had immense Olympic success during the 1970s and 1980s, although suspicions of systematic use of performance-enhancing drugs were amply confirmed after 1991, when the East German archives became accessible to researchers.

China and Taiwan

China had been involved in the Olympic movement since the 1920s. The first Chinese IOC member was elected in 1922 and the IOC had recognised the Chinese NOC (Hill 1992: 40–45). After the communist revolution, many nationalists, including some NOC members, fled to Formosa (now Taiwan), but the NOC retained recognition. Avery Brundage later argued, with considerable disingenuousness, that the NOC had simply changed its address! However, Lord Killanin (President 1972–1980) later stated that there was no trace at Lausanne of any such change of address having been recorded (Hill 1992: 40–45). In 1952 the People's Republic of China (PRC) informed the IOC that it had an established body, the 'All China Athletic Commission', and wished to apply for recognition as an NOC. The Formosans were also seeking recognition and an invite to the 1952 Games. This placed the IOC in a quandary once again. They opted to accept teams from both, in advance of considering recognition for China's NOC (Hill 1992: 42). Despite this diplomatic pragmatism, the Formosans declined to acquiesce and although the China team set off, they reached Helsinki too late to participate (see Espy 1979: 36–37).

In 1954 the IOC recognised the NOC of the PRC while maintaining its recognition of Formosa's. The China committee was known as the 'Olympic Committee of the Chinese Republic' (changed in 1958 to 'Olympic Committee of the People's Democratic Republic of China'). The Formosa committee retained the title the 'Chinese Olympic Committee'. The IOC resorted to the rather slippery claim that it was recognising territories under the control of an NOC and not as nations (Hill 1992: 40–45).

By 1956, the IOC had, on the one hand, successfully persuaded the two German nations to enter one team, but on the other agreed to recognise NOCs from both China and Formosa (see Espy 1979: 44–45). This time a more assertive China objected and did not compete in 1956. At the start of 1956 the third Chinese IOC member, Shou Ti-Tung, elected in 1947, requested that the Formosa Olympic Committee be expelled. Brundage was dismissive. Later in the year, the PRC withdrew from Melbourne in protest and in 1958 it withdrew from the Olympic movement and from all IFs (Hill 1992: 42). After a period of relative openness ('Let a hundred flowers blossom'), China had entered a period of tougher ideological stance (the 'Great Leap Forward') and isolation from 'imperialist' organisations, denouncing Avery Brundage and withdrawing from the IOC (Espy 1979: 63). Chinese IOC member Shou Ti-Tung resigned, dubbing Brundage a 'faithful menial of US imperialists' (see Hill 1992: 40–45).

The IOC attempted to resolve the issue, by insisting that the Formosa committee could not go on purporting to represent China, but must reapply, choosing a name that reflected the territory that it actually controlled. This fairly moderate proposal led to a storm of controversy in the US in which Brundage, who was (falsely) represented as having expelled Formosa, was bitterly criticised (Espy 1979: 65). In 1960 the Formosa NOC proposed that it be known as the Republic of China, in accord with its UN recognition. The IOC accepted this but insisted that at Rome they compete as Formosa. The team carried a sign reading 'Formosa', but displayed a placard reading 'Under Protest'. In 1968 the name the 'Olympic Committee of the Republic of China' was reaffirmed by the IOC (Hill 1992: 40–45). In the 1970s, US foreign policy pursued rapprochement with China, and President Nixon visited China in 1972. In 1971 the UN recognised the PRC and expelled Formosa/Taiwan, giving its seat on the Security Council to China. The IOC resolved that China would be welcomed back if it accepted Olympic rules and the continued presence of Taiwan (Hill 1992: 40–45).

From the mid-1950s, then, the IOC was beginning to experience greater difficulties with managing national contestation, and in 1956, in the evocative words of Charpentier and Boissonnade, 'heavy clouds darkened the Olympic sky' (1999: 259). It was a year of dramatic political events: the escalation of the Algerian war of independence (1954–1962); Russian tanks on the streets of Budapest to crush the local more liberal-minded regime; and the English and French invasion of Egypt in response to Colonel Nasser's nationalisation of the Suez Canal. Spain, Holland, Italy, Switzerland, Iraq and Egypt announced their withdrawal from the Games. Israel, its troops mobilised, sent only a symbolic delegation of three (Charpentier and Boissonnade 1999: 259). A water polo match between Hungary and the USSR turned into a grudge match with, according to some witnesses, the water turning red with blood. Against this backdrop of national contestation there was one positive internationalist development – the Closing Ceremony featured, instead of competitors marching in teams, as in the Opening, 500 representatives of the 4,000 competitors who 'marched as a single cavalcade' (Espy 1979: 58). North Korea sought to enter a team for 1964, but the IOC insisted on a joint Korean team. The North agreed but the South refused. The IOC then threatened that in that case it would admit North Korea. The South remained intransigent – so North Korea was admitted as a separate team (Espy 1979: 82–83). It seems clear that the IOC did not merely reflect political decisions taken elsewhere, but was actively interventionist. It operated, though, not so much in accord with high principle, or in relation to clear constitutional principle, but rather with pragmatic responses to specific circumstances.

Palestine, Israel and the Middle East

Up until the Second World War, Palestine had an Olympic Committee, although, as a 'mandate' territory, it competed under the British flag. So Palestine was invited to compete in 1948. However, the United Nations had recommended the partition of Palestine, and the State of Israel was declared in 1947. The Palestine NOC became the Olympic Committee of Israel, with the intention of competing under the Israeli flag, although some Arab nations objected to the 'Zionist' flag. Under the threat of a boycott, the IOC, once again opting for a short-term pragmatic, if not pedantic, solution, declared Israel ineligible. It argued that as the original Olympic Committee had been given recognition under the national designation of 'Palestine', and as this Palestine committee no longer existed, and since 'Israel' had not applied for recognition, it was ineligible (Espy 1979: 29; and see Trory 1980: 18). Israel's new NOC was subsequently recognised and an Israeli team competed in 1952 in Helsinki. In addition to the PRC, six more countries boycotted the Melbourne

Games: Spain, Switzerland and the Netherlands, to protest the Soviet invasion of Hungary; and Lebanon, Egypt and Iraq, to protest Israel's invasion of the Sinai and the Gaza Strip.

Palestine was accepted as a member of the Olympic Council of Asia in 1986, and the IOC recognised Palestine as a nation for Olympic purposes in 1993, both events triggering reactions of outrage in Israel and among Zionists worldwide. Fighting a rearguard action, Israel attempted, in 1996, to persuade the IOC to bar the use of the word 'Palestine', suggesting instead 'Palestinian Authority, Palestinian Autonomy or Palestinian Delegation'. Palestinian teams have participated in the Olympic Games since 1996. In 1996 a reception hosted by Andrew Young brought together Israel and Palestine Olympic delegates. The Palestine and Israel Olympic Committee delegations were filmed by the world's media exchanging greetings.[2]

In 2004 the PLO leader Yasser Arafat announced that the Palestinians would observe a truce during the 2004 Olympic Games. Since the death of Arafat in November 2004 and the rising power of Hamas in Palestine and the right wing in Israel, attitudes have hardened considerably and the issue of the Palestinian Olympic identity remains a controversial one.

De-colonisation and newly emergent nations

In the post-war era, the last great European empire, the British Empire, was dismantled. A UK weakened in the wake of the war was unable to combat movements for independence. While independence for India (1947) was seen as the watershed, the process of de-colonisation was to be long and drawn out. The Bandung Conference in 1955, organised by the Colombo group of countries (Burma, Ceylon, India, Indonesia and Pakistan), brought together representatives from 24 African and Asian countries to discuss shared economic objectives and the end of colonialism (Espy 1979: 47). In 1962 Indonesia, the host of the Asian Games, refused visas to Taiwan and Israeli competitors. The following year the IOC suspended the Indonesian NOC, which withdrew from the Olympic movement. Indonesian President Sukarno took the initiative in establishing the proposed Games of the New Emerging Forces (GANEFO). An initial conference, with delegates from Cambodia, China, Guinea, Indonesia, Iraq, Mali, Pakistan, North Vietnam, the UAR and the Soviet Union, and observers from Ceylon and Yugoslavia, drew inspiration from the 1955 Bandung Conference (Espy 1979: 81). China is believed to have been the driving force behind these proposals.

The first GANEFO was staged in 1963 with a second scheduled for Cairo in 1967. Part of the geopolitical substructure of this, of course, was the impact of the Sino-Soviet split which meant that China and the Soviet bloc were competing with each other as well as with the West for influence in the 'Third World' (Lutan and Hong 2005). A session of the GANEFO council was held in Beijing in 1965 and it was decided to hold an Asian GANEFO at the same time as the Olympic-approved Asian Games (Espy 1979: 109). Cairo pulled out of staging the next GANEFO in 1967 for financial reasons. The IOC took seriously the threat of GANEFO and its ability to win regional support in Africa, and manoeuvred carefully to protect its power base (Gitersos 2011). The IOC was particularly keen to avoid any splits, and as early as 1964 the Indonesian NOC had been reinstated (Field 2011). China, during the cultural revolution, became more inward looking and, in Espy's words,

191

'GANEFO died a quiet death' (1979: 110). After this brief episode in separatism, Third World countries became more focused on the Olympic Games, utilising the event as a symbolic opportunity to announce their independent presence on the world stage – and the number of NOCs rose steadily to reflect these aspirations. The numbers of competing nations grew steadily up till 1976, with a dip in 1980 caused by the US-led boycott.

Apartheid and South Africa

A 'cultural boycott' played a significant role in the isolation and stigmatisation of the South African apartheid regime. The sports boycott of South Africa led the way, giving the issue a high profile and encouraging the extension of the boycott into other areas. Although it also required well-directed pressure from campaigning individuals, organisations and countries, it could be argued that the IOC was a leading force in the sporting boycott.

South Africa first competed in 1908 in London and had sent a team to every Games since then. No black competitors were ever chosen by the exclusively white South African Olympic Committee. This appears not to have been an issue for the IOC, which in the 1950s had no African members. It was only in 1959 that campaigning began within the IOC, led by the Soviet Union member, Alexei Romanov (Ramsamy 1984: 45). In 1961, South Africa became a republic and began to introduce additional laws enforcing segregation. In 1963 the IOC met with the African NOCs who insisted that no invitation be issued to South Africa for the 1964 Games. The IOC asked the South African NOC to make a public statement opposing racial discrimination; when there was no response, the South Africans were excluded from 1964. Fighting back with a diplomatic offensive, which involved rallying its supporters within the IOC and offering some rather vague and meaningless conciliatory statements, South Africa was able to secure an IOC invitation for 1968. However, a campaign to fight back was mounted by the Supreme Council for Sport in South Africa (SCSA) and the South African Non-Racial Olympic Committee (SANROC), with the support of black African states and black activists in the US, led by Harry Edwards. The threat of a boycott by around 40 countries forced the IOC to make a U-turn and ban South Africa. The arrogant response of South Africa, warning the IOC not to meddle in its domestic affairs, was sufficient to alienate the support that it still had in the IOC, and in 1970 South Africa was expelled from the organisation (Ramsamy 1984: 45–48).

At the start of the 1960s, the IOC had been seeking, in vain, reassurance from the South African NOC that apartheid in sport did not exist, or would be eradicated. The South African National Olympic Committee (SANOC) seemed unable or unwilling to oppose the South African government publicly and so South Africa were not invited to take part in 1964 (Espy 1979: 87). Although many on the IOC were not crusaders against racism, the organisation nonetheless deserves some credit for being one of the organisations to outlaw South Africa. The whole story highlights the growing symbolic power of the Olympic Games, and presages the era of boycotts and political protests. In 1966 the SCSA was formed – largely to campaign against South Africa. Some compromise proposals from SANOC, involving a mixed team at the Olympics, persuaded the IOC to readmit them. This triggered a huge reaction in the NOCs and elsewhere, with many countries and individuals threatening to boycott. The IOC was forced into constructing a face-saving formula for getting the South Africans to withdraw. South Africa was expelled from the IOC in 1970, and only re-admitted in 1991, after apartheid came to an end.

CONCLUSION

Given the complex issues that the IOC has had to manage during the twentieth century, it is a considerable achievement that the movement has never split, or suffered any significant defections. Indeed, it may be because of the peculiar construction of the IOC – dominated as it has been by European aristocracy – that its very closeness to the dominant classes of powerful nations has enabled it to function, at times as an alternative (if self-serving) form of diplomacy. Nor is this influence limited to Western Europe. After the division of Europe and the emergence of communist nations in the East, the IOC was able to absorb and clasp to its bosom the new apparatchiks of Eastern Europe, who had influence within their countries. By the mid-1970s, though, the apartheid issue and the Cold War were to trigger a wave of boycotts in which, in the television era, the huge symbolic force of the Games became clearer and more dramatic than ever before. It is striking that it was in this period that the appointment of Juan Antonio Samaranch as IOC President was made. Samaranch was the most ambassadorial of presidents, using his own diplomatic background and delicate utilisation of the art of public tact and private pressure to preserve and enhance the power of the IOC. He was also to be responsible for a ruthless IOC revolution, removing the obstacle of the term 'amateur' from the constitution, dispensing with long-serving Secretary Monique Berlioux and working with Horst Dassler of Adidas to transform the system of selling sponsorships. The new president had doubtless learned about ruthlessness in the pursuit of political ends in his earlier career. In November 1967 he had been on his knees in front of the fascist General Franco, taking the oath of office prior to becoming a National Councillor (see Boix *et al.* 1994, picture on rear cover). Samaranch, it appears, was a loyal supporter of the Spanish fascists and remained so right up to Franco's death in 1975, just five years before he assumed the presidency of the IOC (see Jennings 1996; Jennings and Sambrook 2000).

NOTES

1 Of the 70 IOC members in 1936, here are some examples. After the Games, Count Baillet Latour became an honorary member of the Nazi sports organization. Count Clarence von Rosen, Master of the Horse to the King of Sweden, was involved in the Swedish Nazi movement. Lord Aberdare opposed the boycott and claimed he had never heard of any Olympic athlete being boycotted or impeded because of his non-Aryan origin. Sir Noel Curtis-Bennett said those advocating a boycott were 'a lot of well-meaning busybodies who try to mix sport and politics'. Dr Karl Ritter von Halt was a sport official in Nazi Germany. Marquis Melchior de Polignac was involved in collaborationist organisations with the Nazi occupiers during the Second World War. Francois Piétri was the Vichy ambassador to Spain from 1940 to 1944. Jewish labourers from a local concentration camp worked on estates in Austria owned by the family of Prince Francois-Joseph von Liechtenstein. William May Garland was a founder

193

member of the exclusive Jonathan Club in California, which did not admit men of colour until 1987.
2 www.meor1996.org.

FURTHER READING

Allison, L. (ed.) (1993) *The Changing Politics of Sport*, Manchester: Manchester University Press.
Charpentier, H. and Boissonnade, E. (1999) *La Grande Histoire des Jeux Olympiques*, Paris: Editions France-Empire.
Hill, C. (1992) *Olympic Politics*, London: Manchester University Press.
Tomlinson, A. and Young, C. (eds) (2006) *National Identity and Global Sports Events*, Albany: State University of New York Press.

CHAPTER 9

POLITICS AND THE OLYMPICS

It is often thought that the English journalist and author George Orwell condemned sport outright as simply 'war minus the shooting' (see Davison 1998: 442). He certainly did not think it was a great means by which to solve problems in international relations. But he also recognised that it was not the cause of such problems: 'big scale sport is itself, I think, merely another effect of the causes that have produced nationalism' (Davison 1998: 442–443). Orwell was writing just after Moscow Dynamo (a team of Soviet soldiers) had played a series of matches in Britain, in 1945, shortly after the end of the Second World War. His closing point was that 'you do make things worse by sending forth a team of eleven men, labelled as national champions, to do battle against some rival team, and allowing it to be felt on all sides that whichever nation is defeated will "lose face"' (Davison 1998: 443). Whether we entirely accept his analysis or not, we can see that Orwell was acutely aware of the *symbolic* politics of sport.

Despite Rule 50.2 in the 2015 version of the Olympic Charter, which states that 'No kind of demonstration or political, religious or racial propaganda is permitted in any Olympic sites, venues or other areas' (IOC 2015: 93), the modern Olympic movement has had to contend with wars, boycotts, protests, walkouts and even a terrorist attack (Sadd 2014). As the Olympics have become a global televisual event, it has become more available for symbolic political action. From the late 1960s onwards the Olympic Games have been caught up in symbolic politics, taking two main forms: the *promotional* opportunities offered by the Games to enhance reputations – by competing, winning medals and hosting them, as well as refusing to participate in them through different forms of boycott – and the opportunity to *protest* about a perceived social injustice by 'seizing the platform' that the Games offer through such a globally mediated mega-event (Price 2008). In addition, the Games have developed amidst changes in economic ideologies – from state-led, mixed economies to privatised neo-liberal economic orthodoxies.

As the previous chapter indicated, in the period between 1968 and 1984 the Olympic Games became the site of more highly focused symbolic political contestation in which the boycott became a significant political weapon.[1] This chapter examines the promotional and protest politics of the Games by focusing on three main trends in international relations and political economy: the emergence of boycotts and political theatre, particularly between the 1960s and the end of the 1980s; the growth of national and place promotion as a form of reputational politics; and the growth of the Olympics as an economic investment opportunity, as neo-liberalism increasingly became the 'common sense' of international political economy from the 1980s onwards. These trends are in tension and overlap, so that, for example, the 1984 Summer Olympics in Los Angeles can be seen to illustrate each of them. At the same time, focusing initially on events such as the Black Power salutes in the 1968 Olympic Games in Mexico which triggered a period of boycotts and political theatre (in 1976, 1980 and 1984), we seek to highlight the process whereby that form of politics has largely been marginalised in favour of promotional politics in more recent Games. This chapter thus continues to explore the international political and economic context that shaped the politics of the Games from the 1960s onwards, while also identifying the development of the politics of legacy and sustainability mentioned in earlier chapters.

POLITICS AT THE GAMES

It is possible to describe the politics at the Olympic Games in terms of a number of different contrasts and features. According to Toohey and Veal (2007: 87–118), for example, there have been several different forms of political *interference* in the Olympic Games: *internal politics* within the nation where the Olympics are being staged; *international rivalries*, based on either different political or ideological disputes and the use of the Games to advance national agendas; competitors using the Games as a forum for *political demonstrations* against their national governments; non-participants using the Games to *further their political causes*; participating nations trying to equate Olympic success with their *social, economic and political superiority*; and *politics within the IOC* impacting on Olympic policy. It is easy to illustrate these.

As we have seen in the previous chapter, the Games awarded to Berlin in 1916 provided the earliest example of the second type of political situation facing the Olympic Games. When the First World War began in 1914, pressure was exerted by the Allied powers to move the Games. As the Games could not be relocated to an alternative site they were cancelled, for the first time in the history of the modern Games, although they continue to be counted officially by the IOC as the sixth (VI) Olympic Games. Berlin in 1936 was the location of the infamous 'Nazi Games'. Problems stemmed from the issue of discrimination against Jews in Germany under the Nazi regime. To compensate for the growing world opposition, the Nazis spared no effort in their preparations.

The 1936 Olympic Games were intentionally awarded to Berlin so that Germany could show that it had regained its status among European countries. With the Nazis in power, however, Adolf Hitler used the event as a platform to demonstrate his theories about racial superiority. Although the 'Nazi Games' were a very powerful propaganda exercise, the attempt to claim Aryan superiority through athletic performance failed, as African-American Jesse Owens became the hero of the Games, winning four gold medals. During the long jump competition, Owens' German rival, Luz Long, publicly befriended him in front of the Nazis. Long was killed during the Second World War, but Owens kept in touch with his family for many years after the war.

Following the war, the 1948 Olympics in London took on a greater political significance as participation came to symbolise political recognition and legitimacy. Germany and Japan were not invited to London because of their wartime roles, while the Soviet Union was invited but did not participate. To limit Britain's responsibility to feed the athletes, it was agreed that the participants would bring their own food. No new facilities were built, but Wembley stadium had survived the war and proved adequate. The male athletes were housed in a Royal Air Force camp in Uxbridge and the women were housed at Southlands College (now part of Roehampton University) in dormitories. The 1948 London Games were the first to be shown on television, although very few people in Britain yet owned sets. Though there had been much debate as to whether or not to hold the 1948 Olympic Games, and there was concern about the outcome, they turned out to be a popular success. Approximately 4,000 athletes participated, representing 59 countries.[2]

In 1956, Egypt withdrew from the Melbourne Games due to the Suez Canal conflict. The same year, there were revolts in Poland and Hungary against the regime in Moscow, which led to Soviet troops firing on unarmed crowds in Budapest – and fights breaking out between Hungarian and Soviet athletes in Melbourne.

The first Asian country to host the Olympics, Tokyo in 1964, spent $3 billion rebuilding the city to show off its post-war success. Yoshinori Sakai, who was born on the day that Hiroshima was destroyed by an atomic bomb, was chosen as the final torchbearer. Sporting success is often tied to nationalistic attempts to promote social, economic and/or political superiority. Here Olympic medal tables take on the role of describing the outcomes of a proxy war. How successful this is in actually convincing populations of national supremacy or developing national pride is subject to some dispute, however (see Hilvoorde *et al.* 2010).

Finally, the internal make-up and politics of the IOC have impacted on Olympic Games outcomes. As we have shown in Chapter 3, the IOC is a self-elected, self-regulating association and, until 1981, it consisted virtually entirely of men. After evidence of corruption in the 1990s, the IOC felt obliged to investigate the claims. The main reform measures that resulted – to do with the organisation, sport and athlete issues, the host city selection process, financial control and transparency and membership – are also discussed in Chapter 3. The political debate then and since is nicely summed up in the titles of two books published in the 2000s: *The Olympic Turnaround* (Payne 2005) and *The Great Olympic Swindle* (Jennings and Sambrook 2000). On the one hand, the IOC is now seen as efficient, reformed and recovered. On the other hand, it is seen as remaining manipulative, promotional, and not fundamentally reconstructed at all.

THREE TRENDS IN THE POLITICS OF THE GAMES

In this section we attempt to classify the politics of the Olympic Games in the past 50 years. Broadly speaking, we discern three trends: the use of boycotts as a form of political theatre – to abstain, as an individual or group, from engaging with the Olympics or some related organisation as an expression of *protest*; the use of the Olympics for reputation *promotion* (for a cause, a socio-political or economic ideology, or a host city, region or national location); and the development of *neo-liberalism as the common-sense* context for the staging of the Olympic Games. Figure 9.1 outlines recent Olympic Games in terms of their best fit with each of these trends. The rest of this chapter explores the trends and identifies features of each of the Games that illustrate them.

Boycotts and political theatre	Promotional and reputational politics	Neoliberalisation of the Games
1968 Mexico	1972 Munich	1976 Montreal
1980 Moscow	1992 Barcelona	1984 Los Angeles
1984 Los Angeles	2000 Sydney	1996 Atlanta
1988 Seoul	2004 Athens	2012 London
	2008 Beijing	
	2016 Rio de Janeiro	

Figure 9.1 Three trends in the politics of the Olympic Games, 1968–2016.

Boycotts and political theatre at the Olympic Games[3]

Boycotts have occurred at the Olympic Games for three main reasons: as part of the Cold War; because of apartheid, 'race' or imperialism; and in terms of nations being divided by political or ideological differences. As Bairner and Molnar (2010: 163) suggest, however, 'the number of boycotts associated with the Olympics is somewhat ironic as one of the original ideas behind the establishment of the modern Games was to create a free international sporting community that no nation-state would manipulate to its political advantage'. They add: 'Clearly, this aim has not been realized so far.'

As we saw in Chapter 8, it was the Helsinki Games in 1952 that marked the beginning of Cold War tensions. Capitalist West Germany participated for the first time, and the USSR participated in the Olympics for the first time since the Russian Revolution of 1917. The USSR initially planned to house its athletes in Leningrad and fly them into Finland each day. In the end, separate housing facilities for communist/Eastern bloc athletes were set aside. East Germany was denied its request to be included, and a German team made up entirely of West German athletes attended. From 1956 to 1964 the two Germanys were forced to reach their own Olympic truce and compete as a joint team.

As mentioned above and in Chapter 8, three separate protests affected the Melbourne Games in 1956, each in its way related to differences between capitalist and communist

Olympics	Boycott	Explanation/other issues
London 1948		The two major Axis powers of the Second World War, Germany and Japan, were not invited; the Soviet Union was invited but did not send any athletes.
Helsinki 1952	People's Republic of China (PRC)	The PRC was protesting at the Republic of China (Taiwan) being recognised by the IOC – the PRC did not return to Olympic competition until the 1980 Winter Games. The Soviet Union attended for the first time, but East Germany was denied its request to be included and a Germany team made up entirely of West German athletes attended.

Olympics	Boycott	Explanation/other issues
Melbourne 1956	Egypt, Iraq and Lebanon (Suez Crisis); Netherlands, Spain and Switzerland (Soviet Union's invasion of Hungary); People's Republic of China (protesting at the Republic of China (Taiwan) being allowed to compete (under the name 'Formosa').	Egypt was invaded by Israel, the United Kingdom and France after Egypt nationalised the Suez canal; the political frustrations between the Soviet Union and Hungary boiled over during a men's water polo semi-final – the 'blood in the water' match.
Tokyo 1964	Indonesia and North Korea (after the IOC banned teams that took part in the 1963 Games of the New Emerging Forces).	South Africa expelled from the IOC due to apartheid. South Africa would not be invited again until 1992.
Mexico City 1968		'Black Power' salute performed by Tommie Smith and John Carlos, African-American athletes who came first and third in the 200 metres race, during the medal award ceremony. The Tlatelolco massacre, ten days before the Games began – more protesters were shot by government forces.
Munich 1972		Munich massacre – members of the Israeli Olympic team were taken hostage by the Palestinian terrorist group Black September.
Montreal 1976	Tanzania led boycott of 22 African nations.	IOC refused to bar New Zealand, despite the New Zealand rugby union team's tour of South Africa.
Moscow 1980	US President Jimmy Carter issued a boycott of the Games to protest the Soviet invasion of Afghanistan and a total of 62 eligible countries failed to participate.	A substitute event, titled the Liberty Bell Classic (also known as the 'Olympic Boycott Games'), was held at the University of Pennsylvania in Philadelphia by 29 of the boycotting countries.
Lake Placid 1980	The Republic of China (Taiwan) refused to compete under the name of 'Chinese Taipei'.	To date, the only case of boycotting the Winter Olympic Games.
Los Angeles 1984	The Soviet Union and 14 of its allies; Iran and Libya also boycotted the Games.	The Eastern bloc organised its own multi-sport event, the 'Friendship Games'.
Seoul 1988	North Korea; Albania, Cuba, Ethiopia, Madagascar, Nicaragua and the Seychelles.	North Korea was (and still is) technically at war with South Korea.
Sochi 2014	In August 2008, the government of Georgia called for a boycott of the 2014 Winter Olympics; in late 2013 rights activists also called for a boycott on the basis of new Russian legislation related to 'non-traditional' sexual relations.	In response to Russia's participation in the 2008 South Ossetia war. Sochi is within 20 miles of Abkhazia, a disputed territory claimed by Georgia.

Figure 9.2 Boycotts and political issues at selected Olympic Games, 1948–2014.

Sources: Bairner and Molnar (2010); Hill (1996); Toohey and Veal (2007).

countries. The People's Republic of China (PRC) withdrew after the IOC recognised Taiwan, and would not return to the Olympic movement until 1980. Egypt, Iraq and Lebanon protested at Israel's invasion of the Sinai Peninsula, while Spain, Switzerland and the Netherlands boycotted the Games over the Soviet invasion of Hungary. The conflict between the USSR and Hungary erupted during the Games when they faced each other in the water-polo semi-final. The referee abandoned the game after a fierce exchange of kicks and punches. Hungary, leading at the time, was credited with a victory. The match became known as the 'blood in the water' match.

Over 60 nations, including West Germany and Japan, boycotted the Moscow Games in 1980 to protest at the Soviet invasion of Afghanistan. The American-led boycott reduced the number of participating nations from 120 to 81, the lowest number since 1956. Countries such as Britain and France supported the boycott, and the UK government under Margaret Thatcher placed enormous pressure on British athletes not to take part. Because the British Olympic Association (BOA) had no direct government funding it was able to resist and allow athletes to participate if they wished. Partly due to a lack of competition, the Moscow Games became quite successful for the British athletes, who finished ninth overall. The exact number of boycotting nations is difficult to determine, however, as a total of 62 eligible countries failed to participate, but some of those countries withdrew due to financial hardships, only claiming to join the boycott to avoid embarrassment. A substitute event, titled the Liberty Bell Classic (also known as the Olympic Boycott Games), was held at the University of Pennsylvania in Philadelphia by 29 of the boycotting countries.

Following the Western boycott of the 1980 Games, the USSR led a boycott by 14 socialist nations of the 1984 Games based in Los Angeles. The absentees claimed the Los Angeles Olympic Committee was violating the spirit of the Olympics by using the Games to generate commercial profits. The Eastern bloc organised its own multi-sport event, the Friendship Games, instead. For different reasons, Iran and Libya also boycotted the Games. US media tycoon Ted Turner also launched the Goodwill Games following this period. The first Goodwill Games, held in Moscow in 1986, featured 182 events and attracted over 3,000 athletes representing 79 countries. The Games were later bought from Turner by Time Warner Australia, who organised the Brisbane 2001 Games, before announcing that it would be the last.

For the first time since the 1972 Munich Games, there was no organised boycott of the 1988 Olympics in Seoul. North Korea stayed away as it was still technically at war with South Korea, and it was joined by Albania, Cuba, Ethiopia, Madagascar, Nicaragua and the Seychelles. Otherwise the Games went on with little interruption, and their success represented a major milestone on the journey from dictatorship to democracy for South Korea. IOC President Juan Antonio Samaranch seemed to manoeuvre very cleverly to avoid a boycott in 1988 – stringing the North Koreans along with largely empty promises of shared events – for example, the marathon run across the demilitarised zone. With Samaranch appearing as the great conciliator, North Korea appeared to lose most of the support it had.

The 1980s thus saw the second peak of Cold War politics during the Reagan years, and the sudden collapse of the Soviet Union at the end of the decade. The boycotts of 1980 and 1984 required the politicians to struggle quite hard to get support. Hence in 1980 the BOA, not having government funding, was able to resist the pressure of Margaret Thatcher to a certain extent. Similarly in 1984 the Soviets were not able to carry the whole communist bloc with them as they sought to boycott the Los Angeles Games. Arguably this began to discredit the boycott as a weapon – because the Games go on, and no one remembers who was not there.

The Rome Games in 1960 marked the end of South African participation in the Olympic Games for 32 years. The 1960 Olympics also saw the coming to prominence of African-American athletes, such as Wilma Rudolph and Cassius Clay (later to change his name to Muhammad Ali) and also marathon-runner Abebe Bikila, running barefoot, who became the first black African Olympic champion. Free of other major political disruptions, the Rome Games became a showcase for Italy, attracting a record 5,348 athletes from 83 countries. In the 1960s many countries had curtailed their sporting links with South Africa and Rhodesia because of their apartheid policies. In 1963 South Africa was expelled from the Olympics due to apartheid. It would not be invited again until the 1992 Olympics. This expulsion did not, however, immediately apply to the Paralympic Games. South Africa made its Paralympic Games debut in 1964 and continued to compete until 1976.

Despite the existence of boycotts prior to it – for example in 1964 Indonesia and North Korea both withdrew from the Tokyo Games after the IOC decision to ban teams that took part in the 1963 Games of the New Emerging Forces (GANEFO) – arguably it was the Mexico City Games in 1968, and the Black Power demonstration that took place there, that triggered a sustained period of boycotts as political theatre at the Olympics for the next two decades (including 1976, 1980 and 1984).

Before the Mexico City Olympics in 1968, many Mexicans believed that spending large amounts of money in the name of sport was unjustified. Many argued that the money should have been spent on housing or welfare resources instead. Then, ten days before the Opening Ceremony, the most violent response to a demonstration by students about government policy occurred. The Tlatelolco Massacre involved more than 200 protesters being shot by government forces. The Mexico student murders, although largely neglected at the time in the mainstream media and since in most books about the Games (certainly compared to the massive prominence given to the Munich hostage story, see below), contributed to the sense that the Olympics was a politically useful platform that could be 'seized' (Price 2008).

BOX 9.1 THE TLATELOLCO MASSACRE, MEXICO CITY, 1968

The Tlatelolco massacre, also known as the 'Night of Tlatelolco', was a government massacre of student and civilian protesters and bystanders that took place during the afternoon and night of 2 October 1968, in the Plaza de las Tres Culturas in the Tlatelolco section of Mexico City. While at the time government propaganda and the mainstream media in Mexico claimed that government forces had been provoked by protesters shooting at them, government documents that have been made public since 2000 suggest that the snipers had in fact been employed by the government.

New declassified information about the massacre is available thanks to a collaboration between *Proceso* magazine in Mexico and the US National Security Archive. The National Security Archive has investigated the Tlatelolco massacre since 1994 through records obtained under the Freedom of Information Act and archival research in both Mexico and the US. At the time, Mexico was still ruled by the Institutional Revolutionary Party (PRI) and absolute secrecy continued to surround the tragedy at Tlatelolco.

Although estimates of the death toll range from 30 to 1,000, with eyewitnesses reporting hundreds of dead, the Archive's Mexico Project Director Kate Doyle has only been able to find evidence for the death of 44 people. At least information about who died as a result of the ferocious violence unleashed by government forces in the Plaza of the Three Cultures in October 1968 is now available.

(Source: www.gwu.edu/~nsarchiv/NSAEBB/NSAEBB201/
index.htm; last accessed 17 November 2010)

The year 1968 was one of global unrest: Europe was rocked by student protests, the Vietnam War raged on, Martin Luther King and Robert Kennedy were assassinated and the USSR invaded Czechoslovakia. Meanwhile at the Olympics, East Germany competed separately for the first time. Tommie Smith and John Carlos, who finished first and third in the 200 metres, gave the Black Power salute during the US national anthem as a protest against racism in the US. White Australian Peter Norman, who finished second, also wore a badge supporting the same cause as Smith and Carlos, but has mostly been written out of the history of this moment (Osmond 2010).

BOX 9.2 THE BLACK POWER 'SALUTE'

On 16 October 1968, Tommie Smith won the 200-metre race in a world-record time of 19.83 seconds, with Australia's Peter Norman second and John Carlos in third place. The two US athletes received their medals shoeless. Smith wore a black scarf and Carlos had his tracksuit top unzipped. All three athletes wore Olympic Project for Human Rights badges. Both US athletes intended to bring black gloves to the event, but Carlos forgot his. It was Peter Norman who suggested that Carlos wear Smith's left-handed glove, this being the reason for him raising his left hand, as opposed to his right, differing from the traditional Black Power salute. When the US national anthem – 'The Star-Spangled Banner' – played, Smith and Carlos delivered the salute with heads bowed, a gesture that became front-page news around the world. That such a relatively small gesture could create such a response paved the way to the Olympics becoming a major platform for the playing out of political theatre for at least the next two decades (for more details see Carlos with Zirin (2011); Waller *et al.* (2012); Harvey *et al.* (2014: 72–76)).

The Olympic Games as promotional opportunity:
from boycotts to boosterism

The largest Games staged to date at the time was the 1972 Olympics in Munich, West Germany. Twenty-seven years after the Second World War, the Games were supposed to represent peace. Despite the iconic architecture, and with competitions well under way, the Munich Games are most often remembered for the terrorist attack that resulted in the death of 11 Israeli athletes. With five days of the Games to go, eight Palestinian terrorists belonging to the Black September group broke into the Olympic Village, killing two Israelis and taking nine other members of the Israeli Olympic team hostage. The Palestinians demanded the release of 200 prisoners from Israel. In an ensuing battle, all nine Israeli hostages were killed, as were five of the terrorists and one policeman. IOC President Avery Brundage took the decision to continue the Games after a 34-hour suspension. Seventeen people were killed in total, but it is still unclear what actually happened in the shoot-out. Key questions still remain unanswered satisfactorily, including: Who killed the Israeli hostages? The police or the hostage-takers? IOC President Brundage was pilloried for stating that 'the Games must go on', but could he have done otherwise? What would another IOC president do in similar circumstances?

In Montreal in 1976 around 30 African nations staged a last-minute boycott after the IOC allowed New Zealand to compete. Some of the teams withdrew after the first day. New Zealand's All Blacks rugby team had recently played in the racially segregated South Africa, which had been banned from the Olympics since 1964. The controversy prevented a much anticipated meeting between Tanzanian Filbert Bayi – the former world record holder in both the 1,500 metres and the mile – and New Zealand's John Walker, who had surpassed both records to become the new world record holder. Walker went on to win the gold medal in the 1,500 metres.

Taiwan also withdrew when communist China pressured Canada (its trading partner) to deny the Taiwanese the right to compete. In Montreal in 1976 the high cost and construction of facilities for the Games attracted criticisms. The event began and concluded with many unfinished facilities. Partly in response to this the internal politics of the Olympics in Canada have been hard fought ever since. In Toronto a group opposing a bid, Bread not Circuses, was formed and became one of the strongest anti-Olympic organisations in the world. It lobbied against Toronto's 1996 and 2008 Olympic Games bids and the Vancouver bid for the 2010 Winter Games. Bread not Circuses argued that the perceived profits from the event were only short-term 'economic steroids'. Some local politicians argued that Toronto should apply to host the 2024 Summer and Paralympic Games in the wake of hosting the 2015 Pan American Games. When the deadline for submitting bids passed in September 2015, however, Toronto was not among the bidding cities and the city mayor cited 'other priorities' (BBC Sport 2015).

The period 1988–1992 was a watershed in the shift from boycott to 'boosterism' at the Olympic Games. Barcelona in 1992 was and continues to be seen as a huge success, especially for urban redevelopment, thus inaugurating the idea of (and emphasis on) the Games as a tool for boosterism – urban promotion, (re-)design and legacy. The 1992 Barcelona Games also marked the first Olympic Summer Games since the end of the Cold

War. Latvia, Lithuania and Estonia fielded separate teams, while the rest of the former Soviet Union competed as the 'Unified Team'. Germany competed under one flag for the first time since 1964, while post-apartheid South Africa (including Nelson Mandela) was invited, ending a 32-year ban.

The neo-liberalisation of the Games

In many ways, the Los Angeles Games of 1984 were the tipping point in the shift to the next phase of the politics of the Olympics. The 1984 Games figure in two columns in Figure 9.1 under 'boycotts' and 'neo-liberalisation'. After Montreal in 1976 a critique of quasi-Keynesian government policy approaches in the advanced capitalist economies, including sports mega-events, began to develop. A new economic orthodoxy began to emerge – referred to in the UK as Thatcherism and in the US as Reaganomics – which emphasised the failure of state-produced solutions to social and economic problems (including the staging of Olympic Games) and which instead valorised the hosting of more privatised Games (Gruneau and Neubauer 2012). Explicitly ideological, this approach impacted on the 1984 Games in a way which made popular capitalism and neo-liberalism the common sense of the rest of the 1980s and since. The collapse of 'actually existing socialism' and the demise of the USSR by the end of the 1980s complemented this development. Rather than reprise the old Cold War antagonisms, the politics of hosting the Olympics now revolved around boosters and sceptics involved in debates over the branding and promotion of cities as 'world class' destinations, and the politics of environmental sustainability and legacy. Critics and sceptics now had to find different ways of seizing the platform. The Los Angeles Games were not only a pivotal moment in the evolution of the Olympics, they also helped to legitimate a sweeping neo-liberal political project in the US, with influences that have been felt across the globe since then (Gruneau and Neubauer 2012).

While the bombing of electricity pylons was undertaken in an attempt to interrupt the Barcelona Opening Ceremony, nevertheless the 1992 Games are always heralded as a success. They presented the idea to the world that the Olympics could be used to channel the aspirations of other cities and regions to redevelop and refashion huge parts of their territory. The age of urban and regional 'boosterism', linked to notions of legacy, environment and sustainability, was born. Based upon ideas that the collective public interest would best be served by urban entrepreneurialism and wealth creation via trickle-down economics, the politics of redistribution gave way to a politics of recognition, or identity politics. The neo-liberalisation of cities, matched by a similar political and economic development in the hosting of the Olympic Games (as discussed in Chapter 5), involves urban restructuring and illustrates well what Harvey (2008) has called 'accumulation by dispossession'. As local communities are displaced, and their right to the city threatened, resentment and anger against corporate power and wealth can develop. How this manifests itself, though, is not predictable (Watt 2013).

The neo-liberalisation of the Olympics has involved: governance structures bypassing local municipal political structures; indirect public subsidies going to the IOC – since national public resources have to be spent in support of and with the promise of showcasing 'world

204

class' events; and other attempts to enhance the reputational status and attractiveness of host locations, while cutbacks have occurred elsewhere in public spending and investment. The IOC retain control of the newly commercialised Games while OCOGs and national governments bear the risk, especially the financial and security risks. Cities bid to host the Games as a means of public diplomacy, and national governments use the opportunity to operate forms of soft power.

It was in this way that the Atlanta Games in 1996 were held without any governmental support. This led to a commercialisation of the Games and the extensive involvement of corporate money in it was 'ambivalently perceived' (Bairner and Molnar 2010: 155). In addition, a pipe bomb exploded in Atlanta's Centennial Olympic Park on 27 July 1996, during the Games, killing two people and injuring a further 110. Although the incident was referred to as a terrorist bomb, the motive or group responsible was never determined. Approximately 10,000 athletes participated in Atlanta, representing 197 countries (including Hong Kong and the Palestinian Authority). The choice of Atlanta saw the commercially driven modernisers/neo-liberalisers win out over tradition. The problems with Atlanta, and then with corruption, appear to have led to a shame-faced IOC voting to give the 2004 Summer Olympics to Greece.

The Sydney Games in 2000 were the largest ever, with 10,651 athletes competing in 300 events. Despite its size, the event was well organised and renewed faith in the Olympic movement after the 1996 Atlanta bombing. The Australians chose Aboriginal athlete and national hero Cathy Freeman to light the Olympic torch. In 2004 the Olympic Games returned to its origins when Athens hosted the XXVIII Olympiad. Greece was the birthplace of the ancient Olympic Games more than 2,000 years ago, and Athens staged the first modern Olympic Games in 1896. However, 2004 was the most guarded Olympic Games in history and the biggest – and most expensive – peacetime security operation ever (see Chapter 12 for a discussion of security at the Olympics).

The 2008 Games, staged in Beijing, provoked outrage from human rights groups who said that allowing China to host the Games legitimised its repressive regime. Protesters also claimed that China would use the Games as a propaganda tool. Supporters of the Games argued that the Olympics would accelerate the progress of social liberalisation in China. Taiwan government officials strongly supported the Beijing Games, believing that the event would reduce the risk of China using force against its neighbour. Arguably, the choice of Beijing as host was over-determined by political and economic judgements – Tiananmen Square may have happened in 1989, but by the 2000s China was a very big and growing market.

Ironically it was the attempt to use the Olympic torch relay as a global rallying call – and at the same time as an opportunity for sponsors to be seen to be associated with the Olympics – that proved most costly to the image of the Beijing Olympics. The torch relay opened the door for conflict and thus brought back political theatre to the Games (Horne and Whannel 2010). While in Beijing the organisers of the Games were using 'One World One Dream' as one of their key slogans, around the world the torch was followed by protests – about human rights in China and the relationship between China and Tibet – as the photographs taken during the London leg in April 2008 show.

Figure 9.3 The battle of the flags. The 2008 Summer Games, staged in Beijing, provoked outrage from human rights groups who said that allowing China to host the Games legitimised its repressive regime. Here the flags of Tibet and China vie for position in Central London during the torch relay in April 2008.

Figure 9.4 Tibet and China clash. Protesters and counter-demonstrators make their case during the 2008 torch relay in Central London in April 2008.

Sport mega-events, political contestation and consumer culture

We have discussed the build-up to Rio 2016 and the aftermath of London 2012 at the beginning of this book. Both illustrate the different forms of political contestation that the contemporary Olympics attract (Horne 2016). These range from the politics of rights – of

206

workers and citizens to the city – to debates about the politics of legacy discourse. The politics of public opposition and political activism to London 2012 and other recent Olympics have been considered elsewhere (Sadd 2014; Giulianotti *et al.* 2014; Boykoff 2014a, 2014b). The growing disinclination to act as hosts for the Olympics and other sports mega-events since then – including the four cities withdrawing their candidacy from the Winter Olympic Games and Edmonton withdrawing from a bid to host the Commonwealth Games – has led some commentators to ask where sports mega-events are going (Grix 2014).

Part of the answer is that while sport, and sports mega-events such as the Olympics especially, may appear superficially as credible tools of social and economic development, many scholars, politicians and citizens have come to realise that they do so in ways that do not challenge inequalities or neo-liberal policies. As Zimbalist (2015: 122) writes: 'Hosting sports mega-events, then, tends to reinforce the existing power structure and patterns of inequality.' In fact, the hosting of sports mega-events may have been a most convenient shell for the promotion of neo-liberal agendas, since they do not deviate from top-down notions of economic and social development.

The shift of the two biggest sports events organisers, the IOC and FIFA, towards holding mega-events in the 'global South' (South Africa in 2010, Brazil in 2014 and Rio in 2016) and developing market economies (Russia, the Winter Olympics in Sochi in 2014 and hosting the Football World Cup in 2018) connects with recent attempts to link sport and social development.[4] But mega-events in the South are compromised by the weaker position of the host countries to bear the burden of hosting and the opportunity costs being relatively much higher than in the advanced economies (Darnell 2010). In this way they highlight the contradictions of the contemporary politics of the Olympic Games.

Much recent writing on sport has shown how the three main features of contemporary capitalism – globalisation, commodification and inequality – shape and contour contemporary sport and sports mega-events, such as the Olympics. Featherstone (2007: xviii) has noted that 'if there is an emergent global culture, consumer culture has to be seen as a central part of this field'. For Featherstone, in these circumstances consumption cannot be seen as an 'innocent act', but rather as 'part of the chains of interdependencies and networks which bind people together across the world in terms of production, consumption and the accumulation of risks'. Studying sport and especially sports mega-events under such circumstances focuses on the way they have become transnational cultural forms in and through which consumer culture is fuelled. With sports mega-events, two features of consumer culture are highlighted: *transformation* and *consumerisation*. Mike Featherstone (2007: xxi) remarks that central to consumer culture is the transformation of 'lifestyle, living space, relationships, identities, and, of course, bodies'. It was noticeable that 'transformation' was a key element in Rio's bid to host the 2016 Olympics and was maintained in the merchandising afterwards (Figure 9.5). We argue that consumerisation – the process of the construction of people with consumer values and outlooks – has impacted on personal and collective identities and the development of new lifestyles (Horne 2006).

Consumer culture itself has a developmental history of transformations, and as Lee (1993: 135) suggests, the growing importance of cultural and service markets since the 1970s

Figure 9.5 'Transformação' merchandise for Rio 2016'.

BOX 9.3 BUILDING BRICS BY BUILDING STADIA

The acronym 'BRIC' (standing for Brazil, Russia, India, China) was coined in 2001 by the Goldman Sachs economic consultant Jim O'Neill ('Building better global economic BRICs', Goldman Sachs, Global Economics Paper No. 66, 30 November 2001). The term has since been extended to include South Africa (hence BRICS) and become a common umbrella term in business, media, academic and government rhetoric about the future potential of these 'emerging giants', in particular the threat/ opportunity that these economies present to the developed world. The regionalised perspective of BRICS encourages a commodified picture of these countries around major risks/opportunities: investment, global hegemony and social transformation. The BRICS can be seen as the West/North's dream of a new East/South with geopolitical status and power to rival the developed world. Indeed, much BRICS discourse echoes Cold War rhetoric (for more detail on the BRICS see Bond and Garcia 2015).

208

Consideration of individual BRICS and mega-events, and associated media representations, reveal four main challenges around consumption, construction, containment and communication:

1 *Consumption*: sport (and sports mega-events) becomes a central rather than peripheral cultural form in the growth and spread of capitalist consumer cultures – tourism, consumerisation and global visitor destinations. This creates an issue about the possibility of *under-consumption* – are the Games really that popular?

2 *Construction*: designing, building, engineering, sustaining 'iconic' facilities prompts the traditional questions: Will the facilities be ready on time? At the stated costs? And of adequate standard? Will the facilities be more a form of monumentalism, reflecting wider international political and economic power relationships, than a contribution to the communities where they are built? (see Horne 2007b).

3 *Containment*: security and surveillance technologies connected with sports mega-events were a developing market before 9/11. Social control and surveillance may be important, but for whom? And of whom? As with other major sports events in South America, great preparations over security have been evident during the build up to the two mega-events held in Brazil in 2014 and 2016 (McLeod-Roberts 2007).

4 *Communication*: reaching the world audience; managing the message. What happens when things go wrong? The perils of media coverage of countries in the South to the North, and East to the West, have been explored by Dimeo and Kay (2004) and Horne and Manzenreiter (2012). Studies have demonstrated that developing countries run several risks when hosting large events, not least of which is being portrayed negatively in the global media. Coverage of events in developing nations is always prone to negative responses when something goes wrong.

has represented a dematerialisation of the commodity form and the growth of 'experiential commodities' including cultural events, heritage attractions, theme parks, commercialised sport and other public spectacles. Echoing Harvey (1989), Lee concludes that the rapid growth of these experiential commodities represented a 'push to accelerate commodity values and turnovers' (Lee 1993: 20) and 'make more flexible and fluid the various opportunities and moments of consumption' (Lee 1993: 137). Hence the last two decades of the twentieth century saw the restless search for novel ways to expand markets in the advanced capitalist economies and develop new ones elsewhere. Lee (1993: 131) suggests that this explains the spread of consumerism to the rest of the world, the development of a vast children's market and 'the deeper commercial penetration and commodification of the body, self and identity'. Sport has been part of this transformation and sports mega-events have been transformed in turn.

Consumption for symbolic purposes and status value might be thought to be the preserve of the affluent in the advanced capitalist countries. Indeed, substantial numbers of the world's population – including between one-third and one-quarter of those people who live in the advanced capitalist countries – are mainly interested in consumption for material provision rather than 'for show'. Yet the idea of consuming goods for their symbolic value as much as if not more than for their use value is not restricted to these post-industrial societies. By the end of the twentieth century consumerism had spread as a global 'culture-ideology' mainly for two reasons (Sklair 2002: 108ff.): first, capitalism has entered a globalising phase and, second, the technical and social relations that structure the mass media have 'made it very easy for new consumerist lifestyles to become the dominant motif' (Sklair 2002: 108). Hence '"consumerism" may influence even the symbolic life of the poor' (Bocock 1994: 184) and sport is one means of bringing this about.

Of course, contemporary sport is not simply a set of commercial media spectacles, even if it often seems that way. Sport as an active practice continues to be undertaken and played by millions more participants than the relatively small number of elite athletes whose performances are routinely broadcast on national and, increasingly, international media networks. In addition, many more people than actually participate in it *follow* any particular sport. Popular involvement in sport is one of the major accomplishments of the 100 or so years since modern sport was established. But sport is not naturally followed any more than people naturally go shopping. Sport consumers and audiences are *made*, not born.

Sport *consumerisation* appears initially to have relied upon local and national affiliations. Globalisation has offered the opportunity to expand this process of consumerisation, and the mass media of communications have played a major role in the creative process whereby sport is transformed. In turn, as mediated sport has become an accepted part of everyday life-worlds, it has also come to have an influence on consumption choices and aspirations for particular consumer goods and lifestyles. Hence sport today – especially through a focus on large-scale ('mega') mediated events and celebrity accomplishments – plays a major role in the maintenance of consumer culture, through marketing, advertising and other promotional strategies.

The crisis of capitalist financial regulation in 2007 and 2008 – in which vast sums of public money were used to support banking and other financial institutions floundering after the poor judgements and speculative dealings by private financiers – is a useful reminder that government intervention to support and maintain capitalism is not an aberration. Whether it is more appropriate to describe this new phase in the development of neo-liberalism 'disaster capitalism', based on the 'shock doctrine' (Klein 2007; Loewenstein 2015) or 'celebration capitalism' (Boykoff 2014a), it is undeniable that economic regimes of the contemporary era increasingly use, or formulate, crises to reshape the economy in the interests of business.

The Olympic Games clearly provide a positive, uplifting, even inspiring diversion during times like these and some would argue therefore that there should be more serious and pressing topics for a social scientist to research. Boykoff (2014a) argues, however, that the processes and politics of hosting sports mega-events are precisely a manifestation of a globalised 'celebration capitalism', whereby public resources are made available to private

210

interests and for private benefit. Darnell and Millington (2016) suggest, however, that there are important points of continuity between neo-liberalism and celebration capitalism. The notion of celebration capitalism helps to explain the successful re-inscription of neo-liberal development philosophy in the new millennium. If the logic and policies of neo-liberalism have retained their hegemonic status despite events such as the 2008 financial crisis, this is likely due to a reinvention of neo-liberal logic in ways that have built consent within the current context. Celebration capitalism through sports mega-events may therefore signal less of a break from neo-liberalism, and more the latest, 'improved', version of neo-liberal policy.

CONCLUSION

As this chapter (and the book as a whole) suggests, the Olympic Games are a global spectacle attracting vast audiences, but also a deeply political phenomenon. Researching the costs and benefits of sports mega-events is itself a political activity. It can involve researching the powerful – the elite of business leaders and government officials – as well as leaders of sports organisations who gather together to formulate hosting bids or to stage events after a successful bid has been made. It can also involve research into the ongoing activities of organisations more sceptical of the benefits of the event which are themselves investigating the claims made by mega-event promoters or 'boosters'.

It is difficult to accept that the politics of the Olympic Games should be understood as a continuing form of imperial power, as Brohm (1978) once suggested. Today, the politics of the Olympics revolves around such issues as containment – terrorism, security, surveillance and civil rights associated with restrictions on freedom of movement and expression – and human rights and rights to freedom from eviction and to adequate housing (Harvey *et al.* 2014; Kuhn 2015). Such issues came to prominence during the Beijing Olympiad – for example, the protests surrounding the torch relay in 2008 (Horne and Whannel 2010), but also affected several thousand people in London associated with the 2012 Games, and will continue into 2016 in Brazil with the Rio Olympics and beyond. The tensions between the politics of redistribution and the politics of recognition remain a part of these developments and are explored in Chapter 11.

NOTES

1 At the same time American athlete Leahseneth ('Lacey') O'Neal coined the less widely used term 'girlcott'. Speaking for black women athletes, she advised that the group would not 'girlcott' the Olympic Games as they were still focused on being recognised (www.sports-reference.com/olympics/athletes/on/lacey-oneal-1.html [last accessed 19 August 2010]).
2 See, for example, this newspaper report from the time: www.guardian.co.uk/politics/ 1948/jul/29/past.comment (last accessed 25 October 2010).
3 As with much of this book, the focus of this chapter is on the Summer Olympic Games. We hope to remedy this in future work. The Winter Olympics have not had so many instances of boycotts, although at the 1980 Winter Olympics, Taiwan (referring to itself as the Republic of China, ROC) refused to compete under the name of 'Chinese Taipei'.

It is the only case of boycotting the Winter Olympic Games. In August 2008, however, the government of Georgia called for a boycott of the 2014 Winter Olympics, held in Sochi, Russia, in response to Russia's participation in the 2008 South Ossetia war. Sochi is within 20 miles of Abkhazia, a disputed territory claimed by Georgia. In 2013 and 2014 calls were also made to boycott the Sochi Olympics on the basis of new legislation in Russia placing restrictions on expressions of non-heterosexual sexual preferences (see Boykoff 2016 for further discussion).

4 On the IOC webpage 'Olympism in Action' promises to build 'a better world through sport' (www.olympic.org/olympism-in-action [last accessed 25 September 2015]).

FURTHER READING

Boykoff, J. (2014) *Activism and the Olympics: Dissent at the Games in Vancouver and London*, New Jersey: Rutgers University Press.

Hayes, G. and Karamichas, J. (eds) (2012) *Olympic Games, Mega-Events, and Civil Societies: Globalisation, Environment, and Resistance*, Basingstoke: Palgrave.

Horne, J. (2016) 'Sports mega-events: three sites of contemporary political contestation', *Sport in Society*. DOI: 10.1080/17430437.2015.1088721

CHAPTER 10

FESTIVAL, SPECTACLE, CARNIVAL AND CONSUMPTION

In 1984 one of us wrote 'the Olympic Games cannot be both a television spectacle and a people's festival' (Whannel 1984: 41). It was a polemical point made by a young man, and clearly the Olympic Games as a cultural practice embraces aspects of both festival and spectacle. Yet the challenge does point to the different visions of the Olympic Games, the tensions between them, and the difficulty of holding on to both festival and spectacle in the same globalised mega-event. For most, the London Olympics of 2012 were an occasion for partying, picnicking and just happily milling-around, but were also surrounded by security fences, gates, scanners, cameras, sensors, comprehensive databases and hazard profiles. As with previous Games, a significant proportion of the tickets for the major events were parcelled out to the 'Olympic family', including their corporate friends, sponsors, media organisations, VIPs and celebrities. It was not promising terrain for a people's party. However, the presence of such a major event in a big city did have a galvanising effect – people wanted to celebrate and party. The Olympic Games were not confined to stadia, but were viewed in homes, bars, malls and parks, where an atmosphere of festivity and jollity did develop. The Olympic Park became a festive cockpit. There were spontaneous events, informal celebrations, casual merry-making and carnivalesque costumes.

In advance of the Games, the portents for joyous people's festivity were not especially encouraging. During construction, the Olympic Park became the site of symbolic contestation. The Park was surrounded by a high blue fence, some miles in length, which was utilised by graffiti artists and local artist groups who adorned it with various acts of creativity. In response, the ODA reportedly introduced a daily patrol, in which a man cycled around the perimeter fence, phoning in reports of any outbreaks of art or vandalism, depending on one's perspective. A quad bike would then set off, driven by a man with a pot of blue paint, who would erase the damage and restore the pristine blueness. As the Olympic project developed, the fence began to be decorated with 'official' artwork, some from local schools, and sponsors' banners began to appear. So, in the spirit of maintaining the blueness, some local artists took to painting over the sponsors' banners with their own pot of blue paint. (For discussion of the reaction of people to the Olympic experience, see Cohen 2013; Powell and Marrero-Guillamón 2012; Perryman 2013).

One of the sites of wider festivity was supposed to be the 'Cultural Olympiad'. In the UK, the Cultural Olympiad encountered problems. When the Olympic budget was first planned, large National Lottery sums were redirected from the arts to the Olympic project.

Figure 10.1 The Blue Fence, with its mixed messages of 'welcome' and 'keep out', neatly catching some of the contradictions of the Olympic project.

The impact of this was to produce hostility to the Olympics among the arts community, which initially responded in lukewarm fashion to the invitation to contribute to the Cultural Olympiad. Those organisers who pursued the possibility of Olympic-related projects found that funding was limited, that they were not able to approach competitors to the existing Olympic sponsors, that most sponsorship opportunities were already taken up by the Olympic Organising Committee, and that the brief and the mission were ill-defined and uninspired. In addition, the project appeared to have little resonance with the British public – up to 2010 only 2 per cent of the British population had even heard of it (Collins and Palmer 2012: 138). Despite these problems, the Cultural Olympiad was able to regroup, build momentum and, in the end, mount a wide-ranging programme of events, which, according to their evaluation, were experienced by a large portion of the population (see Garcia 2013).

The IOC certainly make grand claims for it being the largest celebration of culture and the arts in the history of the modern Olympic and Paralympic Games. In the years leading up to the Games, more than 14 million people participated in or attended cultural events across the UK. Nearly 170,000 people attended 8,300 cultural workshops on various art forms. The Cultural Olympiad drew the participation of 25,000 artists representing all 204 NOCs. The Cultural Olympiad culminated with the 12-week London 2012 Festival, which drew 19.5 million people, including 16.5 million attendances at free events. More than three million people paid to participate in London 2012 Festival events, including more than 1,450,000 who attended museum and gallery exhibitions and over 600,000 people who attended events, performances and exhibitions as part of the World Shakespeare Festival. Performances included 130 world premieres and 85 UK premieres (IOC 2012).

And yet, one wonders how many of these experiences were genuinely moving, challenging or memorable. There is a marked tendency for official Cultural Olympiad events to be affirmative rather than interrogative. One of the stranger manifestations of the cultural dimension illustrates a rather uncomfortable attempt to manage Olympism in the age of

214

commercial sponsorship: the Coubertin Olympic Awards Competition, run by the International Pierre de Coubertin Committee and the Institute of Business Ethics, offers an annual essay prize. The competition challenges students to write a research essay on how the Olympic ideals of fairness, integrity and openness can help businesses balance commercial success with their social responsibilities.[1] Here, once again, the contradictions and tensions at the heart of the Olympic movement are at work – the address to idealism harnessed to the public relations (PR) needs of corporate capitalism and the Olympic sponsors.

The most interesting art may well have been generated not by the Cultural Olympiad but by the responses of artists to the Olympic construction site between 2006 and 2012 (see Powell and Marrero-Guillamón 2012). The art documented in this book, and the discussion of visual representation, space and politics in it, appears to us far more interesting than any of the activities seen or read about that were included in the Cultural Olympiad, which seemed, by contrast, largely affirmative and celebratory – loath to allow any flies in the ointment, spanners in the works or grit in the machinery.

The imperatives of security tend to push organising committees towards a suspicion of the general public, who are perceived more as an element that needs to be controlled, channelled and organised, rather than as active participants whose spontaneity can contribute to the festivity. At major sporting events, authorities often provide giant screens for the many people who do not have tickets. This has the merit, from the perspective of social control, of encouraging the corralling of people in specific areas that can be more conveniently policed.

Figure 10.2 The Water Cube, Beijing 2008. Olympic building is increasingly concerned to be 'iconic', but security needs often mean that non-ticket holders are restricted to a distant view.

215

Figure 10.3 The main stadium, Beijing 2008. The new spectacular style of public space: this could be an arts centre, a museum or a shopping mall. Space for festivity, temple of spectacle and consumption, or both?

Even in Beijing, screens were established around the city. In the last few days before the 2008 Games, though, there appeared to be a loss of nerve regarding street crowds. Many (although not all) of the live screens reportedly remained blank during the Opening Ceremony. Chinese citizens were urged to stay off the streets and watch the Opening Ceremony at home, on television. On the first days of the Games, the 'live' screens in the centre of Beijing were showing, not live sport, but tedious edited highlights of earlier events, including a long sequence of Chinese leaders greeting foreign dignitaries. During London 2012, live screens were available around the country, in parks, bars, public squares and shopping malls. The Westfield shopping mall, one of the largest in Europe, opened in 2011. Cleverly positioned in the space between the Olympic Park and the two stations (Stratford and Stratford International) that serve it, the mall was, metaphorically and literally, the gateway to the Olympics. We entered and left through the temple of consumption, a temple that is still pulling in the crowds long after the Olympic circus has packed its tents and left (for further discussion of the public sphere in Beijing and London, see Brownell 2013).

The emergence of the modern Olympic Games drew on festival – the Much Wenlock Games were and remain festive in character. As the Games developed so did its rituals,

216

including the spectacle of the Opening and Closing Ceremonies. Before television, of course, these forms of spectacle had a very different character – they were designed for the spectators present in the arena and not for the electronic spectators around the world. This chapter considers the relation between the festive and spectacular aspects of the Olympic movement. First, though, the very terms we are utilising here – festival, spectacle, carnival and consumption – need further examination.

THE FESTIVE, THE SPECTACULAR AND THE CARNIVALESQUE

'Festival' is about festivity and therefore fun. It is by definition exceptional – festival is different from, and interrupts, everyday life. It is celebratory. Often, it required religious sanction. It is also cyclical and recurrent, which gives it a timeless dimension. In this sense the major occasions of sport, cyclical and recurrent, and causes for celebration, are also festive. Festival is collective or communal – the focus is on the shared participatory nature of the experience more than on any particular performance. Yet spectacle and festival are hard to separate entirely. When Walter Benjamin (1999) discusses nineteenth-century shopping arcades and walking in the city, or when Richard Dyer (1978) discusses entertainment, they are referencing communal and shared pleasures, yet also referencing spectacle – whether the spectacle of window shopping or of film viewing. The terms denote, not so much definable objects, as ways of seeing and ways of being. In the second half of the nineteenth century the emergence of branded goods, chain stores and advertising shifted shopping from the functional to the spectacular mode (see Bowlby 1985), and the present-day mall has become a cathedral in which popular leisure and spectacular consumption interact. Festivities typically involve the provision of entertainment, the consumption of food and drink and the retailing of commodities, as well as spontaneous communality.

One common element of festivity is the firework display. Are fireworks spectacle? Fireworks are interesting in that, at their most spectacular, they are conventionally laid on by the authorities as a show, a spectacle. But fireworks also induce a sense of wonder which never dulls. A firework display is, arguably, a form of spectacular entertainment, but an intriguing one. It is all but impossible to represent or relay fireworks. They are transient – gone as soon as they appear. They cannot be represented – they cannot be effectively televised, photographed or even painted – they have to be witnessed in person. No mode of representation can adequately capture the experiential dimension of a firework display. A firework display can be free or admission can be charged – although fireworks are not readily confined within the view of people in a stadium. A firework is a commodity but a firework display resists commodification – it cannot be encompassed within a room, a hall or even a stadium – it is a process and not a product, ephemeral in nature, not open to repetition.

The 'digitally enhanced fireworks' featured in the television coverage of the Beijing 2008 Opening Ceremony caused a huge controversy, in which accusations of fakery were bandied about. Part of the firework display was 'real' and live, but other parts appeared to have been pre-recorded and used to enhance the television image. Such accusations, though, only make sense if one is conceptualising the Olympics as an event that is televised, rather than as a television event. Clearly the Opening Ceremony is precisely a constructed artifice in the tradition of show business, and how it is constructed has always involved smoke and mirrors. One of the authors was in Beijing during the evening of the Opening Ceremony, although not inside the stadium. While there clearly were real fireworks, the full display could not be properly seen either from inside the stadium or from immediately outside it. Fireworks covered a large geographical area. (The previous day, batteries of firework mortars could be seen in various parts of the city, including Tiananmen Square, a few miles south of the Olympic Stadium). Only on television could the whole production, complete with digital augmentation, be properly perceived. Festivity and spectacle are enmeshed on such occasions.

The word 'spectacle' denotes the pleasures involved in watching, and to some extent therefore a relation between an event, performance or object and an observer. In this sense it references a less participatory model of pleasure than does the term 'festivity'. Spectacle has been somewhat under-interrogated – in that it comes laden with two readings. The first, derived from the Roman Circus, is that it was a mere distraction with the purpose of political control, and the second, derived from Guy Debord (1967/1970) is that it performs an ideological role in consumer capitalism. So in leftist critical discourse the term is, almost inevitably, weighted down with strong connotations of negativeness and irredeemability. Broudehoux (2007: 389) argues that 'Beijing's spectacular Olympic preparations have in many ways acted as a propaganda tool and an instrument of pacification to divert popular attention from the shortcomings of China's rapid economic transformation, accompanied by rampant land speculation, corruption, and uneven development'. So spectacle becomes associated with oppression and control, and can be utilised to mask poverty and social exclusion.

The term has acquired, in a range of analytic traditions, a negative character. In diverse writing by Theodor Adorno, Guy Debord, Daniel Boorstin and Jean Baudrillard, spectacle is regarded as ideological, a mode of commodification, as empty and as all-pervasive. Machiavelli, as Kellner (2003) has pointed out, advised the productive use of spectacle for political control. Martin Jay argued that Debord's critique of commodity fetishism is similar to the puritan critique of idolatry (see Frow 1997). MacAloon (2006b) has criticised the tendency for the term 'spectacle' to become a baggy catch-all concept.

The leftist critique of spectacle has certainly been haunted by a tendency to collapse back into one-dimensionalism. Commodification, commercialisation, globalisation and spectacle, even when utilised to analyse complex social contradictions, tend to become merely negative warning signs. There is a need to deconstruct the term 'spectacle'. Kellner, in *Media Spectacle* (2003), refers to mega-spectacle (OJ, 9/11, Princess Diana) but does not offer a clear definitional statement. However, it is surely hard to understand contemporary popular culture without some sense of spectacle. All forms of entertainment that establish some form of distance separation or boundary between performance and audience can be considered as, in part, forms of spectacle. This does not in itself require a negative or pejorative use of the term 'spectacle'. Maurice Roche (2000) has drawn attention to the multi-dimensional character of mega-events – modern and non-modern, national and non-national, mediated and non-mediated. Horne (2011a) also highlights the combination of symbolic and material dimensions, and outlines the way such events function as lightning conductors, accelerating global flows and connections with modernity.

218

The word 'carnival' denotes a special and particular form of festivity. While carnival has an everyday meaning – associated with parades, extravagant costumes and excess – it has been given a more precise meaning in the writing of Bakhtin, especially in *Rabelais and His World* (1965). Carnival in this sense involves inversion, subversion and transgression. Normal power relations are inverted: temporarily, the powerless acquire the trappings of power, while the powerful are mocked or rendered powerless, the established order is subverted, there is a suspension of norms and conventions and laws are transgressed. Carnival has become associated with masks and costumes that reveal the performative aspect of gender roles and sexual relations. Carnival might imply a degree of temporary licence allowed by authority, but often carries the sense of danger and excitement that such authority might be overturned, disobeyed or defied. In Bakhtin's discussion of Rabelais, the world of the carnivalesque is one of spontaneity, informality and irreverence: 'these images are opposed to all that is finished and polished, to all pomposity, to every ready-made solution in the sphere of thought, and world outlook' (Bakhtin 1965: 3).

A key feature of carnival for Bakhtin is the absence of a clear distinction between performers and spectators: carnival 'does not acknowledge any distinction between actors and spectators. Footlights would destroy a carnival, as the absence of footlights would destroy a theatrical performance'. Participation is essential to carnival, which has to be, temporarily, all-embracing, and 'everyone participates because its very idea embraces all the people. While carnival lasts, there is no other life outside it. . . . Such is the essence of carnival, vividly felt by all its participants' (Bakhtin 1965: 7). Discussion of an application of the term carnival can be somewhat utopian: in the Brazilian carnival, although mass participation is a feature, it is also possible to distinguish between performers and spectators, especially now that the floats are paraded through the 90,000-capacity Sambadrome, designed by Neimeyer and built in 1984. So even in its carnivalesque form, festival and spectacle are inevitably enmeshed – there is not a neat distinction to be made between them. All these terms present problems of definition and distinction. All are frequently used in a common-sense manner, in rather vague and general ways (see Manzenreiter's 2006 critical discussion of these terms, especially 'spectacle'; and MacAloon's 1999 critique of 'spectacle').

As discussed in Chapter 6, MacAloon (1999) sees the Olympic Games as a 'modern secular ritual'. He identifies four genres of Olympism as cultural performance – spectacle, festival, ritual and game (MacAloon 1984: 242). In recent years, though, it can be argued that there have also been manifestations of carnivalesque behaviour at major sporting events – face-painting, joke banners, dressing in elaborate costumes and coordinated costumes, often with a degree of arbitrariness (e.g. Viking hats). The Mexican wave, which does not coordinate with and is not a response to on-field action, often arises when the action is dull, and is a reassertion of the primacy of the spectator (we can make our own amusement). This form of behaviour, while it may be amusing and/or disruptive, is plainly not in any deep sense subversive. By contrast, if, as in the situationist slogan, 'revolution is the festival of the oppressed', it can be argued that the carnivalesque character of recent anti-capitalist and anti-globalisation street demonstrations is a more pertinent instance of the political character of carnival than the carnivalesque manifestations at sport events. Boje (2001), for example, refers to the carnival of resistance to globalisation discourse, and Boykoff (2014c) refers to the 'festival of dissent', in which activists from the Homeless Workers

Movement marched on the São Paulo stadium during the 2014 World Cup (also see Chapter 1). A Pew Research poll found that 61 per cent of Brazilians felt the World Cup had used resources better spent on education, health care and social services (Boykoff 2014c). But the oppressed surely deserve a wider concept of festival. Indeed the informal structure, if not anti-structure, of popular festivities is in itself an assertion, a self-validation, a celebration of the community of the popular.

Official public events, though, often involve a combination of spectacle, displays of political power and demonstrations of technological mastery. The most advanced uses of digital technology in the simulation programmes of military planning and video games and the combination of digital and mechanical technologies in theme parks have converged. In official public leisure the crowd is managed and controlled. There are, though, no clear distinctions that can be made. All forms of festival and carnival involve some element of spectacle. Spectacles are rarely without some dimension of the festive, and some outbreak of the carnivalesque. It cannot be claimed that spectators are ever entirely and simply passive. Equally, the claim that in carnival the distinction between performer and spectator is erased does not stand up to examination – there is a difference between being on the float and off the float, for example. Nevertheless, if one accepts a schematic application in which these terms can help to clarify parameters, their use can then offer some purchase on understanding the Olympic Games and its particular articulation of elements of spectacle, festivity and carnival.

ANALYSING THE SPORTS SPECTACLE

The work of Victor Turner is regarded as important in this context, and Dayan and Katz (1992: 231) suggest that 'festive events deserve a theory that takes specific account of their festive dimension: that is what Victor Turner has taught us'. Influenced by Turner, MacAloon (1984) produced a schematic analysis of the relation of rite, drama, festival and spectacle. One interesting interface between spectacle and festival can be seen in the cultural practices that have evolved around the growing use of large screens in city centres and parks, relaying live pictures of major sporting events. Audiences picnic, drink, celebrate. Carnivalesque modes of dress appear. Major sport events cut into the structured regularities of everyday life. They prompt people to stay up into the early hours, or to drink beer at breakfast while watching live broadcasts of sport events in bars. These rituals disrupt the time of work discipline. They are part of a tradition of 'dysfunctional' practices that constitute resistances to the tyranny of work – celebrating St Monday, taking a 'sickie', the three-hour lunch break, doing nothing. They belong to a defiant hedonistic culture, associated with drink, sex and being 'bad'.

Indeed, at many major events the organisers have nurtured and encouraged such settings. At the Torino Winter Olympics in 2006, the organisers established an Olympic plaza in which many of the medal ceremonies were staged. Just as the spaces of the city have become more festive at times of major sport events, the stadium experience has become more controlled. This is typified by the giant card stunts, much loved by television and by sponsors and advertisers. They reduce the spectators to a participant in a ritual they cannot perceive or enjoy. They become the serfs of the television production centre, responding to a command by waving an abstraction – a card that is merely one cell of a giant mosaic.

220

Where and how in this interface of spectacle and festival are politics articulated? If popular culture is conceived as the interface between organised political discourse and popular common sense, then politics lies partly in the process whereby discursive elements are legitimised or delegitimised. So what are the moments of instability, destabilisation, ruptures, breaks and challenges? And what are their conditions of existence? Given that the dominant political configuration is neo-liberal, then how can the discursive elements of neo-liberalism be disarticulated? How can the truly festive be retrieved from corporate control?

A challenging politics attempts to expose the crimes of the powerful, unmasking details of their wealth and where it comes from. It also endeavours to publicise the conditions of poverty. The key test is political effectivity. Clearly joyous, spontaneous and carnival elements temporarily reinscribe the communal and the social in civil society, suggesting new relations of individual and collective, real space and cyber space. But when the mode of the music changes, do the walls of the city really shake? It is instructive here to pay attention to the physical environment of public space. Just as during the nineteenth century

Figure 10.4 Beijing shopping mall. Inside an upmarket shopping mall in central Beijing, directly opposite the grand hotel commandeered in its entirety for the duration of the Games by the IOC, this spectacular display reproduces the running track as a catwalk for fitness chic.

Figure 10.5 Westfield Shopping Mall, Stratford.

the railway station became the new cathedral – the new grand public architecture – in the twentieth century the sport stadium was the new cathedral. In the London 2012 Games the stadium moves closer to that other modern cathedral of consumption, the shopping mall. The stadium provides and enables the spectacle of perfectly honed bodies in competitive movement. The mall offers the spectacle of the commodity. Sport and leisure wear in the form of the branded goods of Nike and Adidas link the stadium and the mall.

As we noted in Chapter 9, Boykoff (2014a) maintains that the Olympics Games are the quintessential example of 'celebration capitalism', a specific formation of capitalism that in many ways slices against the neo-liberal zeitgeist. For him it is the flipside of Naomi Klein's concept of 'disaster capitalism': both disaster capitalism and celebration capitalism occur in states of exception – catastrophe and exuberance, respectively. With both disaster capitalism and celebration capitalism, undercutting democratic processes is commonplace. For Olympic host cities, the Games offer the opportunity to exhibit celebratory exceptionality and this justifies the special legislation, the extra security, the infrastructure improvements and the freedom from taxation. In theory, Boykoff (2013: 60) suggests, 'celebration capitalism could be a Keynesian pump-primer for the economy', but at present this is not how celebration capitalism functions in the context of the Olympic Games.

VORTEXTUALITY AND THE DISPERSED SPECTACLE

The combination of sporting spectacle and global media produce, in the case of the Olympic Games, an intense reification of place and time – the elaborate and expensive campaign to be awarded the Games, the subsequent seven-year countdown, the construction of grandiose iconic architecture and the two-week vortextual focus on the host city. The Olympics are a vortextual spectacle – they suck attention in with a considerable intensity, temporarily dominating the news agenda (see Whannel 2010). Around the world, for two brief weeks, television screens, newspaper pages, internet sites, blogs and twitterings focus upon the Olympic Games. The Olympic site is briefly the centre of the world. But the Olympics are also a dispersed spectacle. They can be and are consumed around the world on television, on internet sites, and through the print media. Giant live screens are provided in parks, city squares and shopping malls. (This is all even truer of the Football World Cup, which is in the end more effective in calling up the patriotic subject).

Global televised mega-events have both a centrifugal and centripetal character. They are about both convergence and fragmentation. Everything focuses on the host city or host nation, and yet they can be consumed everywhere. Furthermore, they are in some ways more readily consumed at a distance. Being in Beijing in August 2008 felt too close – like trying to watch Cinerama in the front row. Conversely, the embedded, immediate and experiential nature of 'being there' has come to seem a partial and incomplete experience compared to the sense of completion, comprehensiveness and technological mastery bestowed by television. We would suggest here three phases in the development of the sport spectacle. First, pre-television, major events could only be fully experienced at the site, as with a world's fair. Second, television extended the live immediacy of the sport to the domestic sphere around the world. Third, the ubiquity of the electronic image, digitalisation and the new media have rendered this image in two ways – (1) the image has become better, sharper, closer, more analytic (replays) than the live experience can be, and (2) it is available, indeed unavoidable, everywhere in public spaces (at least metropolitan ones) in bars, in malls, in streets.

So the Games, like the Football World Cup, have become a dispersed spectacle – the existence of a global audience with their own shared and embedded experiences is as important a part of the event as the spectators at the site. Olympic images are also disseminated across multiple media platforms in a variety of forms – merchandising, mascots, computer games, ring-tones, wallpaper. An interesting dimension of the dispersed spectacle is the massive visibility, during the Opening Ceremony, of officials and athletes capturing the scene on their cameras and mobile phones. The resultant images could travel around the world as readily as broadcast television. So the World Cup and the Olympic Games have spawned forms of dispersed spectacle that could be seen as forms of de-territorialisation, yet in the reification of place and promotion of cities there is also a re-territorialisation.

But the Games are dispersed not only in space, but also through time. The launching of a bid and the winning of a bid might be celebrated through a series of public events which mobilise the spectacular and the festive and even to a degree the carnivalesque. The torch relay provides a further set of occasions dispersed around the world (although, after the

2008 torch relay was utilised for human rights protests, Olympic insiders correctly predicted that this would be the last global torch relay to be staged). Even when the Games conclude, the party can continue. In September 2008, after Beijing, the Australian team were paraded through the centre of Sydney in an event which also included a trailer for London featuring (you can probably guess) a red London bus, umbrellas and bowler hats, and a band playing the *Dad's Army* theme tune. Global television events such as the Olympic Games and the Football World Cup, then, have become dispersed spectacles – they occur not simply at the site but around the world in myriad locations – homes, cafés, bars, malls, squares and parks – framed by a range of national and local hopes and fantasies, consumed in ways which are shaped by gender, class and ethnic formations, assumptions and expectations.

Experiencing the Games

In 2008, Whannel spent a day tracking the Beijing torch relay when it came through central London, which contributed to an article by Horne and Whannel (2010); and both authors had a range of experiential encounters with the Olympic Games in London in 2012. We include the following observations, not as any form of systematic ethnographic obser-vation, but simply as a report of our own experiences and reflections. Whannel, who lives in Central London, was in London throughout the Games, and Horne spent some time in the city. Together, they attended the final of the women's football at Wembley Stadium, and viewed the marathon from the City of London. Whannel attended a rehearsal of the Opening Ceremony in the company of sports historian, activist and former Olympic athlete Bruce Kidd. Whannel also attended the canoe slalom, the water polo, BMX cycling and taekwondo (the taekwondo with Bruce Kidd and John Horne), and a morning of athletics in the main stadium. He spent an evening with Australian sports sociologist David Rowe, watching people watching the Games in various bars. Like millions, both Horne and Whannel watched a great deal of the Games on television – at home, in bars and on giant screens in public spaces.

Horne stayed with a friend in Leyton, within walking distance of the Olympic site, and one Tube stop further along from Stratford, for the second week of the event. Leyton High Street had been beautified and Leyton Tube station had signs indicating that it was an alternative place to alight in order to get to the Olympic Stadium. Few people used it, however, which led to some local stall holders complaining that they had been short-changed with grand promises of thousands of passing Olympic customers. The local London Olympic Borough, Waltham Forest, had initiated an ethnic food market and contracted it out to a company called North London Business, but then published a route to the Olympic Park that led visitors to go a different way.[2]

Despite the potentially disastrous withdrawal of the main private security provider (G4S) at the last moment, requiring the Army to be deployed, the security was, in our experience, fairly light-touch and friendly in character. It was a considerable PR success for the British Army.[3] The large regiment of well-trained and jolly volunteers ('Games Makers') were also popular with the public. There was a party atmosphere, and at times a degree of patriotic fervour. It was all quite un-British and un-London in character. Festivity was especially

Figure 10.6 Crowds watching the cycling as Bradley Wiggins speeds by on his way to a gold medal. Photograph courtesy of Stephen McCubbin.

Figure 10.7 Street spectators watching the marathon in the City of London, near the Monument.

visible in the open-air and free events – road cycling and the marathon. The month of the Games constituted a brief and exceptional period.

The remarkable temporary transformation in the mood of London and Londoners was widely commented on. Not usually the most friendly of cities, Londoners seemed to respond to the Olympic situation by behaving unusually – smiling, talking to strangers, appearing cheerful. Once the Olympics were over, Londoners, Whannel included, appeared happy to revert to their normal, more sombre and grumpy personas. Travelling on London transport was different than usual. The trains were generally quieter and groups of people were happy to talk to each other about what they were going to see and where they had been, as well as the weather, which remained good. One city commuter was overheard remarking, of the unaccustomed quietness of his train, 'If this is the Olympics I wish we could have it every week.' One of the reasons for the lack of overcrowding on public transport and absence of traffic jams on the roads was the deliberate alarm tactics initiated by LOCOG in advance publicity to the effect that transport hubs would be very over-crowded and that Londoners should consider avoiding work, their regular commuting times or simply leave the city. As a result, the city was much quieter than usual. Transport ran smoothly, traffic was free of jams and the controversial Olympic-traffic-only lanes were frequently open to general traffic also.

Many of the people that Horne spoke to were not from London and had come down from the north or other parts of the UK for a few days to sample the Olympics. Visiting museums and other city centre attractions, which were usually busy, was delightful, as queues were very short or non-existent. The drop in visitor numbers was later confirmed both by a friend of Horne's who worked at one of them and by reports about attendance figures from other museums and galleries.[4] Horne took advantage of his location and walked to the Stratford site from Leyton on a couple of occasions. On his walks he encountered Olympic athletes waiting for taxis to transport them away from the Olympic Park at the back of the site, groups of police waiting to go on duty and a large queue inside the John Lewis store inside the recently opened Westfield's Stratford City shopping mall. The department store had advertised itself as providing a perfect view of the Olympic site from its third floor and by the second week of competition it had become a 'must see' attraction. When Horne visited, the wait time to reach the third floor was 45 minutes and the store was charging £1 per person. He asked an employee if there was an alternative to waiting and they showed him a similar view that was available without charge from the second floor.[5]

Horne met friends from Germany, Brazil, Canada and the US, as well as the UK, during his stay in London. With these people he visited some of the Games-related sites that had temporarily been staged during the Olympics in places such as Hyde Park (the Sochi 2014 display and Africa House), Somerset House (Brazil House), the British Library (the Olympic philately exhibition, Olympex 2012) and the East End of London (part of a trail of different statues of London 2012 mascots Wenlock and Mandeville).[6] Immediately after the Games Horne attended an academic symposium about the Olympics in Oxford. The mood of the meeting was very celebratory. On the way to Oxford the morning after the Closing Ceremony Horne encountered his first delay on the London Underground in a week of travelling . . . was this normal service resumed?

Figure 10.8 John Lewis store in Westfield: queue to view

CONSUMPTION: WESTFIELD AND THE STRATFORD CITY MALL

While public focus fell on the Olympic Games, far less attention was paid to the associated development of a large shopping mall. Given the substantial degree of public investment in the Games, the issue of legacy has become a central topic. While the real legacy value of, and future economic support for, many of the sporting venues have been questioned, one aspect of the Olympic project seems likely to produce a successful and highly profitable legacy. The huge shopping mall built by Westfield is perfectly situated in both space and time. With prestigious anchor tenants such as John Lewis and Marks & Spencer, it neatly spans the space between Stratford International Station and Stratford Station, providing excellent transport links to much of London. The entrances to these stations provided direct access to the mall, which also contained the main entrance route into the Olympic Park. The mall benefited from the Olympic publicity and the procession of up to 100,000 people per day during the Olympic fortnight in summer 2012.

For such a key development, the various bodies involved in the Games were surprisingly coy about it. It was fairly hard to find any references to the Stratford City Development or Westfield on the websites of LOCOG, the ODA, the LDA, the Mayor's Office, the Department of Transport or London and Continental Railways. It was extremely difficult to find any clear financial information about the relation of public and private investment in the site. Even in an otherwise impressive and comprehensive study of Olympic cities from the perspective of urban development (Poynter and MacRury 2009), there were only a few fleeting references to the Westfield Mall.

Like the Games itself, the Stratford City Mall has its origins in government policy for regeneration in the docklands, the Thames Gateway and the lower Lea Valley. In 2002, two developers, Chelsfield and Stanhope, formed Stratford City Developments and proposed a £3.5 billion mixed development at Stratford, in East London, on a 150-acre site on the route of the Channel Tunnel rail link, then under construction. Newham Council granted planning permission in October 2002. At this point the proposed development comprised five million square feet of office space, two million square feet of retailing, 4,850 homes and 2,000 hotel rooms, along with schools, libraries and other public facilities. It was originally planned to begin construction in 2006, completing by 2020 (*The Times* 20 October 2002). Just months after Newham granted planning permission, the government was won over to the Olympic idea, considerably enhancing the value of the Stratford development, should London win.

But the Stratford City development plans were making slow progress. Both companies had a record in the field: Chelsfield handled the Paddington basin scheme, while Stanhope were responsible for the Broadgate development (*The Times* 10 September 2004). But Chelsfield were already troubled by internal problems when they got planning permission, and their sale of Wentworth Golf Club had triggered a boardroom row. The Chelsfield stake interested three companies (Westfield, Multiplex and Aldersgate). It appears that the three formed a consortium, Duelguide, which acquired the Chelsfield stake, sometime between October and December 2004. However, Multiplex was already in serious financial trouble caused by its involvement in building the new Wembley Stadium, on which by May 2005 it estimated its losses to be around £45 million (Horne and Whannel 2012).

Just two months later, in July 2005, the London bid was successful and both land and proposed development suddenly became worth significantly more. In December 2005, Aldersgate, together with associates, acquired the Multiplex share of Duelguide, paying £127.5 million for the Multiplex rights in the Stratford City development site and its stake in the Global Switch business. Those who now had a stake in the development were: London and Continental Railways (LCR), which owned the leasehold of the 170-acre site; Stanhope, and the two partners in Duelguide, Aldersgate and Westfield. But the various companies did not establish an easy rapport, Westfield and Aldersgate in particular having a difficult relationship. Under pressure from an increasingly impatient LCR, the companies agreed to a proposed 'shoot-out' auction in which the highest-bidding partner would buy the others out. But in May 2006, under more pressure from LCR and the various public bodies (ODA, LDA, the Mayor's Office), Stanhope agreed to sell its stake. Aldersgate were reported as being prepared to pay between £50 million and £55 million and seemed the favourite, but Frank Lowy, Westfield Chairman (in Europe with his 244 ft yacht for the Football World Cup), had not given up (*Independent on Sunday* 14 May 2006).

In June it was announced that Westfield had acquired full ownership of Stratford City Developments, buying the Aldersgate stake for around £150 million (*The Age*

13 June 2006). On 2 March 2007, the ODA, LCR and Westfield announced they were now in exclusive talks with the Australian-based property consortium Lend Lease to develop the Olympic Village and Zones 2–7 of Stratford City, which comprised housing, commercial and hotel development. Westfield retained responsibility for Zone 1, comprising the main shopping mall, as well as residential, leisure, hotel and office facilities (ODA Media Release 2 March 2007).

By the start of 2008, Westfield were evidently keen to commence work on Stratford City, although some final contractual details remained unresolved, and they were permitted to establish building contracts under licence.[7] By March, Westfield were clear that the mall could be open by 2011, and the ODA had agreed to provide some infrastructure, such as roads and bridges. Westfield also had infrastructural spending commitments under the terms of the S106 Planning Agreement negotiated with the LDA.[8] By April 2008 clear physical progress was visible.[9] In May 2008 it was announced that LCR was selling the land to Westfield. This was rather surprising, given that back in March 2007 LCR Managing Director (Stations and Property) Stephen Jordan had said: 'LCR is pleased to be working with all parties, not only to provide essential infrastructure for a successful Games in 2012, but to provide key elements of legacy – the homes and jobs people need' (ODA Media Release 2 March 2007). It appeared to mean that Westfield now became the sole landowner and sole developer for the Stratford City project.

It was reported in the *Observer* (24 August 2008) that Westfield's Frank Lowy had per-suaded the ODA to hand over what was understood to be in excess of £100 million to ensure that the mall would be open in time for the 2012 Games. It is hard to understand quite why Westfield needed an incentive for an outcome very much to their own advantage, and according to the *Observer*, Culture Select Committee members would

2001	November	Stratford site for Games preferred to Wembley
2002		Chelsfield and Stanhope form Stratford City Developments and propose a £3.5bn mixed development in East London, on a 150-acre site on the Channel Tunnel rail link route then under construction
	October	Newham Council granted planning permission
2003	15 May	London bid to go ahead
2004	19 October	Westfield, Multiplex and Aldersgate form a consortium, Duelguide
2005	6 July	IOC awards Games to London
2005	December	Aldersgate acquires the Multiplex share of Duelguide
2006	May	Westfield buys Stanhope stake in the Stratford development
	June	Westfield buys Aldersgate stake in Stratford City Developments
2008	March	Westfield mall could be open by 2011. ODA agrees to provide some infrastructure, such as roads and bridges
	May	LCR sells the land to Westfield
	17 July	The *Guardian* reports that Westfield persuaded the government to contribute tens of millions of pounds to ensure the mall will be open for the Games
2011		Westfield's Stratford City opens

Figure 10.9 The Stratford site and the Westfield mall.

Sources: company websites, company press announcements, newspaper reports.

push ODA officials for an answer. It would seem that this article may well be referring to the infrastructural work that the ODA agreed to undertake in the S106 Planning Agreement. In November 2010, with the main building work complete, major retailers signed up, and with just one year until the official opening Westfield chose to cash in by selling half of their development to a consortium of Dutch and Canadian finance houses for £871 million (*Daily Telegraph* 23 November 2010). In doing so, they retain significant control and a substantial stake in the future of the mall, while also recouping a significant amount upfront.

When infrastructural development is carried out by a combination of public and private agencies, it can be difficult to unravel cost and benefit, or public finance and private finance. The Westfield London mall at White City/Shepherd's Bush is a case in point. A new station at Shepherd's Bush on the West London Line has been constructed by Westfield, together with Network Rail, prior to Transport for London (TfL) taking over responsibility for overground services (TfL Board Meeting 6 February 2008). Westfield gained massively in becoming the focal point of shopping in the area, boosted by re-organisation of transport, with TfL rerouting many bus routes away from the existing town centre and to the

Figure 10.10 The Westfield advertisement. The Westfield mall, with its dream location between the station and Olympic Park, combines elements of an upmarket shopping, leisure and entertainment location.

new Westfield shopping mall (Morris and Evans 2008). It is relevant to ask whether the negotiations leading to the signing of S106 Planning Agreements are adequately transparent and accountable.

CONCLUSION

While the British press made much of the dramatic increase in the London 2012 budget, little focus fell on the disbursement of this budget. In all the public furore about the costs of the Olympic Games which raged from February to May 2007, there was a significant absence. There was very little, if any, discussion of where the £10 billion was actually going. Who would receive this money, and to do what? Who was gaining? Aeron Davis has argued that business journalism is 'highly dependent on information and advertising subsidies'; that a 'Financial Elite Discourse Network' has grown up; and that 'in effect, business news has been captured by financial elites' (Davis 2000: 82–89). Our understanding of business and financial issues through journalism is likely to be limited by the shaping and framing work of the PR operations of powerful corporations. The Olympic Games has become an enormous lever for moving public policy, uncorking infrastructural investment – public investment, private gain. The key dynamics are associated with globalising processes, transnational corporations, urban renewal, consumption and the new urbanism (see discussion in Chapter 5 and Poynter *et al.* 2016). In such a context, it could be argued that festivity becomes a side-effect, rather than a partner, of spectacle. Areas of festivity were regulated spaces, subject to surveillance, wrapped within the maternal embrace of the Olympic family. They were cockpits for an affirmative culture of self congratulation.

NOTES

1 www.culturalolympics.org.uk (last accessed 23 October 2015).
2 www.huffingtonpost.co.uk/2012/08/13/olympic-food-market-leyton-petition_n_1771817.html (last accessed 23 October 2015).
3 www.telegraph.co.uk/finance/newsbysector/supportservices/10070425/Timeline-how-G4Ss-bungled-Olympics-security-contract-unfolded.html (last accessed 23 October 2015).
4 www.theguardian.com/culture-professionals-network/culture-professionals-blog/2012/sep/03/london-2012-museum-attendance-figures-fall (last accessed 23 October 2015).
5 www.dailymail.co.uk/news/article-2183478/Westfield-Stratford-John-Lewis-charges-visitors-2-view-Olympic-Park-floor.html (last accessed 23 October 2015)
6 www.bl.uk/press-releases/2012/may/olympic-philatelic-collecting-brought-to-life-at-the-british-library (last accessed 23 October 2015); http://memoirsofametrogirl.com/2012/08/06/wenlock-mandeville-mascot-olympic-discovery-trails-london (last accessed 23 October 2015).
7 ODA: Minutes of 23rd Board Meeting: 28 February 2008.
8 ODA: Minutes of 24th Board Meeting: 27 March 2008.
9 ODA: Minutes of 25th Board Meeting: 24 April 2008.

FURTHER READING

Cohen, P. (2013) *On the Wrong Side of the Track? East London and the Post Olympics*, London: Lawrence & Wishart.

Powell, H. and Marrero-Guillamón, I. (eds) (2012) *The Art of Dissent: Adventures in London's Olympic State*, London: Marshgate Press.

Sinclair, I. (2011) *Ghost Milk: Calling Time on the Grand Project*, London: Hamish Hamilton.

PART III

THE FUTURE OF THE OLYMPICS

CHAPTER 11

LEVEL PLAYING FIELDS

Shortly after the London 2012 Olympic and Paralympic Games sociologist Kath Woodward (2013: 2–3) wrote:

> the Olympics and Paralympics have generated excitement and massive interest, and the athletes who have taken part have become heroic figures in the public arena. It has all worked way beyond the dreams of the organizers and the scepticism of many critics and political activists. The legacy of the games remains uncertain but the duration of the events . . . has been an undisputed success. . . . The Paralympics and its athletes have generated as much interest and support as has the Olympics which preceded them; so-often socially inflected embodied differences have become ordinary and pass unremarked. . . . London 2012 has offered a celebration of the ordinariness of many of the differences between and among people and downplayed the markers of inequality. . . . This is not to say that the games themselves were not marked by inequalities, which also operated routinely.

There are a number of complexities being communicated here. The excitement of the event is captured in combination with recognition that inequalities persisted during and after the sporting party has taken place. This chapter examines issues of access and equity at the Olympic Games in this light. It considers: the composition of the IOC; inequality at global, regional and national levels marking the relationship between affluent and poor countries that compete at the Olympics; social class and the exclusion of professionals; the involvement of women in the Olympics; 'race' and racism; disability sport and the Paralympic Games; and relates these to other forms of social inequality that provide a context within which the Olympic Games take place. It examines the contrast between the rhetoric and the practice of Olympism.

As we have seen, despite reforms since the 1990s, the governance of the Olympics is still dominated by European men, often with an aristocratic social background. The commitment to amateurism, only abandoned since the early 1980s, gave the Games a distinct social class character. The first black member of the IOC was invited to join in 1963; the first women members were accepted in 1981. Women were excluded entirely from the early Games, and only since the 1980s has the full programme of events begun to be opened to them. Even here there remain areas of contestation and controversy, such as ski jumping. The Paralympic Games, despite a long struggle for inclusion, are still staged as a separate event. Through 'The Olympic Programme' (TOP) major corporations, most notably NBC and its parent company General Electric, are in a position to exercise a shaping influence on the development of the Games. This chapter poses an underlying question: 'Who are the Games for?'

Maurice Roche (2000: 41) outlined four ways in which sports mega-events, such as the Olympic Games, 'provided opportunities and arenas for the display and exercise of "civil society" in addition to "the state" both at national and international levels' at the turn of the nineteenth century. Specifically focusing on the modern Olympic Games and the IOC, established in 1894, Roche argues that the Games were connected to four developing ideas about global citizenship: *universal citizenship* and the associated discourse on human rights; *mediatised citizenship* and the right to participate in the Olympics as a media event; *movement citizenship* and the right to participate in the Games as a sports organisation and a movement; and *corporate citizenship* or the position of the IOC as a collective actor in global civil society.

Here we primarily focus on the first and third of these forms of citizenship – the extent to which the Olympics offer a level playing field to those who wish to participate, and thus contribute to the expansion of human rights. As a 'movement', the IOC claims to be quite different from other sports organisations and their mega-events. The problem is that – even if the Olympics were seen by progressives and reactionaries alike as a positive cultural innovation 100 years or more ago – this was essentially a dream built upon a particular set of values and relationships (embodied in the ideology of nineteenth-century amateurism, and based on Western, masculine and (upper) social class-based moral conceptions) that simply no longer apply.

Members of the IOC today, and many sports people and physical educators, still believe that sport has a higher social and moral purpose, but elite sport has also become a more integral part of capitalist consumer culture, and mega-events such as the Summer Olympic Games are its commercial spectacles. The Olympics uses its difference as a 'movement' with an ideology (Olympism) different from other world cups and commercial events (such as the FIFA World Cup, or Cricket or Rugby Union World Cups) to provide it with its own distinctive 'brand'.[1] Anti-commercialism can thus enhance commercial value. However, the IOC faces two main challenges – around democracy and fair play.

Under siege since the 1990s about its undemocratic procedures, it remains 'a self-recruiting and secretive elite international club, directly accountable and accessible to nobody but itself' (Roche 2000: 207). Despite the establishment of an ethics commission and various other sub-committees attempting to bring about Olympic reform, since the 1990s, the IOC has had difficulty, beyond those people ready to accept its ideology, in convincing others that it is operating according to the highest standards of democratic governance. This situation has not been aided by the increase in revelations of cheating in sport, and especially the use of performance-enhancing drugs, in a context where the chasm between the rewards from success and the anonymity derived from losing has widened considerably. This and other contemporary challenges for the Olympics are considered in more detail in the final chapter.

In order to assess whether there can be a levelling of the playing field through the Olympic Games, this chapter will outline the four key social divisions that underpin the world of sport and the Olympics specifically: social class, 'race', gender and disability/para-sport. Sport, fairness and a level playing field are difficult to achieve since inequalities in material conditions give rise to massive disparities in resources between nations, which tables showing medals per capita or GDP reveal, and which media constructions of valiant but ultimately unsuccessful athletes such as 'Eric the Eel' portray. Media portrayals of Olympic athletes are generally positive, viewing athletes as trying hard despite the odds, but the reality is that over half of participating nations and their athletes do not obtain a medal of any colour.

First, though, we want to briefly consider the way the IOC has positioned itself with respect to global inequalities. With the recognition that social and economic inequality has been growing at global, regional and national levels (Piketty 2014; Wilkinson and Pickett 2009), a consensus developed among the member countries of the United Nations (UN) to adopt declarations to reduce poverty, hunger, gender inequality, illiteracy, child mortality and environmental degradation. These were made tangible in the 'Millennium Development Goals' (MDGs) that operated from 2000 to 2015. The UN held a Sustainable Development Summit in New York in September 2015 and adopted 17 broad follow-up 'Sustainable Development Goals' (SDGs) and 169 specific targets to run from 2016 until 2030. Since the 1990s, the idea of using sport for, or in, development of 'sport for development and peace' has increasingly been adopted by academics and practitioners and also influenced policy makers at the UN (Levermore and Beacom 2009). Sport has increasingly been seen to be able to make a contribution to enduring global problems, including the challenges associated with health, education, gender equity, and the promotion of peace (Darnell 2012). The IOC gained status as a Permanent Observer to the United Nations in 2009, which means the IOC's representatives can attend sessions and the work of the UN General Assembly as well as maintain permanent offices at UN Headquarters. This position has undoubtedly contributed to the growth of the view that UN goals could be assisted through links to sports programmes. At the UN Summit in September 2015, President Bach addressed the members and pledged wholehearted support for the '2013 Agenda for Sustainable Development', while thanking UN member states 'for recognising the contribution of sport to sustainable development and to advancing the Sustainable Development Goals'.[2] In particular, Bach identified sports contribution to health, educational opportunity, gender equality for women and girls, the promotion of peace and the strengthening of global partnerships.

In the most economically developed countries, meanwhile, nationalism spurs on the search for gold medal success via the production of elite athletic bodies and highly specialised athletes. The cost of Olympic gold medals has been growing (Donnelly 2009). The Olympics cannot escape from the social context (including existing beliefs and ideologies) of their formation or of their current manifestation. Olympic change through time tends to reflect, rather more than refract, wider social changes, although it can send out strong messages that help construct certain beliefs about sporting abilities and opportunities. Generally, though, the IOC follows social change – economic, political, ideological and cultural – rather than leading or promoting it. But this is not a criticism of the Games alone since arguably sport and sports institutions generally are more conservative forces than forces for progressive social change. The next sections focus on the four main social divisions and areas of political debate in this light.

SOCIAL CLASS: OLYMPIC SPORT AS A VEHICLE FOR OVERCOMING CLASS HOSTILITY AND DIFFERENCES

Social class has played a major role in influencing the construction of, organisation of, consumption of and participation in modern sport. Class was central to the formation of modern sports culture, and the Olympics were part of that. Class position (of origination) and class of destination are linked through ideas about social mobility. Sport is a powerful symbol of mobility and change in social status. Class has an important influence on sport participation and the character of specific sport cultures. For the first 80 years, the IOC upheld the notion of amateurism and outlawed professionalism in Olympic sport. This partly reflected the social background of Coubertin and his other IOC members, who largely viewed their position as one of being social class conciliators. Sport offered a means of 'calming' proletarian 'bitterness' (Coubertin 2000 [1920]: 225). As sociologist Pierre Bourdieu (1978) once noted, sport has been 'an object of struggles between the fractions of the dominant class and also between the social classes'. Nowhere is this more apparent than in inclusion and exclusion at the Olympic Games and in the Olympic movement.

As we have discussed in Chapter 6, Coubertin arrived at his view of sport and physical education from studying the English public school system. This was a highly elitist system based on the wider British class structure. During the nineteenth century the use of organised athletics and 'athleticism' as an educational ideology 'became established as the "essence of school life"' (Simon 1975: 8; Mangan 1981). Key features of this ideology were anti-intellectualism, anti-individuality and conformity. Athleticism was thus a form of character training, developing physical and moral courage, loyalty and cooperation and the ability both to command and to obey (Mangan 1975). Dunning (1975) argues that mid-nineteenth-century public school reforms in Britain, including an emphasis on athleticism and muscular Christianity, represented a compromise between rising industrial bourgeois and declining aristocratic interests. Reform led to the 'incipient modernisation' of team games (especially association football or 'soccer') into modern sports by stimulating the development of codified rules designed to 'civilise' the games and equalise participants. Who played whom in the games fixtures, however, became one of the key indicators in defining not just the status of schools, just as it did in the 'Ivy League' in American universities, but also the structure of the public school network as a whole. As de Honey (1975: 27–31) noted, by 1902 there was a relatively close community of 64 boys' schools which interacted with each other in two or more activities, including rowing, athletics, gymnastics, rifle shooting, cricket, rugby, association football, racquets and fencing. Interaction in activities with differential prestige attached to them created different social levels of schools.

Rather than signalling the embourgoisement (or downward cultural mobility) of the aristocratic elite, it can be said that the reformed public schools were thus able to capture middle-class talent (Gruneau 1981: 355). In this way English public schools came to play a formative role in the reproduction and 'promotion of gentry-class power' (Wilkinson 1964: ix) in the nineteenth century. Wilkinson identified public schools as a political system with a political role: 'maintaining order by ethical restraint rather than by law' (1964: ix). The English (and Scottish) public schools selected and reinforced certain values and created a specific public school ethos, as well as a social stratum, that prided itself on public service, among other things. The aim was to create a boy who was capable of loyally obeying 'his supervisors and who at the same time could command a regiment or head a government' (Arnstein 1975: 236). According to Bertrand Russell, 'the concept of the gentleman was invented by the aristocracy to keep the middle classes in order' (Arnstein 1975: 235). By 'capturing' the nouveaux riches within the category of gentlemen, the public school 'acted as an "escape-valve" in the social system' (Arnstein 1975: 235). It was this elitist social class context that most influenced Coubertin (as we discuss in Chapter 6).

It is well known that there are social class differences in leisure, and a reasonable expectation or hypothesis would be that they have been exacerbated by the recession that followed the banking crisis of 2008–2009 (Roberts 2015). Two surveys of leisure activities benefitting from state funding in the UK, *Taking Part* and the *Active People Survey*, revealed that overall sport participation remained stable between 2005–2006 and 2011–2012, with just over half the adult population (age 16 and over) taking part at least once in the four weeks preceding interviews (Roberts 2015: 135–136). Yet when social class is taken into account it is evident that 'wider economic class inequalities have led to wider social class differences in leisure' (Roberts 2015: 145). To what extent does social class influence who plays, who competes, and who wins gold medals in elite sport and Olympic sport today?

Despite a longstanding sports policy rhetoric about securing 'Sports for All' in the UK and the successful Olympics bid presentation in 2005, which placed such a lot of emphasis on inspiring more people, especially young people, to participate in sport, overall participation rates in recreational sport in the United Kingdom did not significantly alter then, or since (Girginov and Hills 2008: 2097–2100). Ten years after winning the bid and near the third anniversary of London 2012, the former Olympics Minister Tessa Jowell declared that the situation was 'back to where we started in 2002' (quoted in Gibson 2015c: 7). Ever since the implementation of spending cuts by the Conservative and Liberal Democrat coalition government in 2010 there had been a growing concern about the Olympic Games participation legacy. Six months after the coalition's formation in 2010, the education department announced plans to close 450 school sports partnerships that had linked primary and secondary schools to encourage the sharing of facilities and funding specialist coaches. Although there was a reaction by educationalists and parents that saw some of these arrangements saved, by 2015 Sport England revealed in its half-yearly *Active People Survey* that there had been a fall of 220,000 in the number of people of all ages taking part in sport for half an hour each week. The number of people swimming regularly had dropped by three-quarters of a million. The decline in sports participation was most marked among the poor and pointed to a post-Olympics legacy failure (Williams 2015).

Prior to the London bid, data cited by academics such as Holt and Mason (2000: 6–9), the Office for National Statistics (1998) and sportscotland (2002) all showed the continuance of stratified sports cultures in Britain. Rowe and Moore (2004) suggested three reasons for the decline in participation since the 1990s: people had competing demands on their time; people had a greater number of leisure choices, many of which promote more sedentary behaviour; and the quality of the sports infrastructure (for participants) had been declining. As a consequence of lack of investment over the previous 30 years, some 500 recreational sports centres had been closed, and local authorities estimated that they required £500 million to upgrade existing facilities (*Guardian* 21 August 2004).

Research conducted in the past 25 years confirms the continuing relationship between independent schools, elite sport performance and social class (Evans and Bairner 2012; Horne 2006: 146–149; Horne *et al.* 2011). A research project on *The Development of Sporting Talent 1997* (English Sports Council 1998) interviewed 924 (approximately 500 men and 420 women) of Great Britain's top sportsmen and women in 11 sports – athletics (track and field), cricket (male and female), cycling, hockey, judo, netball, rowing, Rugby League, Rugby Union (male and female), sailing and swimming. Athletics produced the 'most typical elite sports people' – someone educationally well qualified, from a higher socio-economic group, who had had a family member involved in sport. Of participants, 29 per cent were from the professional and managerial social class (AB), 32 per cent were from the clerical and non-manual class (C1), 28 per cent were from the skilled manual (C2) and 12 per cent were from semi-skilled and unskilled manual classes (DE). This compared with 19 per cent AB, 34 per cent C1, 21 per cent C2 and 25 per cent DE in Great Britain's population as a whole. In rowing, over 50 per cent of elite rowers were educated at independent schools, compared to only 5 per cent of the GB population as a whole. Rugby League had the most manual/working-class profile (67 per cent were C2, D or E), while in Rugby Union 41 per cent of elite male players and 24 per cent of elite female players were educated at independent schools. Of elite sailing athletes, 24 per cent were educated at independent schools; 61 per cent were from AB, 22 per cent were from C1, 17 per cent were from C2, and none came from D or E social class backgrounds. Swimming contained the most 'upper-class' profile of all the sports – 21 per cent had attended independent schools, 69 per cent were from AB, 24 per cent were from C1, and only 6 per cent were from C2, D or E social classes.

The authors of the report that summarised the data noted that the opportunity to realise sporting potential was still significantly influenced by an individual's social background. They concluded that:

> a precociously talented youngster born in an affluent family with sport-loving parents, one of whom has (probably) achieved high levels of sporting success, and attending an independent/private school, has a 'first-class ticket' to the sporting podium. His or her counterpart, equally talented but born in less favoured circumstances, at best has a third-class ticket and at worst no ticket at all.
> (English Sports Council 1998: 13)

This conclusion was underscored following the Sydney Summer Olympic Games in 2000, when a survey suggested that 80 per cent of British medal winners at the Games went to independent schools (*Guardian* 21 August 2004).

At the Beijing Games in 2008, 'Team GB' secured 47 medals across 12 sports disciplines – athletics (track and field), boxing, cycling, equestrianism, gymnastics, kayaking, pentathlon, rowing, sailing, swimming, taekwondo and windsurfing. As many were team events, there were 70 individual athletes in total who were medal holders. Five athletes won more than one medal: Chris Hoy (cycling, three gold); Rebecca Adlington (swimming, two gold); Jason Kenny (cycling, one gold, one silver); Tim Brabant (kayaking, one gold, one bronze); and Tina Cook (equestrianism, two bronze). Of these, 41 per cent (28 athletes) were educated at independent schools, 13 per cent (nine) were from religious or faith (voluntary-aided) schools and 46 per cent (32) were from state comprehensive schools (also referred to as 'maintained schools'). This compared nationally with approximately 7 per cent of school pupils in the independent sector and 93 per cent in the state 'maintained' sector. Former independent school students were clearly over-represented among the medal winners in Team GB: they took 31 per cent of the gold medals, 44 per cent of the silver medals and 45 per cent of the bronze medals. A similar disproportionate number of Team GB medal winners in 2012 – 37 per cent – had previously attended private schools (Smith *et al.* 2013). Research by the Sutton Trust (2012) suggested that athletes who attended independent schools were five times over-represented among the state-educated gold medal winners relative to their proportion in the population.

We know that models of the potential for behaviour to change resulting from people's exposure to sports mega-events, such as the Olympic Games, need to be improved to properly understand the complexity of motivations to participate in sport and physical activity (Coalter 2004). Rather than 'trickle-down' or 'role model' speculation, Coalter suggests that participation change agents may need to be 'embedded' and/or involved at the grassroots level. Research by Mackintosh *et al.* (2015) and Such (2014) suggest that the messages about 'active' participation stemming from major sports events need to be examined in terms of their transmission through families. Such (2014) concludes:

> The effects of sport mega events do not, as other research has shown, 'trickle down' to the general population and get us out of our armchairs, but 'diffuse' or 'trickle through and around' our relational everyday lives. It is my suggestion that it is through family and peer networks that sport legacy policy could lever longer-term outcomes.

Horne *et al.* (2011) and Shilling (2007) pose similar questions about the existence of multiple social capitals (especially cultural, symbolic and physical capital; that is *embodied* cultural capital) related to social class operating in and through families and schools that impact on the propensity of individuals to participate in sport. Related to these capitals, or resources, are the body pedagogics (Shilling 2004) that frame and shape physical capital. Future research will be needed to explore these questions in order to investigate the participation legacies of the Olympic Games, and other major sports events.

'RACE' AND THE IOC: OLYMPIC SPORT AS A VEHICLE FOR TESTING 'RACIAL' DIFFERENCES

Bairner and Molnar (2010: 3–4) identified three main forms of the politics of 'race' associated with the Olympics. First, there is institutional racism among member nations, which was particularly evident in the Games of 1904 (St. Louis and the Anthropology Days) and 1936 (Berlin and the attempt to assert the superiority of the Aryan 'race' and the Nazi regime). Second is the opportunity to protest/demonstrate overcoming racism – 1968 (Mexico City) stands out here, as we have mentioned in Chapter 9. Third is the relationship between ethnicity, 'race' and sports performance. The 1904 Anthropology Days, for example, were essentially racial contests set up to measure and demonstrate 'race' as an explanation of performance. But this 'science' of differences has not disappeared despite declarations since the Second World War about the imprecision in using the concept of 'race', and within sport it remains a debating point to this day (see, for example, Entine 2000; Hoberman 1997).

Carrington (2010: 15) consciously avoided discussing what he calls the 'rather obvious markers that readers might have expected to encounter' in a book about 'race' and sport: for example Muhammad Ali, the failed boycott of the 1968 Olympics and the political protests staged at them. In attempting to think about 'race' and sport 'beyond *Beyond a Boundary*' (the widely acclaimed book written by C.L.R. James in 1963), Carrington argues that analysis of sport in 'an age still marked by the historical scars of Empire and racial exclusion' remains an essential task, especially to consider the 'importance of sporting spectacles' in shaping national identities (Carrington 2010: 163–165). He hoped that the London Olympics in 2012 might provide 'an important public space within which to re-imagine the national story'. Rather than ignoring it, acknowledging the history of racism and 'race' in Britain in all its complexity in shaping the present could be valuable. He hoped that the 2012 Olympics 'might just signal the revival of a truly multicultural nation finally at ease with itself' (Carrington 2010: 165).

In the event, the Summer Olympics of 2012 'came to London in the context of a national debate over race and multiculturalism which both questioned what it means to be British and identified sport as a way to shore up and provide substance to Britishness' (Carrington 2013: 107). Some commentators, such as Winter (2013), noted that while London 2012 was promoted as a progressive, inclusive, multicultural project, it did not set out to address the 'social, political and economic realities of the most disenfranchised' members of the black and minority ethnic (BME) communities. Instead he argues that the Games sought to discipline marginalised communities and individuals who did not comply with or aspire to the collective celebration. Similarly Hylton and Morpeth (2012: 387) suggested BME communities in the neighbouring 'Olympic Boroughs' were caught in the contradiction of both being promoted as ambassadors and stakeholders of London 2012 and as problems to be fixed by it: 'reified by Olympic stakeholders as fragmented and disadvantaged, therefore requiring an Olympic makeover to manage these social issues'. Carrington (2013: 108–109) also suggests that while the London 2012 Opening Ceremony designed by film-maker Danny Boyle did 'serve to reinvigorate a sense of the lived realities of contemporary multiracial Britain', it did so *without* providing 'any account of Empire': 'imperial British history without Empire, blacks arriving from the colonies in a story without colonisation'. While sport appears to have the capacity to create social bonds and identifications that cut across racial, ethnic and religious divides – think Nicola Adams, Mo Farah and Jessica Ennis – it is not evident, writing three years later, that London 2012 sparked a new inclusive Britishness.

Evidence gathered in the past 25 years by public agencies and academic researchers in the UK points to some of the issues and challenges ahead. UK Sport estimated that 10.3 per cent of its funded athletes were from BME groups, which compared favourably with the 7.9 per cent of the 2001 UK population from such communities. Analysis of the GB Team that represented Great Britain at the 2008 Beijing Olympic and Paralympic Games showed that 7 per cent of the athletes in the GB Olympic squad and 3.6 per cent of athletes in the GB Paralympic squad were from BME groups. UK Sport estimated that 16 per cent of the coaches who were part of the GB Olympic Team for the Beijing Olympic 2008 Games were from BME groups (Long *et al.* 2009). Yet research into the relationship between black and Asian people and sport since the 1990s has demonstrated the historical and contemporary extent of racism in various British sports – athletics, basketball, cricket, rugby league and rugby union, football, hockey, boxing and others (for example, see the collections edited by Carrington and McDonald 2001 and Jarvie 1991b).

Few systematic studies into non-white people's participation in sport at grassroots level have been undertaken. It is apparent that levels of participation in sport are not equal for all ethnic groups. In 1996, 46 per cent of white adults had participated in one activity (excluding walking) during the previous four weeks, compared with 41 per cent of black people, 37 per cent of Indians and 25 per cent of Pakistanis and Bangladeshis (Sport England 1999a). Ethnic minorities remain under-represented in their use of local authority swimming pools (Sport England 1999b).

Analysis of sports-specific participation by ethnic minorities has not been possible due to the small sample sizes, but in 2000 Sport England published *Sports Participation and Ethnicity in England National Survey 1999/2000*. This was the first large-scale survey (with 3,000 non-white adult respondents) focusing on England. It found that 49 per cent of ethnic minority men compared with 54 per cent of white men had participated in sport in the previous four weeks. Of ethnic minority women, 32 per cent, compared with 39 per cent of white women, had participated in sport in the previous four weeks. The survey found that 39 per cent of black Caribbean and Indian people, 31 per cent of Pakistani people and 30 per cent of Bangladeshi people participated in sport. Compared with the general population, few ethnic minorities declared walking as a physical activity (e.g. only 19 per cent of Bangladeshi women compared to 44 per cent of the total population). The findings showed differences between the participation of men and women. Swimming had a low priority, whereas football involvement among men was about the national average (10 per cent).

Such research into the physical activity of BME people – in Britain as elsewhere – has tended to focus on two main themes. On the one hand are *equity issues*; to do with what Coakley (2003) calls the 'sports opportunity structure', the preserving of prejudices despite black excellence in sport, and 'stacking' – the over-representation of black athletes in certain positions in team sports deemed to require less intelligence. Various anti-racism campaigns (for example, 'Let's Kick Racism Out of Football' in 1993/1994, now renamed 'Kick it Out', 'Hit Racism for Six!' in cricket in 1995 and 'Football against Racism in Europe' (FARE) in 2002) have developed in response to these issues. On the other hand, research has begun to look at *resistance to* or *accommodation with* racism through the consumption of sport. While some black people have used sport as a route of black cultural resistance to racism and positive identity formation (Carrington and McDonald 2001), others, especially male youth in the US, have been enticed into following their 'hoop dreams' (Brooks-Buck and Anderson 2001).

The mass media play a major role in the creation of such aspirations. According to Brookes (2002: 107ff.), research into media representation has developed to challenge the conceptual notion of stereotyping. The increasing commodification of sport has affected the way black people are represented in the sports media and targeted as consumers. These ideas relate to developments in the theoretical conception of personal and social identity which have emerged in the past 25 years, especially the idea that identity is an ongoing process. This last idea questions the value of the concept of stereotype and suggests instead that 'racial identity is not stable, essential or consistent; it is dynamic, complex and contradictory' (Brookes 2002).

Similarly, Carrington (2010) argues that it is useful to 'read the politics of sport and race diasporically'. Cassius Clay's performance in boxing at the 1960 Olympic Games in Rome placed the African-American at the centre of attention (Hylton 2009: 18–19). When in the 1960s the civil rights movement in the US was at its height, John Carlos and Tommie Smith promoted the Black Power movement to a global audience in Mexico City in 1968 (Hylton 2009: 11). In this way, 'black' national stars have acquired global significance through involvement in sports events that have been mass mediated. Several other of the most 'iconic moments in African-American sporting history occurred *outside* of the United States' – Jesse Owens in Berlin in 1936 and Wilma Rudolph in Rome in 1960. Hence, Carrington argues, 'African-American athletes are associated more with international geographical markers than with American ones' (Carrington 2010: 58).

Yet these accomplishments also promote an expectation of performance by black athletes. Hylton (2009: 81–82) describes how he showed a photograph of Kostas Kenderis winning the 200-metre sprint final at the 2000 Sydney Olympic Games to students. He asked them what was wrong with the photograph. The consensus of his students was that a white sprinter had actually finished ahead of black athletes. If black achievement in track and field has become the conventional wisdom, so too has under-performance in other Olympic events. Hence Eric Moussambani's swim in Sydney made him a universal representative of black Africans in water in the British media (as 'Eric the Eel'). By contrast, Eddie Edwards' ski-jumping performance in Calgary in 1988 (nicknamed 'Eddie the Eagle') did not get reduced to deficiencies in his biology or make him a representative of an entire continent (Carrington 2004: 89).

Media coverage of the 2012 Olympics, and all Olympic Games subsequently, needs to be examined in terms of the racialised construction of potential and previous Olympic champions. As Carrington (2010: 137–140) notes, media discussion after both the decision to award London the hosting of the 2012 Olympics (on 6 July 2005) and the bombing of London Underground trains and a bus the following day (on 7 July 2005, often referred to as '7/7') raised the issue of multiculturalism in Europe. If 6 July involved a positive and strong celebration of multiculturalism and the development of a tolerant, open and diverse city, media reaction to the events of the following day suggested that multiculturalism had fanned the flames of intolerance, segregation and ethnic tension. Both reactions also demonstrated the potential power of sport to influence, aid in or even thwart the creation of ethnically diverse communities in the UK.

GENDER: OLYMPIC SPORT AS A VEHICLE FOR THE DEMONSTRATION OF GENDER DIFFERENCES[3]

'The inclusion of women at the Olympic Games would be "impractical, uninteresting, unaesthetic, and incorrect"' (Pierre de Coubertin, 1912 cited in Donnelly and Donnelly 2013a: 12). Coubertin's views about the role and place of women in sport, and those of many of his fellow members of the IOC, have thrown a shadow over the Olympic movement since its inception. Struggles over women's right to participate, equality in the number of events available to them and the organisation of the Olympic movement more generally have taken place (Harvey *et al.* 2014: 42–66; Hargreaves 1984, 1994, 2000; Bandy 2010). Despite this, as Hargreaves (1994) also demonstrated, some men have supported the inclusion of women in sport and the Olympics in particular. Inclusion has involved debates about the number of female participants, the number of events and the leadership opportunities open to women.

The IOC had no women members until as recently as 1981, when it appointed two; it has been making attempts to catch up since. By 1995 still only seven out of 107 IOC members were women. It established a 20 per cent threshold goal for the inclusion of women in National Olympic Committees (NOCs), National Governing Bodies (NGBs) and International Federations (IFs). In 2014, 23 of the 102 members of the IOC were women (22.6 per cent) and four members of the 15-member IOC Executive Committee were female (IOC 2014b: 58–59).

Women's sporting participation at the Olympic Games has, however, recently shown greater improvement (Donnelly and Donnelly 2013a). At the Opening Ceremony of London 2012 President Rogge declared that the Games represented 'a major boost for gender equality' with three milestones reached: a higher percentage of women athletes than any previous Summer Olympics; women competitors in every sport; and no countries preventing women from participating. At London 2012 the 26 Olympic sports were organised into 36 different competitions (for example, cycling had four competitions or disciplines as they are described in the Olympic Charter – BMX, mountain bikes, road and track races). These 36 competitions were organised into 302 events for which medals were awarded (for example, there were ten boxing events for men and three boxing events for women). There were 136 women's events and 166 men's events (Donnelly and Donnelly 2013a: 16). Figure 11.1 outlines the changes in women's participation at the Summer Olympics from 1900 to 2012.

Year	Host	Women	Men	Women's sports/events
1900	Paris	22	975	4/2
1904	St. Louis	6	645	1/1
1908	London	37	1,971	1/2
1912	Stockholm	48	2,359	3/6
1920	Antwerp	65	2,561	2/6
1924	Paris	135	2,954	5/11
1952	Helsinki	519	4,436	6/25
1960	Rome	610	4,736	6/29
1972	Munich	1,059	6,075	8/43
1980	Moscow	1,125	4,238	12/50
1988	Seoul	2,194	6,197	17/86
1996	Atlanta	3,512	6,806	21/108
2000	Sydney	4,069	6,582	25/132
2008	Beijing	4,637	6,305	26/137
2012	London	4,835	6,068	26/136

Figure 11.1 Gender and participation at selected Summer Olympic Games: 1900–2012.

Sources: Donnelly and Donnelly (2013a); IOC (2010a); Toohey and Veal (2007: 199).

Despite the fact that London 2012 was hailed as the 'Women's Games' – in so far as it featured female athletes in every national team for the first time ever, women's competitions in every event, the introduction of women's boxing as an Olympic discipline and the first-ever (knowingly) pregnant Olympic competitor (Harvey *et al.* 2014: 42) – as Donnelly and Donnelly (2013a: 5) suggest in a *gender equality audit* of London 2012, it would be incorrect to assume that gender inequality in participation at the Olympics is a thing of the past. There remain at least four areas of inequality still evident between male and female athletes and teams: differences in funding and sponsorship; differences in publicity and media representation; the re-emergence of sex-testing for female athletes (see also Donnelly and Donnelly 2013b); and gender-based structural and rule differences that exist in sports and the Olympic programme.

It is worth considering how we got to this point. Women were first included in the 1900 Olympic Games in Paris. According to the IOC, at those Games there were 22 female participants, or 2.3 per cent of the total number of competitors (IOC 2010a). In Beijing in 2008 the 42 per cent participation rate for women was a record, up from less than 12 per cent in 1960 (Rome), 22 per cent in 1980 (Moscow) and 38 per cent in 2000 (Sydney). In London in 2012 there were 136 women's events and 166 men's events. Of these, 48 events were gender exclusive, 39 events were open to men only (23.5 per cent of men's events) and nine events were open to women only (6.6 per cent of women's events). In total 1,233 more men than women competed in London (Donnelly and Donnelly 2013a: 6).

Despite Coubertin's view that 'If some women want to play football or box, let them, provided the event takes place without spectators, because the spectators who flock to such competitions are not there to watch as sport' (Coubertin 2000 [1928]: 189), in August 2009 the IOC agreed to the request from the International Amateur Boxing Association (IABA) to allow women to take part in boxing. Hence in London in 2012 women's boxing took place for the first time at the Summer Olympics (Woodward 2014b). In April 2011, the IOC also announced that for the first time women's ski jumping would be permitted to take place at the Winter Olympic Games in Sochi (Russia) in 2014. The International Ski Federation, the world governing body, supported the inclusion of this event, while the IOC appeared to resist (see Box 11.1). What is also noteworthy about this attempt to gain approval for another (women's) event at the Olympics is that a Canadian judge ruled in

---

BOX 11.1 WOMEN'S SKI JUMPING: THE STRUGGLE TO BECOME AN OLYMPIC EVENT

Ski jumping (for men) has been part of the Winter Olympics since the first Games in Chamonix Mont-Blanc in 1924. The existence of a men's competition without a women's competition has become a major bone of contention as the field of elite female competitors has grown. In May 2006, the International Ski Federation (FIS) decided to allow women to ski jump at the 2009 Nordic World Ski Championships in Liberec, Czech Republic (won by Lindsey Van of the United States), and then to have a team event for women at the 2011 world championships in Oslo. Women have competed on the Continental Cup circuit since 2005.

246

In 2006, FIS also decided to submit a proposal to the IOC to allow women to compete at the 2010 Winter Olympics in Vancouver. In November that year the Executive Board of the IOC rejected the proposal for a women's ski jumping event in 2010. The reason given was the low number of athletes as well as few participating countries in the sport. The Executive Board noted that women's ski jumping had yet to be fully established internationally. Jacques Rogge stated that women's ski jumping would not be an Olympic event because 'we do not want the medals to be diluted and watered down', referring to the relatively small number of potential competitors in women's ski jumping. It has been noted that while the number of women in ski jumping is not insignificant, the field has a much wider spread in terms of talent, in that the top men are all of a similar level of strength competitively, while the women are more varied, even in the top tiers. Supporters of women's ski jumping argued, on the other hand, that there were 135 top-level female ski jumpers in 16 countries, saying that was more than the number of women competing at that level in some other sports that were already in the Winter Games.

A group of 15 competitive female ski jumpers filed a suit against the Vancouver Organizing Committee (VANOC), claiming that conducting a men's ski jumping event without a women's event in the Vancouver Winter Olympics in 2010 would be in direct violation of Section 15 of the Canadian Charter of Rights and Freedoms. The ski jumpers wanted a court declaration that VANOC must either hold women's ski jumping in 2010 or cancel all ski jumping events. VANOC argued that the IOC decides which sports are allowed in the Games and that the national Charter did not apply to it. For its part, the IOC had insisted that its decision to keep women's ski jumping out of the Vancouver Games was based on technical merit, not discrimination. The arguments associated with this suit were heard in court in April 2009 and a judgment was made in June 2009 against the ski jumpers. The judge ruled that although the women were being discriminated against, the issue was an IOC responsibility and thus not governed by the Canadian Charter. The court further ruled that the Canadian Charter of Rights and Freedoms did not apply to VANOC. Subsequently three British Columbia judges unanimously denied an appeal on 13 November 2009.

In 2006, the IOC had said that past world championships were one of several criteria used to determine which of several possible new events would be included in the 2010 Winter Olympics. 'Events must have a recognized international standing both numerically and geographically, and have been included at least twice in world and continental championships.' The statement said the decision not to include curling mixed doubles and women's ski jumping in the 2010 Winter Games 'was made as their development is still in the early stage thus lacking the international spread of participation and technical standard required for an event to be included in the programme'. But advocates for the inclusion of women's ski jumping say the IOC formally dropped that requirement in 2007.

In October 2010 the IOC's ruling Executive Board chaired by the then President Jacques Rogge held a joint meeting with the National Olympic Committees.

The Executive Board considered whether to include women's ski jumping for a third time. Gian-Franco Kasper, President of FIS, reported that he was 'very optimistic' that all five proposed ski events would win approval, if not immediately then in the coming months. 'They don't need additional courses or anything built', he said. 'And there is enough space in the programme.' However the IOC delayed the decision until April 2011. The IOC's Executive Board claimed that they needed more time before making a final decision and this was eventually made by President Rogge after FIS had staged their World Championships. The IOC had said that it believed including the events would increase universality, gender equality and youth appeal, and in general add value to the Games, but it wanted more time to study them. After the World Championships held in Oslo in February 2011, President of the FIS Gian-Franco Kasper said he was very optimistic that ski jumping for women would be in the Sochi Olympics in 2014. Final approval from the IOC, however, had to wait until the meeting in April 2011.

(Sources: Nybelius and Hofmann 2015; Hofmann 2011; Vertinsky *et al.* 2009)

2009, ahead of the 2010 Winter Olympics in Vancouver, that although the women were being discriminated against, the issue was an IOC responsibility and thus not governed by Canadian laws. The court further ruled that the Canadian Charter of Rights and Freedoms did not apply to VANOC, the Organising Committee of the 2010 Winter Olympic Games.

Women's participation in sport in general still attracts debate in many countries (Lenskyj 2013; Kietlinski 2011). Some scholars suggest that over 100 years after its formation, modern sport is a 'rather less reliable ally of hegemonic masculinity' (Rowe 1995: 130). Others argue that sport, via its links with consumer culture, continues to play a part in the assertion and affirmation of specific hegemonic ideals of masculinity (Day 1990). Fischer and Gainer (1994), for example, analysed a range of research studies investigating the relationship between gender and sport and concluded that:

> the consumption of sports is deeply associated with defining what is masculine and, concurrently, what is not feminine. It has been noted that participating in and watching sports lead to a range of masculinities, and each of them relies for its definition on being distinct from femininity.

> (Fischer and Gainer 1994: 101)

Their conclusion is shared by historical studies that have emphasised how sport was a gender-distinguishing activity, related to a changing gender order – for example, in the US between the 1840s and 1890s, and in the UK between the 1820s and 1880s (Burstyn 1999; Whitson 1994). The 'gendering' of sport by men involved various techniques, including definition, direct control and ignoring and/or trivialising women's sport or their involvement in sport. For men, sport was a primary socialising experience – into masculine identities, hierarchical social bonding and various forms of masculinity. Hence women faced marginalisation in their consumption of sport. The macho (or 'fratriarchal') culture of sport is repeatedly reinforced with every media report of the sexual misbehaviour of young

248

male elite athletes or men associated with the administration of the sport. Only analysis of the social meanings and interactions of specific subcultural groups, the media portrayal of women as athletes and the gendered consumption of sport (for example, Wellard 2002; Fleming 1995) can reveal the nature of women's and men's practices and settle these kinds of questions with respect to the Olympic Games.

Vertinsky *et al.* (2009) use a framework developed by McDonagh and Pappano (2008) to examine the history of women's ski jumping, and document the modes of regulation which have developed around female participation in ski jumping competitions and women's historical exclusion from the Olympic Games. Vertinsky *et al.* approach sport as a socially constructed space and system, which over 100 years since its establishment still privileges the male body as superior. Sport therefore is viewed as not simply reflecting social and gender realities, but as playing a key role in constructing them. Hence in their view,

> a central problem with organized sport has been the way that sport-related policies – especially those enforcing sex segregation – have codified historical myths about female physical inferiority, fostering a system which, while offering women more opportunities than ever before, has kept them from being perceived as equal athletes to men.
>
> (Vertinsky *et al.* 2009: 44)

From this approach, sex segregation in sport does not reflect actual sex differences in athletic ability, but instead helps to construct and enforce the premise that males are inherently athletically superior to females. This premise has been built on three assumptions (which Vertinsky *et al.* call the 'three Is'), which have their origins in nineteenth-century beliefs about the female sporting body and women's proper role in society: female *inferiority* compared to males; the need to protect females from *injury* in competition; and the *immorality* of females who compete directly with males.

Challenging these assumptions, they suggest – following McDonagh and Pappano (2008) – requires moving through a four-stage process: (1) challenging the prohibition of women from participating in certain sports activities; (2) allowing women to participate in sports activities on a sex-segregated basis; (3) accommodating women in sports programmes on a sex-integrated basis; and (4) permitting women to choose whether they prefer a sex-integrated or sex-segregated context for their sports activities (i.e. on the basis of voluntary, rather than coercive, sex segregation). The problem is that it is not a straightforward process, but one based on struggles that can mean setbacks as well as forward momentum (Hofmann 2011; Hofmann and Preuss 2005). A report for the Women's Sports Foundation (WSF) (2009), *Women in the 2000, 2004 and 2008 Olympic and Paralympic Games*, concluded that:

> While progress has been made, the Olympic Games are an enormous undertaking where progress and inequalities co-exist. In 2008, the IOC projected 45% for women, but it appears that this increase in percentage was the result of a modest participation increase for women and a decrease in the participation of male athletes. The participation gap between female and male athletes has closed over

the last two Olympiads primarily by cutting the men's field. This is also true of the gap between female and male Paralympians. Several adjustments were made in the 2008 Paralympic program, which offers fewer classifications for male athletes, while increasing the number of classifications for female athletes.

(WSF 2009: 3)[4]

In 2008 the WSF report noted that certain countries had not incorporated more females into their Olympic teams. While the Olympic Solidarity Program was available to assist with funding for nations facing financial difficulties, some countries claim cultural and religious sanctions preclude the inclusion of women on their Olympic teams. Nonetheless, some countries with religious constraints have sent women to the Games. For example, Egypt sent 16 women (over 16 per cent of the total team) to the 2004 Summer Olympics. Egypt has been cited as being different from other Islamic countries because of its secular interpretation of Islam (Walseth and Fasting 2003), but other Muslim nations have also increased the number of female athletes (accounting for 60 per cent of Senegal's delegation in 2004).

An illustration of the way the rules of sport impact differently on Muslim female athletes occurred in 2012. Saudi Arabia sent two women athletes to the Olympic Games for the first time. The Saudi team insisted that the judoka Wojdan Ali Seraj Abdulrahim Shaherkani would not compete without wearing a hijab (a veil that covers the head and chest), while the International Judo Federation (IJF) insisted that she remove the hijab on safety grounds. The IOC resolved the matter with both sides agreeing that Ms Shaherkani wear a modified head cover (Donnelly and Donnelly 2013a: 15).

Testing of sex type remains one of the most significant markers of sport, and elite Olympic sport especially, as a gendered activity (Donnelly and Donnelly 2013a: 14–15; Horne *et al.* 2013: 114–119). Mokgadi Caster Semenya, the South African middle-distance runner and world champion, won the gold medal in the women's 800 metres at the 2009 World Championships. Afterwards, questions were raised about whether Semenya had an intersex condition that might give her an unfair advantage over the other racers. She was withdrawn from international competition until 6 July 2010, when the IAAF cleared her to return to competition. The result, however, was that 'all international women athletes were left with the legacy of a new "fem test" based on testosterone levels' (Donnelly and Donnelly 2013a: 15). Analysis of international newspaper coverage before and during the 2004 Summer Olympics in Athens demonstrated that the media still tend to focus on women's appearance and bodies rather than their athletic performance (Markula 2009). Women competitors in more 'feminine' sports – such as archery, badminton, swimming, diving, gymnastics and volleyball – tended to attract more attention than women in 'masculine' ones that exhibit size, power, strength, speed and contact.

The WSF (2009: 2) report concluded that the IOC has recently 'made noteworthy attempts to support the inclusion of greater numbers of women in the international sporting scene'. Initiatives include the Women and Sport Commission and the Fourth IOC World Conference on Women and Sport, held in 2008. However, changes have been less far-reaching in the NOCs, the IFs and the International Paralympic Committee. The WSF report considered that most of them still 'struggle to meet the IOC's request that women be represented at a minimal 20% standard in leadership positions' (WSF 2009: 2).

The need to encourage women to be involved in leadership positions and organisations – from the grassroots levels to the upper echelons of competitive Olympic and Paralympic sport – remains ongoing. One of the barriers to this is that the marketing of exercise – evidenced in health and fitness magazines as well as mainstream women's magazines – is often not for physiological fitness or psychological health, but in pursuit of physical perfection or sexual attractiveness. Women are more likely to engage in exercise – non-competitive physical activity – rather than sport. Image-making and commercialisation of the sexual body in sport has developed for women athletes, but increasingly in the last two decades for men also (Whannel 2000). Is the impact on men and women the same?

Research by Sassatelli (1999) and Fishwick (2001) suggested that some women are able to find in exercise and health clubs an important space for self-development lacking in other parts of their lives. Yet considerably fewer opportunities exist for women to work in professional sport than men. Sport offers women new ways of spending leisure time and exercising economic power. But it arguably also helps to confirm and reinforce their role and position in society. It offers both liberation and constraint, challenging some social norms or conventions while incorporating some people into others. The recent attempt to encourage women as consumers of sportswear, as well as spectators at big events, may suggest a decline in the peripheral nature of sport to women compared with men. But there are many ways that women remain on the outside of sport – and Olympic sport especially. As Lenskyj (2013: 131ff.) argues, Olympic sport still 'privileges certain gendered, classed, raced and sexualized sporting bodies'.

DISABILITY SPORT: PARALYMPISM AS A VEHICLE FOR BLURRING DIFFERENCES

The London 2012 Games (thankfully for some people) only had two official mascots: Wenlock and Mandeville. Readers of earlier chapters will recognise where the first name comes from – Much Wenlock in Shropshire, which hosted games in the nineteenth century, and was visited by Coubertin as he was searching for models for his modern Olympics (see Chapter 6). Mandeville, on the other hand, derived from the name of the hospital that hosted the first ever 'Paralympic' Games – Stoke Mandeville Hospital in Aylesbury, Buckinghamshire, a few miles to the north of London.

Aside from Team GB athletes, such as Tanni Grey-Thompson, the undeniable poster boy of the Paralympic Games in 2012 was South African double-amputee Oscar Pistorius (Horne 2013: 119–120). His trial and subsequent conviction for killing his girlfriend, Reeva Steenkamp, in 2013 should have nothing to do with the Paralympic Games. However, such is the nature of his celebrity through association with the Games that his trial became global news. Pistorius was acquitted of murder but found guilty of 'culpable homicide' (the South African equivalent of manslaughter). In December 2015, however, South Africa's Supreme Court of Appeal (SCA) overturned that conviction and replaced it with one of murder. At the time of writing Pistorius is on bail awaiting sentencing.

It is now a requirement of potential Olympic hosts that the Paralympics and 'regular' Olympic events must be included in any candidacy file. In the past decade the IOC has embraced the International Paralympic Committee (Cashman and Darcy 2008). Do these

Figure 11.2
Pearly Mandeville
in the East End of
London.

developments mark a significant move from the two events existing in separate spheres to consecutive staging of the Games? In the future will we see a genuinely combined Games? This section marks a note of caution about these developments and suggests that struggles over the meaning and place of para- or disability sport will continue (Brittain 2015; Smith and Thomas 2012).

Sainsbury's, the large British supermarket chain, acted as sponsor of the 2012 Paralympics, and Channel 4 (C4) covered the Paralympics exclusively and extensively on television. C4 ran a series of advertisements featuring the strap line 'Thanks for the warm up' towards the end of the Summer Olympics. Using the song 'Harder than you think' by American rap group Public Enemy as the theme tune, C4 produced almost an equal amount of saturation coverage of the Paralympics as the BBC had of the Olympic Games in 2012. But did this award-winning coverage on TV and in the press signal a major step forward for disabled people and athletes?

According to Colin Barnes (1992), disabled people have identified ten commonly recurring disabling stereotypes in the mass media. These are the disabled person as:

1. pitiable and pathetic;
2. an object of curiosity or violence;
3. sinister or evil;
4. super cripple;
5. adding atmosphere;
6. laughable;
7. his/her own worst enemy;
8. a burden;
9. non-sexual;
10. unable to participate in daily life.

Studies of impairment and disability representation took off in the 1980s. Disabled people were found, to a large extent, to be absent from much of the mainstream media. There were few, if any, disabled characters in soap operas or other long-running TV dramas. When they did appear, little attention was paid to the ordinary features of their lives – love, romance or sex – and the focus was primarily on the interaction of disabled people with health and social care professionals. Drama was focused on how they managed their impairment. Television portrayals seemed to be underpinned by themes such as pity, fear, menace, loathing, innocence and courage (Cumberbatch and Negrine 1992). They dealt with personal tragedies and special achievements.

Similar critiques have been made of newspaper coverage of disability. The press tended to focus on health, fundraising and charity, as well as on the personal tragedy dimensions of stories about people with disabilities. Researchers identified a fairly consistent negative cultural stereotyping of people with impairments. Media representations have tended to be underpinned by cultural rules about 'able-bodied-ness' (Barnes 1992). Attempts to offer alternative counter-representations could run the risk of alienating the audience and producing fear. Historical research into media representations of people with disabilities reveals a fascination with what have been described as 'spectacles of difference'. These serve to reinforce the image of a disabled person either as a tragic but brave victim of a crippling condition, or as a pitiable and pathetic individual. Reviewing research into media representations of disabled people, Barnes and Mercer (2003) identified the issue of *cultural domination* – 'in which groups experience symbolic devaluation' (Barnes and Mercer 2003: 88) – as a central concern. But they also suggested that there has been a change in the way disabled people are represented, with more disabled people appearing in soap operas and drama series as 'ordinary' (Barnes and Mercer 2003). The coverage of disabled sport may be another area where changes are under way.

Despite the acknowledgement that the mass media and other cultural representations play a constitutive role in the social definition and reproduction of meanings of disability, compared to research into the representation of women and BME people in sport, there has been very little that focuses on the media representation of disabled athletes or people with disabilities participating in sport (Goggin and Newell 2000). As Anderson (2000: 107) notes: 'Throughout history, disabled sport has been somewhat marginalised by the media. Although as exciting and emotive as any sport, disabled sport has not received much media coverage.' In fact, film archives do demonstrate that disabled sports people were often represented as examples of 'the super cripple' (Howe 2011, 2013).

Systematic analysis of the media coverage of the Paralympic Games and disability sport in general has only recently begun to develop (see, for example, Schantz and Gilbert 2001; Schell and Duncan 1999). Thomas and Smith (2003) published an analysis of the British media coverage of the 2000 Paralympic Games held in Sydney. Their study focused on the print media and examined the language and images used to portray athletes' performances. They reached four main conclusions:

1   There was a tendency for the print media to provide medicalised descriptions of disability (with an emphasis placed on the athletes overcoming their medical problems).
2   The photographic images often hid the athletes' impairments.
3   Female Paralympic Games athletes were less likely to be portrayed in active poses than male athletes.
4   The images tended to reinforce stereotypical perceptions of disability and reaffirm notions of able-bodied-ness (through an emphasis, for example, on how Paralympic Games athletes sought to emulate able-bodied athletes).

Hence the eight British newspapers that Thomas and Smith gathered data from produced a view of disability as individualised rather than socially constructed and tended, they argued, to trivialise disabled people's athletic performances. The portrayal of disabled people often produces an individualised account of disability. Disabled people are often viewed as dependent, reported in a way which is patronising and objectifying, and with images that tend to direct attention away from the social factors that create disability. These tendencies are a feature of much news and documentary reporting, of which sports reporting can be considered a part. It also may be because disabled people are rarely involved in the decision-making processes in the media about what should and should not be shown or reported. When asked how she felt her sport was covered in the media, Tanni Grey-Thompson, the winner of nine Paralympic gold medals for Britain, said:

> We do pretty well, for a minority sport. The coverage is still probably a bit too nice. The print media are getting bolder but there is a feeling that broadcasters don't want the criticism to seem too harsh.
>
> (*Daily Telegraph* 16 September 2003)

Yet, as research has revealed, disabled female athletes have less coverage (Schantz and Gilbert 2001; Schell and Duncan 1999) than disabled male athletes, those with cerebral palsy and learning difficulties have less coverage than other disabled athletes and wheelchair athletes receive greater media attention than others – possibly because they are perceived to deviate less from cultural notions of able-bodiedness than the others.

While Thomas and Smith (2003) offer a welcome contribution to the literature, there are a number of omissions. As noted above, they focused on representations of the 2000 Paralympic Games from a selection of only eight national English newspapers (and adopted an unusual classification system that linked the *Guardian* and the *Sun/News of the World* together as 'liberal', and the *Daily Mail* and *The Times* together as 'conservative'). Because of this, they ignored regional daily newspapers, the local press and magazines (including niche sports magazines). In addition, they did not consider reporting of the 2000 Paralympic Games by television, radio or the internet (Goggin and Newell 2000). The focus on representations, while consistent with much of the international research previously cited, ignores the production of sport as news as well as entertainment (Whannel 1992; Horne *et al.* 2013: 87–104) in the broadcast media. In addition, by failing to take into account audience reception and readings of the media messages, they ignore important developments in media analysis that have occurred in the past decade.

In a discussion of sports journalism, difference and identity, Tudor (1998) noted that there have been three typical defences against the suggestion that sports reporting sustains patterns of inferential racism: 'lazy journalism'; 'reflecting society'; and 'things are improving'. We would suggest that the twin of 'inferential racism' might be called 'inferential handicapism' and that these three defences have been deployed when accusations have been made about the marginalisation of disabled people in the mainstream media and the coverage, or lack of it, of disabled sport. Yet as Tudor showed, each of these responses can be shown to be deficient. The first tends to individualise the issue when it is a more collective phenomenon. The second ignores the selecting, amplifying and spreading role of the media – the tabloid press, for example, often tends to assume a homogeneous public in appealing to crude populist assumptions. The third, while acknowledging problems in the past, fails to consider the extent to which the media have failed to challenge racism (or handicapism) in the present. There are some examples of media coverage of people with disabilities being discriminated against in sport or in sport situations – for example, Casey Martin, the American golf player who sued the Professional Golf Association for the right to use a golf cart in tournaments (reported in the *Guardian* 16 January 1998), and Shelley Anne Emery, the woman in a wheelchair whose image was digitally removed from a photograph of the England cricket team celebrating a Test Match win over South Africa, published in the *Sun* (reported in the *Guardian* 19 August 1998). There are also examples of disabled people being praised for their accomplishments in sport. Some might argue that this is merely perpetuating a culture of pity towards the disabled. An understanding of the history of the representations of disabled athletes in the media in all its forms is an essential prerequisite for assessing the impact of these changes. Yet to date there has been very little research undertaken into the history of the mass media involvement in disability sport in Britain, or, despite its prominence in the disability sports calendar, the social significance of the Paralympic Games (on this see Brittain 2009, 2012).

With the growth of the Paralympic Games, and in the US programmes such as 'Sporting Chance', which provide disabled people with opportunities to participate in sport, 'marketers are now addressing this market', according to Shank (2002: 412). In the US, Nixon (2000: 425) notes that 'We have even seen athletes with disabilities on "Wheaties" cereal boxes, a site where some of the most prominent American sports heroes have been displayed.' It can be argued that the development of the Paralympic Games has involved a transformation of their purpose from making disabled people into good worker-citizens, via participation in wholesome sport, into making them good consumer-citizens through their consumption of the expanded sports spectacle. Sport may become a major conduit for the production of what can be termed 'commodity disabilism' or the treatment of disability as a commodity. This will be accompanied by changes in the representation of disabled athletes in the media in all its forms. Some researchers have identified how this is already under way (Duncan and Aycock 2005).

Braye *et al.* (2013) argue that while the vision of the International Paralympic Committee (IPC) to use the Paralympic Games as a vehicle to achieve a more equitable society is a laudable one, the 2012 Paralympic Games, and Paralympic sport generally, has had very little positive impact on the everyday lives of disabled people in the UK. A survey of the opinions of disability activists in the UK before 2012 found that negative views towards the Paralympics existed prior to the media coverage on C4 (Braye *et al.* 2012). Braye *et al.* (2013) argue that the more positive, 'legacy of change' rhetoric, widely portrayed by the media after the 2012 Paralympics, did not address the sort of concerns research discussed earlier in this section reveals, that illustrates the ways in which the media itself can also contribute to undermining such positive messages. Nor, Braye *et al.* (2013) argue, did it adequately cover the barriers and inequalities disabled people face on a daily basis.

One of the contradictory features of the 2012 Paralympics, for example, was the role of French IT company Atos. The IPC had been in partnership with Atos since 2002 as a sponsor and marketing agency for the Paralympics. During 2012 a controversy arose over Atos as it was also contracted by the UK Department for Work and Pensions (DWP) to implement a Work Capability Assessment (WCA) used to assess disabled people's fitness to work. Critics suggested that the WCA strategy lacked integrity, was poorly implemented and ultimately removed vulnerable disabled people's benefits with tragic consequences. Despite the in-depth media coverage of the Paralympics and praise for the achievements of the Paralympians, opportunities for disabled people in Britain, outside of elite Paralympic athletes, were being eroded and have been restricted by coalition government welfare policy over the same period (Roan 2013). After undergoing a WCA between 2011 and 2014 and being found 'fit for work', 2,380 people with disabilities died.[5]

CONCLUSION

We began this chapter by referring to the mixed messages that come out of any assessment of the Olympics after London 2012. We also referred to Maurice Roche, who argued that, in addition to being a movement, the Olympics offered several other forms of global citizenship. With regard to universal citizenship, he suggested, 'arguably the negatives outweigh the positives in the Olympic record' (Roche 2000: 203). That within 27 years of the cessation of hostilities in 1945 all three Axis powers (Italy, Japan and (West) Germany) had hosted at least one Olympic Games might suggest otherwise, but Roche argues that the IOC has not tended to take 'a consistent and strong line on the human rights record' of the host nations. Equally, the likelihood that the Olympics as a media event will become fully available to all people in the world, via the internet, is another of those arguments about new media technologies that is based as much on hope as on experience. It is difficult to imagine that the IOC will allow internet coverage of the Games to compromise the major element in its funding – exclusive broadcasting rights revenue. Hence the media coverage of the mega-event has tended to be both commercialised and nationalised – in so far as the sports covered (the 'feed') tends to be determined by national TV companies' choices in line with the involvement of its athletes and the anticipated tastes of its viewers. It is in this way that international mega-events can be transformed into forums for national(ist) introspection.

As a collective actor in global civil society, the IOC has had to deal with another two issues concerning its integrity: the process of bidding to act as host and the development of the idea of an 'Olympic truce'. Regarding the first, as we have seen, Olympic city bidding corruption and the role of agents in helping to win bids was a focus of investigative journalism for much of the 1990s, and especially after 1998 and the revelations surrounding the bribes that enabled the success of Salt Lake City in obtaining the 2002 Winter Olympic Games. The Olympic truce idea, in conjunction with the United Nations, is a contribution to international civil society in so far as it seeks the preservation of human life and peaceful coexistence. Yet through this the UN risks 'being associated with an association which is committed to commercialism, global capitalism and consumer culture' (Roche 2000: 214–215).

Roche also draws attention to the phenomenological impacts of sports mega-events. In particular he looks at their role in providing time-structuring resources – both interpersonal and public – and suggests that the 'once in a lifetime' opportunity discourse so often associated with them is one of the main reasons for their popularity, at least among many of those who live in the cities and locations that host them. Roche (2003) argues that mega-events are socially memorable and culturally popular precisely because they mark time between generations and thus provide a link between what he calls the everyday lifeworld (micro social sphere) and the meso and macro social spheres. They are 'a special kind of time-structuring institution in modernity' (Roche 2003: 102). Hughes (1999), too, notes that underpinning the economic strategies captured by such notions as 'selling places', 'place marketing' and the 'creative city', the idea that ludic space might be an economically valuable use of land has come to the fore. The ludic city, though, might also be seen as valuable for the growth of sociality and the consideration of alternative ways of relating to each other as human beings rather than simply being for commercial gain (see Latham 2003).

Consumer identities and consumer spaces are produced by trademarked mega-events, including the Olympic Games (Magdalinski *et al.* 2005). At the same time, sport, culture and (pop) music events enable flows and mobilities of people and non-human entities. In the midst of these, new social identities and understandings – interlinked through social class, gender, ethnic, bodily and national differences – may be produced, resisted or sustained. Cashman (2006: 21–22) suggests that memory regarding sports mega-events such as the Olympic Games can take three forms – individual or private memory, spontaneous collective memory, and cultivated public memory. This begs the question, however, about who does the sustaining of memory – at the grassroots, citizens, the media or politicians – and for what ends. There can be a tendency when recalling events towards what Cashman refers to as 'Olympic reductionism' (2006: 25). Here, memories are reduced to the highlights – 'a few events which are repeatedly mentioned in public discourse' – and usually only the official achievements. In the popular memory of sports mega-events, how it is possible to go beyond these official accounts is an important question that continues to need to be addressed.

NOTES

1 The IOC Annual Report for 2014 is subtitled 'Credibility, Sustainability and Youth'.
2 www.olympic.org/news/ioc-president-calls-sport-a-natural-partner-for-realisation-of-sustainable-development-goals-during-speech-to-the-united-nations/247232 (last accessed 30 September 2015).
3 This section, as with much of the rest of the book, focuses on the *Summer* Olympic Games. For discussion of the gendered nature of the Winter Olympics see Lenskyj (2013: 99–104) and Donnelly and Donnelly (2015).
4 www.womenssportsfoundation.org/home/research/articles-and-reports/athletes/2000-2004-and-2008-olympic-report (last accessed 28 September 2015).
5 www.independent.co.uk/news/uk/politics/over-4000-people-have-died-soon-after-being-found-fit-to-work-by-the-dwp-s-benefit-tests-10474474.html (last accessed 27 October 2015).

FURTHER READING

Howe, P.D. (2008) *The Cultural Politics of the Paralympic Movement*, London: Routledge.
Hylton, K. and Morpeth, N. (2012) 'London 2012: "race" matters and the East End', *International Journal of Sport Policy and Politics* 4 (3), 379–396.
Lenskyj, H. (2013) *Gender Politics and the Olympic Industry*, Basingstoke: Palgrave Macmillan.
Smith, A., Haycock, D. and Hulme, N. (2013) 'The class of London 2012: some sociological reflections on the social backgrounds of Team GB athletes', *Sociological Research Online* 18 (3).

CHAPTER 12

THE 'DARK SIDE' OF THE OL

This chapter considers recent developments affectin~~~~~
and other mega-events. The Olympic movement can b~~~~~
tional sporting bodies by the manner in which, fro~~~~~ proclaimed its
moral mission. From the time of de Coubertin's concer~~~~~ the fitness of youth and the
need for an internationalist perspective, the discourse of Olympism began to develop.
A recent formulation announced that the Olympic movement stands for 'a healthier,
more equal, and more tolerant society, freed from prejudice and division, and untarni-
shed by discrimination and injustice' (121st Session and 13th Congress of the IOC,
Copenhagen 2009).

The Olympic movement is hugely successful in that it has evolved a global mega-event that
grips the imagination and signifies human aspirations – faster, higher, stronger. It also faces
a series of challenges, associated with commercialism, corruption, drug-use, gambling, the
environment and security, to name only a few. Since the processes of commercialisation
in the Olympics began to grow more rapidly, from the start of the 1980s, the contradictions
have sharpened, and the tensions heightened. Institutions taking decisions involving
millions of dollars are always likely to involve a certain amount of corruption. In the case
of the Olympics, the choice of sites, with a great deal at stake, is taken in a secret ballot by
an electorate of barely 100, who are not answerable to anyone for how they vote. Whole
teams of people within bidding committees devote much of their time for two or more
years considering how best to win votes from among this tiny electorate. The Olympic
'product' is, judging by the large sums paid by television corporations and sponsoring
corporations to obtain the rights, a highly valuable one. Yet this brand is dependent on its
image and is hence vulnerable and can be tarnished – by corruption, but also by potential
scandals involving performance-enhancing drugs, gambling and the fixing of results, and
over-zealous security measures that conflict with the potential festival of sport.

The Olympics maintains its environmental credentials are good, yet every Games is also
accompanied by stories of displaced people, demolished housing and environmental
damage. Significant air miles are clocked up by the 30,000 or more people that, as competitors, officials, administrators, consultants, researchers and journalists, are part of the
Olympic travelling circus. The very success of this high-profile global mega-event has
required ever-greater investment in security, to the extent that the Games have become
for the security industry an invaluable exercise in research and development paid for by
the public purse.

...re, we review some of the main challenges that the Olympic
...esent. We offer focused consideration of three of the main concerns
...tion, doping and security at the Games – to indicate just some of the
...temporary scale of mega-events can create temptations for organisers,
...vernments to go way beyond the Olympic ideals and enter what we call the
...of the Olympics, and arguably sports mega-events generally.

CORRUPTION RISKS IN THE IOC AND OTHER MEGA-EVENT ORGANISATIONS

The hidden world of corruption in world sport, which the indefatigable investigative journalist Andrew Jennings has been unmasking for 30 years, began to unravel in 2015, as a result of an FBI investigation into FIFA. Much of this story commences with Horst Dassler, who drove the sports business through Adidas and then in the 1980s also through ISL (see Chapter 4). As a young man in the 1950s, Dassler was a pioneer in ensuring that as many sports teams and individuals as possible wore Adidas, achieved originally by giving them as gifts, and subsequently by what he used to refer to, with a wry smile, as 'insoles', which he made clear were payments for wearing his brand of shoes and clothing. Despite the concerns of the then IOC President, Avery Brundage, these payments became routine. In a highly competitive business, Dassler sought an edge by nurturing links with up-and-coming officials in sport governing bodies around the world, including, for example, former FIFA President Sepp Blatter and current IOC President Thomas Bach, who was a member of his 'international relations' team (Jennings 2014).

Dassler was instrumental in ensuring that Havelange became FIFA President, and Samaranch became IOC President. He boosted the careers of many other sports officials including Primo Nebiolo and Sepp Blatter. A wide network of favours, inducements, corrupt practices, kickbacks and bribes spread throughout the world of sport governing bodies. The payment of bribes to influence the vote on venues for mega-events became routine. Only recently, and partly after many years of investigative journalism by Andrew Jennings, have many of the suspicions and allegations begun to harden into proof. It now seems likely, for example, that several top former FIFA executives may be facing jail sentences.

The time when international sport governing bodies could turn a blind eye, drag their feet, make light of accusations and impose minimal reprimands may be coming to an end. For the IOC, an organisation with a self-proclaimed moral mission, and many members of high integrity, the record of corrupt or questionable behaviour among some of its members is not impressive. Thomas Bach was a protégé of both Dassler and Samaranch. He was an Adidas executive and according to the *Guardian*, a German television documentary contained allegations that he was part of Dassler's inner circle, helping place favoured candidates in sporting federations and paying inducements to sport stars (*Guardian* 14 September 2013). Readers might like to investigate the alleged involvement in corruption of such people as João Havelange (former President of FIFA), Lamine Diack (former President of the IAAF), Guy Drut (former Minister of Youth Affairs and Sport in France), Lee Kun-Hee (former chairman of the Samsung corporation), Kim Un-yong (former Vice-President of the IOC), Bob Hasan (former IOC member) and

260

Primo Nebiolo (another former President of the IAAF), who have all been IOC members (Jennings 2014).

But individuals are easier to identify than complex systems. This can leave the structure or system enabling corruption intact. The structure of the system is the elephant in the room; just as the 'criminogenic environment of the financial system' (Sayer 2015: 273) was responsible for the economic crash of 2007–2008, it is necessary to consider the problems of international sport as part of a systemic crisis. This section sketches some of the ways in which corruption risks enter into the planning and hosting of sports mega-events. We argue that it is important to understand that the sources, forms and consequences of corruption vary: 'Corruption is not an external or superficial feature but rather is embedded within political and economic systems. Its precise role and effects will depend on the configurations and dynamics of such systems' (Williams 1999: 488).

Corruption remains a slippery concept to define precisely and discussion of it tends to create binaries: the Western and Eastern blocs of nations, developed and developing societies, democratic and authoritarian regimes, regulated and self-regulated organisations and associations (see Figure 12.1). The power to define corruption may be said to lie with the dominant party and usually that means those in the left-hand column of the figure. Hence Africa, South America and Asia are often considered to be the continents and subcontinents particularly affected by corruption.

This creates the potential for accusations of overstepping territorial jurisdiction, as has happened with respect to the role of the FBI and the US Attorney General in the crisis at FIFA (Sopel 2015) and the basis for concerns that the action taken was politically motivated against Russia (host of the 2018 World Cup) and Qatar (host of the 2022 World Cup). But this also raises the question of how else are BINGOs (business-oriented international non-government organisations) like FIFA or the IOC to be regulated?

Why should corruption matter in sport? Because sport matters: as we have argued in this book, sport in its mega-event form is used to political effect by hosts; elite sport has become a transnational multi-billion dollar industry; and it engages with the everyday lives of billions of people across the globe. However as Maennig (2005) indicates, it is useful to distinguish between two types of corruption in sport: *competition corruption* and *management corruption*. Whereas competition corruption relates to doping and match fixing, which we discuss next, this section focuses on the latter, management corruption. In sports mega-events this relates to activities such as vote rigging and the use of undue influence in elections or the selection of hosts, and embezzlement, fraud and bribery. That is, it involves non-competition decisions made by sports officials, associations and governing bodies.

West	East
Developed	Developing
Democratic	Authoritarian
Regulated	Self-regulated

Figure 12.1 Binaries and corruption.

According to Maennig (2005), corruption in sport is as old as the ancient Olympic Games. Offenders had to erect columns of shame (*zane*) at their own expense, or that of their city, at the entrance to the Olympic stadium to atone for their actions. In contemporary sport he suggests that it is no greater 'nor more widespread than in other areas of social life' (Maennig 2005: 215). However, there have been two tendencies: competition judges and officials have become involved more frequently in corruption; and the number of cases of management corruption in sport has been increasing (Maennig 2005: 201). To examine this, we need to consider the context, types and circumstances when corruption can occur in sports mega-events.

Since the 1980s, and the growth of neo-liberalism as the new economic orthodoxy and the rolling back of the social democratic consensus, rent-seeking behaviour – 'seeking control of assets and resources that can be used to extract rent from users' (Sayer 2015: 53) – has become the economic imperative. This has had implications for elite sport and especially its flagship mega-events, the Olympic Games and the men's Football World Cup. At the same time as there has been a massive growth in commercial interest involvement in sport – creating a 'global media sports cultural complex' (Rowe 2011: 34) in which the role of corporate media and sponsors especially has become bigger and bigger – regulatory systems and demands for greater transparency and accountability in governance have also emerged. In these circumstances, suspicions about the practices of self-regulating bodies claiming relative autonomy from local jurisdictions, such as international sports associations like the IOC and FIFA, have grown.

As the IOC and FIFA, among other sports organising bodies, have become BINGOs, journalists and sociologists and other social scientists have sought to investigate shortcomings in their operations (Simson and Jennings 1992; Jennings 2006; Sugden and Tomlinson 1998, 2003; Tomlinson 2014). At the same time, as we have seen in this book, several features of the sports mega-events that these bodies oversee have become attractive and have been used by states for different non-sporting ends – economic, urban, and social development, nation building and signalling (by branding the nation) and to assist in economic and political liberalisation. As Houlihan (2002: 194) noted, the 'willingness of governments to humble themselves before the IOC and FIFA through lavish hospitality and the strategic deployment of presidents, prime ministers, royalty and supermodels, is a reflection of the value that governments place on international sport'.

In a relatively simplistic formula, Klitgaard (1988: 75) suggested that 'corruption = monopoly + discretion – accountability'. Where and when can corruption in sports mega-events occur? Maennig (2005: 208) suggests that in circumstances where a sport (or sports event) enjoys high levels of popularity and attractiveness which make it capable of generating large cash flows, economic rents 'result from the fact that . . . the relevant international sports bodies have a unilateral monopoly over the awarding of sporting title honours'. Hence management corruption in relation to sports mega-events can take a number of forms: for example, acquiring certain positions in sports associations, influencing the allocation of broadcasting or other media rights or fixing the allocation of construction contracts for stadium or facilities building.

As transient events, sports mega-events also enjoy four broad, if overlapping, phases when corruption can occur – the bid phase, the preparatory phase, the games time phase and the post-games phase:

1	The awarding of host city/nation status – although this assumes that benefits do flow from hosting, the negative impact would stem from the loss of potential image, income and employment 'gains' in those locations, mostly cities, not selected.
2	The production of the bid document – the potential host can inflate expectations in order to impress voters.
3	The negotiation and allocation of rights (for example for broadcasting, sponsorship and merchandise).
4	The awarding of contracts for the construction of sports venues and facilities by the host Organising Committee and/or 'delivery authority'.
5	The 'delivery authority' in subcontracting to, for example, small to medium enterprises to undertake work in preparation for the event.

One constant potential source of corruption is, of course, the governance (internal procedures) of international sports associations and related sports bodies involved in sports mega-events, as the crises at FIFA in 2015 and that in the IOC in the 1990s demonstrate.[1] Expanding good governance in sport requires greater transparency, accountability, integrity and democracy. It may be possible to identify ways in which the risk of corruption could be better managed in sports mega-events (see Figure 12.2). However, putting new rules into practice is difficult since changing the culture of an organisation – tacit, unwritten, unofficial ways of doing things – requires changing the rituals, routines and daily practices of the organisation. Where corruption is proven, there is a need perhaps to focus on anti-corruption and cronyism in the re-engineering of an organisation (Spicer 2015).

It is possible that Michael Garcia, the former US prosecutor who investigated allegations of wrongdoing with regard to the 2018 and 2022 World Cup hosting decisions, was correct when he said as he resigned from FIFA that 'No independent governance committee, investigator, or arbitration panel can change the culture of an organization' (cited in Affleck 2015). This may be especially the case for organisations with the distinctive characteristics of international sports associations that create the potential for corruption (Pielke Jr 2015) mixed with an enduring belief in the 'Great Sport Myth' – an almost unshakeable belief about the inherent purity and goodness of sport (Coakley 2015). One way forward may be to demand that sports governing bodies have to start operating as big businesses, 'using

---

1 Provide and publicise clear codes of conduct to measure behaviour and misbehaviour.
2 Reduce the surpluses potentially accrued by host cities and governing organisations to provide the wider global sports 'family' with a greater share.
3 Have a high degree of transparency – including detailed documentation of decision-making processes, monitoring of executive and administrative bodies by an internal auditing department to monitor staff, reducing degrees of discretion and freedom of information legislation applicable to sport.
4 Create financial incentives to offset temptations for corruption by insiders.
5 Install systematic internal auditing and control measures in sports bodies – which should bear direct responsibility for any crimes committed by subordinates.

Figure 12.2 Five means of managing corruption risks in sports mega-events.

Source: adapted from Maennig (2005) and Tanzi (1998).

best business practices' (TI 2012, cited in Pielke Jr 2015), possibly using Play the Game sports governance indicators and other means of managing corruption risks. But it needs to be remembered that operating in an organisational 'culture of ethical failure' (Klein 2014: 334) is a systemic problem, not one of individual agents alone. At the time of writing, under the FIFA presidency of IOC member Sepp Blatter at least eight of FIFA's 23 executive committee members have been implicated in scandals in the past three years. If FIFA members take bribes over choice of hosts, why should it be assumed that IOC members do not?

Indeed, the Olympics, with their strong ethos of fair play and amateurism, are not immune to corruption; in the 1990s the IOC was rife with corrupt practices (Simson and Jennings 1992; Jennings 1996, Lenskyj 2002), and this came to a head before the 2002 Games at Salt Lake City in Utah, when Marc Hodler, an IOC member, broke ranks and revealed that people had been bribed to vote for cities bidding for the right to host the Games. Salt Lake City, having failed to win their earlier bid to host the Games, realised that they would have to change tactics and offer bribes. IOC members and their relatives received benefits from city officials. The Olympics have been tarnished by the revelations of corruption, which most importantly highlights the need for reform of the governance of sport. Corruption is clearly closely linked to economic factors, given the enormous financial benefits that can accrue from sporting success or, in the case of the Olympics, from hosting such an enormous event, but the desire for economic gain is not the only factor to be addressed. There are cultural and social factors in play too. Corruption takes a variety of forms, including what Maenigg refers to as *competition corruption*.

DOPING, TESTING AND SECRECY

Doping is currently seen as a form of *competition corruption* in sport. It has not always been seen in this way, however (Dimeo 2007). While drug use in sport existed prior to the post-Second World War/Cold War period, it was in the 1950s and 1960s that individuals began to pursue the use of pharmaceuticals to significantly enhance athletic performance. To understand the differing reactions to it, we have to consider the changing meaning of sport and of the Olympic Games. Three interrelated developments from the 1950s onward have shaped Olympic sport, and therefore the response to doping, according to Beamish (2010: 64–65).

First, there has been the increased professionalisation of the Games' athletes – the IOC formally removed the exclusion of professionals in 1974. Beamish (2010: 65) argues that the change of the 'eligibility code' in 1974 to allow professional athletes to compete at the Olympics did 'more than fundamentally change the type of athletes participating in the Games; it opened the way to athletes whose motivation, commitment and actions were directly antithetical to Coubertin's "spirit" of sport', the bedrock of Olympism. Second was the Cold War, which led to the development of heavily resourced, national, high-performance sports systems on either side of the ideological barrier. Third, there has been an increased use of science and technology in athletic preparation, or what Miah and Garcia (2012: 96–102) refer to as the *technologisation* of modern sport. So the contradiction between a transhistorical vision of sport, essentially rooted in nineteenth-century values, enshrined in Coubertin's ideas and a modernist athletic spectacle, seeking

264

to apply rational, efficient, scientific techniques to performance, continues to exist and create issues for the Olympic movement.

As we noted in Chapter 3, the Olympic principles embedded in the Olympic Charter encompass a vast range of articles setting out approved principles and practices. Over time the Charter has expanded to accommodate change. This bureaucratic edifice is both generative and reflexive of contemporary social norms and organisation, but resonates with the origins and founding principles of the modern games and of the principles upon which they were based. What makes the governance of the Olympics distinctive is the explicitly stated ideals, Olympism, and the concept of an Olympic movement which incorporates and expresses particular sporting values, ones that originally explicitly and emphatically excluded the participation of women, and asserted the values of militaristic, white, aristocratic, masculinity (Woodward 2012).

The Olympic system involves a complex set of processes that have been modified and transformed in light of social and cultural changes, such as the wider participation of women in sport and the implementation of race equality legislation, and most notably and most recently in response to charges of corruption and deception in the late 1990s. The Olympic system came late to ethical regulation, with an Ethics Commission only being set up in 1999, the same year as the World Anti-Doping Agency (WADA) was established in a climate of controversy and crisis for the IOC when there was not only media coverage of administrative corruption, but also revelations of drug abuse by athletes and coaches. Also in this context, and before WADA was formally set up, it was not helpful for the then President Samaranch to proclaim in 1998 that the IOC's anti-doping list should in fact be reduced because, '[d]oping is everything that, firstly, is harmful to an athlete's health and, secondly, artificially augments his performance. . . . If it's the second case . . . it's not doping' (cited in Ritchie 2012: 418). WADA was eventually established, following the IOC 'World Conference on Doping in Sport' held in Lausanne in 1999. As an independent body, WADA monitors drug use world-wide, sets global standards, supports laboratory technology to improve detection and created the World Anti-Doping Code, which most countries have adopted (Ritchie 2012: 419).

Debates about doping reflect different political viewpoints and ideological positions and have occurred at different phases of Olympic history. Hence social context is important for understanding the responses to various incidents. Scholars have also taken different approaches to the subject, dealing with doping in relation to ethical arguments, policy and legal aspects, deviant behaviour and subcultures of sport, as well as socio-historical accounts of the development of drug use in the Olympics (Ritchie 2012: 411–414). As we have seen with other aspects of the Olympics, when it comes to doping and the idea that there is, or ought to be, some direct, immutable and unproblematic link between sport and healthy practices, we encounter contradictory premises. In this light, Mansfield and Malcolm (2015: 188, 190) critically assess what they refer to as the 'sport–health ideological nexus' and argue that 'Olympic sport entails considerable health costs for both participants and wider communities'.

There has broadly been a shift in the past 60 years from seeing doping exclusively as outright cheating (during the Cold War period) to seeing it as bad for the image of sport, in a period of more intense commercialisation of sport. Throughout the period two sports

265

have faced the greatest scrutiny – road cycling, and track and field athletics. Arguably it was the death of Danish cyclist Knud Enemark Jensen, who collapsed and died during the road race at the 1960 Summer Games in Rome, that led the IOC to address the use of performance-enhancing substances, and it established its first Medical Committee to investigate drug use shortly afterwards. Several other memorable examples and responses to doping have taken place in connection with the Tour de France. British cyclist Tommy Simpson died in 1967 from use of amphetamine, which led to limited drug testing at the Olympic Games in Mexico in 1968. The Festina team's use of EPO (erythropoietin) in 1998, at which there was evidence of organised doping programmes for entire teams, led to the Festina team being expelled from the Tour, and hastened the formation of WADA. More heightened concerns about cycling followed from the doping revelations about Lance Armstrong in 2012 that led to him being stripped of all the Tour de France titles he had won between 1999 and 2005.

If it was the Soviet Union and the German Democratic Republic (GDR) that developed systematic and scientific doping techniques during the 1950s, these techniques soon spread to the West. Soviet weightlifters were using testosterone during the 1950s, but it was an American doctor who developed an anabolic steroid that had the same benefits, but without the unwanted side-effects. By 1970 the use of steroids in sport was believed to be widespread (Moore 2012: 70). There is a history of sport governing bodies trying to turn a blind eye to the use of performance-enhancing drugs – there were, for example, no positive drug tests at Moscow in 1980. The level of positive drug test results during the 1970s and 1980s was strikingly low, and yet now, 30 years or more on, analysis of the pattern of world records from the 1970s into the era of more rigorous drug testing has revealed some performances from that time that inevitably give rise to suspicions. In 1980, after the Moscow Games, a German scientist developed a way of testing the ratio between testosterone and epi-testosterone, which could identify testosterone users (athletes stopped using steroids in time for traces to disappear but could use testosterone right up to competition). In 1982 the IOC added testosterone to its banned drugs list, and the new test was used at the World Athletics Championships in Helsinki in 1983. Again, no positive drug tests were reported at 1983, although rumours published in the Norwegian paper *VG* said that several samples had been positive (Moore 2012: 66–67). The lack of positives at 1983 led to suspicions that the IAAF were covering up positive test results. At the Pan American Games, also in 1983, paranoia spread among athletes that this time the testers were serious. Twelve US athletes withdrew and flew home, and many others also withdrew claiming injury (Moore 2012: 72). In the Los Angeles Olympics of 1984, 11 positive samples were reported, but another nine were discovered. The only copy of codes enabling identification of the athletes involved mysteriously disappeared from the hotel room of an IOC member (Moore 2012: 111–113).

One of the most dramatic incidents in track and field athletics, which also presented a turning point from discourses of concern for the health of the athlete to moral censure expressed in the language of fair play and its converse, cheating, was the case of Ben Johnson, who was found guilty of using anabolic steroids, and during the 1988 Olympic Games in Seoul was stripped of his 100 metres gold medal. Many years later, evidence has emerged, gathered together in a book, *The Dirtiest Race in History* (Moore 2012) and subsequently made into a television documentary of the same title, that six of the eight finalists in the 100 metres had a record of using performance-enhancing drugs at some point in their careers. Given the common practice of ceasing to use steroids three weeks before competition, the positive test of Johnson's sample in itself remains something of a puzzle, and Johnson himself believes that the beer he drank in the testing waiting room may have been spiked (Moore 2012).

For a long time there has been a battle between drug cheats and drug testers. Every time a new mode of testing is introduced, the drug cheats manage to resort to new harder-to-detect methods. The rise of use of steroids, which can be taken during training but then dropped before competition, led to the development of testing away from competition and the so-called Athletes' Biological Passport, a map of bio-markers from blood samples. Additionally, the shift since 2000 from sampling athletes' urine to sampling their blood came about as drugs were being used that mimicked natural substances, making them more difficult to detect in urine.

Public censure has contributed to stronger anti-doping policies being introduced by all major sports. The introduction of year-round testing and comprehensive biological profiling of athletes has become far more elaborate, but the various pharmacological means utilised by athletes to evade the tests have also grown in sophistication. Drugs such as tetrahydrogestrinone have been developed to evade detection in use, as was demonstrated in the case of the English sprinter Dwain Chambers in 2003 (Cashmore 2005: 227–266). Some of the concerns about doping in sport are presented within a medicalised discourse of concern for the athletes involved and the health problems related to drug use. Hence Beamish (2010: 67) argues for the 'development of the best harm-reduction strategies possible'. Wider issues relate to the extent of drug abuse and the damage to world sport and the reputation and ethos of sport in general.

The IOC is not slow to trumpet its anti-drug programmes, proclaiming that the 2012 Games had the most comprehensive testing programme of any Olympic Games in history. More than 5,000 tests – 4,005 urine and 1,057 blood – were conducted during the Games, after extensive pre-Games testing by NOCs and IFs. Games tests were conducted on the top five competitors, plus two at random in each race. A WADA-accredited laboratory located in Harlow used state-of-the-art technologies. The facilities were open 24 hours a day, seven days a week, with a team of more than 150 anti-doping scientists from several countries (IOC 2012).

Athletics (with all respect to gymnastics and swimming) is the central Summer Olympics sport and throughout much of the world it commands the biggest headlines and the largest TV audiences. If the credibility of athletics was to be undermined to the extent that happened with cycling in the 1990s and 2000s it would be a major problem for the sport and the Olympic Games especially. There have long been suspicions that positive test results are covered up to preserve the chances of a particular star performer or to preserve the clean image of the sport itself. Revelations first broadcast by WDR/ARD television in Germany in 2014, and subsequently published by *The Sunday Times* in the UK in August 2015, seemed to suggest a systematic cover-up of positive tests and suspicious blood patterns by the sports governing body, the IAAF.

Under the front-page headline 'Revealed: sport's dirtiest secret', *The Sunday Times* report by journalists Calvert and Arbuthnott (2015: 1) was based on the leaking of 12,000 blood-test samples taken from athletes between 2001 and 2012. Analysis of thousands of test results by sport scientists suggested that one-third of medals, including 55 golds, were won in endurance events at the Olympic Games and Athletics World Championships by athletes with suspicious blood tests. Ten of the medals won at London 2012 were done so by athletes who had recorded suspicious test results in preceding years. The allegations suggested that the IAAF had not acted promptly on these findings, but this was refuted by the organisation. The IAAF argued that profiling is a complicated process in which fluctuations in readings do not necessarily indicate the use of illegal performance-enhancing techniques. A subsequent WADA Commission found that the IAAF council could not have been unaware of the extent of doping in athletics and the non-enforcement of applicable anti-doping rules, and the controversy surrounding track and field athletics continues to be debated. The dilemma for sport governing bodies is that rigorous testing and subsequent disqualifications can have a major impact on public confidence in any sport, especially if it plays such a central part in the Olympics.

SECURITY, RISK AND SURVEILLANCE

Ever since the establishment of payment for admission to enclosed arenas, the interface between inside and outside has required fences and control mechanisms to prevent those not entitled to enter from entering. In the 'risk society', both actual risk and the heightened sensitivity to risk have dramatically increased surveillance, boundaries and monitoring (Beck 1992). In the post-9/11 environment, of course, both risk and fear have become more significant. Corporate architecture has resorted to modern versions of the devices of medieval castles – the moat, the drawbridge and the portcullis – to reduce the threat of unauthorised incursion.

The Olympic Games survived a previous period, between 1968 and 1984, when its very visibility as a global event gave it great power as a platform for symbolic political acts (as discussed in Chapters 8 and 9). The perceived threat that, once again, the Olympic Games might be utilised as such a platform has pushed security expenditure to new heights. It is not clear that these expenditures are subject to adequate scrutiny – which politician, after all, wants to be on record as having cut the security budget? Among its many other roles, as with previous Games, the London Olympics functioned as a test-bed for 'state-of-the-art' security technologies.

Much of the academic research on security and sports mega-events focuses on three main overlapping issues regarding:

1 *security legacies* of sports mega-events (e.g. Bennett and Haggerty 2011; Fussey *et al.* 2011; Fussey and Coaffee 2012b);
2 *security risks* and the infrastructures and technologies used in an attempt to manage those risks (Fussey and Coaffee 2012a; Giulianotti and Klauser 2010, 2012; Richards *et al.* 2011); and
3 the overall *security spectacle* that characterises sports mega-events (e.g. Boyle 2012; Boyle and Haggerty 2009, 2011; Fussey *et al.* 2011).

Each of these themes is briefly discussed in what follows.

MacAloon wrote about the vibrant presence of festival outside the stadiums, which goes unwitnessed by those who do not attend and observe. He did, though, acknowledge the impact of security from as early as 1976, commenting that Montreal introduced security measures that 'radically segregated credentialed from un-credentialed participants, and this security effect has been multiplied one-hundredfold since the 1970s' (MacAloon 2006b: 21). Indeed the Games have always provided both a challenge and an opportunity for the cultures of control. The relevant authorities have generally attempted to 'cleanse' the site, the surrounding area, and indeed sometimes much of the city, of its 'undesirables'. American writer Richard Schweid, who spent a year in Barcelona in 1991–1992, recounts that in the build-up to the Games, the municipal government cancelled all licences and permissions to work the Ramblas during the Games. 'Officials did not want the usual horde of beggars, buskers, street musicians, mimes, jugglers, shell-game hustlers and fire-eaters asking tourists for their time and change.' Prostitutes were moved to the Zona Franca, a warehouse district on the edge of Barcelona. However, Schweid observes, the city did allow some regular street entertainers to remain. He also notes that during the Games the police were not notably in evidence and that the city carried out its role of host to perfection (Schweid 1994: 176).

The IOC makes clear that security is the responsibility of the host city, while ensuring that securitisation does not obstruct the sporting facilities or Olympic spirit (Coaffee 2011: 118). The IOC limits its own involvement to taking out insurance against total or partial cancellation (Houlihan and Giulianotti 2012: 709). This means that in recent Games, security has become an increasing challenge as the number of people involved and the costs keep growing. Coaffee (2011: 122) noted that over 25,000 security personnel were deployed in Barcelona in 1992 and in Atlanta in 1996. In Sydney in 2000 approximately 5,000 police, 3,500 defence personnel and up to 7,000 contract security staff were deployed (Lenskyj 2002). Security, in recent Games, has become an increasing challenge and the numbers have increased accordingly.

Immediately after the destruction of the World Trade Center on 11 September 2001, major sporting events in the US were subject to unprecedented security. For the Winter Olympics in Salt Lake City in 2002, a '52-mile no-fly zone was imposed around the entire Games site, and sharpshooters were placed on various mountaintop positions to protect specific competition venues' (Galily 2015). The heightened atmosphere of fear triggered by 9/11 meant that the Organising Committee for Athens 2004 came under pressure from the European Union and the US to increase spending on security. In the event, Greece spent a record $1.5 billion on security, using more than 70,000 security forces. American troops provided a training exercise, practising responses to dirty-bomb attacks and hijackings. Chemical sensors, CCTV cameras and hidden microphones were installed, controlled by computer surveillance. Patriot missiles, fighter planes and US battleships were deployed. O'Neill (2005: 1) argued that the city was 'under US occupation for the duration of the Games (albeit at the invitation of the Greek authorities), as both shorelines and airspace fell under the command of US and Greek troops'. There is, of course, a genuine dilemma for any Organising Committee, as Cohen (2005: 6) points out:

No one wants a 'Fortress Olympics' yet both athletes and spectators need a safe environment. The danger is that risk management drives the whole enterprise and stifles the aleatory principles that alone make the games a joyful occasion worth remembering.

In the wake of 9/11, there was a much more comprehensive form of security planning for the next Summer Olympics, Athens 2004, including real-time updating and sharing of intelligence. An Olympic Advisory Group (OAG) was established, with representatives from Australia, France, Germany, Israel, Spain, the UK and the US. Nine separate operational readiness security exercises were staged between 2001 and 2004. An Olympic Intelligence Centre operated 24 hours per day from the start of July 2004 (Hinds 2007: 23). According to Bowe and Rodriguez (2012):

> One report revealed that Greek law enforcement and intelligence agencies installed more than 1,000 surveillance cameras in Athens in advance of the 2004 Summer Olympics – and then continued to make use of them for policing purposes long after athletes and spectators had packed up and left. . . . Chinese authorities installed a whopping 200,000 cameras and employed other surveillance measures in an effort to make Beijing secure. And, in a move that drew widespread condemnation, the Chinese government ordered foreign-owned hotels to install Internet monitoring equipment to spy on hotel guests.

Security costs for the Olympic Games increased from $179.6 million at Sydney 2000 to $1.5 billion for Athens 2004, and the exceptional case of $6.5 billion for Beijing in 2008 (see Figure 12.3; for details see Yu *et al.* 2009). For London 2012, the original published security budget of £337 million grew to over £1 billion, but typically a lot of security spending was 'off budget', hidden in general police or security budgets. The UK already makes extensive use of CCTV; indeed, six years before the London Olympics, the BBC reported in November 2006 that there were already 4.2 million cameras in the UK. The British Security Industry Authority (BSIA) estimated that by 2013 there were 5–6 million of them. Robot drone aircraft had already been deployed in the UK in the Olympic context – for example, at the Olympics handover party in 2011 in the Mall. Although technical and legal issues prevented any extensive use of drones for surveillance during the 2012 Games, around 25 police authorities had acquired drone planes and their use gained ministerial approval in October 2012.[2] As has often occurred before, the Olympics in London was used to test new security technologies (*Guardian* 22 February 2010).

	Number of athletes	Security cost per athlete ($)	Tickets sold	Security cost per ticket ($)	Security cost ($ million)
Los Angeles 1984	6,829	11,627	5,720,000	14	79.4
Seoul 1988	8,391	13,312	3,300,000	33	111.7
Barcelona 1992	9,356	7,072	3,021,740	22	66.2
Atlanta 1996	10,318	10,486	8,384,290	13	108.2
Sydney 2000	10,651	16,062	6,700,000	27	179.6
Athens 2004	10,500	142,857	5,300,000	283	1,500
Beijing 2008	10,942	607,022	6,500,000	1,021	6,642
London 2012	10,568	181,545	8,200,000	223	1,918

Figure 12.3 Security costs per athlete and per spectator at Olympic Games 1984–2012.

Source: adapted from Hinds 2007; Boyle and Haggerty 2009; Houlihan and Giulianotti 2012; IOC 2014.

In a whole range of ways, then, a culture of control has become a more prominent feature of the Olympic Games in which ordinary people – residents of local communities in the immediate host areas and visitors alike – are seen as a risk that has to be managed. Legislation prevents unauthorised use of Olympic-related words, as we discussed in Chapter 10, and even allowed the London Organising Committee right of entry to homes to search for 'pirated', i.e. unauthorised, Olympic goods, as well as banners for protests. Major sports events utilise the crowd, but as 'extras', enabling the visual card stunts that can only be seen properly on television, and channel spontaneous behaviour into regimented behaviour, such as the rituals of victory ceremonies, cup-giving, the playing of loud music. Characteristically, at major football events today, stadium anthems like Queen's 'We are the Champions' are played over the public address system, drowning out and eliminating the possibility of any spontaneous responses to the joy of victory.

In common with previous Games, festivity was contained and controlled by order and organisation at London 2012. London handled security by allowing fun in delimited spaces, subject to surveillance and policing. A picnic in the Olympic Park could be very pleasant, but restrictions on items that could be brought in (for example, water) resulted in long queues at the relatively small number of free drinking water taps. The further from the intense cultures of control that must inevitably dominate the Park, the more chance the festive and even the carnivalesque has to thrive. However, the gap between the performers and spectators in the arenas and the people in the public spaces of London was always clear.

London 2012 was initially asked to provide over 15,000 police, 13,500 defence force personnel and close to 15,000 contract security staff. In the days leading up to the London 2012 Games, there was a significant addition of 3,500 defence personnel as concerns arose that G4S, the leading contract security provider, would not be able to supply the agreed number of private security staff. This increased the total number of defence personnel to approximately 17,000; almost twice the number of troops then deployed in Afghanistan (Whelan 2014). The Command Perimeter Security System (CPSS) at the Olympic Park in Stratford included

> a 17.5km, 5,000V electric fence topped with 900 daylight and night vision surveillance CCTV cameras. . . . Wireless-capable cameras . . . can be quickly deployed, removed and set up somewhere else according to demand or requirement, allowing security operators to identify trouble spots and move the cameras to areas where they are most needed.
>
> (Courtney 2012)

The needs of the Olympic Games helped enable a much greater linking up of such technology. Courtney (2012) noted that:

> thousands of CCTV cameras already installed in London, many owned by either the 33 local authorities or Transport for London (TfL), are to be integrated into a single system via a specialised software set-up that uses high-speed broadband links and automatic number plate recognition software, giving the Metropolitan Police and other security bodies the ability to track any individual's progress through the city.

He added:

> it seems unlikely that the systems installed for 2012 will be simply torn down again rather than assimilated into wider TfL or other local authority surveillance networks; it has been estimated that most of the 1,200 cameras deployed in Athens during the 2004 Olympic games are still in use by the authorities.

Thus it is that security and surveillance technologies,

> often initially implemented in an attempt to 'secure' sports mega events, continue to function post the event in everyday life, and with the familiar logic of 'mission creep' end up being used for other purposes than they were originally developed.
> (Whelan 2014: 395)

Security occurred in other ways; at its peak, on so-called 'Super Saturday' (4 August 2012) when 'Team GB' won six gold medals, BT prevented an average of 11,000 malicious requests per second.[3] The number of detected malicious site visit attempts rose from around two million a day at the beginning of the Games to a peak of nine million a day.[4] Yet all this accumulated experience constituted a valuable resource for private companies to trade on in consultancy services to future hosts of mega-events. One clear legacy for the government left by the London Olympics was the enhancement of surveillance equipment and expertise. For some years, the security needs of the Olympic Games have helped stimulate research and development in the security industry.

Fussey *et al.* (2011) describe how London implemented its version of the conventional Olympic 'total' security model. In addition to proactive policing and intelligence efforts being directed towards potential threats, key elements of the total security model included at least three key stages. The first involved intense planning for 'resilience', should the goal of 'prevention' fail and security problems such as a terrorist attack eventuate during the Games. The second stage involved reconfiguring public and private space into security infrastructures through the development of 'island' security and sophisticated 'defensible space' techniques at key sites. The third stage concerned the deployment of advanced surveillance and real-time monitoring of people and space, much of which involved expanding the existing network of surveillance technologies in the host city.

These measures were also accompanied by an intense 'military urbanism' that played a crucial role in the overall 'securitisation' of the Olympic Games and at the same time the increased securitisation of urban public space. As Boyle and Haggerty (2009: 270) put it, 'Militarization of event security also means the militarization of cities' as security systems 'become familiar and routinised – the increasingly normalised spectacle of security'.

Thus Boyle and Haggerty (2012) argue that security spectacles and the planning for extreme events that underpin them are largely about providing the illusion of 'absolute security' and an attempt to control uncertainty. In the same vein, Houlihan and Giulianotti (2012: 705–706) suggest that the recent period of the Olympics might be regarded as hyper-security, in which resources are allocated not on the basis of probability but of possibility, and intense aversion to risk. London 2012 was regularly described by politicians and security chiefs as the biggest ever security challenge for the UK. Hence we have seen

272

the emergence of a new field of expertise around the management of unease. Security advances during work for mega-events constitutes a very tangible and commercially valuable legacy of the Games. The state-of-the-art developments around mega-events have constituted a significant field of technological and systemic innovation. The security operation for Beijing 2008 drew on experience from Athens 2004, the Winter Olympics in Turin in 2006, the 2006 Commonwealth Games and the 2006 Asian Games (Hinds 2007: 24).

At the same time, as Whelan (2014: 396) writes:

> There is little doubt that many of these developments are about the 'security spectacle' rather than bearing a correlation to actual security risks. For example, the show of military 'strength' during London 2012 – involving an aircraft carrier docked on the Thames, several RAF fighters, fixed long-range surface-to-air missiles deployed at several locations and portable missiles on the top of apartment buildings close to Olympic sites, Unmanned Aerial Vehicles or 'drones', and the more traditional positioning of tactical teams and snipers – would be considered far beyond any probable threat to the Olympics.

Given the unpredictable nature of modern terrorist acts, security is largely a form of public show. In reality we don't know whether to expect shooting, bombing or suicide bombers. Nor do we really know where the attacks might come from. For a decade after 2001, Al-Qaeda was represented in the media as the main threat, until the idea of a more diffuse loose network of semi-autonomous groups became the dominant model. ISIS had not even emerged at the time of the London Games, yet now is represented in the West as the prime mover of international terrorism. Yet for all the focus on so-called Islamist radicalisation, since 2005 the fringe Irish republican groups remain a threat, although no one appears to be rushing to establish de-radicalisation programmes for them.

Despite a range of incidents, it is not self-evident that attacking popular gatherings such as sport is a main priority among groups resorting to political violence. It does not, unlike the attack on the Taj Mahal Palace Hotel in Mumbai in 2008, offer a dramatised symbolic assault on a rich elite. It does have great potential for generating a significant backlash among the sector of the public who they may be aiming to impress. Despite this, security for mega-events can now command almost all the resources it requires. Few politicians wish to be on record as having refused a budgetary increase to security, in case something does happen. As is typical of risk assessment, there is confusion between the likelihood and the consequences of an incident. The process of thinking the unthinkable, made necessary post-9/11, is almost inevitably, short of hard evidence.

Assessing the success of the security operation for London 2012, Robert Raine, the former Director of Olympic and Paralympic Security at the UK Home Office, argued that a 'new benchmark' had been set in respect of inter-agency security coordination, and that this was a key factor in ensuring that London 2012 was secure (cited in Rosemont 2015). Boyle and Haggerty (2009: 262–263) suggest that there has been a bifurcation between the mechanistic aspects of security provision and the representational dimension. Given that the elimination of all risk is impossible, the provision of an appearance of absolute security becomes important, hence the public spectacle of security. Greece saw the Olympics as an ideal opportunity to transform itself into a counter-terrorism superpower whose knowledge and technologies could be marketed internationally (Boyle and Haggerty 2009: 266). Hence we can see this as another area in which capital, seeking new ways to accumulate, is benefiting from funding from public sources; public expenditure generating private profit through the monetisation of public safety.

CONCLUSION

This chapter has focused on three of the main challenges that currently confront the Olympics. We might have looked at others, for example gambling and match-fixing, commercialisation, and the environment, but we have already touched on the second and third in the earlier parts of the book. In the build-up to the 2012 London Olympics the then IOC President Jacques Rogge was quoted as saying that match-fixing and betting were not only embedded in football and cricket but also were a serious risk to Olympic sport. Rogge acknowledged the temptation to cheat among athletes who are not highly paid, but attributed cheating to 'human nature' (cited in Gibson 2011: 12).

An explanation that stresses the social processes would give greater emphasis to the networks and financial systems of gambling which permeate contemporary sport, and also the processes that facilitate the operation of betting syndicates and the proliferating cultures of gambling, rather than prioritising a generic human condition. Temptation has to operate within the wider social field of possibilities, and gambling is ubiquitous in the culture of sport. The Olympics does face a threat from the combination of gambling and match-fixing that has already had a significant impact on football and cricket. There is nothing new about gambling, but since the rise of the internet from the 1990s onwards, online gambling has grown very rapidly to become a large and lucrative industry. The scale of online transactions is immense. In some countries de-regulation has contributed to this growth, while in others regulation has always been lax. In many, national-based regulatory systems have proved to be inadequate for the digital era.

A 2011 report in the Australian *Economist* indicated that, on average, every adult Australian loses just under AUD1,300 per year. Australians spend AUD22 billion per year on gambling, nearly five times the spending on foreign aid. Sports betting alone brought in AUD600 million of revenue in 2011 (Horn 2011). During the American Super Bowl there are now so many gambling options that people can even bet on the coin toss. Even where betting is restricted the spending is huge; illegal wagering on the 2005 Men's NCAA Basketball Tournament was estimated at $2.5 billion (Delaney 2007).

The sheer volume of transactions has led to constant innovation, especially in the form of spot betting (where gamblers wager not on the ultimate outcome but on the smallest detail of a contest) – for example, in football the time at which the first corner is conceded, or in cricket the number of no balls called within a specific number of overs. Such events have proved easy to arrange, provided a specific individual can be bribed. The normalisation of gambling and the involvement of professional sportspeople in it leaves them vulnerable to pressure to abet match-fixing. A European study found that an estimated €8 million of betting profits generated by match-fixing in Germany alone and at least €2 million was paid in bribes to those involved (Europol 2013).

The salary of top performers in many sports may seem to make them immune to such inducements, and some proven instances of match-fixing have occurred at lower levels of sports. However, most Olympic competitors are not earning huge salaries. In addition, any use of performance-enhancing drugs can render a sportsperson, however wealthy, vulnerable to blackmail. To date there have been no documented cases of the rigging of any aspects of Olympic competition. It would be naive, though, to assume that the Olympic Games are completely immune from these dangers, as IOC members are well aware.

Commercialisation of the Olympic Games is so well established as to be almost taken for granted. The 1984 Olympics has become regarded as the point at which commercialisation of the Games entered a new and more dramatic era (Tomlinson and Whannel 1984). The economics of the gigantic global spectacle provide two problems for the Olympic movement. The first is that it has become too big, with too much money at stake. The second is the more intangible danger of the bubble bursting. The large revenues do not constitute a protection against loss for hosting cities. Flyvbjerg and Stewart (2012) suggested a link between the Athens Olympics and the economic problems now faced by Greece, and argued that 'cost overrun and associated debt from the Athens 2004 Games has contributed to a Greek "double dip" in the financial and economic crises of 2007–2012' (Flyvbjerg and Stewart 2012). As we have previously argued, the long-term benefits of hosting can be hard to quantify precisely, but there is growing evidence that the huge costs involved may be discouraging future bidders (Zimbalist 2015). In 2008 and 2012 tourism numbers dropped during the Summer Olympic Games. Scholarly studies suggest that there is not a demonstrable positive economic impact from hosting. Numbers of bidding cities dropped from 12 in 1997 for the 2004 Games to three in 2013 for the 2020 Games. In the Winter Olympics, too, the number of bidders has dropped from nine in 1995 for the 2002 Games in Salt Lake City to just two in 2014 for the 2022 Games (Zimbalist 2015). As we have seen, the IOC are already reviewing the bidding process to try to attract more interest, and it is the case that the IOC, like the British Royal Family, may be very stuffy and in some ways out of touch, yet are also extremely adaptable and adept at surviving.

As part of a significant, if discreet, re-branding of the Olympic movement that has been under way since the Salt Lake City scandal broke in 1998, environmental concerns have been given a higher profile, with candidate cities expected to outline their 'green' credentials and plans to use renewable and sustainable resources. The IOC has some reason to be proud of the initiatives it has taken in this area and their partial successes. However, the staging of giant global events, involving the construction of expensive facilities and the travel of thousands of competitors, spectators and media people, is inevitably questionable on ecological grounds. Climate change could eventually threaten the very viability of the Winter Games. According to one report, across the US winter temperatures have warmed 0.16 degrees Fahrenheit per decade since 1895; the rate of warming has more than tripled to 0.55 degrees Fahrenheit per decade since 1970. The proportion of total winter precipitation falling as snow has decreased in the north-eastern and western US, with concurrent decreases in snowpack in both regions. Visitors to skiing areas can drop by as much as 30 per cent in years of low snowfall (Burakowski and Magnusson 2012). The estimated $12.2 billion US winter sports industry has already felt the direct impact of decreased winter snowpack and rising average winter temperatures. Snow depths could decline in the west by 25 to 100 per cent. The length of the snow season in the north-east will be cut in half.[5] A study in the *Journal of Sustainable Tourism* showed that under current climate conditions 85 per cent of all Swiss skiing areas are snow-reliable. This number would drop to 63 per cent if temperatures were to rise by 2 °C, an outcome which is currently looking hard to avoid (Koenig and Abegg 1997). Mega-events like the men's Football World Cup and the Olympic Games, however powerful they like to represent themselves as being, can never be free of wider processes of change – as James Dorsey has commented so pithily, 'Qatar is too hot, Beijing has no snow' (Dorsey 2015).

After 2016 the Olympic Games, Summer and Winter, enters what may come to be known as its 'East Asian' era, as Pyeongchang (South Korea), Tokyo (Japan) and Beijing (China) host the 2018, 2020 and 2022 Games, respectively (see Figure 12.4). Already each of these future events has attracted some form of controversy. Although we have not discussed the Winter Olympics in great detail in this book, it is noticeable that critics have identified the

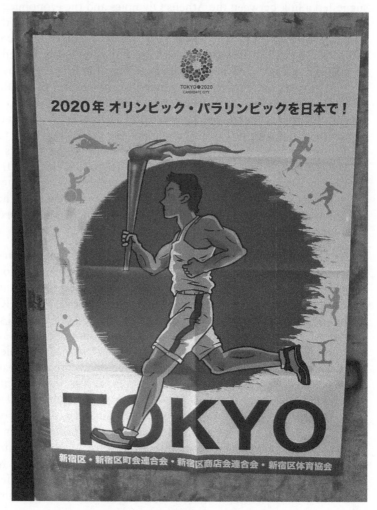

Figure 12.4
Poster for Tokyo as Candidate City for the 2020 Olympic and Paralympic Games.

environment as a major fault line in the 2018 and 2022 Winter Games, while Tokyo has faced problems developing an appropriate venue for the 2020 Games.

In the past, the governing bodies of world sport have not always been able to act effectively as stewards of the public interest in sport, whether it is in the area of corruption, the use of performance-enhancing drugs, commercialisation, environmental protection or the escalation of excessive security. In all these areas, the world of sport has become beset with rumour, gossip, innuendo, allegation and refutation. These are the dark, murky areas of the Olympics and sports mega-events generally. The challenge in forthcoming years will be whether those involved with the organisation of sports mega-events will recognise the value of the scholarship available, as discussed in this book, that critically assesses the Games, that might just provide the insights required to illuminate the way forward.

NOTES

1 In the final week of May 2015, 14 FIFA officials and marketing executives were indicted by US prosecutors led by the Attorney General Loretta E. Lynch, describing alleged bribery schemes and other corruption charges. Additional charges relating to bribes allegedly known about by other FIFA officials emerged shortly after. The indictment was for corruption in the Confederation of North, Central American and Caribbean Association Football (CONCACAF), one of the confederations associated with FIFA, alleging bribes and kickbacks estimated at more than $150 million over a 24-year period. Although re-elected a few days later, FIFA President Blatter stepped down in June as law enforcement officials in the US confirmed that he was also part of the focus of the federal corruption investigation (Borden et al. 2015). At the same time it was revealed that a former member of the FIFA executive and General Secretary of CONCACAF, Chuck Blazer, had turned FBI informant and admitted to receiving bribes to select South Africa as the host for the 2010 World Cup between 2004 and 2011 at a trial in New York in 2013. At his testimony, which was only made public in May 2015, he pleaded guilty to racketeering, wire fraud conspiracy, money laundering, income tax and banking offences. The New York judge hearing his testimony added to the acronym list by which FIFA is referred by describing it as a 'Rico' enterprise – a 'racketeering influenced corrupt organization'.
2 'Minister endorses use of drones by British police', 1 October 2012 (www.wired.co.uk/news/archive/2012-10/01/british-police-more-drones [accessed 1 September 2015]).
3 Sports Video Group (http://sportsvideo.org/main/blog/2014/10/bts-lessons-learned-at-londonolympics-provide-roadmap-for-tokyo-2020).
4 'Multi-layered security provided foolproof protection for communication services at London 2012', London 2012 Network Protection Factfile.
5 'Climate impact changes on winter tourism economy' (available online at: www.nrdc.org/globalwarming/climate-impacts-winter-tourism.asp [accessed 3 July 2015]).

FURTHER READING

Bennett, J. and Haggerty, K. (2011) Security Games: Surveillance and Control at Mega-Events, London: Routledge.

Maennig, W. (2005). 'Corruption in international sports and sport management: forms, tendencies, extent and countermeasures', *European Sport Management Quarterly* 5 (2), 187–225.

Richards, A., Fussey, P. and Silke, A. (eds) (2011) *Terrorism and the Olympics: Major Event Security and Lessons for the Future*, London: Routledge

Ritchie, I. (2012) 'The use of performance-enhancing substances in the Olympic Games: a critical history', in H. Lenskyj and S. Wagg (eds) *The Palgrave Handbook of Olympic Studies*, Basingstoke: Palgrave, pp. 410–429.

BIBLIOGRAPHY

Abend, Lisa (2014) 'Why nobody wants to host the 2022 Winter Olympics: hosting the Games is too expensive' *Time*, 3 October (available online at: http://time.com/3462070/olympics-winter-2022; last accessed 23 October 2015).

Affleck, J. (2015). 'Sepp Blatter's FIFA exit opens door for prosecutors, reformers', *Conversation* (available online at: https://theconversation.com/sepp-blatters-fifa-exit-opens-door-for-prosecutors-reformers-42729; last accessed 5 June 2015).

Allison, L. (ed.) (1986) *The Politics of Sport*, Manchester: Manchester University Press.

Allison, L. (ed.) (1993) *The Changing Politics of Sport*, Manchester: Manchester University Press.

Almeida, M., Joseph, J., Palma, A. and Soares, A.J. (2013) 'Marketing strategies within an African–Brazilian martial art', *Sport in Society* 16 (10), 1346–1359.

Alves, M.H.M. and Evanson, P. (2011) *Living in the Crossfire: Favela Residents, Drug Dealers, and Police Violence in Rio de Janeiro*, Philadelphia: Temple University Press.

Alvito, M. (2007) 'Our piece of the pie: Brazilian football and globalization' *Soccer and Society* 8 (4), 524–544.

AMPVA (2012) *Plano Popular da Vila Autódromo: Plano de Desenvolvimento Urbano, Econômico, Social e Cultural*, Rio de Janeiro: AMPVA (Associação de Moradores e Pescadores da Vila Autódromo).

Anderson, B. (1983) *Imagined Communities*, London: Verso.

Anderson, J. (2000) 'Disability sports', in R. Cox, G. Jarvie and W. Vamplew (eds) *Encyclopedia of British Sport*, Oxford: ABC-CLIO (pp. 105–107).

Anderson, P. (2007) 'Jottings on the conjuncture', *New Left Review* 48 (second series) November/December: 5–37.

Anderson, P. (2011) 'Lula's Brazil', *London Review of Books* 33 (7), 3–12.

Andrews, D., Schulz, J. and Silk, M. (2010) 'The Olympics and terrorism', in A. Bairner and G. Molnar (eds) *The Politics of the Olympics*, London: Routledge (pp. 81–92).

Anholt-GfK Roper (2014). 'Germany knocks USA off top spot for "best nation" after 5 years' (available online at: www.gfk.com/news-and-events/press-room/press-releases/pages/germany-knocks-usa-off-best-nation-top-spot.aspx; last accessed 1 December 2014).

Anon. (2012) *Official Review: London 2012 Olympic Games*, London: Haymarket Media Group.

Anthony, D. (1986) *Britain and The Olympic Games: Rediscovery of a Heritage*, Birmingham: City of Birmingham.

Anthony, D. (1997) 'Coubertin, Britain and the British: a chronology', *Journal of Olympic History* 5 (3), 18.

Appadurai, A. (1996) *Modernity at Large*, Minneapolis: University of Minnesota Press.

Arbena, J.L. (1986) 'Sport and the study of Latin American history: an overview', *Journal of Sport History* 13 (2), 87–96.

Arbena, J.L. (1995) 'Nationalism and sport in Latin America, 1850–1990: the paradox of promoting and performing "European" sports', *International Journal of the History of Sport* 12 (2), 220–238.

Arbena, J.L. (ed.) (1999) *Latin American Sport: An Annotated Bibliography, 1988–1998*, Westport, CT: Greenwood Press.

Arbena, J.L. (2001) 'The later evolution of modern sport in Latin America: the North American influence', *International Journal of the History of Sport* 18 (3), 43–58.

Archer, R. and Bouillon, A. (1982) *The South African Game: Sport and Racism*, London: Zed Books.

Aris, S. (1990) *Sportsbiz: Inside the Sports Business*, London: Hutchinson.

Arnstein, W.L. (1975) 'The survival of the Victorian aristocracy', in F.C. Jaher (ed.) *The Rich, the Well Born, and the Powerful: Elites and Upper Classes in History*, Secaucus, NJ: Citadel Press (pp. 202–257).

Bailey, P. (1978) *Leisure and Class in Victorian England*, London: RKP.

Bairner, A. and Molnar, G. (2010) 'The politics of the Olympics: an introduction', in A. Bairner and G. Molnar (eds) *The Politics of the Olympics*, London: Routledge (pp. 3–14).

Bakhtin, M. (1965) *Rabelais and his World*, Cambridge, MA: MIT Press.

Bale, J. (2008) 'From the Anthropological Days to the Anthropological Olympics', in S. Brownell (ed.) *The 1904 Anthropology Days and Olympic Games: Sport, Race, and American Imperialism*, Lincoln, NE, and London: University of Nebraska Press (pp. 324–342).

Bale, J. and Moen, O. (eds) (1995) *The Stadium and the City*, Keele: Keele University Press.

Bale, J. and Sang, J. (1996) *Kenyan Running: Movement Culture, Geography and Global Change*, London: Frank Cass.

Bandy, S. (2010) 'Politics of gender through the Olympics: the changing nature of women's involvement in the Olympics', in A. Bairner and G. Molnar (eds) *The Politics of the Olympics*, London: Routledge (pp. 41–57).

Barbassa, J. (2015) *Dancing with the Devil in the City of God: Rio de Janeiro on the Brink*, New York: Touchstone.

Barnes, C. (1992) *Disabling Imagery and the Media*, Halifax: Ryburn Publishing.

Barnes, C. and Mercer, G. (2003) *Disability*, Cambridge: Polity Press.

Barney, R.K., Wenn, S.R. and Martyn, S.G. (2002) *Selling the Games: The IOC and the Rise of Olympic Commercialism*, Salt Lake City: University of Utah Press.

Bateman, D. and Douglas, D. (1986) *Unfriendly Games: Boycotted and Broke*, Glasgow: Mainstream.

Bauman Lyons Architects (2008) *How to be a Happy Architect*, London: Black Dog.

BBC Sport (2007) 'Brazil will stage 2014 World Cup' (available online at: http://news.bbc.co.uk/sport1/hi/football/internationals/7068848.stm; last accessed 12 June 2014).

BBC Sport (2015) '2024 Olympics: LA, Hamburg, Rome, Budapest & Paris bid', 16 September (available online at: www.bbc.co.uk/sport/0/olympics/34266181; last accessed 25 September 2015).

Beamish, R. (2010) 'The politics of performance enhancement in the Olympic Games', in A. Bairner and G. Molnar (eds) *The Politics of the Olympics*, London: Routledge (pp. 58–68).

Beck, U. (1998) *Democracy without Enemies*, Cambridge: Polity.

Belanger, A. (2009) 'The urban sport spectacle: towards a critical political economy of sports', in B. Carrington and I. McDonald (eds) *Marxism, Cultural Studies and Sport*, London: Routledge (pp. 51–67).

Bellos, A. (2002) *Futebol: The Brazilian Way of Life*, London: Bloomsbury.

Bellos, A. (2014) *Futebol: The Brazilian Way of Life*, 2nd edition, London: Bloomsbury.

Benchimol, J.L. (1990) *Pereira Passos: um Haussmann tropical: a renovação urbana da cidade do Rio de Janeiro no início do século XX*, Rio de Janeiro: PCRJ, Secretaria Municipal de Cultura, Turismo e Esportes, Departamento Geral de Documentação e Informação Cultural.

Benjamin, W. (1999) *The Arcades Project*, translated by Howard Eiland and Kevin McLaughlin; prepared on the basis of the German volume edited by Rolf Tiedemann, Cambridge, MA and London: Belknap Press.

Bennett, C.J. and Haggerty, K.D. (2011) *Security Games: Surveillance and Control at Mega-Events*, Oxford: Routledge.

Bennett, T. (1991) 'The shaping of things to come: Expo' 88', *Cultural Studies* 5: 30–51.

Bernstock, P. (2014) *Olympic Housing: A Critical Review of London 2012's Legacy*, Farnham: Ashgate.

Billings, A. (2008) *Olympic Media: Inside the Biggest Show on Television*, London: Routledge.

Billings, A.C., Eastman, S.T. and Newton, G.D. (1998) 'Atlanta revisited: prime-time promotion in the 1996 Summer Olympics', *Journal of Sport and Social Issues* 22 (1), 65–78.

Birley, D. (1993) *Sport and the Making of Britain*, Manchester: Manchester University Press.

Boadle, A. (2014) 'World Cup leaves Brazil costly stadiums, poor public transport', *Reuters* (available online at: www.reuters.com/article/2014/06/05/us-brazil-worldcup-infrastructure-idUSKBN0EG23H20140605; last accessed 12 June 2014).

Bocock, R. (1994) *Consumption*, London: Routledge.

Boix, J., Espada, A. and Pointu, R. (1994) *L'héritage trahi*, Paris: Editions Romillat.

Boje, D.M. (2001) 'Carnivalesque resistance to global spectacle: a critical postmodern theory of public administration', *Administrative Theory and Praxis* 23 (3), 431–458.

Bond, P. and Garcia, A. (eds) (2015) *BRICS: An Anti-capitalist Critique*, London: Pluto.

Boorstin, D. (1961) *The Image: A Guide to Pseudo-Events in America*, New York: Harper & Row.

Borden, S., Schmidt, M.S. and Apuzzo, M. (2015). 'Sepp Blatter decides to resign as FIFA President in about-face', *New York Times*, 3 June, A1 (also available online at: www.nytimes.com/2015/06/03/sports/soccer/sepp-blatter-to-resign-as-fifa-president.html?_r=0; last accessed 5 June).

Bose, M. (2012) *The Spirit of the Game: How Sport Made the Modern World*, London: Constable.

Bourdieu, P. (1978) 'Sport and social class', *Social Science Information* 17 (6), 819–840.

Bowater, D. (2015). 'Brazil Rio: rare victory for residents in regeneration battle', *BBC News*, Latin America & Caribbean, 4 February (available online at: www.bbc.co.uk/news/world-latin-america-31090761; last accessed 31 July 2015).

Bowe, R. and Rodriguez, K. (2012) 'Spy games', *Electronic Frontier Foundation* (available online at: www.eff.org/deeplinks/2012/07/spy-games; last accessed 18 July 2012).

Bowlby, R. (1985) *Just Looking: Consumer Culture in Dreiser, Gissing and Zola*, London: Methuen.

Boykoff, J. (2013) 'Celebration capitalism and the Sochi 2014 Winter Olympics', *Olympika* 22, 39–70.

Boykoff, J. (2014a) *Celebration Capitalism and the Olympic Games*, London: Routledge.

Boykoff, J. (2014b) *Activism and the Olympics: Dissent at the Games in Vancouver and London*, New Brunswick, NJ: Rutgers University Press.

Boykoff, J. (2014c) 'Why you should root for the World Cup protesters', *Guardian*, 10 June.

Boykoff, J. (2016) 'Sochi 2014: politics, activism and repression', in R. Gruneau and J. Horne (eds) *Mega-Events and Globalization: Capital and Spectacle in a Changing World Order*, London: Routledge (pp. 131–148).

Boyle, P. and Haggerty, K. (2009) 'Spectacular security: mega-events and the security complex', *International Political Sociology* 3 (3), 257–274.

Boyle, P. and Haggerty, K. (2011) 'Civil cities and urban governance: regulating disorder in Vancouver', in *Urban Studies special issue: Security and Surveillance at Sport Mega-events*, 48 (15), 3185–3201.

Boyle, R. and Haynes, R. (2014) 'Watching the Games', in V. Girginov (ed.) *Handbook of the London 2012 Olympic and Paralympic Games. Volume Two: Celebrating the Games*. London: Routledge (pp. 84–95).

Braathen, E., Mascarenas, G. and Sorboe, C. (2015) 'Rio's ruinous mega-events', in P. Bond and A. Garcia (eds) *BRICS: An Anti-capitalist Critique*, London: Pluto, pp. 186–199.

Brailsford, D. (1969) *Sport and Society: Elizabeth to Anne*, London: RKP

Braye, S., Dixon, K. and Gibbons, T. (2012) '"A mockery of equality": an exploratory investigation into disabled activists' views of the Paralympic Games', *Disability and Society* 28 (7), 984–996.

Braye, S., Gibbons, T. and Dixon, K. (2013) 'Disability "Rights" or "Wrongs"? The claims of the International Paralympic Committee, the London 2012 Paralympics and Disability Rights in the UK', *Sociological Research Online* 18 (3).

Brent Heritage (2002) 'Wembley' (available online at: www.brent-heritage.co.uk/wembley.htm; last accessed 18 August 2010).

Briggs, A. (1991) 'Mass entertainment: the origins of a modern industry', in A. Briggs, *Serious Pursuits: Communications and Education, Collected Essays Vol. 3*, Hemel Hempstead: Harvester Wheatsheaf (pp. 38–61).

Brittain, I. (2009) *The Paralympic Games Explained*, London: Routledge.

Brittain, I. (2012) *From Stoke Mandeville to Stratford: A History of the Summer Paralympic Games*, London: Common Ground.

Brittain, I. (2015) 'Olympic Agenda 2020 Recommendations and the Paralympic Movement', in Deslandes, A., DaCosta, L.P. and Miragaya, A. (eds) *The Future of Sports Mega-events*, Rio de Janeiro: Engenho Arte e Cultura.

Brohm, J.-M. (1978) *Sport: A Prison of Measured Time*, London: Ink Links.

Brookes, R. (2002) *Representing Sport*, London: Hodder.

Brooks, B. and Barchfield, J. (2015) 'AP investigation: filthy Rio water a threat at 2016 Olympics' (available online at: http://bigstory.ap.org/article/a098d8884ff74c53988b 8932ce2f0d44/ap-investigation-dirty-rio-water-threat-2016-olympics; last accessed 30 July 2015).

Brooks-Buck, J. and Anderson, E. (2001) 'African American access to higher education through sports: following a dream or perpetuating a stereotype?' *Widening Participation and Lifelong Learning* 3: 26–31.

Broudehoux, A.-M. (2004) *The Making and Selling of Post-Mao Beijing*, London: Routledge.

Broudehoux, A.-M. (2007) 'Spectacular Beijing: the conspicuous construction of an Olympic metropolis', *Journal of Urban Affairs* 29 (4), 383–399.

Broudehoux, A.-M. (2016) 'Mega-events, urban image construction, and the politics of exclusion', in R. Gruneau and J. Horne (eds) *Mega-Events and Globalization: Capital and Spectacle in a Changing World Order*, London: Routledge (pp. 113–130).

Brown, S. (2012) 'De Coubertin's Olympism and the laugh of Michel Foucault: crisis discourse and the Olympic games', *Quest* 64, 150–163.

Brownell, S. (1995) 'The stadium, the city and the state: Beijing', in J. Bale and O. Moen (eds) *The Stadium and the City*, Keele: Keele University Press (pp. 95–110).

Brownell, S. (ed.) (2008) *The 1904 Anthropology Days and Olympic Games: Sport, Race, and American Imperialism*, Lincoln, NE and London: University of Nebraska Press.

Brownell, S. (2013) 'The Olympic public sphere: the London and Beijing opening ceremonies as representative of political systems', *The International Journal of the History of Sport*, 30 (11), 1315–1327.

Building Design (2008) 'World Architecture 100' (available online at: http://emag.digitalpc. co.uk/cmpi/world arch08.asp; accessed 17 December 2009).

Burakowski, E. and Magnusson, M. (2012) 'Climate impacts on the winter tourism economy in the United States', University of New Hampshire (available online at: http://protectourwinters.org/climate_report/report.pdf; last accessed 3 July 2015)

Burstyn, V. (1999) *The Rites of Men: Manhood, Politics and the Culture of Sport*, Toronto: Toronto University Press.

Cairns, G. (2015) 'The hybridization of sight in the hybrid architecture of sport: the effects of television on stadia and spectatorship', *Sport in Society*, 18 (6), 734–749.

Calvert, J. and Arbuthnott, G. (2015) 'The doping scandal. Revealed: sports dirtiest secret', *Sunday Times*, 2 August, pp. 1–2.

Campbell, D. (2014) 'London Olympics borough is the most physically inactive in England', *Guardian*, November.

Cano, I., Borges, D. and Ribeiro, E. (2012) *Os Donos do Morro: uma avaliação exploratória do impacto das Unidades de Polícia Pacificadora (UPPs) no Rio de Janeiro*, Rio de Janeiro: FBSP/LAV/UERJ.

Carlos, J. with Zirin, D. (2011) *The John Carlos Story: The Sports Moment that Changed the World*, Chicago: Haymarket Books.

Carrington, B. (2004) 'Cosmopolitan Olympism, humanism and the spectacle of "race"', in J. Bale and M.K. Christensen (eds) *Post-Olympism? Questioning Sport in the 21st Century*, Oxford: Berg (pp. 81–98).

Carrington, B. (2010) *Race, Sport and Politics*, London: Sage.

Carrington, B. (2013) 'Streets of flames and summer games', in M. Perryman (ed.) *London 2012: How Was It For Us?* London: Lawrence & Wishart (pp. 97–116).

Carrington, B. and McDonald, I. (eds) (2001) *'Race', Sport and British Society*, London: Routledge.

Cashman, R. (2006) *The Bitter-Sweet Awakening*, Sydney: Walla Walla Press.

Cashman, R. (2011) *Sydney Olympic Park 2000 to 2010: History and Legacy*, Petersham: Walla Walla Press.

Cashman, R. and Darcy, S. (2008) *Benchmark Games: The Sydney 2000 Paralympic Games*, Sydney: Walla Walla Press.

Cashman, R. and Harris, R. (2012) *The Australian Olympic Caravan from 2000 to 2012: A Unique Olympic Events Industry*, Petersham: Walla Walla Press.

Cashman, R. and Horne, J. (2013) 'Managing Olympic legacy', in S. Frawley and D. Adair (eds), *Managing the Olympics*. Basingstoke: Palgrave (pp. 50–65).

Cashmore, E. (2005) *Making Sense of Sports*, 4th edition, London: Routledge.

Chappelet, J.-L. and Kubler-Mabbott, B. (2008) *The International Olympic Committee and the Olympic System: The Governance of World Sport*, London: Routledge.

Charpentier, H. and Boissonnade, E. (1999) *La Grande Histoire des Jeux Olympiques*, Paris: Editions France-Empire.

Chatziefstathiou, D. (2012) 'Pierre de Coubertin: man and myth', in H. Lenskyj and S. Wagg (eds) *The Palgrave Handbook of Olympic Studies*. Basingstoke: Palgrave Macmillan (pp. 26–40).

Chatziefstathiou, D. and Henry, I. (2012) *Discourses of Olympism: From the Sorbonne 1894 to London 2012*, London: Palgrave.

Chernushenko, D. (1994) *Greening our Games: Running Sports Events and Facilities that Won't Cost the Earth*, Ottawa: Centurion.

Clendinning, A. (2006) 'Exhibiting a nation: Canada at the British Empire Exhibition, 1924–1925', *Histoire sociale/Social History* 39 (77), 79–107.

Clift, B and Andrews, D. (2012) 'Living Lula's passion? The politics of Rio 2016', in H. Lenskyj and S. Wagg (eds) (2012) *The Palgrave Handbook of Olympic Studies*, Basingstoke: Palgrave Macmillan (pp. 210–229).

Coaffee, J. (2011) 'Strategic security planning and the resilient design of Olympic sites', in A. Richards, P. Fussey and A. Silke (eds) *Terrorism and the Olympics: Major Event Security and Lessons for the Future*, London: Routledge.

Coakley, J. (2003) *Sports in Society*, 8th edition, New York: McGraw-Hill.

Coakley, J. (2015). 'Assessing the sociology of sport: on cultural sensibilities and the great sport myth', *International Review for the Sociology of Sport* 50 (4–5), 402–406.

Coalter, F. (2004) 'Stuck in the blocks? A sustainable sporting legacy', in A. Vigor, M. Mean and C. Tims (eds), *After the Gold Rush: A Sustainable Olympics for London*, London: Institute for Public Policy Research/Demos (pp. 91–108).

Coffey, A. (2010) 'Brazil Olympics may send poor families packing' (available online at: www.globalpost.com/dispatch/study-abroad/100519/brazil-olympics-rio-favelas; accessed 20 November 2010).

Cohen, P. (2005) 'The Olympics story', *Rising East Online* 1, January.

Cohen, P. (2013) *On the Wrong Side of the Track? East London and the Post Olympics*, London: Lawrence & Wishart.

Cohen, P. and Watt. P. (2016) *A Hollow Legacy? London 2012 and the Post Olympic City*, London: Palgrave.

COHRE (2007) *Fair Play for Housing Rights: Mega-events, Olympic Games and Housing Rights*, Geneva: Centre on Housing Rights and Evictions.

COHRE (2008) *One World, Whose Dream? Housing Rights Violations and the Beijing Olympic Games*, Geneva: Centre on Housing Rights and Evictions.

Collins, Sandra (2007) *The 1940 Tokyo Games: The Missing Olympics*, London: Routledge.

Collins, S. and Palmer, C. (2012) 'Taste, ambiguity and the Cultural Olympiad', in J. Sugden and A. Tomlinson (eds) *Watching the Olympics: Politics, Power and Representation*, London: Routledge.

Comitê Popular da Copa e das Olimpíadas do Rio de Janeiro (2013) *Megaeventos e Violações dos Direitos Humanos no Rio de Janeiro* (available online at: http://rio.portalpopulardacopa.org.br; last accessed 12 June 2014).

Cook, T.A. (1908) *The Cruise of the Branwen (Being a Short History of the Modern Revival of the Olympic Games)*, London: privately published, copy in British Library.

Cornwell, R. (2009) 'Yield of dreams', *The Independent*, 17 April, p. 48.

Coubertin, P. de (1888) *L'Education en Angleterre* Paris: Hachette.

Coubertin, P. de (1890) *Universités trans-Atlantiques*, Paris: Libairie Hachette.

Coubertin, P. de (1917) *Un artisan d'energie française*, Paris: Henri Didier, Librarie Éditeur.

Coubertin, P. de (2000) *Pierre de Coubertin 1863–1937, Olympism: Selected Writings*, Lausanne: IOC.

Courtney, M. (2012) 'CCTV at the 2012 Olympics: the great zoom boom', *EandT: Engineering and Technology Magazine*, 7 (7).

Crilley, D. (1993) 'Architecture as advertising: constructing the image of redevelopment', in G. Kearns and C. Philo (eds) *Selling Places: The City as Cultural Capital, Past and Present,* Oxford: Pergamon Press (pp. 231– 252).

Crompton, J.L. (2006) 'Economic impact studies: instruments for political shenanigans?' *Journal of Travel Research* 45, 67–82.

Cuellar, J.E. (2013) 'Latin America, football and the Japanese diaspora', *Soccer & Society* 14 (5), 722–733.

Culf, A. (2005) 'The man who is making a £2bn mark on London', *Guardian*, 27 October 2005, Sport section, p. 8.

Cumberbatch, G. and Negrine, R. (1992) *Images of Disability on Television*, London: Routledge.

Cunneen, C. (2000) 'Public order and the Sydney Olympics: forget about the right to protest', *Indigenous Law Bulletin* 5 (1), 26–27.

Cunningham, H. (1980) *Leisure in the Industrial Revolution*, London: Croom Helm.

Curi, M. (2008) 'Samba, girls and party: who were the Brazilian soccer fans at a World Cup? An ethnography of the 2006 World Cup in Germany', *Soccer & Society* 9 (1), 111–134.

Curi, M., Knijnik, J. and Mascarenhas, G. (2011) 'The Pan American Games in Rio de Janeiro 2007: consequences of a sport mega-event on a BRIC country', *International Review for the Sociology of Sport* 46 (2), 140–156.

Curran, J., Gaber, I. and Petley, J. (2005) *Culture Wars: The Media and the British Left*, Edinburgh: Edinburgh University Press.

Darnell, S. (2010) 'Mega sport for all? Assessing the development promises of Rio 2016', in R. Barney, J. Forsyth and M. Heine (eds) *Rethinking Matters Olympic*, 10th International Symposium for Olympic Research, London, Ontario (pp. 498–507).

Darnell, S. (2012) *Sport for Peace and Development: A Critical Sociology*, London: Bloomsbury Academic.

Darnell, S. and Millington, R. (2016) 'Modernization, neoliberalism and sports mega-events: evolving discourses in Latin America', in R. Gruneau and J. Horne (eds) *Mega-Events and Globalization: Capital and Spectacle in a Changing World Order*, London: Routledge (pp. 65–80).

Davies, W. (2015) 'Rio losing its battle to clean up waterways for the Games', BBC News, Latin America & Caribbean, 15 March (available online at: www.bbc.co.uk/news/world-latin-america-31980723 (last accessed 23 October 2015).

Davis, A. (2000) 'Public relations, political communication and national news production in Britain 1979–1999', PhD thesis, Goldsmiths College, University of London.

Davis, J.A. (2012) *The Olympic Games Effect: How Sports Marketing Builds Strong Brands*, 2nd edition, Solaris: John Wiley & Sons.

Davison, P. (ed.) (1998) *I Belong to the Left, 1945: The Complete Works of George Orwell, Vol. 17*, London: Secker & Warburg.

Day, I. (1990) *'Sorting the Men Out from the Boys': Masculinity, a Missing Link in the Sociology of Sport*, Sheffield: Sheffield City Polytechnic.

Dayan, D. and Katz, E. (1992) *Media Events: The Live Broadcasting of History*, Cambridge, MA: Harvard University Press.

DCLG (2015) *London 2012 Olympics Regeneration Legacy Evaluation Framework*, AMION Consulting Limited Department for Communities and Local Government.

DCMS (2008) *Guide to Safety at Sports Grounds*, London: Department of Media, Culture and Sport.

Debord, G. (1967/1970) *Society of the Spectacle*, Detroit, MI: Black & Red.

Delaney, T. (2007) 'Basic concepts of sports gambling: an exploratory review', *New York Sociologist* 2, 93–102.

Dias, C. and Andrade Melo, V. de (2011) 'Leisure and urbanisation in Brazil from the 1950s to the 1970s', *Leisure Studies* 30 (3), 333–343.

Dimeo, P. (2007) *A History of Drug Use in Sport: 1876–1976*, London: Routledge.

Dimeo, P. and Kay, J. (2004) 'Major sports events: image projection and the problems of the "semi periphery": a case study of the 1996 South Asia Cricket World Cup', *Third World Quarterly* 25 (7), 1263–1276.

Donnelly, M., Norman, M. and Donnelly, P. (2015) *The Sochi 2014 Olympics: A Gender Equality Audit*, Toronto: Centre for Sport Policy Studies, University of Toronto.

Donnelly, P. (1996) 'Prolympism: sport monoculture as crisis and opportunity', *Quest* 48 (1), 25–42.

Donnelly, P. (2009) 'Own the podium or rent it? Canada's involvement in the global sporting arms race', *Options Politiques/Policy Options*, December: 41–44.

Donnelly, P. and Donnelly, M. (2013a) *The London 2012 Olympics: A Gender Equality Audit*, Toronto: Centre for Sport Policy Studies, University of Toronto.

Donnelly, P. and Donnelly, M. (2013b) *Sex Testing, Naked Inspections and the Olympic Games: A Correction to the London 2012 Olympics – A Gender Equality Audit*, Toronto: Centre for Sport Policy Studies, University of Toronto.

Dorsey, J. (2015) 'Mega events: Qatar is too hot, Beijing has no snow', James Dorsey Sport and Politics Blog (available online at: www.huffingtonpost.com/james-dorsey/mega-events-qatar-is-too_b_7916384.html; last accessed 22 August 2015).

Duncan, M.C. (2001) 'The sociology of ability and disability in physical activity', *Sociology of Sport Journal* 18 (1), 1–4.

Duncan, M.C. and Aycock, A. (2005) 'Fitting images: advertising, sport and disability' in J. Jackson and D. Andrews (eds) *Sport, Culture and Advertising*, London: Routledge (pp. 136–153).

Dunning, E. (1975) 'The origins of modern football and the public school ethos', in B. Simon and I. Bradley (eds) *The Victorian Public School*, Dublin: Gill & Macmillan (pp. 168–176).

Durry, J. (n.d.) *Pierre de Coubertin: The Visionary*, Lausanne: IOC.

Dyer, R. (1978) 'Entertainment and utopia', *Movie* 24: 2–13.

Economist, The (1996) 'The zillion dollar games', 22 July: 13.

Eichberg, H. (1998) *Body Cultures: Essays on Sport, Space and Identity*, London: Routledge.

Eisinger, P. (2000) 'The politics of bread and circuses: building a city for the visitor class', *Urban Affairs Review*, 35, 316–333.

English Sports Council (1998) *The Development of Sporting Talent 1997: An Examination of the Current Practices for Talent Development in English Sport*, London: English Sports Council.

Entine, J. (2000) *Taboo*, New York: Public Affairs.

Espy, R. (1979) *The Politics of the Olympic Games*, Berkeley: University of California Press.

Essex, S.J. (2011) 'The Winter Olympics: driving urban change, 1924–2014', in J.R. Gold and M.M. Gold (eds) *Olympic Cities: City Agendas, Planning and the World's Games, 1896–2016*, Abingdon and New York: Routledge (pp. 56–80).

Essex, S. and Chalkley, B. (1998) 'Olympic Games: catalyst of urban change', *Leisure Studies* 17 (3), 187–206.

Essex, S. and Chalkley, B. (2003) 'Urban transformation from hosting the Olympic Games', Centre d'Estudis Olimpics (UAB) (available online at: http://olympicstudies.uab.es/lectures/web/pdf/essex.pdf; last accessed 21 March 2015).

Essex, S.J. and Chalkley, B.S. (2007) 'The Winter Olympics: driving urban change 1924–2002', in J.R. Gold and M.M. Gold (eds) *Olympic Cities: City Agendas, Planning and the World Games, 1896–2012*, London: Routledge.

European Tour Operators Association (2006) *Olympic Report*, London: ETOA.

Europol (2013). 'Update: results from the largest match-fixing investigation in Europe' (available online at: www.europol.europa.eu/content/results-largest-football-match-fixinginvestigation-Europe; last accessed 20 December 2015).

Evans, J. and Bairner, A. (2012) 'Physical education and social class', in G. Stidder and S. Hayes (eds) *Equity and Inclusion in Physical Education and Sport*, London: Routledge.

Ewen, S. (1988) *All Consuming Images*, New York: Basic Books.

Ewing, K.D. (2006) *Global Rights in Global Companies: Going for Gold at the UK Olympics*, London: Institute of Employment Rights.

Faulhaber, L. and Azevedo, L. (2015) *SMH 2015: Remoções no Rio de Janeiro Olímpico*, Rio de Janeiro: Mórula.

Featherstone, M. (2007) *Consumer Culture and Postmodernism*, 2nd edition, London: Sage.

Field, R. (2011) 'The Olympic movement's response to the challenge of emerging nationalism in sport: an historical reconsideration of GANEFO', PhD Thesis, University of Manitoba, Winnipeg.

Finley, M. and Pleket, H. (1976) *The Olympic Games: The First Thousand Years*, London: Chatto & Windus.

Fischer, E. and Gainer, B. (1994) 'Masculinity and the consumption of organised sports', in J.A. Costa (ed.) *Gender Issues and Consumer Behaviour*, London: Sage (pp. 84–103).

Fishwick, L. (2001) 'Be what you wanna be: a sense of identity down at the local gym', in N. Watson and S. Cunningham-Burley (eds) *Reframing the Body*, Basingstoke: Palgrave (pp. 152–165).

Fleming, S. (1995) *Home and Away: Sport and South Asian Male Youth*, Aldershot: Avebury (pp. 152–165).

Flower, R. (1982) *The Palace: A Profile of St. Moritz*, London: Debrett.

Flyvbjerg, B. (2014). 'What you should know about megaprojects and why: an overview', *Project Management Journal* 45 (2), 6–19.

Flyvbjerg, B. and Stewart, A. (2012) *Olympic Proportions: Cost and Cost Overrun at the Olympics 1960–2012*, Oxford, Saïd Business School Working Papers.

Folha de São Paulo (2014) 'O Mundial e as despesas do governo' (available online at: www1.folha.uol.com.br/infograficos/2014/05/82605-o-mundial-e-as-despesas-do-governo.shtml; last accessed 12 June 2014).

Frampton, K. (2005) 'Introduction: the work of architecture in the Age of Commodification', in W. Saunders (ed.) *Commodification and Spectacle in Architecture*, Minneapolis: University of Minnesota Press (pp. ix–xviii).

França, R. (2015) 'Transcarioca completa 1 ano com altos e baixos, transportando 230 mil passageiros por dia' *O Globo*, 24 May.

Frawley, S. and Adair, D. (eds) (2013) *Managing the Olympics*, Basingstoke: Palgrave Macmillan.

Freeman, J. (2014) 'Raising the flag over Rio de Janeiro's favelas: citizenship and social control in the Olympic city', *Journal of Latin American Geography*, 14 (1).

Friedman, M., Andrews, D. and Silk, M. (2004) 'Sport and the façade of redevelopment in the postindustrial city', *Sociology of Sport Journal* 21 (1), 119–139.

Frow, J. (1997) *Time and Commodity Culture: Essays in Cultural Theory and Postmodernity*, Oxford: Clarendon Press.

Fussey, P. (2012) '(In)security and the re-ordered Olympic City', *CJM: Criminal Justice Matters* (incorporating the ISTD bulletin) 88, 22–24

Fussey, P., Coaffee, J., Armstrong, G. and Hobbs, D. (2011) *Securing and Sustaining the Olympic City: Reconfiguring London for 2012 and Beyond*, Farnham: Ashgate.

G1 (2013) 'Protestos pelo país têm 1,25 milhão de pessoas, um morto e confrontos', (available online at: http://g1.globo.com/brasil/noticia/2013/06/protestos-pelo-pais-tem-125-milhao-de-pessoas-um-morto-e-confrontos.html; last accessed 12 June 2014).

Gaffney, C. (2008) *Temples of the Earthbound Gods: Stadiums in the Cultural Landscapes of Rio de Janeiro and Buenos Aires*, Austin: University of Texas Press.

Gaffney, C. (2010) 'Mega-events and socio-spatial dynamics in Rio de Janeiro, 1919–2016', *Journal of Latin American Geography* 9 (1), 7–29.

Gaffney, C. (2013) 'Virando o jogo: the challenges and possibilities for social mobilization in Brazilian football', *Journal of Sport and Social Issues* (published online – abstract available at http://jss.sagepub.com/content/early/2013/12/16/0193723513515887. abstract; last accessed 8 September 2014).

Gaffney, C. (2014) 'A World Cup for whom? The impact of the 2014 World Cup on Brazilian stadiums and cultures', in P. Fontes and B. Buarque de Hollanda (eds) *The Country of Football: Politics, Popular Culture & The Beautiful Game in Brazil*, London: Hurst & Co. (pp. 187–206).

Gaffney, C. (2016) 'The urban impacts of the 2014 World Cup in Brazil', in R. Gruneau and J. Horne (eds) *Mega-Events and Globalization: Capital and Spectacle in a Changing World Order*, London: Routledge (pp. 167–185).

Galicia, H. (2015) 'Porto Maravilha and the rehabilitation policy of central areas' (available online at: https://raquelrolnik.wordpress.com/2015/07/16/o-porto-maravilha-e-a-politica-de-reabilitacao-de-areas-centrais; last accessed 31 July 2015).

Galily, Y., Yarchia, M. and Tamirb, I. (2015) 'From Munich to Boston, and from theater to social media: the evolutionary landscape of world sporting terror', *Studies in Conflict & Terrorism*, Published online 25 August.

Garcia, B. (2001) 'Enhancing sport marketing through cultural and arts programmes: lessons from the Sydney Olympic Arts Festivals', *Sport Management Review*, 4 (2), 193–219.

Garcia, B. (2013) *Cultural Olympiad Evaluation: Final Report*, Liverpool: Institute of Cultural Capital.

Garcia, B. and Cox, T. (2013) *London 2012 Cultural Olympiad Evaluation: Final Report*, Institute of Cultural Capital, University of Liverpool/Liverpool John Moores University.

Garcia, B. and Miah, A. (2006) 'Ever-decreasing circles: the profile of culture at the Olympics', *Locum Destination Review*, 18, 60–62.

Garcia, G. (2014). 'Copa do Mundo não melhorou imagem do país no exterior, aponta índice britânico', *Brazilian News* 14, 18–24 November.

Gathorne-Hardy, J. (1977) *The Public School Phenomenon*, Harmondsworth: Penguin.

Gems, G. (2008) 'Anthropology Days, the construction of whiteness, and American imperialism in the Philippines', in S. Brownell (ed.) *The 1904 Anthropology Days and Olympic Games: Sport, Race, and American Imperialism*, Lincoln, NE and London: University of Nebraska Press (pp. 189–216).

Gibson, O. (2011) 'IOC leader lauds London as 2012 preparations enter final straight', *Guardian* 26 July, pp. 12–13.

Gibson, O. (2014) 'IOC unveils its Olympic vision in blaze of Monaco back-slapping', *Guardian*, 8 December (available online at: www.theguardian.com/sport/blog/2014/dec/08/ioc-olympic-vision-monaco-gay-rights-tv-channel; last accessed 21 October 2015).

289

Gibson, O. (2015a) 'How the Olympics failed', *Guardian*, Sport Section, 6 July, p. 1.

Gibson, O. (2015b) 'Japan scraps 2020 Olympic stadium plan', *Guardian*, 18 July, p. 17.

Gibson, O. (2015c) 'Coalition wasted Olympic school sport legacy: Jowell', *Guardian*, 6 July, p. 7.

Girginov, V. (ed.) (2010) *The Olympics: A Critical Reader*, London: Routledge.

Girginov, V. (ed.) (2013) *Handbook of the London 2012 Olympic and Paralympic Games. Volume One: Making the Games*. London: Routledge.

Girginov, V. (ed.) (2014) *Handbook of the London 2012 Olympic and Paralympic Games. Volume Two: Celebrating the Games*. London: Routledge.

Girginov, V. and Collins, M. (2013) *Routledge Special Issue Collection on the Olympic and Paralympic Games. Knowledge Creation: Bibliometrics and General Trends* (available online at: http://explore.tandfonline.com/page/pgas/theme-of-the-month-sports/april; last accessed 12 October 2015).

Girginov, V. and Hills, L. (2008) 'A sustainable sports legacy: creating a link between the London Olympics and sports participation', *International Journal of the History of Sport* 25 (14), 2091–2116.

Girginov, V. and Parry, J. (2005) *The Olympic Games Explained*, London: Routledge.

Gitersos, T.V. (2011), 'The sporting scramble for Africa: GANEFO, the IOC and the 1965 African Games', *Sport in Society: Cultures, Commerce, Media, Politics*, 14 (5), 645–659.

Giulianotti, R. (2005) *Sport: A Critical Sociology*, Cambridge: Polity.

Giulianotti, R. and Klauser, F. (2010) 'Security governance and sport mega-events: toward an interdisciplinary research agenda', *Journal of Sport and Social Issues*, 34 (1), 49–61.

Giulianotti, R. and Klauser, F. (2012) 'Sport mega-events and "terrorism": a critical analysis', *International Review for the Sociology of Sport* 47 (3): 307–323

Giulianotti, R. and Robertson, R. (eds) (2007) *Globalization and Sport*, Oxford: Blackwell.

Giulianotti, R., Armstrong, G., Hales, G. and Hobbs, D. (2014) 'Global sport mega-events and the politics of mobility: the case of the London 2012 Olympics', *British Journal of Sociology* (available online at: http://onlinelibrary.wiley.com/doi/10.1111/1468-4446.12103/abstract; last accessed 16 March 2015).

Giulianotti, R., Armstrong, G., Hales, G. and Hobbs, D. (2015) 'Sport mega-events and public opposition: a sociological study of the London 2012 Olympics', *Journal of Sport and Social Issues*, 39 (2), 99–119.

Glancey, J. (2008a) 'Secrets of the Bird's Nest', *Guardian*, G2, 11 February, pp. 23–27.

Glancey, J. (2008b) 'Architecture', *Guardian*, G2, 11 December, pp. 22–23.

Glancey, J. (2009) 'The wow years', *Guardian*, G2, 8 December, pp. 17–20.

Goff, B. and Simpson, M. (2012) *Thinking about the Olympics: The Classical Tradition and the Modern Games*, London: Bristol Classical Press.

Goffman, E. (1974) *Frame Analysis: An Essay on the Organization of Experience*, New York: Harper & Row.

Goggin, G. and Newell, C. (2000) 'Crippling Paralympics? Media, disability and Olympism', *Media International Australia* 97: 71–84.

Gold, J. and Gold, M. (eds) (2007) *Olympic Cities*. London: Routledge.

Gold, J.R. and Gold, M.M. (2011) *Olympic Cities: City Agendas, Planning and the World's Games 1896–2016*, 2nd edition, London: Routledge.

Goldblatt, D. (2014) *Futebol Nation: A Footballing History of Brazil*, London: Penguin.

Gordon, C. and Helal, R. (2001) 'The crisis of Brazilian football: perspectives for the twenty-first century', *International Journal of the History of Sport* 18 (3), 139–158.

Gotham, K.F. (2016) 'Beyond bread and circuses: mega-events as forces of creative destruction', in R. Gruneau and J. Horne (eds) *Mega-Events and Globalization: Capital and Spectacle in a Changing World Order*, London: Routledge (pp. 31–47).

Graham, C.G. (1986) *Leni Riefenstahl and Olympia*, Metuchen, NJ and London: Scarecrow Press.

Grant Thornton UK (2013) *Report 5: Post-Games Evaluation – Meta-Evaluation of the Impacts and Legacy of the London 2012 Olympic Games and Paralympic Games*, For Department for Culture, Media & Sport, prepared by Grant Thornton, Ecorys, Loughborough University, Oxford Economics, Future Inclusion.

Gratton, C., Shibli, S. and Coleman, R. (2006) 'The economic impact of major sports events: a review of 10 major UK sports events', in J. Horne and W. Manzenreiter (eds) *Sports Mega-Events: Social Scientific Analyses of a Global Phenomenon*, Oxford: Blackwell (pp. 41–58).

Gravelaine, F. de (1997) *Le Stade de France: Au coeur de la ville pour le sport et le spectacle*, Paris: Le Monteur.

Greenberg, S. (1987) *Guinness Olympic Games: The Records*, London: Guinness Superlatives.

Greene, S.J. (2003) 'Staged cities: mega-events, slum clearance, and global capital', *Yale Human Rights and Development Law Journal* 6: 161–187.

Grix, J. (ed.) (2014) *Leveraging Legacies from Sports Mega-Events*, Basingstoke: Palgrave.

Gruneau, R. (1981) 'Elites, class and corporate power in Canadian sport: some preliminary findings', in J. Loy, G. Kenyon and B. McPherson (eds) *Sport, Culture and Society: A Reader on the Sociology of Sport*, Philadelphia: Lea & Febiger (pp. 348–371).

Gruneau, R. (1984) 'Commercialism and the modern Olympics', in A. Tomlinson and G. Whannel (eds) *Five Ring Circus: Money, Power and Politics at the Olympic Games*, London: Pluto Press (pp. 1–15).

Gruneau, R. (2002) 'Foreword', in M. Lowes, *Indy Dreams and Urban Nightmares*, Toronto: Toronto University Press (pp. ix–xii).

Gruneau, R. and Horne, J. (eds) (2016) *Mega-Events and Globalization: Capital and Spectacle in a Changing World Order*, London: Routledge.

Gruneau, R. and Neubauer, R. (2012) 'A gold medal for the market: the 1984 Los Angeles Olympics, the Reagan era, and the politics of neoliberalism', in H. Lenskyj and S. Wagg (eds) *The Palgrave Handbook of Olympic Studies*. Basingstoke: Palgrave Macmillan (pp. 134–162).

Guedes, C. (2011) '"Changing the cultural landscape": English engineers, American missionaries, and the YMCA bring sports to Brazil – the 1870s to the 1930s', *International Journal of the History of Sport* 28 (17), 2594–2608.

Gutman, R. (1988) *Architectural Practice: A Critical View*, Princeton: Princeton Architectural Press.

Guttmann, A. (1978) *From Ritual to Record*, London: Columbia University Press.

Guttmann, A. (1984) *The Games Must Go On: Avery Brundage and the Olympic Movement*, New York: Columbia University Press.

Guttmann, A. (1992) *The Olympics: A History of the Modern Games*, Chicago: University of Illinois Press.

Guttmann, A. (2006) 'Berlin 1936: the most controversial Olympics', in A. Tomlinson and C. Young (eds) *National Identity and Global Sport Events: Culture Politics and Spectacle in the Olympics and World Cup*, New York: SUNY (pp. 65–82).

Hain, Peter (1970) *Don't Play With Apartheid*, London: Allen & Unwin.

Hall, C.M. (2001) 'Imaging, tourism and sports event fever: the Sydney Olympics and the need for a social charter for mega-events', in C. Gratton and I. Henry (eds) *Sport in the City*, London: Routledge (pp. 166–183).

Hall, C.M. (2005) 'Selling places: hallmark events and the reimaging of Sydney and Toronto', in J. Nauright and K. Schimmel (eds) *The Political Economy of Sport*, Basingstoke: Palgrave (pp. 129–151).

Hall, C.M. and Hodges, J. (1997) 'The politics of place and identity in the Sydney 2000 Olympics: sharing the spirit of corporatism', in M. Roche (ed.) *Sport, Popular Culture and Identity*, Oxford: Meyer & Meyer (pp. 95–111).

Hall, S., Critcher, C., Jefferson, T., Clarke, J. and Roberts, B. (1978) *Policing the Crisis: Mugging, the State and Law and Order*, London: Macmillan.

Hampton, J. (2008) *The Austerity Olympics: When the Games Came to London in 1948*, London: Aurum Press.

Hannigan, J. (1998) *Fantasy City: Pleasure and Profit in the Postmodern Metropolis*, London: Routledge.

Hardin, B. and Hardin, M. (2003) 'Conformity and conflict: wheelchair athletes discuss sport media', *Adapted Physical Activity Quarterly* 20 (3), 246–259.

Hargreaves, J.A. (1984) 'Women and the Olympic phenomenon', in A. Tomlinson and G. Whannel (eds) *Five-Ring Circus: Money, Power and Politics at the Olympic Games*, London: Pluto Press (pp. 53–70).

Hargreaves, J.A. (1994) *Sporting Females: Critical Issues in the History and Sociology of Women's Sport*, London: Routledge.

Hargreaves, J.A. (2000) *Heroines of Sport: The Politics of Difference and Identity*, London: Routledge.

Hart-Davis, D. (1986) *Hitler's Games*, London: Century.

Harvey, D. (1989) *The Condition of Postmodernity*, Oxford: Blackwell.

Harvey, J., Horne, J., Safai, P., Darnell, S. and Courchesne-O'Neill, S. (2014) *Sport and Social Movements: From the Local to the Global*, London: Bloomsbury Academic.

Hayes, G. and Horne, J. (2011) 'Sustainable development: shock and awe – London 2012 and civil society', *Sociology* 45 (5), 749–764

Hayes, G. and Karamichas, J. (2012a) 'Introduction: sports mega-events, sustainable development and civil societies', in G. Hayes and J. Karamichas (eds) *Olympic Games, Mega-Events and Civil Societies*, Basingstoke: Palgrave (pp. 1–27).

Hayes, G. and Karamichas, J. (2012b) *Olympic Games, Mega-events and Civil Societies: Globalization, Environment, Resistance*, Basingstoke: Palgrave Macmillan.

Hill, C. (1992) *Olympic Politics*, London: Manchester University Press.

Hill, C. (1994) 'The politics of Manchester's Olympic bid', *Parliamentary Affairs* 47, 338–355.

Hill, C. (1996) *Olympic Politics: Athens to Atlanta 1896–1996*, 2nd edition, Manchester and New York: Manchester University Press.

Hiller, H. (2003) 'Toward a science of Olympic outcomes: the urban legacy', in M. de Moragas, C. Kennett and N. Puig (eds) *The Legacy of the Olympic Games 1984– 2000*, Lausanne: IOC (pp. 102–109).

Hilvoorde, I. van, Elling, A. and Stokvis, R. (2010) 'How to influence national pride? The Olympic medal index as a unifying narrative', *International Review for the Sociology of Sport* 45 (1), 87–102.

Hinds, A. (2007) 'Fortress Olympics: counting the cost of major event security', *Jane's Intelligence Review*, 19 (5).

Hoberman, J. (1995) 'Toward a theory of Olympic internationalism', *Journal of Sport History* 22: 1–37.

Hoberman, J. (1997) *Darwin's Athletes: How Sport has Damaged Black America and Preserved the Myth of Race*, Boston: Houghton Mifflin.

Hodges, E. (2014) 'The social and environmental costs of Rio's Olympic golf course', Rio on Watch, 22 August (available online at: www.rioonwatch.org/?p=17283; last accessed 24 September 2015).

Hofmann, A. (2011) 'A never ending story: women's struggle for acceptance in ski jumping', *Journal of the New England Ski Museum* 80, Winter: 1–11 (available at www.skimuseum.org/doc198.html; last accessed 8 March 2015).

Hofmann, A. and Preuss, A. (2005) 'Female eagles of the air: developments in women's ski-jumping', in M. Lämmer, E. Mertin and T. Terret (eds) *New Aspects of Sport History:* Proceedings of the 9th ISHPES Congress, Cologne, Germany, Cologne: Academia Verlag (pp. 202–209).

Hollins, S. (2011) 'The Summer Olympic Games and the environment: a 20-year perspective', *Leisure Studies Association Newsletter*, 88, 50–56.

Holt, O. (2005) 'Bored of the rings', *GQ Sport* 1 (1), 16–20.

Holt, R. (1989) *Sport and the British: A Modern History*, Oxford: Oxford University Press.

Holt, R. (1992) 'An Englishman in the Alps: Arnold Lunn, amateurism and the invention of Alpine ski-racing', *International Journal of the History of Sport*, 9 (3), 421–432.

Holt, R. and Mason, A. (2000) *Sport in Britain, 1945–2000*, Oxford: Blackwell.

Home Affairs Select Committee (2012) 'Olympics security', Seventh Report of Session 2012–2013, HC 531-I, 21 September 2012 (available online at: www.publications. parliament.uk/pa/cm201213/cmselect/cmhaff/531/531.pdf; accessed 1 June 2015).

Honey, J.R. de S. (1975) 'Tom Brown's universe: the nature and limits of the Victorian public schools community', in B. Simon and I. Bradley (eds) *The Victorian Public School*, Dublin: Gill & Macmillan (pp. 19–33).

Horn, J. (2011) 'Caught in the game: the rise of the sports betting industry', *The Monthly Essays* (available online at: www.themonthly.com.au/issue/2011/november/1320384446/ jonathan-horn/caught-game; last accessed 22 July 2015).

Horne, J. (2006) *Sport in Consumer Culture*, Basingstoke: Palgrave.

Horne, J. (2007a) 'The "four knowns" of sports mega-events', *Leisure Studies* 26 (1), 81–96.

Horne, J. (2007b) 'World Cup Cricket and Caribbean aspirations: from Nello to Mello', *North American Congress on Latin America (NACLA) Report on the Americas* 40 (4), 10–14.

Horne, J. (2010) 'The politics of hosting the Olympic Games', in A. Bairner and G. Molnar (eds) *The Politics of the Olympics*, London: Routledge (pp. 27–40).

Horne, J. (2011a) 'Architects, stadia and sport spectacles: notes on the role of architects in the building of sport stadia and making of world-class cities', *International Review for the Sociology of Sport* 46 (2), 205–227.

Horne, J. (2011b) 'Sports mega-events and the shaping of urban modernity in East Asia', in M. Baskett and W.M. Tsutsui (eds) *Olympian Desires: Building Bodies and Nations in East Asia*, Folkestone: Global Oriental, (pp. 183–198).

Horne, J. (2012) 'The four "Cs" of sports mega-events: capitalism, connections, citizenship and contradictions', in G. Hayes and J. Karamichas (eds) *Olympic Games, Mega-Events, and Civil Societies: Globalisation, Environment, and Resistance*, Basingstoke: Palgrave (pp. 31–45).

Horne, J. (2013) 'Sporting mega-events, urban modernity, and architecture', in D. Andrews and B. Carrington (eds) *A Companion to Sport*, Oxford: Wiley/Blackwell (pp. 427–444).

Horne, J. (ed.) (2014a) *Leisure, Culture and the Olympic Games*, London: Routledge.

Horne, J. (2014b) 'Managing World Cup legacy', in S. Frawley and D. Adair (eds) *Managing the Football World Cup*, Basingstoke: Palgrave Macmillan (pp. 7–24).

Horne, J. (2016) 'Sports mega-events: three sites of contemporary political contestation', *Sport in Society* (available online at: www.tandfonline.com/doi/full/10.1080/174304 37.2015.1088721; last accessed 23 October 2015).

Horne, J. and Manzenreiter, W. (2006) 'An introduction to the sociology of sports mega-events', in J. Horne and W. Manzenreiter (eds) *Sports Mega-Events: Social Scientific Analyses of a Global Phenomenon*, Oxford: Blackwell (pp. 1–24).

Horne, J. and Manzenreiter, W. (2012) 'Olympic tales from the east: Tokyo 1964, Seoul 1988 and Beijing 2008', in H. Lenskyj and S. Wagg (eds) *The Palgrave Handbook of Olympic Studies*, Basingstoke: Palgrave Macmillan (pp. 103–119).

Horne, J. and Silvestre, G. (2016) 'Brazil, politics, the Olympics and the FIFA World Cup', in A. Bairner, J. Kelly and J. Lee (eds) *The Routledge Handbook of Sport and Politics*, London: Routledge

Horne, J. and Whannel, G. (2010) 'The "caged torch procession": celebrities, protesters and the 2008 Olympic torch relay in London, Paris and San Francisco', *Sport in Society* 13 (5), 760–770.

Horne, J. and Whannel, G. (2012) *Understanding the Olympics*, London: Routledge.

Horne, J., Tomlinson, A. and Whannel, G. (1999) *Understanding Sport: An Introduction to the Sociological and Cultural Analysis of Sport*, London: E & FN Spon.

Horne, J., Lingard, R., Forbes, J. and Weiner, G. (2011) 'Capitalizing on sport: sport, physical education and multiple capitals in Scottish independent schools', *British Journal of Sociology of Education*, 32, 861–879.

Horne, J., Tomlinson, A., Whannel, G. and Woodward, K. (2013) *Understanding Sport: A Socio-cultural Analysis*, London: Routledge.

Houlihan, B. (2002) 'Political involvement in sport, physical education and recreation', in A. Laker (ed.), *The Sociology of Sport and Physical Education*, London: Routledge (pp. 190–210).

Houlihan, B. (2008) 'Doping and sport', in B. Houlihan (ed.) *Sport and Society: A Student Introduction*, 2nd edition, London: Sage (pp. 375–394).

Houlihan, B. and Giulianotti, R. (2012) 'Politics and the London 2012 Olympics: the (in)security Games', *International Affairs*, 88 (4), 701–717.

House of Commons Committee of Public Accounts (2013) *The London 2012 Olympic Games and Paralympic Games: Post-Games Review*; Fortieth Report of Session 2012–13; Report, together with formal minutes, oral and written evidence; HC 812; published on 19 April 2013, London: The Stationery Office.

House of Lords Library (2012) House of Lords Library note, for background reading for the debate to be held on Thursday 8 November on Olympic and Paralympic Games Legacy, Dorothy Hughes 6 November 2012, LLN 2012/037

Howe, P.D. (2008) *The Cultural Politics of the Paralympic Movement*, London: Routledge.

Howe, P.D. (2010) 'Disability, Olympism and Paralympism', in A. Bairner and G. Molnar (eds) *The Politics of the Olympics*, London: Routledge (pp. 69–80).

Howe, P.D. (2011) 'Cyborg and supercrip: the Paralympics technology and the (dis)empowerment of disabled athletes', *Sociology*, 45 (5), 868–882.

Howe, P.D. (2013) 'Supercrips, cyborgs and the unreal Paralympian', in M. Perryman (ed.) *London 2012. How Was It for Us?*, London: Lawrence & Wishart (pp. 130–141).

Howell, D. (1990) *Made in Birmingham: The Memoirs of Denis Howell*, London: Queen Anne Press.

Hughes, G. (1999) 'Urban revitalization: the use of festive time strategies', *Leisure Studies* 18 (2), 119–135.

Humphrey, J. (1986) 'No holding Brazil: football, nationalism and politics', in A. Tomlinson and G. Whannel (eds) *Off the Ball: The Football World Cup*, London: Pluto (pp. 127–139).

Hutchins, B. and Mikosza, J. (2010) 'The Web 2.0 Olympics: athlete blogging, social networking and policy contradictions at the 2008 Beijing Games', *Convergence: The International Journal of Research into New Media Technologies*, Special issue on Sport in new media cultures, 16 (3), 163–183.

Hylton, K. (2009) *'Race' and Sport: Critical Race Theory*, London: Routledge.

Hylton, K. and Morpeth, N. (2012) 'London 2012: "race" matters and the East End', *International Journal of Sport Policy and Politics* 4 (3), 379–396.

Ilha Pura (2015) Video (available online at: http://ilhapura.com.br; last accessed 23 October 2015).

Inglis, S. (2000) *Sightlines: A Stadium Odyssey*, London: Yellow Jersey.

Inglis, S. (2005) *Engineering Archie: Archibald Leitch – Football Ground Designer*, London: English Heritage/HOK.

IOC (n/d) *Sponsor Handbook: A Celebration of the Olympic Centennial*, Lausanne: The Olympic Programme.

IOC (2004) *Olympic Charter*, Lausanne: IOC.

IOC (2007a) *Olympic Charter*, revised 7 July, Lausanne: IOC.

IOC (2007b) *Sexual Harassment and Abuse and Abuse in Sport: Consensus Statement (February), IOC Medical Commission Expert Panel*, Lausanne: IOC.

IOC (2009) *Olympic Marketing Fact File*, Lausanne: IOC.

IOC (2010a) www.olympic.org/en/content/Olympic-Games/All-Past-Olympic-Games/Summer/Beijing-2008; last accessed 19 August 2010.

IOC (2010b) *The Olympic Summer Games: Factsheet*, Lausanne: IOC.

IOC (2012) *IOC Factsheet: London 2012 Facts and Figures Update*, November 2012, (available online at: www.olympic.org/Documents/Reference_documents_Factsheets/London_2012_Facts_and_Figures-eng.pdf)

IOC (2014a) *Olympic Charter*, Lausanne: IOC.

IOC (2014b) *Annual Report 2014: Credibility, Sustainability and Youth*, Lausanne: IOC.

IOC (2015) *Olympic Charter*, Lausanne: IOC.

Jacob, S. (2010) 'In a meeting with the Mayor of Rio, Vila Autódromo reaffirms desire to stay' (available online at: www.catcomm.org/en/?p=2642; accessed 20 November 2010).

James, C.L.R. (1963) *Beyond a Boundary*, London: Stanley Paul.

Jarvie, G. (1991a) *Highland Games: The Making of the Myth*, Edinburgh: Edinburgh University Press.

Jarvie, G. (ed.) (1991b) *Sport, Racism and Ethnicity*, London: Falmer.

Jarvie, G. (1992) 'Highland gatherings, Balmorality, and the glamour of backwardness', *Sociology of Sport Journal* 9 (2), 167–178.

Jarvie, G. (2006) *Sport, Culture and Society*, London: Routledge.

Jenkins, S. (2014) 'The World Cup and Olympics threaten to overwhelm Rio: yet there is time to create a sensation out of disaster', *Guardian* (available online at: www.theguardian.com/cities/2014/apr/23/world-cup-olympics-rio-de-janeiro-brazil-sensation-disaster; last accessed 12 June 2014).

Jennings, A. (1996) *The New Lords of the Rings: Olympic Corruption and How to Buy Gold Medals*, London: Pocket Books.

Jennings, A. (2000) 'The great Olympic illusion', programme broadcast on BBC2, 29 August (transcript available online at: http://news.bbc.co.uk/1/hi/programmes/correspondent/901405.stm; last accessed 20 December 2015).

Jennings, A. (2006) *Foul! The Secret World of FIFA: Bribes, Vote Rigging and Ticket Scandals*, London: HarperCollins.

Jennings, A. (2012) 'The love that dare not speak its name: corruption and the Olympics', in H. Lenskyj and S. Wagg (eds) *The Palgrave Handbook of Olympic Studies*, Basingstoke: Palgrave Macmillan (pp. 461–473).

Jennings, A. (2014) 'Meet the IOC', *The Nation*, 26 January.

Jennings, A. and Sambrook, C. (2000) *The Great Olympic Swindle*, London: Simon & Schuster.

Jennings, W. (2012) *Olympic Risks*, Basingstoke: Palgrave Macmillan.

John, G. and Sheard, R. (2000) *Stadia: A Design and Development Guide*, 3rd edition, Oxford: Architectural Press.

John, G., Sheard, R. and Vickery, B. (2006) *Stadia: A Design and Development Guide*, 4th edition, Oxford: Architectural Press.

Jones, P. (2006) 'The sociology of architecture and the politics of building', *Sociology* 40 (3), 549–565.

Karamichas, J. (2005) 'Risk versus national pride: conflicting discourses over the construction of a high voltage power station in the Athens metropolitan area for demands of the 2004 Olympics', *Human Ecology Review* 12 (2), 133–142.

Karamichas, J. (2013) *The Olympic Games and the Environment,* Basingstoke: Palgrave Macmillan.

Kavestos, G. (2012) 'The impact of the London Olympics on property prices', *Urban Studies*, 49 (7), 1453–1470.

Kellner, D. (2003) *Media Spectacle*, London: Routledge.

Kelly, W.W. (2011) 'The Olympics in East Asia: nationalism, regionalism, and globalism on the center stage of world sports', in W.W. Kelly and S. Brownell (eds) *The Olympics in East Asia: Nationalism, Regionalism and Globalism on the Center Stage of World Sports*, New Haven, Conn.: Yale University: Yale CEAS Occasional Publications, Volume 3.

Keys, B. (2006) *Globalizing Sport: National Rivalry and International Community in the 1930s*, Cambridge, MA and London: Harvard University Press.

Kidd, B. (1984) 'The myth of the ancient games', in A. Tomlinson and G. Whannel (eds) *Five Ring Circus*, London: Pluto (pp. 71–83).

Kidd, B. (1992) 'The Toronto Olympic commitment: towards a social contract for the Olympic Games', *Olympika: International Journal of Olympic Studies* 1: 154–167.

Kidd, B. (2010) 'Epilogue: the struggles must continue', *Sport in Society* 13 (1), 157–165.

Kidd, B. and Donnelly, P. (2000) 'Human rights in sports', *International Review for the Sociology of Sport* 35 (2), 131–148.

Kietlinski, R. (2011) *Japanese Women and Sport*, London: Bloomsbury Academic.

King, A. (2004) *Spaces of Global Cultures: Architecture Urbanism Identity*, London: Routledge.

Klein, N. (2007) *The Shock Doctrine*, London: Penguin/Allen Lane.

Klein, N. (2008) 'The Olympics: unveiling police state 2.0', *Huffington Post*, www.huffingtonpost.com/naomi-klein/the-olympics-unveiling-po_b_117403.html; posted 7 August; last accessed 10 December 2010.

Klein, N. (2014) *This Changes Everything*, London: Allen Lane.

Klitgaard, R. (1988). *Controlling Corruption*, Berkeley: University of California Press.

Knight, D.R. (1978) *The Exhibitions: Great White City 70th Anniversary*, London: Barnard & Westwood.

Knijnik, J.D., Horton, P. and Oliveira Cruz, L. (2010) 'Rhizomatic bodies, gendered waves: transitional femininities in Brazilian Surf', *Sport in Society* 13 (7/8), 1170–1185.

Knott, S.M. (2008) 'Germans and others at the "American Games": problems of national and international representation at the 1904 Olympics', in S. Brownell (ed.) *The 1904 Anthropology Days and Olympic Games: Sport, Race, and American Imperialism*, Lincoln, NE and London: University of Nebraska Press (pp. 278–300).

Koenig, U. and Abegg, B. (1997) 'Impacts of climate change on winter tourism in the Swiss Alps', *Journal of Sustainable Tourism* 5 (1): 46–58.

Krüger, A. (1993) 'Book review of J. Boix and A. Espada El deporte del poder: vida y milagro de Juan Antonio Samaranch (Madrid: Ediciones temas de hoy, 1991)', *International Journal of Sports History* 10, 291–293.

Krüger, A. (2003) 'Germany: the propaganda machine', in M. William and A. Krüger (eds), *The Nazi Olympics*, Urbana and Chicago: University of Illinois Press (pp. 17–43).

Krüger, A. and Murray, W. (eds) (2003) *The Nazi Olympics: Sport, Politics and Appeasement in the 1930s*, Champaign and Urbana: University of Illinois Press.

Krüger, A. and Riordan, J. (1996) *The Story of Worker Sport*, Leeds: Human Kinetics.

Kuhn, G. (2015) *Playing As if the World Mattered: An Illustrated History of Activism in Sports*, Oakland: PM Press.

Kuper, S. (1994) *Football Against the Enemy*, London: Orion.

Larson, J. and Heung-Soo Park (1993) *Global Television and the Politics of the Seoul Olympics*, Boulder, CO: Westview.

Larson, M. (1994) 'Architectural competitions as discursive events', *Theory and Society* 23 (4), 469–504.

Latham, A. (2003) 'Urbanity, lifestyle and making sense of the new urban cultural economy', *Urban Studies* 40 (9), 1699–1724.

Lauermann, J. (2015) 'Boston's Olympic bid and the evolving urban politics of event-led development', *Urban Geography* (available online at: www.tandfon line.com/doi/abs/10.1080/02723638.2015.1072339; last accessed 23 October 2015).

Lee, H. (2012) 'Gilbert West and the English contribution to the revival of the Olympic Games', in Barbara Goff and Michael Simpson (eds) *Thinking about the Olympics: The Classical Tradition and the Modern Games*, London: Bristol Classical Press (pp. 109–121).

Lee, M. (1993) *Consumer Culture Reborn*, London: Routledge.

Lee, M. (2006) *The Race for the 2012 Olympics: The Inside Story of How London Won the Bid*, London: Virgin.

Lee, P.-C., Bairner, A. and Tan, T.-C. (2010) 'Taiwanese identities and the 2008 Beijing Olympic Games', in A. Bairner and G. Molnar (eds) *The Politics of the Olympics*, London: Routledge (pp. 129–144).

Lennartz, K. (1983) *Deutschlands an den Olympischen Spielen 1900 in Paris und 1904 in St Louis (German Participation at the Olympic Games: 1900 in Paris and 1904 in St Louis)*, Bonn: Carl Diem Institut.

Lenskyj, H. (2000) *Inside the Olympics Industry: Power, Politics and Activism*, Albany: State University of New York Press.

Lenskyj, H. (2002) *The Best Olympics Ever? Social Impacts of Sydney 2000*, Albany: SUNY Press.

Lenskyj, H. (2008) *Olympic Industry Resistance Challenging Olympic Power and Propaganda*, Albany: State University of New York Press.

Lenskyj, H. (2012) 'The case against the Olympic Games: the buck stops with the IOC', in H. Lenskyj and S. Wagg (eds) *The Palgrave Handbook of Olympic Studies*, Basingstoke: Palgrave Macmillan (pp. 570–579).

Lenskyj, H. (2013) *Gender Politics and the Olympic Industry*, Basingstoke: Palgrave Macmillan.

Lenskyj, H. and Wagg, S. (eds) (2012) *The Palgrave Handbook of Olympic Studies*, Basingstoke: Palgrave Macmillan.

Lever, J. (1995/1983) *Soccer Madness: Brazil's Passion for the World's Most Popular Sport*, Prospect Heights: Waveland Press.

Levermore, R. and Beacom, A. (eds) (2009) *Sport and International Development*, Basingstoke: Palgrave.

Levine, R.M. (1980) 'Sport and society: the case of Brazilian futebol', *Luso-Brazilian Review* 17 (2), 233–252.

Levine, R.M. (1999) *Father of the Poor? Vargas and His Era*, Cambridge: Cambridge University Press.

Levine, R.M. and Crocitti, J.J. (eds) (1999) *The Brazil Reader: History, Culture, Politics*, Durham, NC: Duke University Press.

Levy, A. (2004) *Small Island*, London: Headline.

Liao, H. and Pitts, A. (2006) 'A brief historical review of Olympic urbanization', *International Journal of the History of Sport* 23 (7), 1232–1252.

Lippe, Gerd von der (2008) 'Female ski-jumpers in Norway: against nature', in M. Lämmer, E. Mertin and T. Terret (eds) *New Aspects of Sport History*, Proceedings of the 9th ISHPES Congress, Cologne: Academia Verlag (pp. 331–335).

Llewellyn, M.P. (2012) *Rule Britannia: Nationalism, Identity and the Modern Olympics*, London: Routledge.

Loewenstein, A. (2015) *Disaster Capitalism: Making a Killing Out of Catastrophe*, London: Verso.

London 2012 (2004) *Candidate File*, London: London 2012.

London 2012 Olympics regeneration legacy evaluation framework (2015) AMION Consulting Limited Department for Communities and Local Government, Queen's Printer and Controller of Her Majesty's Stationery Office.

Long, J., Hylton, K., Spracklen, K., Ratna, A. and Bailey, S. (2009) *Systematic Review of the Literature on Black and Minority Ethnic Communities in Sport and Physical Recreation*, Leeds: Sporting Equals and the Sports Councils/Carnegie Research Institute, Leeds Metropolitan University.

Lovesey, P. (1979) *The Official Centenary History of the AAA*, London: Guinness Superlatives.

Lowerson, J. (1993) *Sport and the Middle Classes, 1870–1914*, Manchester: Manchester University Press.

Lowes, M. (2002) *Indy Dreams and Urban Nightmares*, Toronto: Toronto University Press.

Lutan, R. and Hong, F. (2005) 'The politicization of sport: Ganefo – a case study', *Sport in Society* 8 (3), 425–439.

Maas, K. and Hasbrook, C. (2001) 'Media promotion of the paradigm citizen/golfer: an analysis of golf magazines' representations of disability, gender and age', *Sociology of Sport Journal* 18 (1), 21–36.

MacAloon, J.J. (1981) *This Great Symbol: Pierre de Coubertin and the Origins of the Modern Olympic Games*, Chicago: University of Chicago Press.

MacAloon, J.J. (1984a) 'Olympic Games and the theory of spectacle in modern societies', in J.J. MacAloon (ed.) *Rite, Drama, Festival, Spectacle: Rehearsals Toward a Theory of Cultural Performance*, Philadelphia: Institute for the Study of Human Issues (pp. 241–280).

MacAloon, J.J. (ed.) (1984b) *Rite, Drama, Festival, Spectacle: Rehearsals Toward a Theory of Cultural Performance*, Philadelphia: Institute for the Study of Human Issues.

MacAloon, J.J. (1996) 'Humanism as political necessity? Reflections on the pathos of anthropological science in Olympic contexts', *Quest* 48 (1), 67–81.

MacAloon, J.J. (1999) 'Anthropology at the Olympic Games', in A.M. Klausen (ed.), *Olympic Games as Performance and Public Event*, New York and Oxford: Berghahn Books (pp. 9–26).

MacAloon, J.J. (2006a) *This Great Symbol: Pierre de Coubertin and the Origins of the Modern Olympic Games*, 2nd edition, London: Routledge.

MacAloon, J.J. (2006b) 'The theory of spectacle: reviewing Olympic ethnography', in A. Tomlinson and C. Young (eds) *National Identity and Global Sports Events*, New York: State University of New York Press (pp. 15–39).

MacAloon, J.J. (2008) '"Legacy" as managerial/magical discourse in contemporary Olympic affairs', *Journal of the History of Sport*, 25 (14), 2060–2071.

McCann, B. (2008) *The Throes of Democracy: Brazil Since 1989*, London: Zed Books.

McCann, B. (2014) *Hard Times in the Marvelous City: From Dictatorship to Democracy in the Favelas of Rio de Janeiro*, Durham, NC and London: Duke University Press.

McCusker, P. (2008) 'Bring back the Morpeth Olympics', *The Journal*, 11 April (available online at: www.nebusiness.co.uk/business-news/latest-business-news/journal-business-news/2008/04/11/bring-back-the-morpeth-olympics-51140–20749347; accessed 10 July 2010).

McDonagh, E. and Pappano, L. (2008) *Playing with the Boys: Why Separate is Not Equal*, New York: Oxford University Press.

McFee, G. (1990) 'The Olympic Games as tourist event', in A. Tomlinson (ed.) *Sport in Society: Policy, Politics and Culture*, Brighton: Leisure Studies Association.

McIntosh, P. (1952) *Physical Education in England since 1800*, London: Bell.

Mackintosh, C., Darko, N. and May-Wilkins, H. (2015) 'Unintended outcomes of the London 2012 Olympic Games: local voices of resistance and the challenge for sport participation leverage in England', *Leisure Studies*, DOI: 10.1080/02614367. 2015.1031269

McLeod-Roberts, L. (2007) 'Paramilitary games', *NACLA Report on the Americas* 40 (4), 20–25.

McNeill, D. (2004) *New Europe: Imagined Spaces*, London: Hodder Arnold.

McNeill, D. (2009) *The Global Architect*, London: Routledge.

McPhail, T. and Jackson, R. (eds) (1989) *The Olympic Movement and the Mass Media*, Calgary: Hurford Enterprises.

Maennig, W. (2005). 'Corruption in international sports and sport management: forms, tendencies, extent and countermeasures', *European Sport Management Quarterly* 5 (2), 187–225.

Magdalinski, T., Schimmel, K. and Chandler, T. (2005) 'Recapturing Olympic mystique: the corporate invasion of the classroom', in J. Nauright and K. Schimmel (eds) *The Political Economy of Sport*, London: Palgrave Macmillan (pp. 38–54).

Malcolmson, R.W. (1973) *Popular Recreations in English Society 1700–1850*, Cambridge: Cambridge University Press.

Mallon, B. and Buchanan, I. (2000) *The 1908 Olympic Games: Results for All Competitors in All Events with Commentary*, Jefferson and London: McFarland.

Mandell, R. (1976) *The First Modern Olympics*, Berkeley: University of California Press.

Mandell, R. (1987) *The Nazi Olympics*, Urbana: University of Illinois Press.

Mangan, J.A. (1975) 'Athleticism: a case study of the evolution of an educational ideology', in B. Simon and I. Bradley (eds) *The Victorian Public School: Studies in the Development of an Educational Institution*, Dublin: Gill & Macmillan (pp. 147–167).

Mangan, J.A. (1981) *Athleticism in the Victorian and Edwardian Public School*, Cambridge: Cambridge University Press.

Mangan, J.A. (1987) 'Social Darwinism and upper class education in late Victorian and Edwardian England', in J.A. Mangan and J. Walvin (eds) *Manliness and Morality: Middle Class Masculinity in Britain and America*, Manchester: Manchester University Press (pp. 135–159).

Mangan, J.A. (2000) *Athleticism in the Victorian and Edwardian Public School*, revised edition, London: Frank Cass.

Mangan, J.A. (2001) 'The early evolution of modern sport in Latin America: a mainly English middle-class inspiration?', *International Journal of the History of Sport* 18 (3), 9–42.

Mangan, J.A. and Dyreson, M. (eds) (2010) *Olympic Legacies: Intended and Unintended*, London: Routledge.

Mansfield, L. and Malcolm, D. (2015) 'The Olympic Movement, sport and health', in J. Baker, P. Safai and J. Fraser-Thomas (eds) *Health and Elite Sport: Is High Performance Sport a Healthy Pursuit?* Abingdon: Routledge (pp. 187–203).

Manzenreiter, W. (2006) 'Sport spectacles, uniformities and the search for identity in late modern Japan', in J. Horne and W. Manzenreiter (eds) *Sports Mega-Events: Social Scientific Analyses of a Global Phenomenon*, Oxford: Blackwell (pp. 144–159).

Markula, P. (ed.) (2009) *Olympic Women and the Media: International Perspectives*, London: Palgrave.

Marschik, M., Mullner, R., Spitaler, G. and Zinganel, M. (eds) (2005) *Das Stadion: Geschichte, Architektur, Politik, Okonomie*, Vienna: Turia & Kant.

Marshall, P.D., Walker, B. and Russo, N. (2010) 'Mediating the Olympics', *Convergence: The International Journal of Research into New Media Technologies*, Special issue on sport in new media cultures 16 (3), 263–278.

Marvin, C. (2008) '"All under heaven": megaspace in Beijing', in M. Price and D. Dayan (eds) *Owning the Olympics: Narratives of the New China*, Ann Arbor: University of Michigan Press (pp. 229–259).

Marx, K. (1976 [1867]) *Capital: A Critique of Political Economy Vol. I*, Harmondsworth: Penguin.

Marx, K. (1981) *Capital: A Critique of Political Economy, Vol. 3*, introduced by Ernest Mandel; translated by David Fernbach, Harmondsworth: Penguin in association with *New Left Review*.

Mason, T. (1995) *Passion of the People? Football in South America*, London: Verso.

Matthews, G.R. (2005) *America's First Olympics: The St Louis Games of 1904*, Columbia and London: University of Missouri Press.

Meade, T. (1997) *'Civilizing' Rio: Reform and Resistance in a Brazilian City, 1889–1930*, Pennsylvania: Pennsylvania State University Press.

Merrifield, A. (2002) *Metromarxism: A Marxist Tale of the City*, New York: Routledge.

Miah, A. and Garcia, B. (2012) *The Olympics: The Basics*, London: Routledge.

Miah, A., Garcia, B. and Zhihui, T. (2008) '"We are the media": non-accredited media and citizen journalists at the Olympic Games', in M.E. Price and D. Dayan (eds) *Owning the Olympics: Narratives of the New China*, Ann Arbor: University of Michigan Press (pp. 320–345).

Miles, S. (2010) *Spaces for Consumption: Pleasure and Placelessness in the Post-Industrial City*, London: Sage.

Miles, S. and Miles, M. (2004) *Consuming Cities*, Basingstoke: Palgrave.

Miller, D. and Dinan, W. (2007) *A Century of Spin: How Public Relations Became the Cutting Edge of Corporate Power*, London: Pluto.

Minnaert, L. (2012) 'An Olympic legacy for all? The non-infrastructural outcomes of the Olympic Games for socially excluded groups (Atlanta 1996–Beijing 2008)', *Tourism Management* 33 (2), 361–370.

Minton, A. (2009a) *Ground Control: Fear and Happiness in the Twenty-First-Century City*, London: Penguin.

301

Minton, A. (2009b) 'These cities within cities are eating up Britain's streets', *Guardian*, 16 December, p. 30.

Minton, A. (2012) *Ground Control: Fear and Happiness in the Twenty-First-Century City*, 2nd edition, London: Penguin.

Montalban, M.V. (2004 [1991]) *An Olympic Death*, London: Serpent's Tail.

Montenegro, C. (2013) 'Copa pode provocar despejo de 250 mil pessoas, afirmam ONGs', *BBC Brasil* (available online at: www.bbc.co.uk/portuguese/noticias/2013/06/130614_futebol_despejos_cm_bg.shtml; last accessed: 12 June 2014).

Moore, K. (1986) 'Sport, politics and imperialism: British Empire Games from 1881–1930', in *Proceedings of the Fourth Annual Conference*, London: British Society of Sports Historians.

Moore, K. (1987) 'The Pan-Britannic Festival: a tangible but forlorn expression of imperialism', in J.A. Mangan (ed.) *Pleasure Profit Proselytism*, London: Frank Cass (pp. 144–162).

Moore, K. (1989) 'The warmth of comradeship: the first British Empire Games and imperial solidarity', *International Journal of the History of Sport* 6 (2), 242–251.

Moore, K. (1991) 'A neglected imperialist: the promotion of the British Empire in the writing of John Astley Cooper', *International Journal of the History of Sport* 8 (2): 256–269.

Moore, R. (2012) *The Dirtiest Race in History*, London: Bloomsbury.

Moragas, M. de, MacAloon, J. and Llinés, M. (1996a) *Olympic Ceremonies: Historical Continuity and Cultural Exchange*, Barcelona and Lausanne: Olympic Museum, IOC.

Moragas, M. de, Rivenburgh, N.K. and Larson, J.F. (eds) (1996b) *Television in the Olympics*, London: John Libbey.

Morin, G. (1998) *La Cathédrale inachevée*, Montreal: XYZ editeur.

Morris, J. and Evans, N. (2008) 'Keeping the environment at the top of the agenda', in James Morris and Natalie Evans (eds) *The Million Vote Mandate*, Policy Exchange and Localis.

Mosey, R (2010) Interview with Roger Mosey, BBC Olympics Director, in *Convergence: the International Journal for Research on New Media Technologies*, Autumn.

Müller, F., van Zoonene, L. and de Roode, L. (2008) 'The integrative power of sport: imagined and real effects of sports events on multicultural integration', *Sociology of Sport Journal* 25 (4), 387–401.

Munoz, F. (2006) 'Olympic urbanism and Olympic villages: planning strategies in Olympic host cities, London 1908 to London 2012', in J. Horne and W. Manzenreiter (eds) *Sports Mega-Events: Social Scientific Analyses of a Global Phenomenon*, Oxford: Blackwell (pp. 175–187).

Murray, W.J. (1987) 'The French workers sports movement and the Popular Front victory (1939)', *International Journal of the History of Sport* 4 (2), 203–230.

National Audit Office (2008) *Preparing for Sporting Success at the London 2012 Olympic and Paralympic Games and Beyond*, London: Stationery Office.

Neves, E. (2015) 'A um ano da Olímpiada, Rio corre para despoluir a Baía de Guanabara', *Veja Rio*, 6 February (available online at: http://vejario.abril.com.br/materia/cidade/a-um-ano-da-olimpiada-rio-corre-para-despoluir-a-baia-de-guanabara; last accessed 23 October 2015).

Newman, R (2012) 'How the Olympics will cost London', USNews.com, 9 November (available online at: www.usnews.com/news/blogs/rick-newman/2012/03/22/how-the-olympics-will-cost-london; accessed 10 June 2015).

Nichols, G. and Ralston, R. (2015) 'The legacy costs of delivering the 2012 Olympic and Paralympic Games through regulatory capitalism', *Leisure Studies*, 34 (4), 389–404.

Nixon H.L. (2000) 'Sport and disability', in J. Coakley and E. Dunning (eds) *Handbook of Sports Studies*, London: Sage (pp. 422–438).

Nordin, A. (2015) 'Expo Milano: what are worlds fairs for?', *The Conversation*, 7 May (available online at: https://theconversation.com/expo-milano-what-are-worlds-fairs-for-41331; last accessed 7 September 2015).

Nybelius, M.R. and Hofmann, A.R. (eds) (2015) *License to Jump! A Story of Women's Ski Jumping*, Köping: Beijbom Books.

Office for National Statistics (1998) *Living in Britain: Results from the 1996 General Household Survey*, London: Stationery Office.

Official Olympic Games Report (1936) *The Official Report of the Berlin Olympic Games Organising Committee: Berlin, Volume I*, 301–350.

Official Olympic Games Report (1948) *The Official Report of the Organising Committee for the XIV Olympiad*, London: Organising Committee for the XIV Olympiad.

Official Olympic Games Report (1988) *The Official Report of the Organising Committee for the XXIV Olympiad*, Seoul, Korea: Organising Committee for the XXIV Olympiad.

Olds, K. (1997) 'Globalizing Shanghai; the "Global Intelligence Corps" and the building of Pudong', *Cities* 14 (2), 109–123.

Olds, K. (1998) 'Urban mega-events, evictions and housing rights: the Canadian case', *Current Issues in Tourism* 1 (1), 2–46.

Olds, K. (2001) *Globalization and Urban Change: Capital, Culture and Pacific Rim Mega-Projects*, Oxford: Oxford University Press.

de Oliveira, N.G. (2015). *O poder dos jogos e os jogos de poder: interesses em campo na produção da cidade para o espetáculo esportivo (The power of games and the games of power)*, Rio de Janeiro: UFRJ/Anpur.

O'Neill, B. (2005) 'Fortress Olympics', *Rising East Online* 1, January.

O'Neil, T. (1989) *The Game Behind the Game: High Stakes, High Pressure in TV Sports*, New York: Harper & Row.

Osmond, G. (2010) 'Photographs, materiality and sport history: Peter Norman and the 1968 Mexico City Black Power salute', *Journal of Sport History* 37 (1), 119–137.

Oxford Economics (2012) *The Economic Impact of the London 2012 Olympic and Paralympic Games*, a report by Oxford Economics, commissioned by Lloyds Banking Group.

Payne, M. (2005) *Olympic Turnaround*, London: London Business Press.

Payne, M (2006) *Olympic Turnaround: How the Olympic Games Stepped Back from the Brink of Extinction to Become the World's Best Known Brand*, London: Praeger.

Peck, J. and Tickell, A. (2002) 'Neoliberalizing space', *Antipode* 34 (3), 380–404.

Perlman, J. (2010) *Favela: Four Decades of Living on the Edge in Rio de Janeiro*, New York: Oxford University Press.

Perryman, M. (ed.) (2013) *London 2012: How Was It for Us?* London: Lawrence & Wishart.

Petca, A.R., Bivolaru, E. and Graf, T.A. (2013) 'Gender stereotypes in the Olympic Games media? A cross-cultural panel study of online visuals from Brazil, Germany and the United States', *Sport in Society* 16 (5), 611–630.

Philips, D. (2012) *Fairground Attractions: A Genealogy of the Pleasure Ground*, London: Bloomsbury Academic.

Phillips, B. (2000) *Honour of Empire, Glory of Sport: The History of Athletics at the Commonwealth Games*, Manchester: Parrs Wood Press.

Philo, C. and Kearns, G. (1993) 'Culture, history, capital: a critical introduction to the selling of places', in G. Kearns and C. Philo (eds) *Selling Places: The City as Cultural Capital, Past and Present*, Oxford: Pergamon Press (pp. 1–32).

Physick, R. (2007) *Played in Liverpool: Charting the Heritage of a City at Play*, London: Historic England.

Pielke Jr, R. (2015). 'Obstacles to accountability in international sports governance' (available online at: www.transparency.org/files/content/feature/1.2_Obstacles ToAccountability_Pielke_GCRSport.pdf; last accessed 5 June 2015).

Pierson, D. (2010) 'China gushes over high-tech toilets', *The Daily Yomiuri*, 11 October, p. 11.

Piketty, T. (2014) *Capital in the Twenty-First Century*, Cambridge, MA: Harvard University Press.

Pinheiro, D. (2011) 'The President', *Revista piauí* (available online at: http://revistapiaui. estadao.com.br/edicao-58/the-faces-of-futebol/the-president; last accessed 12 June 2014).

Polley, M. (2011) *The British Olympics: Britain's Olympic Heritage 1612–2012*. Swindon: English Heritage.

Polley, M. (2014) 'Inspire a publication: books, journals, and the 2012 Olympic and Paralympic Games', in V. Girginov (ed.) *Handbook of the London 2012 Olympic and Paralympic Games. Volume Two: Celebrating the Games*, Abingdon: Routledge (pp. 255–265).

Polley, M. (2015) 'The 1908 Olympic Games: a case study in accidental and incidental legacies', in R. Holt and D. Ruta (eds) *Routledge Handbook of Sport and Legacy*, Abingdon: Routledge (pp. 59–69).

Porter, L., Jaconelli, M., Cheyne, J., Eby, D. and Wagenaar, H. (2009) 'Planning displacement: the real legacy of major sporting events', *Planning Theory and Practice*, 10 (3), 395–418.

Pound, R.W. (2003) *Olympic Games Study Commission* (Report to the 115th IOC Session, Prague, July), Lausanne: International Olympic Committee.

Pound, R. (2004) *Inside the Olympics: A Behind-the-Scenes Look at the Politics, the Scandals, and the Glory of the Games*, London: Wiley.

Powell, H. and Marrero-Guillamón, I. (eds) (2012) *The Art of Dissent: Adventures in London's Olympic State*, London: Marshgate Press.

Poynter, G. (2005) 'The economics of the Olympic bid', *Rising East Online* 1, January.

Poynter, G. and MacRury, I. (eds) (2009) *Olympic Cities: 2012 and the Remaking of London*, London: Ashgate.

Poynter, G., Viehoff, V. and Li, Y. (eds) (2016) *The London Olympics and Urban Development: The Mega-event City*, Abingdon: Routledge.

Preuss, H. (2004) *The Economics of Staging the Olympic Games: A Comparison of the Games 1972–2008*, Cheltenham: Edward Elgar.

Price, M.E. (2008) 'On seizing the Olympic platform', in M.E. Price and D. Dayan (eds) *Owning the Olympics: Narratives of the New China*, Ann Arbor: University of Michigan Press (pp. 86–114).

Puff, J. (2014) 'Qual o futuro das UPPs no novo governo Pezão?' *BBC Brasil*, 29 October, (available online at: www.bbc.com/portuguese/noticias/2014/10/141026_eleicoes2014_governo_rio_upp_jp_rm; last accessed 22 October 2015).

Puijk, R. (1997) *Global Spotlights on Lillehammer*, Luton: University of Luton Press.

Quanz, D. (1993) 'Civic pacifism and sports-based internationalism: framework of the founding of the International Olympic Committee', *Olympika* 2: 1–24.

Raco, M. (2014) 'Delivering flagship projects in an era of regulatory capitalism: state-led privatization and the London Olympics 2012', *International Journal of Urban and Regional Research* 38 (1), 176–197.

Raine, Robert (2015) 'Reflections on security at the 2012 Olympics', *Intelligence and National Security* 30 (4), 422–433.

Ramsamy, S. (1982) *Apartheid, the Real Hurdle*, London: International Defence and Aid Fund for South Africa.

Ramsamy, S. (1984) 'Apartheid, boycotts and the Games', in A. Tomlinson and G. Whannel (eds) *Five Ring Circus: Money, Power and Politics at the Olympic Games*, London: Pluto Press (pp. 44–52).

Raspaud, M. and Bastos, F. da Cunha (2013) 'Torcedores de futebol: violence and public policies in Brazil before the 2014 FIFA World Cup', *Sport in Society* 16 (2), 192–204.

Real, M. (1986) *Global Ritual: Olympic Media Coverage and International Understanding*, Paris: UNESCO.

Real, M. (1989) *Super Media*, London: Sage.

Reich, K. (1986) *Making It Happen: Peter Ueberroth and the 1984 Olympics*, Santa Barbara, CA: Capra.

Reis, A.C. and Sousa-Mast, F.R. (2012) *Rio 2016 and Sport Legacies: The Legacies of the Olympic Games for Youth at-risk in Rio de Janeiro*, Lausanne: IOC Olympic Studies Centre.

Ren, X. (2008) 'Architecture and nation building in the age of globalization: construction of the national stadium of Beijing for the 2008 Olympics', *Journal of Urban Affairs* 30 (2), 175–190.

Richards, A., Fussey, P. and Silke, A. (2011) *Terrorism and the Olympics: Major Event Security and Lessons for the Future*, London: Routledge.

Rimmer, P. (1991) 'The global intelligence corps and world cities: engineering consultancies on the move', in P. Daniels (ed.) *Services and Metropolitan Development: International Perspectives*, London: Routledge (pp. 146–172).

Rio 2016 OCOG (Rio 2016 Organizing Committee for the Olympic Games) (2009) *Transport Strategic Plan for the Rio 2016 Olympic and Paralympic Games*, Rio de Janeiro: Rio 2016 OCOG.

Rio 2016 OCOG (2014) *Embracing Change: Rio 2016 Sustainability Report*, Rio de Janeiro: Rio 2016 OCOG.

Riordan, J. (1984) 'The Workers' Olympics', in A. Tomlinson and G. Whannel (eds) *Five Ring Circus: Money, Power and Politics at the Olympic Games*, London: Pluto Press (pp. 98–112).

Ritchie, I. (2012) 'The use of performance-enhancing substances in the Olympic Games: a critical history', in H. Lenskyj and S. Wagg (eds) *The Palgrave Handbook of Olympic Studies*, Basingstoke: Palgrave (pp. 410–429).

Ritchie, B. and Hall, M. (1999) 'Mega-events and human rights', in Taylor, T. (ed.) *How You Play the Game: The Contribution of Sport to the Protection of Human Rights*, Sydney: Faculty of Business, University of Technology, Sydney (pp. 102–115).

Ritzer, G. and Stillman, T. (2001) 'The postmodern ballpark as a leisure setting: enchantment and simulated de-McDonaldization', *Leisure Sciences* 23 (2), 99–113.

RKMA (Richard K. Miller & Associates) (2006) *The 2007 Architectural/Engineering/Construction Market Research Handbook*, Loganville, GA: Richard K. Miller & Associates.

Roan, D. (2013) 'Research raises questions over Paralympic Games Legacy', *BBC Sport* (available online at: www.bbc.co.uk/sport/0/disability-sport/20990620; last accessed 18 March 2013).

Roberts, K. (2015) 'Social class and leisure during recent recessions in Britain', *Leisure Studies* 34 (2), 131–149.

Rocha, J. and McDonagh, F. (2014) *Brazil Inside Out: People, Politics and Culture*, Rugby: Latin America Bureau/Practical Action Publishing.

Roche, M. (2000) *Mega-Events and Modernity: Olympics and Expos in the Growth of Global Culture*, London: Routledge.

Roche, M. (2003) 'Mega-events, time and modernity: on time structures in global society', *Time and Society* 12 (1), 99–126.

Rohter, L. (2010) *Brazil on the Rise: The Story of a Country Transformed*, Basingstoke: Palgrave Macmillan.

Rolnik, R. (2009) *Report of the UN's Special Rapporteur on Adequate Housing as a Component of the Right to an Adequate Standard of Living, and on the Right to Non-discrimination in this Context*, New York: United Nations General Assembly.

Rose, A.K. and Spiegel, M.M. (2011) 'The Olympic effect', *The Economic Journal*, June, 652–677.

Rosemont, H. (2012) 'Reassessing the G4S Olympic security affair', *Defencemanagement.com*, 3 October 2012 (longer version of a speech delivered to the Private Military and Security Research Conference at the Royal United Services Institute (RUSI) on 28 September 2012).

Rosemont, H. (2015) 'Reflections on security at the 2012 Olympics', *Humanities and Social Sciences Online*, 1 October (available online at: https://networks.h-net.org/node/28443/discussions/85237/h-diplo-article-review-555-"reflections-security-2012-olympics"-1; last accessed 8 October 2015.

Rowe, D. (1995) 'Big defence: sport and hegemonic masculinity', in A. Tomlinson (ed.) *Gender, Sport and Leisure: Continuities and Challenges*, Eastbourne: University of Brighton (pp. 123–133).

Rowe, D. (1996) 'The global love-match: sport and television', *Media Culture and Society* 18 (4), 565–582.

Rowe, D. (1999) *Sport, Culture and the Media*, Milton Keynes: Open University Press.

Rowe, D. (2004) 'Antonio Gramsci: sport, hegemony and the national-popular', in R. Giulianotti (ed.) *Sport and Modern Social Theorists*, Basingstoke: Palgrave Macmillan (pp. 97–110).

Rowe, D. (2011). *Global Media Sport: Flows, Forms and Futures*, London: Bloomsbury Academic.

Rowe, N. and Moore, S. (2004) *Participation in Sport: Results from the General Household Survey 2002*, Sport England Research Briefing Note, London: Sport England.

Rubio, K. (2009) *Esporte, educação e valores olímpicos*. Itatiba, SP: Casaspi.

Ruhl, J. (1999) 'History and development of the Morpeth Olympic Games', paper presented at the ISHPES Congress, Budapest.

Russell, D. (2006) '"We all agree, name the stand after Shankly": cultures of commemoration in late twentieth-century English football culture', *Sport in History* 26 (1), 1–25.

Rutheiser, C. (1996) *Imagineering Atlanta: The Politics of Place in the City of Dreams*, New York and London: Verso.

Sadd, D. (2014) 'Protesting the Games', in V. Girginov (ed.) *Handbook of the London 2012 Olympic and Paralympic Games. Volume Two: Celebrating the Games*, London: Routledge (pp. 227–238).

Sanati, C. (2015) 'Could fantasy become reality for legalized sports betting?', *Fortune*, 25 June (available online at: http://fortune.com/2015/06/25/legal-sports-betting; last accessed 22 June 2015).

Sánchez, F. and Broudehoux, A.M. (2013) 'Mega-events and urban regeneration in Rio de Janeiro: planning in a state of emergency', *International Journal of Urban Sustainable Development* 5(2), 132–153.

Sánchez, F., Bienenstein, G., Leal de Oliveira, F. and Novais, P. (eds) (2014) *A Copa do Mundo e as Cidades: Políticas, Projetos e Resistências*, Niteroi: Editora da UFF/ Universidade Federal Fluminense.

Sassatelli, R. (1999) 'Interaction order and beyond: a field analysis of body culture within fitness gyms', *Body and Society* 5 (2/3), 227–248.

Sassen, S. (1991) *The Global City*, Princeton, NJ: Princeton University Press.

Saunders, W. (2005) 'Preface', in W. Saunders (ed.) *Commodification and Spectacle in Architecture*, Minneapolis: University of Minnesota Press (pp. vii–viii).

Sayer, A. (2015). *Why We Can't Afford the Rich*, Bristol: Policy Press.

Schantz, O. and Gilbert, K. (2001) 'An ideal misconstrued newspaper coverage of the Atlanta Paralympic Games in France and Germany', *Sociology of Sport Journal* 18 (1), 69–94.

Schausteck de Almeida, B., Coakley, J., Marchi Júnior, W. and Augusto Starepravo, F. (2012) 'Federal government funding and sport: the case of Brazil, 2004–2009', *International Journal of Sport Policy and Politics* 4 (3), 411–426.

Schell, L.A. and Duncan, M.C. (1999) 'A content analysis of CBS's coverage of the 1996 Paralympic Games', *Adapted Physical Activity Quarterly* 16 (1), 27–47.

Schell, L.A. and Rodriguez, S. (2001) 'Subverting bodies/ambivalent representations: media analysis of Paralympian, Hope Lewellen', *Sociology of Sport Journal* 18 (1), 127–135.

Schimmel, K. (2001) 'Sport matters: urban regime theory and urban regeneration in the late-capitalist era', in C. Gratton and I. Henry (eds) *Sport in the City*, London: Routledge (pp. 259–277).

Schimmel, K. (2006) 'Deep play: sports mega-events and urban social conditions in the USA', in J. Horne and W. Manzenreiter (eds) *Sports Mega-Events*, Oxford: Blackwell (pp. 160–174).

Schmidt, C. (2007) *Five Ring Circus: The Untold Story of the Vancouver 2010 Games* (documentary film, available from www.TheFiveRingCircus.com).

Schweid, R. (1994) *Barcelona: Jews, Transvestites and an Olympic Season*, Berkeley: Ten Speed Press.

Shank, M.D. (2002) *Sports Marketing: A Strategic Perspective*, Upper Saddle River: Prentice Hall.

Shapiro, Ari (2014) 'Did London get an economic boost from the 2012 Olympics?', National Public Radio, USA, 3 February (available online at: www.npr.org/sections/parallels/2014/02/03/270950685/did-london-get-an-economic-boost-from-the-2012-olympics; last accessed 16 December 2015).

Shaw, C. (2008) *Five Ring Circus: Myths and Realities of the Olympic Games*, Gabriola Island: New Society Publishers.

Sheard, R. (2001a) *Sports Architecture*, London: Spon.

Sheard, R. (2001b) 'Olympic stadia and the future', in International Union of Architects and IOC, *The Olympic Games and Architecture: The Future for Host Cities*, Lausanne: IOC (pp. 43–47).

Sheard, R. (2005) *The Stadium: Architecture for the New Global Culture*, Singapore: Periplus.

Shilling, C. (2004) 'Physical capital and situated action: a new direction for corporeal sociology', *British Journal of Sociology of Education* 25 (4), 473–487.

Shilling, C. (2007) 'Sociology and the body: classical traditions and new agendas', in C. Shilling (ed.) *Embodying Sociology: Retrospect, Progress, Prospects*, Oxford: Blackwell (pp. 2–17).

Short, J.R. (2004) *Global Metropolitan: Globalizing Cities in a Capitalist World*, London: Routledge.

Silk, M. and Amis, J. (2005) 'Sport tourism, cityscapes and cultural politics', *Sport in Society* 8 (2), 280–301.

Silvestre, G. (2008) 'The social impacts of mega-events: towards a framework', *Esporte e Sociedade*, 4 (10), 1–26.

Silvestre, G. (2012) *An Olympic City in the Making: Rio de Janeiro Mega-event Strategy 1993–2016*, Lausanne: IOC Olympic Studies Centre.

Silvestre, G. (2016) 'Rio de Janeiro 2016', in J. Gold and M. Gold (eds) *Olympic Cities*, 3rd edition, London: Routledge.

Silvestre, G. and de Oliveira, N.G. (2012) 'The revanchist logic of mega-events: community displacement in Rio de Janeiro's West End', *Visual Studies*, 27(2), 204–210.

Simon, B. (1975) 'Introduction' in B. Simon and I. Bradley (eds) *The Victorian Public School: Studies in the Development of an Educational Institution*, Dublin: Gill & Macmillan (pp. 1–18).

Simon, B. and Bradley, I. (eds) (1975) *The Victorian Public School: Studies in the Development of an Educational Institution*, Dublin: Gill & Macmillan.

Simson, V. and Jennings, A. (1992) *The Lords of the Rings: Power, Money and Drugs in the Modern Olympics*, London: Simon & Schuster.

Sinclair, I. (2008) 'The Olympics scam', *London Review of Books* 30 (12), 17–23.

Sinclair, I. (2011) *Ghost Milk: Calling Time on the Grand Project*, London: Hamish Hamilton

Singer, A. (2014) 'Rebellion in Brazil: social and political complexion of the June events', *New Left Review*, 85, 19–37.

Sklair, L. (2001) *The Transnational Capitalist Class*, Oxford: Blackwell.

Sklair, L. (2002) *Globalization: Capitalism and its Alternatives*, Oxford: Oxford University Press.

Sklair, L. (2005) 'The transnational capitalist class and contemporary architecture in globalizing cities', *International Journal of Urban and Regional Research* 29 (3), 485–500.

Sklair, L. (2006) 'Iconic architecture and capitalist globalization', *City* 10 (1), 21–47.

Sklair, L. (2010) 'Iconic architecture and the culture-ideology of consumerism', *Theory, Culture & Society* 27 (5), 135–159.

Smit, B. (2006) *Pitch Invasion: Adidas, Puma and the Making of Modern Sport*, London: Allen Lane.

Smith, A. (2012) *Events and Urban Regeneration*, London: Routledge.

Smith, A. and Thomas, N. (2012) 'The politics and policy of inclusion and technology in Paralympic sport: beyond Pistorius', *International Journal of Sport Policy and Politics* 4 (3), 397–410.

Smith, A., Haycock, D. and Hulme, N. (2013) 'The class of London 2012: some sociological reflections on the social backgrounds of Team GB athletes', *Sociological Research Online* 18 (3).

Sopel, J. (2015). 'Fifa scandal: is the long arm of US law now overreaching', BBC News Online (available online at: www.bbc.co.uk/news/world-us-canada-33011847; last accessed 5 June).

Spence, J. (1988) *Up Close and Personal*, New York: Atheneum.

Spicer, A. (2015). 'With Blatter gone, the hard work of changing FIFA culture starts now', *The Conversation* (available online at: https://theconversation.com/with-blatter-gone-the-hard-work-of-changing-fifa-culture-starts-now-42776; last accessed 5 June).

Spiegel, F. (2007) 'Watkin's Folly to Wembley Stadium' (available online at: http://britishhistory.suite101.com/ article.cfm/watkins_folly_to_wembley_stadium; accessed 18 August 2010).

Sport England (1999a) *Participation in Sport in Great Britain 1996*, London: Sport England.

Sport England (1999b) *Survey of Sports Halls and Swimming Pools in England 1997*, London: Sport England.

Sport England (2000) *Sports Participation and Ethnicity in England National Survey 1999/2000*, London: Sport England.

sportscotland (2002) *Sports Participation in Scotland 2001*, Edinburgh: sportscotland.

Stallard, P. (1996) 'A fractured vision: the world fair comes to Wembley', unpublished paper, University of Sheffield Geography Department.

Steinberg, D.A. (1978) 'The Workers Sport Internationals 1920–28', *Journal of Contemporary History* 13: 233–251.

Steinbrink, M. (2013) 'Festi*favel*isation: mega-events, slums and strategic city-staging: the example of Rio de Janeiro', *Die Erde* 144 (2), 129–145.

Stevens, G. (1998) *The Favored Circle: The Social Foundations of Architectural Distinction*, Cambridge, MA: MIT Press.

Stevens, Q. (2007) *The Ludic City: Exploring the Potential of Public Spaces*, London: Routledge.

Stevenson, D. (1977) 'Olympic arts: Sydney 2000 and the Cultural Olympiad', *International Review for the Sociology of Sport* 32 (3), 227–238.

Stewart, A. (2012) 'Managing the Games franchise is an Olympian feat', *The Conversation*, 25 July (available online at: https://theconversation.com/managing-the-games-franchise-is-an-olympian-feat-7633; last accessed 24 September 2015).

Such, L. (2014) 'Do mega sports events have a legacy?' (available online at: http://discoversociety.org/2014/08/05/do-mega-sports-events-have-a-legacy; last accessed 29 September 2015).

Sudjic, D. (2005) *The Edifice Complex: How the Rich and Powerful Shape the World*, London: Penguin.

Sugden, J. (2012) 'Watched by the Games: surveillance and security at the Olympics', *International Review for the Sociology of Sport* 47 (3), 414–429.

Sugden, J. and Tomlinson, A. (1998) *FIFA and the Contest for World Football*, Cambridge: Polity.

Sugden, J. and Tomlinson, A. (2003) *Badfellas: FIFA Family at War*, Edinburgh: Mainstream.

Sugden, J. and Tomlinson, A. (2012) *Watching the Olympics: Politics, Power, and Representation*, London and New York: Routledge.

Surborg, B., VanWynsberghe, R. and Wyly, E. (2008) 'Mapping the Olympic growth machine: transnational urbanism and the growth machine diaspora', *City* 12 (3), 341–355.

Sutton Trust (2012) 'Over a third of British Olympic winners were privately educated' (available online at: www.suttontrust.com/newsarchive/third-british-olympic-winners-privately-educated; last accessed 29 September 2015).

Taine, Hippolyte (1872) *Notes sur l'Angleterre*, Paris.

Tajima, A. (2004) '"Amoral universalism": mediating and staging global and local in the 1998 Nagano Winter Olympic Games', *Critical Studies in Media Communication* 21 (3), 241–260.

Tanaka, G. (2014) 'Vila Autódromo: resistance symbol in the Olympic Village' (available online at: www.boell.de/en/2014/05/23/vila-autodromo-resistance-symbol-olympic-village; last accessed 20 October 2015).

Tanzi, V. (1998). 'Corruption around the world: causes, consequences, scope, and cures', *IMF Staff Papers*, 45, 559–594.

Taylor Report (1990) *The Hillsborough Stadium Disaster 15 April 1989: Final Report of the Inquiry by the Rt. Hon Lord Justice Taylor*, London: HMSO.

Thielgen, J. (n.d.) 'Genesis and history of the Morpeth Olympic Games', Germany, unpublished,

Thomas, N. and Smith, A. (2003) 'Preoccupied with able-bodiedness? An analysis of the British media coverage of the 2000 Paralympic Games', *Adapted Physical Activity Quarterly* 20 (2), 166–181.

Thrift, N. (2004) 'Intensities of feeling: towards a spatial politics of affect', *Geografiska Annaler Series B* 86, 1: 57–78.

Thrift, N. (2005) 'But malice aforethought: cities and the natural history of hatred', *Transactions of the Institute of British Geographers* 30: 133–150.

Till, J. (2009) *Architecture Depends*, Cambridge, MA: MIT Press.

Tomlinson, A. (1996) 'Olympic spectacle: opening ceremonies and some paradoxes of globalisation', *Media Culture and Society* 18 (4), 583–602.

Tomlinson, A. (1999) 'Staging the spectacle: reflections on Olympic and World Cup ceremonies', *Soundings* 13: 161–171.

Tomlinson, A. (2005a) 'Olympic survivals', in L. Allison (ed.) *The Global Politics of Sport*, London: Routledge (pp. 46–62).

Tomlinson, A. (2005b) 'The making of the global sports economy: ISL, Adidas, and the rise of the corporate player in world sport', in M.L. Silk, D.L. Andrews and C.L. Cole (eds) *Sport and Corporate Nationalisms*, Oxford: Berg (pp. 35–65).

Tomlinson, A. (2014). *FIFA (Fédération Internationale de Football Association): The Men, the Myths and the Money*, London: Routledge.

Tomlinson, A. and Whannel, G. (eds) (1984) *Five Ring Circus: Money, Power and Politics at the Olympic Games*, London: Pluto.

Tomlinson, A. and Young, C. (eds) (2006) *National Identity and Global Sports Events*, Albany: State University of New York Press.

Toohey, K. and Veal, A. (2007) *The Olympic Games: A Social Science Perspective*, 2nd edition, Oxford: CABI.

Trory, E. (1980) *Munich, Montreal and Moscow: A Political Tale of Three Olympic Cities*, Hove: Crabtree Press.

Trumpbour, R. (2007) *The New Cathedrals: Politics and Media in the History of Stadium Construction*, Syracuse: Syracuse University Press.

Tudor, A. (1998) 'Sports reporting: race, difference and identity', in K. Brants, J. Hermes and L. van Zoonen (eds) *The Media in Question: Popular Cultures and Public Interests*, London: Sage (pp. 147–156).

Ueberoth, P. (1985) *Made in America: His Own Story*, New York: Morrow.

UEL/TGiS (2010) *Olympic Games Impact Study: London 2012 Pre-Games Report Final*, October. Report compiled for the Economic & Social Research Council on behalf of the London Organising Committee of the Olympic Games and Paralympic Games Ltd, by the University of East London and the Thames Gateway Institute for Sustainability.

Urry, J. (2002) *The Tourist Gaze*, 2nd edition, London: Sage.

US Soccer (2013) 'The 1994 bid: How the US got the World Cup – Part 3' (available online at: www.ussoccer.com/stories/2014/03/17/14/01/the-1994-bid-how-the-us-got-the-world-cup-part-3; last accessed 12 June 2014).

Vainer, C. (2016) 'Mega-events and the city of exception: theoretical explorations of the Brazilian experience', in R. Gruneau and J. Horne (eds) *Mega-Events and Globalization: Capital and Spectacle in a Changing World Order*, London: Routledge (pp. 97–112).

de Vasconcellos Ribeiro, C.H. and Dimeo, P. (2009) 'The experience of migration for Brazilian football players', *Sport in Society* 12 (6), 725–736.

Vertinsky, P., Jette, S. and Hofmann, A. (2009) '"Skierinas" in the Olympics: gender justice and gender politics at the local, national and international level over the challenge of women's ski jumping', *Olympika*, 18: 43–74.

Vijay, A. (2015) 'After the pop-up games: London's never-ending regeneration', *Environment and Planning D: Society and Space*, 33, 425–443.

Wagg, S. (2015) *The London Olympics of 2012: Politics, Promises and Legacy*, Basingstoke: Palgrave Macmillan.

Wainwright, M. (2008) 'The happy architect', *Guardian*, Society, 19 November, pp. 1–2.

Waller, S., Polite, F. and Spearman, L. (2012) 'Retrospective reflections on the Black American male athlete and the 1968 Olympics: an elite interview with Dr Harry Edwards', *Leisure Studies* 31 (3), 265–270.

Walseth, K. and Fasting, K. (2003) 'Islam's view on physical activity and sport: Egyptian women interpreting Islam', *International Review for the Sociology of Sport* 38 (1), 45–60.

Walters, G. (2006) *Berlin Games: How Hitler Stole the Olympic Dream*, London: John Murray.

Watt, P. (2013) '"It's not for us": regeneration, the 2012 Olympics and the gentrification of East London', *City* 17 (1), 99–118.

Watts, J. (2008) 'China using Games as "warfare", says stadium designer', *Guardian*, 2 August, p. 26.

Watts, J. (2015) 'Rio 2016: "the Olympics has destroyed my home"', *Guardian*, 20 July (available online at: www.theguardian.com/world/2015/jul/19/2016-olympics-rio-de-janeiro-brazil-destruction?CMP=share_btn_link; last accessed 22 October 2015).

Weber, M. (1970) *From Max Weber: Essays in Sociology*, edited by H.H. Gerth and C. Wright Mills, London: Routledge & Kegan Paul.

Wellard, I. (2002) 'Men, sport, body performance and the maintenance of "exclusive masculinity"', *Leisure Studies* 21 (3/4), 235–247.

Whannel, G. (1984) 'The television spectacular', in A. Tomlinson and G. Whannel (eds) *Five Ring Circus: Money, Power and Politics at the Olympic Games*, London: Pluto (pp. 30–43).

Whannel, G. (1992) *Fields in Vision: Television Sport and Cultural Transformation*, London: Routledge.

Whannel, G. (1999) 'From "motionless bodies" to acting moral subjects: Tom Brown, a transformative romance for the production of manliness', *Diegesis: Journal for the Association for Research in Popular Fictions* 4: 14–21.

Whannel, G. (2000) 'Sport and the media', in J. Coakley and E. Dunning (eds) *Handbook of Sport Studies*, London: Sage (pp. 291–308).

Whannel, G. (2002) *Media Sport Stars: Masculinities and Moralities*, London: Routledge.

Whannel, G. (2008) *Culture, Politics and Sport: Blowing the Whistle Revisited*, London: Routledge.

Whannel, G. (2010) 'News, celebrity and vortextuality: a study of the media coverage of the Jackson verdict', *Cultural Politics* 6 (1), 65–84.

Wheeler, R.F. (1978) 'Organised sport and organised labour: the workers' sport movement', *Journal of Contemporary History* 13: 191–210.

Whelan, C. (2014) 'Surveillance, security and sports mega events: toward a research agenda on the organisation of security networks', *Surveillance & Society* 11 (4), 392–404.

Whitson, D. (1994) 'The embodiment of gender: discipline, domination and empowerment', in S. Birrell and C. Cole (eds) *Women, Sport and Culture*, Champaign: Human Kinetics (pp. 353–371).

Whitson, D. (1998). 'Olympic sport, global media, and cultural diversity', in *Global and Cultural Critique: Problematizing the Olympic Games, Fourth International Symposium for Olympic Research* (available online at: http://library.la84.org/SportsLibrary/ISOR/ISOR1998d.pdf; last accessed 5 August 2015).

Whitson, D. (2004) 'Bringing the world to Canada: "the periphery of the centre"', *Third World Quarterly* 25 (7), 1215–1232.

Whitson, D. (2012) 'Vancouver 2010: the saga of Eagleridge Bluffs', in G. Hayes and J. Karamichas (eds) *Olympic Games, Mega-Events and Civil Societies*, Basingstoke: Palgrave (pp. 219–235).

Whitson, D. and Horne, J. (2006) 'Underestimated costs and overestimated benefits? Comparing the impact of sports mega-events in Canada and Japan', in J. Horne and W. Manzenreiter (eds) *Sports Mega-Events: Social Scientific Analyses of a Global Phenomenon*, Oxford: Blackwell (pp. 73–89).

Whitson, D. and Macintosh, D. (1993) 'Becoming a world-class city: hallmark events and sport franchises in the growth strategies of Western Canadian cities', *Sociology of Sport Journal* 10 (3), 221–240.

Wilkinson, R. (1964) *The Prefects: British Leadership and the Public School Tradition – A Comparative Study in the Making of Rulers*, London: Oxford University Press.

Wilkinson, R. and Pickett, K. (2009) *The Spirit Level: Why Equality is Better for Everyone*, London: Allen Lane.

Williams, J. (2009) 'The curious mystery of the Cotswold "Olimpick" games: did Shakespeare know Dover . . . and does it matter?', *Sport in History* 29 (2), 150–170.

Williams, R. (1999) 'Editorial: the new politics of corruption', *Third World Quarterly*, 20 (3), 487–489.

Williams, R. (2015) 'Failure of Olympic legacy shows we are not all in it together', *Guardian*, Sport Section, 20 June, p. 12.

Williamson, T. (2010) 'The 2016 Olympics: a win for Rio?' (Five-part series of articles, available online at: http://rioonwatch.org/?p=83; last accessed 20 November 2010).

Wilson, B. and Millington, B. (2013) 'Sport, ecological modernization, and the environment', in D. Andrews and B. Carrington (eds) *A Companion to Sport*, Oxford: Wiley/Blackwell (pp. 129–142).

Wilson, H. and Sinclair, J. (eds) (2000) 'The Olympics: media, myth, madness', *Media International Australia* 97, Special issue.

Wilson, N. (1988) *The Sports Business*, London: Piatkus.

Winter, A. (2013) 'Race, Multiculturalism and the "Progressive" Politics of London 2012: passing the "Boyle Test"', *Sociological Research Online*, 18 (2), 18.

Women's Sports Foundation (WSF) (2009) *Women in the 2000, 2004 and 2008 Olympic and Paralympic Games*, New York: WSF.

Wong, D.S.Y. (forthcoming) 'The youth Olympic Games', *International Journal of the History of Sport*.

Woodward, K. (2012) *Sex, Power and the Games*, Basingstoke: Palgrave.

Woodward, K. (2013) *Sporting Times*, Basingstoke: Palgrave Macmillan.

313

Woodward, K. (2014a) *Globalizing Boxing*, London: Bloomsbury Academic.

Woodward, K. (2014b) 'Legacies of 2012: putting women's boxing into discourse', *Contemporary Social Science* 9 (2), 242–252.

Yalin, S. (2007) 'The development of the Olympic Press Centre', unpublished MA dissertation, University of Luton (now the University of Bedfordshire).

Young, C. (2010) 'Berlin 1936', in A. Bairner and G. Molnar (eds) *The Politics of the Olympics*, London: Routledge (pp. 93–105).

Young, D.C. (1984) *The Olympic Myth of Greek Amateur Athletics*, London: ARS Publishing.

Young, D.C. (1996) *The Modern Olympics: A Struggle for Revival*, Baltimore: Johns Hopkins University Press.

Young, D.C. (2004) *A Brief History of the Olympic Games*, Oxford: Blackwell.

Yu, Ying, Klauser, F. and Chan, G. (2009) 'Governing security at the 2008 Beijing Olympics', *International Journal of the History of Sport* 26 (3), 390–405.

Zarnowski, C.F. (1992) 'A look at Olympic costs', *Citius, Altius, Fortius* 1 (1), 16–32.

Zhang, T. and Silk, M. (2006) 'Recentering Beijing: sport, space, subjectivities', *Sociology of Sport Journal* 23 (4), 438–459.

Zimbalist, A. (2014) 'Chasing glory: why hosting the Olympics rarely pays off', *The Conversation*, 24 October.

Zimbalist, B. (2015) *Circus Maximus: The Economic Gamble Behind Hosting the Olympics and the World Cup*, Washington, DC: Brookings Institution Press.

Zirin, D. (2009) *A People's History of Sports in the United States: 250 Years of Politics, Protest, People and Play*, New York: The New Press.

Zirin, D. (2014) *Brazil's Dance with the Devil: The World Cup, the Olympics and the Fight for Democracy*, Chicago: Haymarket Books.

Zizek, S. (2005) 'The empty wheelbarrow', *Guardian*, 19 February.

INDEX

All Olympic Games are listed by location and then year, e.g. London 2012, and all other mega-events are listed by name and then year, e.g. World Cup 2014, Empire Games. A reference in *italics* indicates a figure.

the Empire Games 146–47, 168; evolving anthropological theories 157; and multiculturalism debates (London 2012) 242; politics of race 241; racial stereotyping and sports performance in the media 243–44; racism and British sport 243

Ravenstein, Ernest 139

revenues: from 1933–2012 *82*; merchandising *102*; new media rights payments 84; percentage growth in *83*; for the quadrennium 2009–2012 *81*; revenues as percentage of total for each quadrennium *83*; sources *82*; from television rights 84–85, *84–85*; ticketing 82–83, *83*

Rio 2016: academic interest in 3–4; Barra zone 14–16, *19*, 20; bid process 11–12; community displacements 5, 13, 19–20, 22; construction industry opportunities 74–75; costs 17–20, *19*; coverage of 3; criticisms of 13; economic factors 13–14; environmental factors 21; *favela* of Vila Autódromo 23–26, *24*, *25*, *26*, *120*; governance and budget 17–20; graffiti artists *122*; legacy concerns 5, 12; locations 14–17, *15*; Maracanã stadium 14, *16*, 20; Olympic Park 16; projects, responsibilities and estimated costs *19*; public campaign against 28, *120*; security 20; Transformação merchandise *208*; transport 20; urban regeneration and 12, 22–26, 27

Rocha, J. 5

Roche, Maurice 60, 62, 64, 152–53, 162, 218, 236, 256, 257

Rodriquez, K. 270

Rogge, Jacques 245, 247, 274

Romanov, Alexei 192

Rose, A.K. 55

Rowe, N. 239

Salt Lake City bid scandal 33, 69, 264

Salt Lake City Winter Olympics 269

Samaranch, Juan Antonio 32, 61, 71, 98, 185, 200, 260, 265

Saudi Arabia 250

Saunders 119

Schweid, Richard 269

Scott, Bob 32

security: absolute security, appearance of 273–74; Athens 2004 205, 269–270, 273–74; Barcelona 1992 269; Beijing 2008 270; and cleansing of surrounding areas 268–69; costs 269, 270, *270*; and culture of control 271; large screens and crowd control 215–16; legacies of security knowledge 272–73; London 2012 36–37, 224, 270, 271–73; militarization of 272; and Olympics as site of political theatre 268; post-9/11 269–270; Rio 2016 20; scale of, mega events 259; surveillance technology 269, 270, 271–72; Sydney 2000 269; terrorist threat 273

Seoul 1988 266

Sheard, Rod 122

Short, J.R. 118, 125

Silvestre, G. 13–14, 18, 19, 22

ski jumping 246–48, 249

Sklair, Leslie 112, 114, 115

Smith, A. 254–55

Smith, Tommie 202

socio-economic factors: and emergence of the modern Olympic Games 141–42; social development through sport 11, 66, 74, 207, 237

South Africa 4–5, 192–93, 203, 208–9

South Korea 190, 200

Soutsos, Panagiotis 140

Soviet Union: Cold War tensions, Helsinki 1952 189, 198, 200; doping 266; involvement in international competition 187

spectacle: alongside carnival and festival 220; Beijing 2008 opening ceremony 217–18; consumer culture as 217; dispersed spectacles 223–24; modern Olympics as 216–17; negative readings of 218; role of television 223; security spectacle 272–73; spectacles of difference (disabled people) 253; vortextual spectacles 223

Spiegel, M.M. 55

sponsorship deals: 1982 Wold Cup 97; Adidas blueprint for 91; advertising, emergence of 86; growth in 97–98; IOC financial security and 68; strict brand protection 100; torch relay 99; *see also* The Olympic Partner (TOP) Programme

sport: alternative international sports events 172–73, *172*; association with world's fairs 157; commercial and political relations of 126–27; consumer culture and 209; definitions of 134; diffusion through

325

their Facebook pages and arranges them across her screen: rows of moody teenagers. Thinking aloud, she says, "Wouldn't it make sense that he'd play this out close to home? *Home* being the operable concept for a guy whose sisters tormented him. This one girl, Hope Martin-Creech, disappeared the very morning that Ishmael Locke went shopping in her town—Bennington, Vermont, just across the border from Sammy Nelson's upstate cabin."

A click and there is a happy selfie Hope recently posted on Facebook. Her wide smile defies a tapered chin. Lank dirty-blond hair, angled at her jaw, a flyaway wisp off her forehead. Pale brown eyes. Freckles sprinkled across her cheeks and nose. Tattoos of impish figures climbing one side of her neck. "Sixteen. Tenth grade. Lives with her parents and two younger brothers. Good student, no boyfriend, no drugs, no problems. Hasn't been seen since Monday morning when she left for school."

"It makes sense to me," Joan agrees.

Lex says, "Me too."

"We've got DNA profiles from some of the hair samples in the van," Owen says. "Let's see if we can get a sample from this Hope girl. See if there's a match."

Lex says, "If she's not on file, then maybe her parents have her hairbrush. I'll make some calls."

"No," Elsa says, "I'll do it."

Reaching for her phone, she uncrosses her legs abruptly and feels a warm, wet trickle along her shin. It's happened before: the wound weeping too generously for the bandage to hold. Most women fear getting their period on white pants in front of other people. Elsa? Her blood has been known to flow embarrassingly from anywhere.

When your father gets home from work, he kisses you on the cheek and asks how your day has gone. "Fine," you tell him. But you know that he knows, because he has to, doesn't he? The kitchen is too clean for this hour of the day, the house too quiet, everyone in a different room.

24

"It has something to do with his sisters," Elsa says.

The faces of her fellow investigators come into foc
turning to her with surprise as if she'd left the room a
barged back in with an interruption. She *had* left the roo
in a way; she'd zoned out deeply enough to miss a wh
section of their conversation.

Lex asks, "What?"

"His sisters bullied him—three sisters. He coul
reenacting something."

"Or reinventing it," Joan says, in energized agree
"for a better outcome in which he's less hurt.
scratching an unsatisfiable itch, for the third time.'

An unsatisfiable itch. Yes, that's it. Elsa's skin ele
with understanding, telling her they're on the righ
This is how it always happens. This is the feeling :
when the pieces of a case start to fit. Lex was rig
why she's so good at this work, and why it's so
Her skin tells her when a child is within her re
unstoppable, unfixable skin.

Elsa turns back to the list of girls. She pu

"You okay?" The way Lex is looking at her, like a concerned brother. He reads her too well.

"Fine." The phone is already ringing. There's no time to get to the bathroom so she reaches down to adjust the bandage, if only temporarily. Her call is answered halfway through the first ring.

A woman's voice, thin with distress: *"Hello?"*

"Is this Mrs. Martin-Creech, Hope's mother?"

"Yes."

"I don't want to alarm you, Mrs. Martin-Creech, but this is Elsa Myers, I'm with the FBI and I'm calling because—"

The woman says to someone near her, "Ernie—it's the FBI."

A man comes on the line: "This is Detective Sergeant Ernie Bennett."

Elsa introduces herself. "We're looking for a seventeen-year-old girl missing from New York City since Friday, and we've connected her to someone who traveled from here to Bennington in the last twenty-four hours. This man, he's a known repeater, and we're concerned that—"

"You're calling about Hope."

Elsa's bandage breaks loose again; blood moves down her ankle. "Yes."

"She's been missing since yesterday," Bennett tells her, "and this morning we found two items of her jewelry in the woods near her house, so we figure she was in there at one point. Now, with what you're telling me, Special Agent . . ."

"Myers. If he does have Hope," she says, "then he's probably got our girl too. In the past he took them in groups of three."

Bennett falls silent so abruptly, she suspects he's swallowing a curse he won't let loose in front of the frightened mother.

Holding the phone away from her mouth, Elsa asks Lex, "How fast can you get us a copter?"

Lex answers, "Right away."

"Do it."

To Detective Sergeant Bennett, she says, "Hold tight, we'll be there as soon as we can."

25

#getmethefuckoutofhere, Mel types after uploading the selfie of her blazing-red cheek, deleting the addendum #hate-mymom because *that* just feels too harsh. But still. *Post.* And now the cold fact that her mother just slapped her, hard, is out into the vast cyber-cloudy nether-space of whereverness that is Facebook. Part of the conversation. Feels good and right for one split second and then embarrassment sets in.

Delete.

High noon in the hospital parking lot, bright and unfiltered. Mel holds a hand over her eyes and contemplates her next move. She'd stomped down the hall with her mother chasing her saying "You can't leave when Gramp is about to die!" actually saying *die* in her mad voice right there on the cancer ward where everyone really *is* dying and no one needs that kind of tell-it-like-it-is reminder practically shouted in the hallways because it is what it is and they already *know* that. Mel knows Gramp is dying but he isn't dying *today*.

"Well, Mom, you fucking *hit me*."

"*Shhhh.*"

"You don't want anyone to hear about it but you didn't mind *doing it.*"

Ding and the elevator door opened and Mel stepped in and pressed the close-doors button over and over until they finally closed. Her mother just standing there looking shocked that her sweet little daughter would actually leave.

Her mother has never hit her before.

Her aunt has never betrayed her trust before.

Adults are such hypocrites.

She'll go back to the city. Live her *own* life in a way that feels honest.

She swipes her phone for an Uber and, presto, up drives a blue car. Great app. You don't have to wait.

She doesn't see an Uber sign anywhere but the window rolls down and the driver looks at her through his sunglasses and nods so she knows it's her ride. She leans into the air-conditioning, says, "Train station," and gets into the backseat. Some button he's got pinned to his shirt glints for just a second; it's a face, but she can't see whose.

The car curves out of the parking lot and she feels good, really good, making a break for it. The look on her mother's face when the elevator doors closed. She'll head to a friend's place, not home—scare her mother, just overnight.

After about ten minutes she notices fields, not buildings. "Excuse me, sir? Isn't the train station the other way, in town?"

His face looks sweaty, and now she notices a nasty scratch down one side. His left hand stays on the wheel while his right elbow crooks over the seat and he half turns for a quick look at her. When he smiles, a bend in his nose flattens out, but it isn't really a smile. He says, "There's a better train station in the next town."

She doesn't know how one train station can be better than another unless it's closer. But she doesn't ask. This guy gives her the creeps. Just so long as he gets her there.

She thumbs a text to Charlie: Can you meet me Met steps one hour? She should be back in the city by then.

Her mother called him a drug dealer, *but* she doesn't want his drugs and she only sort of likes him, but *still,* if she can get a selfie with him and throw it onto Facebook and *not* delete it, *well,* guess who wins round one? Her mother didn't listen when Mel told her it was a stupid mistake and wouldn't happen again. She just wouldn't listen.

yup will be there

cool

So that's set.

She feels the car swerve to a stop and looks up, expecting they'll be at the train station. But they're not. They are nowhere—not even a house in the distance. The bright blue sky from before has gone all gray, like rain is coming, like they've entered a different world.

He turns around fast, his arm reaching all the way back to snatch her phone right out of her hand. "I like you," he says, and he hurls it out the window.

"What the fuck!"

The back of his hand slams against her cheek so hard, she feels each knobby bone of his knuckles. Pain spitfires through her face, into her brain, silencing her.

"Met your aunt yesterday"—lifting his sunglasses, showing her his eyes—"she was looking for you. Gotta say, you made this pretty easy; usually I have to work harder to get my girl. Only one hospital in Sleepy Hollow. And you—you got right into my car."

She recognizes him now: that weird guy from Ruby's house who watched them, Auntie Elsa whispering, "Shhh."

A worm uncoils in her stomach.

With a click, he locks the doors from up front. She rattles the handle but it won't budge. He jerks the steering wheel and speeds back onto the road.

26

Faded white clapboard, chipped black shutters, a saggy porch. The Martin-Creech house would look neglected if not for the well-tended flower beds seaming the front walk with vibrant color. Deb was also that kind of gardener, Elsa remembers, keen on decorating the outlines. A FOR SALE sign is staked on a front lawn glistening wet from a quick rain amid the familiar chaos of neighbors and visitors who have gathered to help search for Hope.

Every time Elsa thinks that—*search for Hope, look for Hope, hunt for Hope, find Hope*—the banal phrases confront an awful reality. Hope, in this case, is an actual girl, the second girl in a week to go missing at Nelson's hand, her hair now positively identified in his van along with Ruby's and the hair of two of the girls missing since 2012.

Elsa glances around at the hive of state troopers, local detectives, FBI agents, neighbors, and strangers who have come to join the search, and she flashes back to yesterday at the Haverstocks. *Scar tissue,* she thinks; families and communities surging together to heal an unexpected injury. Lex and Joan stand beside her, taking it in.

Just arrived, she group-texts Owen Tate and Rosie Santiago, who stayed behind in New York. *How's it going there?* Elsa doesn't envy them their task of contacting the families of those long-lost missing girls, ripping off the old scabs, poking a finger into the wounds. Asking questions and offering nothing but hopeless answers.

Rosie responds: *Painful. You?*

Circus, zoo, are the first words that spring to mind, but Elsa plugs the defensive sarcasm. Instead, she types, *Still getting the lay of the land.*

Startled by a weight across her shoulders, she looks up from her phone and there is Joan Bailey administering a sideward hug. Elsa doesn't know what to say; she doesn't know if she likes the unexpected affection or if it crosses a boundary. Both, maybe. Fresh off a helicopter flight during which they chatted about irrelevant things, the two women numbing themselves with words while Lex shifted his focus between his phone and the obscurity of passing clouds, Elsa realizes now that that was not idle conversation. Joan had been sussing her out, therapizing her.

Joan says, "I see an agent I know over there. He might have some insight." The behavioral psychologist looks at Elsa with the kind of contemplative pause, ever so slight, that expresses an unspoken request for consent to step away.

"Go ahead." Elsa keeps her tone level, professional, despite a spark of emotion.

Joan crosses the lawn toward a pair of men, one in uniform.

Lex asks, "What was that?"

Ignoring his question, because she doesn't know what it was, not really, she says, "Let's get started."

They go in search of Detective Sergeant Ernie Bennett but cross paths with a tall woman who stops when she sees them. An inch of gray roots borders the center part of her blond hair; her eyes droop, wet, heavy.

"I'm Becky," the woman says. "Hope's mother. You must be Special Agent Myers from New York."

"Elsa, please. This is Detective Lex Cole, NYPD." As she reaches to shake the mother's hand, a wind gust lopes out of nowhere and she has to push hair out of her eyes and tug down a sleeve to fix herself.

"Thank you for coming," Becky says, "thank you so much, this has been such a nightmare."

"We understand," Elsa says. "We're going to do everything we can to help find your daughter. Becky, I know this is awful for you, but do you mind if we jump right in?"

"Please."

"You've been shown the mug shots?"

Becky nods. "I didn't recognize him."

Just then a school bus pulls up and discharges a pair of blond boys, one slightly taller than the other. They wear matching blue backpacks. One has neon-orange sneakers, the other's are green. They shout hellos to their mother, drop their backpacks at her feet, and, ignoring the clumps of people on their lawn, run to the driveway, where a basketball hoop is attached to the front of the garage. A ball is quickly produced and a game started.

Elsa says, "We should speak with Detective Bennett."

"He was in the kitchen a little while ago," Becky offers, "unless he's back out in the field."

In the field. Already she's adopted the lingo of a search.

Becky sighs. Picks up her sons' backpacks. "Check the house first?"

"Sure," Elsa answers. Restless to find the detective, who probably *is* back in the field by now, but also feeling pulled by the family, the sense that there is always something important to learn on the inside. Knowing that houses, and mothers, are rarely as they appear on the surface.

They follow Becky into a comfortable, lived-in kitchen with pushed-aside piles of paper competing with gadgets and condiments for counter space. Ernie Bennett is not there.

Becky catches Elsa glancing at the fridge where the family's last holiday card is prominently displayed: red plaid border, holly boughs, and bells; a tall, handsome father smiling beside his well-groomed wife, their poised teenage daughter, and the two grinning boys. "Tim's a pilot for United," she says. "He was based out of Boston until last year, when they switched him to Chicago."

"That why you're selling the house?" Lex asks.

"He's hardly ever home. We thought it would give us more time together if we moved there."

Elsa asks, "Where is he now?"

"En route here from Anchorage. He's worried sick." In an instant, she seems to melt. "I don't know how much longer I can take this. That other girl . . . what did that man do to her?"

"We don't know." As for what Elsa guesses he did, she won't say.

"Do you really think there's a chance Hope is . . . okay?"

"Definitely." An exaggeration, but it's in everyone's interest to bolster Becky's optimism.

"Maybe Ernie's upstairs," Becky says.

They follow her up a carpeted, bending staircase. No Bennett, but Elsa can't help pausing in Hope's room. It's small and full, the walls painted a faded lilac and covered with whimsical pencil drawings. The intricate illustrations are everywhere that's not blocked by bed, dresser, desk, or bookshelf. A copious assortment of stuffed animals crowd her headboard. On her nightstand, a ceramic bowl is filled with a tangle of rings and bracelets, and a jewelry tree is strung with a webbing of necklaces. By the position of a bookmark, she is halfway through *A Confederacy of Dunces*, presumably for school, unless she's an independent reader.

"I tried to stop her from drawing on the walls when she was little," Becky says, noticing their interest, "but it was useless, so I just let her go at it. I've grown to really like them. I wish there was some way we could take the walls with us when we move."

"She's got talent, that's for sure." Lex steps up for a close look at a group of little figures on a boat, mobilizing to fight a giant wave.

Elsa follows his gaze and before she knows it is pulled into Hope's imaginings, they're drawn with such conviction—the way a tiny hand raises to the monster wave as if to halt it, the bend of a little arm over eyes to block the terrifying sight, a face buried in a cage of spiny fingers, and the one rushing gleefully into the arc of water with a surfboard. That subversive act of resistance speaks to Elsa's heart; she doesn't know this girl, this young artist, and probably never will, but suddenly her desire to reach her before it's too late colludes dangerously with her anxieties over Ruby and her father and Mel, who still hasn't returned her call. Elsa can't save Roy from the disease that's consuming him, unsell the house, or force Mel to forgive her and pick up the phone—she can't pull back time and with it Tara's hand—and she can't uncut her skin this morning, but if she can save these lost, presumably injured girls . . . if she *can* . . . if Ruby and Hope at least can have a future, then maybe . . . maybe what? The impulse lingers in the back of Elsa's mind like an unfinished sentence and all she can think to say to Hope's mother is, "She could be a graphic novelist when she grows up."

"If she wants to. Why not?"

Elsa says, "She has a strong imagination," thinking that that's a good thing. Maybe she fought Nelson. Maybe she's struggling, internally, to keep hold.

Becky settles her hand on a biology textbook open on the desk. "She had a test on Monday. She was up late studying the night before."

A boy's voice sails in from outside—"Mo-ommm!"— and Becky's whole body reacts. She throws open Hope's window. "What is it, Sam?"

"We didn't know where you were."

"I'm right here. Down in a minute, okay?" She leaves the window open onto a lush view of blue hydrangeas. "The boys go back and forth between trying to pretend nothing's happening and worrying they'll lose me next. Look around all you want. I've got to get back outside. If I see Ernie I'll tell him you're here."

As soon as Becky's gone, Elsa says to Lex, "Let's go find him."

He nods but continues to study the wall illustrations. "These pictures are so—" he begins but is interrupted by Elsa's ringing phone.

She glances at the incoming number, tells Lex, "I'll catch up with you outside."

He leaves and she sits on the edge of Hope's bed, her weight sinking into the soft mattress. Feeling that she shouldn't be here, but that she can't pull herself away.

"Agent Myers?" A young man's voice, familiar, deep yet uncertain.

"Charlie?"

"You said to call if I thought of anything else."

"I'm listening."

"It's not about Ruby, though, and maybe I shouldn't have bothered you, but I thought—"

"Just say it."

"Mel was supposed to meet me and she never showed up. I've been calling her but she doesn't answer."

"I don't understand—you made plans with Mel since I saw you?"

"*She* texted *me!*"

"When?"

"Right after I left the police station. She asked me to meet her on the steps of the Met. I don't know why, but I said I'd go; I mean, I *like* her. Anyway, maybe she just blew me off. I wouldn't blame her. But to be honest, I'm kind of paranoid now about not telling you everything, know what I mean?"

"Thanks, Charlie."

"Should I call you if I hear from her?"

"Yes. Yes, please do."

Trembling, Elsa dials Mel and leaves another message: "Mellie, will you *please* call me?"

Next, she tries Tara, who answers with "Did you get my message?"

"Yes, I got it. How's Dad doing?"

"The same. Elsa, I can't believe this, all of it, happening all at once, and I—"

Elsa blurts out, "You *hit* her? You actually fucking *hit* her!"

"I reacted. I was upset. I'm her mother and—"

"I can't talk to you about this right now" is the best Elsa can come up with in lieu of the venom simmering on her tongue. No child deserves to be hit when it isn't in self-defense. But this isn't the time to explain that to her self-righteous, martyred, pampered sister. "I just wanted to make sure she's with you."

"She's at the hotel."

"You saw her there?"

"I've been here all day, with Dad. She stormed out of here like a, like a . . . well, I just assume she's at the hotel. Where else would she be?"

"Call her. If she doesn't answer, call the hotel. If she doesn't answer the room phone, call the front desk and ask them to go into the room."

"Why?"

Elsa doesn't want to invoke Charlie's name; there's no time for Tara's drama. "Just do it."

"Fine. I'll do it. But—"

"Call me after." Elsa hangs up.

Flames of worry lick the edges of her determination not to worry, to keep things in perspective, on the principle that 95 percent of the time, people worry over nothing. Tara will call back and report that Mel has been stewing in the hotel room all day, maybe racking up a big bill on room service in revenge. Elsa feels satisfaction in believing that Mel won't have taken being hit lightly. Mel will have reacted, rejected. Unlike Elsa, who quietly absorbed every assault.

She goes outside to look for Lex and is immediately drawn by the unmistakable sound of Greenberg's voice booming across the lawn. Lex is with him.

"Yello!" Greenberg greets her. "I hear our Mr. Ishmael Locke has himself a different real name."

"Unfortunately," she answers, "that's how it's turning out."

Lex asks Greenberg, "That him?" in continuation of a conversation Elsa missed. Greenberg nods his large bushy head.

"Yup, that's Ernie. Known each other since we were kids. That's how I know Sang McCracken, since you mentioned it." Another reference to something Elsa must have missed. "Met Sang at one of Ernie's annual Fourth of July barbecues."

Striding across the lawn in their direction, the local detective looks like any friendly dad in baggy jeans, sneakers, and a fleece zipper-vest over a T-shirt. But when he speaks, the sharp clip of his words betrays an efficiency you learn only on the job.

"You the folks from New York City?"

Elsa introduces herself. Their hands meet, both gripping harder and a moment longer than necessary. She asks, "Anything new since we spoke?"

"Unfortunately, no. We've got a task force put together in town. Why don't you folks come in with what you have; we'll put everything on the table and see what we can make of it."

To Lex, Elsa says, "Let's find Joan. She'll want to be there."

The three investigators pile into Elsa's car and head toward town along verdurous country roads. On the way, Elsa's cell marimbas a call from Tara. Driving, she says to Lex, "Answer that and put it on speaker. It's my sister."

"Okay." He fishes in her bag and finds her phone.

Tara wails, *"Mel's gone."*

"You're sure?"

"She isn't in our room. She never even went to the hotel. She isn't with any of her friends and she won't answer my calls. I don't know what to do now." Tara groans. "How do I find her? How did you know she wouldn't be there, Elsa?"

"I didn't know. I was hoping she'd be with you."

"She isn't. What do I do now? And don't tell me that teenagers take off sometimes. Some do, some don't—and Mel doesn't."

"I'm going to trace her cell phone," Elsa promises. "I'll call you as soon as I find out where she is."

"You didn't answer me. How did you know to ask me?"

"Talk to you later." Elsa hangs up and catches a glimpse of her phone's wallpaper photo before Lex drops the cell back into her bag: Mel at four, dressed all in princess pink, waving a sparkly plastic star-topped scepter that Elsa bought as a gift. Everyone starts innocent and sweet. Everyone.

"Your niece?" Joan asks from the backseat.

"Yes."

"How old?"

"Sixteen."

Lex asks, "When did this happen?"

"That's why Charlie called me before. Mel asked him

to meet her at the Metropolitan Museum at about one. She never showed."

"And he actually went out of his way to let you know?" Lex says.

"Scared him before, I guess."

Elsa and Lex and Joan lapse into silence as they near the Bennington station house. Little explosions of heat pop along Elsa's skin as she struggles to convince herself that her niece's absence and the girls' abductions are completely unconnected. She steadies her breath and refuses to allow fear to overtake her, reminding herself that Mel's silence is probably intended as punishment for betraying her trust about the drugs. The kid's pissed; who wouldn't be? That's all it is. Nothing bad has happened to Mellie.

But each time one of those girls fell off the radar, wasn't there a plausible explanation at first? She's busy. Her phone's battery ran out. You hurt her, offended her, ignored her, and now it's your turn to see how it feels. And then, suddenly, she isn't ignoring you—she's gone.

27

Mel knows that she was in a forest before and that now she's in a cave: musty damp in her nose and on her face and seeping through her clothes.

At first, when he takes off the blindfold, she can't see anything. The complete darkness is blacker than anything she's ever experienced, a not-seeing that confuses her. Then, gradually, her eyes adjust, which must mean light is filtering in from somewhere.

He pushes her down so she's sitting and she feels sharp rocks through the ass of her jeans. Her bound wrists pull tighter in this position.

"Why are you doing this to me?"

"Say hello to your sisters."

"I don't have any sisters. I'm an only child. I'm—"

"Shut up."

The way he says it, she does.

She starts to make out shapes in the granular light. He's crossed the room and is hunched over something—a toolbox, she thinks, its red color shining through the dull lightlessness of the cave. Something yellow and crumpled near the red box: a nest of rough fabric. A towel, she thinks. Half off the towel, a book.

"Damn it." He slams shut his toolbox. Lifts the towel, looking for something. The book flips over: *The Invisible Man*. A curl of panic as she remembers she's supposed to read the other one, the Ralph Ellison one, this summer for next year's English and she was actually looking forward to it, but now . . .

"What's that about?" Thinking that maybe she can get his mind off whatever tool he's found missing, if that's what just upset him. She doesn't like that he's looking for tools at all, considering. "The book you're reading. I mean, it's so dark in here, how do you read? Unless you have a flashlight."

"I do have a flashlight, since you asked."

"What's the book about?"

Hunched on bent legs, he flattens a hand on the ground to steady himself. Looks at her, his button catching stray light again so this time she can see the face of a little girl. "A scientist uses optics to alter his refractive index so that no one else can see him. That's what he tries to do, but it doesn't work out. This is the third time I've read it. Great book."

"I like to read too. I mean, sometimes not even for school. I like to read in this one chair we have in the living room right next to the window."

"Not me. I like privacy, quiet."

"I like the light from the window."

"My room was the best spot. I put a sign on my door that said *Quiet Zone* but they just ripped it down."

"Who did?"

"Excuse me." An electric undercurrent in his tone now.

He stands abruptly, crouching under the cave ceiling. "I left the nails in the car."

She makes out the whites of his eyes shifting in her direction, stopping when they land on her. He thinks a moment and then he reaches for something, a coil of rope, which he pulls out of a shadow. He ties her ankles together and says, "No funny business while I'm gone."

"I don't have any sisters," she says.

He hunches across the cave quickly. She hears something rip. He returns with a piece of duct tape and presses it hard on her mouth, his large hand covering her nose, and she can't breathe.

She can't breathe.

Then he lets go and dank air surges into her nose.

He crosses the cave again and clicks open his toolbox and suddenly a flashlight beam emanates from his hand. He waves it around the cave, saying, "Take a look. Those are your sisters."

The light lands on the back of a girl lying on her side, brown hair pooled at her neck, the long gentle slope from her shoulder to her waist, her legs ranged long across the rocky dirt floor, cinched at the ankles by filthy rope. Mel watches the back of the girl's ribs, waiting to see them move, looking for even the tiniest evidence of breathing.

The beam jerks to a part of the cave she didn't notice before. In the near-total darkness, the flashlight illuminates another girl. Frazzled blond hair, tattoos up one side of her neck. Bound and connected to some kind of noose that forces her to pitch forward. The rope around her wrists is entwined with several bracelets: the rubber kind they give out at school events, this one yellow, a charm bracelet, and some metal ones, the kind that jangle. Her wide eyes stare fiercely at Mel. When she realizes that Mel sees her, she blinks. Mel blinks in response.

"Chill, girls." He moves toward the mouth of the tunnel until it swallows him and he's all but gone except for his voice, trailing. "When I get back, we are gonna have some fun."

Near the tunnel's entry sits a stack of wood planks—is that what he needs the nails for? *Is he planning to seal them in?* Only when she can't hear him anymore does her brain stop spinning, and then a different, more frantic kind of panic twitches through her. She breathes as loudly as she can through her nose, in and out and in and out, trying to communicate with the other girl. The one who's still alive. When the girl reciprocates in kind, Mel's eyes flood and she drops her head forward and forces herself to stop crying. If her nose gets stuffed she won't be able to breathe, and she won't make it through the next ten minutes.

28

The pillared limestone building in the center of town temporarily housing the local task force reminds Elsa of an old country bank: ornate ceilings and tall windows opening onto a pastoral view. And the windows are clean, sparkling with sunlight. It's nice here, really nice, and yet the realization that she's more at home in the cramped-space, grimy-windowed fogginess of the city makes her feel urban, ruined, and separate. She can't stop thinking about what she did to herself this morning, cutting her leg. A scab is starting to form—she feels the tight pull across her skin—but nonetheless, beneath the film of healing, the voracious jaws are already opening.

Bennett is talking, catching them up, and Elsa forces herself to pay attention. But she thinks and thinks and thinks about Mel. Who hasn't called anyone back. Whose cell signal has still not been triangulated with enough precision to pin down a location. All they've been able to ascertain so far is that the phone is still somewhere on the East Coast.

No, Elsa assures herself, *nothing has happened to Mel;*

she's just headstrong, flipping her mother the bird. She doesn't realize how worried they are about her; if she knew, she'd get in touch.

"We know that right after Hope dropped the chalk," Bennett says, standing at an easel, peeling to a blank page, starting a new list, "she turned toward the woods. Seems we can all agree that that edge of the woods is too densely traversed to pick out individual footprints, but given that the first ring, the copper one, was dropped five hundred yards in, when two sets of tracks are consistent, we know that he led her from the road into the woods. Deeper in, we find the second ring, the glass one." Purple, which according to Becky is often worn on Hope's right forefinger. "So we're guessing he's got her cuffed, and she's dropping rings because she can."

Holding the scrap of blue chalk in the palm of her hand, Elsa wonders how the girl managed to reach into her pocket to get it. But of course, that's assuming she had it in her pocket to begin with, or that she even had a pocket; maybe she was holding it in her hand when he took her. Elsa can see it: The animated Hope who has come alive in her mind—part herself, part Ruby, part Mel, a girl built of impressions—moving languidly toward school, in no hurry, having missed the bus anyway. An idea enters her thoughts. About to draw, she digs into her pocket for the chalk and then . . . what? Sammy Nelson, aka Ishmael Locke, appears in front of her. How does he do it? Does he ask for directions? Or does he come from behind and surprise her? If he surprises her, she drops the chalk before she manages to slip off the first ring. She's smart and intuitive enough to already be thinking about dropping clues. She's right about him. But why doesn't she run? Or does she try?

Without thinking, Elsa reaches down to scratch her leg, and then she corrects the impulse by folding her hands together on the table. She looks at her phone, faceup beside her. It doesn't ring.

"There are caves in these woods," Bennett finishes, "and we think there's a good chance he's got her—or them—in one of them. So that's where we are." He turns to the New York contingent, seated together across the table.

Elsa takes the lead, fast-forwarding through Ruby's disappearance and its connection to Sammy Nelson, who he is, what he's done in the past, and her theory as to his modus operandi. Bennett's people pay close attention, taking in the seriousness of how the two cases appear to be converging. And then the ruminative silence is interrupted by an old-fashioned ringtone that spills from Bennett's cell phone.

He listens, nods, hangs up. Announces: "Someone's turned up at the house with another piece of Hope's jewelry."

A rush to the door as they all hurry back to their cars.

Elsa's nearly at her Beetle, its top bright in the blazing sun, when her cell rings—a caller with an upstate area code. She answers immediately, "Special Agent Myers," hoping it's Mel, or about Mel, or at least about the whereabouts of her phone.

Lex and Joan both wait with Elsa. Around them, investigators slam doors; engines rev, cars race out of the lot. Standing in the sun, blinded by its intensity, Elsa doesn't turn her eyes away. She'll take whatever pain is coming, absorb it, devour it, let it consume her. Joan puts on her sunglasses and Lex lifts a hand to shade his face, both standing protectively close as she listens.

A deep male voice says, "This is Trooper Sullivan. Got something for you on that girl's cell—the signal pings on Route Thirty-Two, just above New Paltz."

"Heading north?"

"Heading nowhere, actually. We watched it a solid five minutes and it's holding still. Thought it might be a rest stop but it isn't. It's a field."

"You found it?" She closes her eyes, trying to divine a sliver of metal in a field of green—a phone. Nestled in the hand of a girl, Mel. Just sitting there, the way kids do, absently texting her friends. Detached from time.

"Not yet, but we're still looking. Just wanted to keep you posted."

Elsa doesn't realize she's trembling until she's in the driver's seat, starting the engine, and feels the weight of Lex's hand on her arm. She shakes him off and drives, wondering how and when Nelson got to Mel. Flashing back to yesterday, walking past the tent, sensing that he was listening. What had they talked about? *Ruby, the gun, Allie—returning to the hospital in Sleepy Hollow.*

Tara's slap resonates on Elsa's own face; she knows exactly how Mel felt, why she bolted, and she wonders for the umpteenth time why she herself never ran when she could have. The poison of rage spreads and spreads until the road in front of her subsumes the past, and she's helpless, because what they did to each other then can't be undone, the seeds cannot be unplanted. The only way for Tara not to have slapped Mel would be if Mel had never been born. And the thought of that is worse than almost anything.

29

Hope opens her eyes—shivering, ravenous, thinking of Jackson.

Jackson is a boy from school. A boy Hope likes, and he knows it.

She'd been with him in her dream just now and shuts her eyes hard and tight, hoping to re-conjure him, but the mildew smell of here and now is too strong and he evaporates.

On the craggy wall behind where the freak was sitting on his towel before he went away, a scant trickle of water drips, drips, drips. Her dry-as-Hades mouth opens and, thirst beckoning, she wills a drop her way. Just one. But she isn't magic and it doesn't come and her animal thirst growls.

And then out of nowhere the other girl comes toward her, the new one, like a rickety tripod, on bound wrists and legs that have somehow come free. Her muddled voice fighting the tape over her mouth, struggling to say something. She looks so bad, so scared, so energized; how Hope felt when she arrived a million hours ago. When the first girl was still breathing. Before she knew that she, too, would die here in this cave. She feels her eyes pool and blinks them clear.

The new girl's face is damp and dirty and she's shaking her head like a dog out of a lake, drops flying. Telling Hope not to cry. That's nice of her, Hope thinks; maybe if they'd met some other time and place, they could have been friends.

The girl hunches over Hope's hands and with bloody stumps of cracked fingernails picks at the ropes. Hope understands; it's how the new girl got her own ankles free. Hope lifts her hands as much as she can, a quarter inch, before the lariat tightens around her neck.

It will never work; it will never work.

She thinks of Jackson, tries to will herself back to the dream. Focuses on what she can remember of his face: roundish cheeks, coppery skin (they say his mother is half American Indian), a natural flare to his nostrils that says *I don't care* but means *I'll be passionate about love when I find out what it is*. He's younger than her by a year. Taller than her by six inches, and she isn't short. She took a bite of his pizza last week and he laughed.

Snap.

Hope widens her eyes and nods and nods. The rope has suddenly gone slack, and she unfurls like a chick out of its shell.

The girl lifts her own hands—her bound, shaking hands. Angles her head, pleading.

Hope shakes out her arms and rotates her neck and kicks her feet and gets to work unknotting the girl's wrists.

30

Becky's hand is trembling, holding a yellow rubber bracelet stamped LIVE STRONG with the ST scratched out and a W etched above it. Broken, roughly, as if bitten apart. Streaked with blood. "She was wearing this yesterday when she left for school."

The young man who delivered it, thick blond hair and a trimmed beard, explains, "I found it at SVC, on campus."

Elsa has heard of Southern Vermont College but knows little about it other than that it occupies the former estate of a nineteenth-century industrialist somewhere in or near Bennington.

"I work part-time at Everett Mansion and sometimes, before I get into my car after work, I go into the woods. Take a walk. Clear my mind. Today something yellow caught my eye. It was bunched up with some pine needles. I've been hearing about that girl on the news and when I saw this, I had a feeling it was hers, or could be hers. And then I noticed something—it isn't wet, but it rained earlier today."

Realizing the possible significance of the find—that

Hope might have dropped it recently, after the rain; that she could be on the move again, either with or without her captor—Elsa turns to Becky and asks, "How well does Hope know the woods?"

"We used to take long walks there," the mother answers, "so she knows it more or less."

The grid of Elsa's forehead tightens. Pulse races. Skin burns. This clever girl thinks for herself; she's a survivor. She dropped clues on purpose—and recently. And Mel, shrewd Mel, would bring ideas of her own. Strength in numbers, Elsa thinks; it's always best to have an ally.

People scatter into the woods, vast and green, and Elsa is moving to join them when she hears her name. She turns and finds Lex facing her, his arms crossed over his chest. His smile isn't encouraging; he's tilting his head. Next to him, Joan stands in perfectly poised professional neutrality. Elsa knows what they're going to say before they say it—she can read it in their eyes—and she's ready for them.

"Elsa," Lex says, "we think you should sit this out."

"No."

"This is personal for you now," Joan says softly, "your niece—"

"No way."

"You can't be clearheaded," Joan argues. "Your judgment will be impaired. Sweetie, no one can operate on all cylinders when a loved one's at risk."

It's the *sweetie* that gets her. One thing Elsa has never been is sweet. She says, "There is no fucking way I'm going to sit this out," and turns toward the woods.

31

The staircase bends at the middle, the two parts joined by a small landing with a window looking out onto the backyard where your old swing set has grown rusty. Only Tara uses it now, occasionally. You have other concerns.

School has gotten harder. There's a boy you like who might possibly like you back. One friend got her period for the first time. Another girl's parents are splitting up. There is a lot for your friends to deal with without adding your own problems into the mix, and besides, what would you say?

Sitting on the lower half of the stairs, fresh from a bout with your mother, you try out excuses for the bruise that might appear on your cheekbone where she hit you with the back of her hand.

"I didn't mean to hit your face," she said. "You moved."

To which you replied, idiotically, "I'm sorry."

You still don't know why *you* apologized to *her*, but in some odd way it feels right. This is a kind of problem you wouldn't know how to begin to discuss with your friends. And so you don't.

The front door opens and Roy walks in. His smile fades when he sees your face. Normally the first thing he asks is "Where's your mother?" but not tonight. He puts down his bag, hangs his coat on the bottom curl of the banister, and sits beside you on your step midway up the first section of staircase.

He says, "Do you want to tell me what happened, Elsie?"

"Why does it matter?" Without acrimony. The truth at the core of your rhetorical question is apparent to both of you. It doesn't matter why it happens. Anything can trigger it. That it happens, and happens, and happens is a fact of your life.

You shrug your shoulders.

Your father sighs.

You've grown too old for him to avoid the question of his culpability, and he says, "If we got a divorce, would you come with me?"

Your heart dances. "Are you? Getting a divorce?"

"It's really just a hypothetical question."

You look at him; you don't quite understand that word.

"I'm just thinking aloud," he clarifies, "wondering what would happen *if.*"

Oh. That means that nothing is changing here. Still, you want him to know: "Yes, I would."

"The only reason I stay is to protect you and Tara."

"But she doesn't hit Tara."

"And between you and me," he says, "we're going to make sure she never does. Right?"

"Right, Daddy." You allow him to take your hand. His, so warm. Something doesn't feel right, but you can't put your finger on it. Finally, you ask, "How does it protect me, though?"

A Map of the Dark

"As long as I'm here, you know you've always got an ally, a friend, nearby. You aren't alone. My eyes are open. I know—we all know—that she takes her anger out on you, honey."

You feel cold, even with his hand still holding yours. He squeezes, as if he senses you drifting and wants to stop you from floating away.

You ask, "Why me?"

"I think it's because you're special." A small, loving smile that you drink in. "You're feisty, you speak your mind, you argue back. And you know what?"

You look at him. It feels like watching a commercial on TV, half of you wanting to believe, the other half holding back.

"You're strong. She can't break you, no matter what."

"My face hurts so much, though."

His eyes squint, inspecting your cheek. "It's not too bad. Listen, do you want to go out to dinner with me tonight? Just the two of us? We can talk about whatever you want to."

You jump at the chance. But over dinner at the local diner, conversation falters; you end up finishing your grilled cheese sandwich mostly in silence, and both of you forgo dessert.

32

Bright daylight weakened by the density of trees, their summer-lush branches arcing high in a forest ceiling. Day becomes artificial evening, and, the farther in Elsa walks, evening becomes premature night punctuated by dream-like flashes of sunshine. Outside sounds are absorbed by bird chatter, insect chirps, breeze-fluttered leaves, the searchers' footsteps soft on a thick carpet of moss and pine needles. Elsa and her group walk, armed, intent, as if connected by an invisible rope of their breathing. As if language has been reduced to only three words, voices repeat, "Ruby!" "Hope!" "Mel!" in an echoing cacophony. Every now and then a voice from somewhere else in the woods intrudes sharply, an unseen searcher, and each time they stop to listen for a note of urgency. Greenberg's voice, in particular, a howl.

A siren crescendos into the now-distant parking lot. An ambulance, at the ready. Dread burrows into Elsa. She takes a deep breath and forges ahead, leading her small group with the map, as if she can read it when her mind is spinning circles around the professionalism she struggles to yoke into place. Maybe Lex and Joan were right, maybe she should recuse herself, since Nelson's crimes have gotten personal. Maybe. But she can't stop. She just can't, now more than ever.

When the beaten path feels limiting, she veers off the trail, and the members of her group scatter into the brush. She ignores the thorny branches slapping at her, tearing her sleeves, and scans every inch of the forest for the girls. Trying not to think about the possibility that Sammy Nelson could be out there too.

Not realizing at first that she's separated from her search party, she reemerges onto the trail and finds herself with a different group, this one including Lex. The side of his neck has a bloody gash. They lock eyes a moment and continue on together.

Half a mile west of their starting point, Elsa's and Lex's phones vibrate simultaneously. Elsa pulls hers out of her pocket and sees that it's a text from Ernie Bennett.

Found it, Everett's Cave, northwest of the mansion.

Elsa responds: Anyone there?

Ruby.

Not Ruby alive, or Ruby dead. Just Ruby.

They have to clamber over jutting stones and then stoop into a narrow opening in order to enter the cave. Then a climb down takes them into darkness, weakly illuminated by Bennett's flashlight. The dark void pulls around Elsa. The mossy damp. The resonant *drip-drip-drip* that grows louder as they proceed.

Bennett shifts his beam upward. "The CSI techs just got here." The dripping is so close now, it gives off echoes.

On the second level, a nest of flowstones and dripping

stalactites. Only a shred of natural light finds its way in. Bennett waves his beam back and forth over the cave to show them, but it's hard to see much of anything until one of the two techs setting up their work area switches on a floodlight. Elsa's stomach bucks when she sees it:

The stack of lumber Nelson loaded into the van at Greenberg's

A filthy towel

A roll of duct tape with a jagged ripped end

A cigarette lighter, orange

An empty Styrofoam cup lying on its side near the towel

A pair of rusty scissors

An unopened bag of carabiner hooks

A coil of steel rope

A flashy new toolbox

A small black handgun that looks identical to the one Elsa saw in Peter Haverstock's workshop

The Invisible Man

A sticky-looking thread of something half dried, reddish, leads Elsa's eye across the cave.

To Ruby.

A wax girl.

Elsa's brain twists and twists; her heart plummets.

They are too late.

Days and hours and minutes *too late.*

Her mind pulls away from her body, like it used to when she was a girl, allowing her to observe the horror from a safe distance. Or a distance, at least. The last time this happened, her mother was dead in front of her. She squeezes her eyes shut and forces her parts back together.

Bennett crouches beside Ruby and says, quietly, as if

he doesn't want the lifeless girl to hear, "We think she's been gone between four and twenty-four hours. She's still in rigor mortis."

Lex silently directs his flashlight to a haphazard pile of rope. A glint of something white brings a soiled feather earring into focus. "Didn't Hope's mother say she was wearing an earring like that when she left for school?"

Yes, Elsa thinks, *yes, yes.* Her eyes hunt for signs of Mel, anything to prove she's also been here, hoping that she wasn't, and in the darkness and panic she sees nothing. She says, "Maybe he doesn't actually have Mel. Maybe—"

Lex's hand on her shoulder is oppressive. She jerks away and heads toward the mouth of the cave. Recalling, suddenly, the thirst that clawed her throat after long hours in her closet. "If it were me in here since yesterday, I'd want water, first thing."

Bennett's voice trails her: "There are a couple of streams and a waterfall nearby. I used to bring my kids here when they were young."

Shaking, Elsa climbs out of the cave, into the tunnel.

Lex and Bennett are right behind her, the flashlight's beam opening the path forward.

33

"Come on, people, let's move it!"

Carrie leads the way, swinging her elbows like she's the captain of a marching band. She's tiny enough to get lost in the profusion of leaves but too bright to miss. Carrie is neon pink, and now, Hope sees for the first time, she carries an emerald-green baton. Behind her, sapphire Velma and Arnold wearing a big gold crown hold hands. This is new. Jesus comes last but he's grown a quarter inch and filled his outlines with rainbow stripes. Hope blinks her eyes. They disappear. Blinks again, and they're back, bigger and brighter than before.

Jesus turns to look directly at her, walking backward. "Don't give up, Hope!"

"I won't." Hope gasps. "I won't." Breathing is harder now. Her lungs feel deflated. Her throat is so swollen it's hard not to choke when she tries to swallow, which she can't anyway because she's out of saliva.

"Where are we going?" she asks the entire board of directors. She pays them to have answers, after all. It's their job.

"Who are you talking to?" the new girl asks. She's smaller than Hope, but stronger.

"Onward," Velma and Arnold say together.

And so they do—move onward. She follows, hoping for the best.

Carrie turns and raises her baton. "The cupcake. Drop the cupcake now. It's time."

Hope rips the cupcake charm off one of her bracelets and drops it. Carrie nods in approval. So does the new girl, who adds, "That's a good idea."

They tramp through the woods.

Everything dims. Hope feels scarily faint.

Jackson.

Her mother.

Her father.

Her brothers.

She forces open her eyes and thrusts her feet forward as daylight seems to drain away. In the dusky forest the entire army of her hundred and twelve little people appear, glowing, perched on leaves like candles on Christmas branches. *Tous ensemble* (Ms. Laroux, ninth-grade French), they raise their batons and lead her forward with a chorus of petty inquisition:

What is a quark?

The smallest unit of matter, makes up protons.

What are molecules?

Two or more atoms held together by *something*.

What is an organelle?

Part of a *something* that has a specific function.

What are the five types of organelles?

Nucleus, mitochondrion, *something something, something, something* body.

Order from smallest to largest.

"I hear water," Hope mumbles, tripping forward.

"No," the new girl says, "not now. We have to keep going."

"I'm so thirsty."

And then, laced into the gurgle of water, the leaf crunch of a footstep. Two.

Someone else's footsteps. *His.*

"Help me," she says to her little people. "Please."

They ignore her and repeat: *Order from smallest to largest.*

A third footstep, closer now.

And a fourth.

But it's an irresistible craving, not fear, that propels her. Water; thirst; molecular compound and human tongue. And then he can have her, if he wants her that badly. She can't fight him anymore, not even in her mind.

"Come with me," she begs the new girl, but she yanks her hand away and runs in the opposite direction.

The gurgling draws Hope forward and there it is: a sparkling, bubbling stream. She falls to her knees, laps at the shallow edge—sweet bliss!

Why couldn't the new girl at least wait for her?

She drinks again but it's not enough.

A plank across the stream promises passage to a clearing on the other side where it's deeper and she could dip in her face and gorge. The thought of it. She moves forward onto the plank, old wood warping underfoot.

The footsteps, faster, harder, louder.

His quick weight heaving onto the plank behind her.

When she's nearly there, it snaps and gravity releases her and as she's flying, her board of directors, *whom she pays to prevent just this kind of mishap*, swarm ahead, repeating the demand:

Order from smallest to largest.

34

Deb is a master gardener; she could be a professional if she wanted to. You learned early that she's happier around plants and have often wondered why she chose to make her living as an elementary school teacher. "*Always* around kids," she's been known to complain, "*never* get a break."

One springtime afternoon, on your way home from school, you and your mother and your sister stop at a landscaping center. Following your mother's instructions, you and Tara carry twenty-pound bags of rocks to the trunk of the car. The rocks are for Deb's garden—she's always creating something new—and you're proud that you're strong enough to assist in the effort. Then, with a heavy bag cradled in your arms, you recognize something vital: You have grown capable; you could resist her next time her rage flies.

Which it does, of course, not long after your realization.

It's just before dinner. You're alone with your mother in the kitchen. Roy isn't home yet, and Tara is at a friend's.

You dig in your heels about something and *that look* overtakes Deb's face, the mask of forced patience falling

257

away, replaced by a contortion that makes your pulse spike.

You can't help yourself; you take off running.

She follows.

At thirteen you're quick but she's a grown woman and catches up with you in the second-floor hallway. She grabs your hair on both sides and smashes your head against the wall. And again. And again. She, enraged. You, in shock.

And then you remember your strength. You can hit back. Maybe you could get through to her if she got a taste of her own medicine.

You draw your hand back and slap your mother's face, hard. Just once. Shouting, *"How do you like it?"*

You've never seen her so surprised. You freeze, terrified of what might come next. You didn't anticipate that this warrior woman who has won every battle in your life would burst into tears and run away to her room and weep. But that is exactly what she does.

The guilt is overpowering. You've hurt your own mother. Proven your point by assaulting *your own mother*.

Her pain haunts you.

After that, the violence stops.

Gradually, over time, a new worry grows: What if someday you should become a mother; won't the cycle inevitably repeat? Because even though the hitting has stopped, the fear of it is still inside you. You are not to be trusted, because she made you in the likeness of her rage.

35

The group of searchers breaks past the dense trees and into the clearing where the nearest stream meanders, but Elsa senses they won't find the girls here. It appears thoroughly undisturbed except for the sounds of cheeping birds and the leafy crunch of the searchers' footsteps. In the near distance you can see the elaborate roofscape of the old mansion that houses the college. From their left tromps a group of half a dozen searchers.

"Water!" Elsa shouts to them. "We're looking for water!"

Bennett points. "This way—there's a reservoir."

They all veer to follow Bennett.

Elsa asks, "How far?"

"Not very—a thousand feet maybe."

As they move deeper into the woods, sunlight fades with an encroaching cloud, and with the loss of visibility, Elsa's heart begins to sink. They'll be too late, she feels it; feels, suddenly, that wrapped in the loss of Ruby is Hope, and wrapped in the loss of Hope is Mel, and wrapped in the loss of Mel is the renewed loss of Deb, and wrapped in the echo of the long-ago loss of Deb, as always, is the loss of herself . . . girls and women ribbed together by a single spine. In one's collapse, they all go down together.

Elsa shakes off the haunted thoughts and tries, tries to push past the inner headwinds of doubt and fear and shame and recrimination.

Lex moves ahead of her, along with two of the faster searchers. As Elsa watches him leave her, emotions conflict: resentment that he's abandoning her, and relief to be alone. Every now and then he glances back at her but he doesn't wait.

After a minute, Greenberg shouts, "I found something!"

In the craggy center of his broad palm he holds a thimble-size enameled pink-and-yellow cupcake frosted with rhinestones. A tiny metal loop shows where it would attach to a chain. Hope must have ripped it off a necklace or bracelet and dropped it as she ran or walked or crawled along. And if Hope was here, Mel could be nearby. Elsa rejects the images flashing through her mind of the girls blanketed under leaves, fallen or buried. No. She won't succumb to that yet.

The terrible thirst chafes at the back of your throat, closet-dark and insistent.

Another stream appears, this one longer. A pair of searchers follow Bennett in that direction, edging north-ward, while the remaining two stay with Elsa. Elsa, skin map tightening, slowed by a pull of dreamlike exhaustion. Soon, everyone has moved ahead of her. As the distance grows, she makes out the edge of what must be the reser-voir Bennett mentioned. She can see searchers, like ants, fanning out around the bank.

She stops walking, so far behind now that there's no

point trying to catch up. Alone and out of breath, she doubles over and gives in to the weight of helpless frustration.

They'll never find Hope.

They'll never find Mel.

Roy is going to die while Elsa is away, her past going with him but never really gone.

She will be forever unmoored. Lost. She has failed at everything.

She sinks to her knees. Pebbles and sticks dig into her flesh, rip through her pants. Her brain is sloggy, heavy; her skin alight. It's foolish to keep working when her father is dying. She *should* take a leave of absence, face the gathering storm head-on, race straight into it.

She should go back to Sleepy Hollow immediately. Sit with her father. Just be there, for whatever it's worth. Talk to him. Listen. It's suddenly clear.

They don't need her help finding the girls; it's presumptuous of her to think that her presence is of any real importance. Between Lex, Joan, Ernie Bennett, Greenberg, and the army of searchers, if the girls are still alive, they'll find them. And if they aren't alive, they'll find them. Everywhere, people swarm, looking. And Elsa does not want to be the one to find Mel if finding her will be anything like finding Ruby.

The pathetic wailing sound leaking through Elsa's tears embarrasses her, and she forces herself quiet, sucking back the flood of self-indulgent remorse. Standing, she brushes leaves off her knees and the palms of her hands.

And then, as the last searcher vanishes into the distance behind the tower of Greenberg, in the growing quiet she becomes aware of a low thrum, gulpy and emotional, as if she hasn't stopped crying, although she is sure that she's no longer making any sound.

A stream babbles somewhere near.

And then the hard crack of wood breaking.

She moves toward the sound, and there it is: water lapping onto a bank of pebbled earth. Just to the left, beyond a thicket of overhanging branches, the broken halves of a long board, someone's intention for a footbridge. It appears to have fallen in and obstructed the flow of water, creating the glurping sound. Her heart sinks lower. She'd thought, for just a moment, that the sound she heard could be someone else crying. That she isn't alone here. That she actually did hear another voice.

She steps into the stream and, pushing aside branches and prickly brush, moves closer for a better look.

And sees them.

Hope, obscured by the brush, wouldn't have been visible to the searchers. You have to veer in sideways, into the stream, or come in from the other direction to see her at all. She must have come across the plank while it was still in place. His sudden weight must have broken it—that crack. And now, here they are: she, curled into the muddy bank; he, kneeling over her.

Through the slick skin of his stream-wet clothes you can see the undulations of strain as his back and shoulders engage in some kind of effort. The cervical knobs of his neck appear grossly pronounced. Beneath him, her body subtly twists, legs barely kicking.

Alive.

Eyes glued to him, Elsa reaches into the water and feels for the Glock holstered to her ankle. She slides off the safety strap, grips the handle, tugs out the gun. Frozen in place, hand underwater, she studies him.

She focuses on the burl of neck and skull where his hair is skewed in all directions, a tender spot a mother might have kissed. She will aim exactly there. If she misses, Hope could die, but if she doesn't try, Hope will die.

She lifts the gun out of the water. And then, in a moment, the wet grip slicks out of her hand. Her weapon lands in the stream with a heavy plop, ripples orbiting. Nelson turns. Sees her.

His eyes blink like shorted neon. Mouth drops. The voice that sails out of him doesn't resemble the one that spoke to her on the Haverstocks' lawn, the voice of nerdy Teddy with his book and his button and his "analog message." This voice is massive, dense, guttural. Untamed. The sound of it spreads across her skin in high-voltage tendrils.

He shouts: *"You!"* And, like a bird of prey, launches himself in her direction.

She staggers backward, trying not to fall, and then pivots in an effort to skirt around him to get to Hope. Takes two steps, three, and then he lands on her, huge and powerful. Forces her down into the water until she's submerged. Eyes open, sinking in the up-bubbles of underwater breath, hands flailing on the streambed, drowning and drowning and drowning with shame for all her failures before this monster, who is herself, who is her mother, who is her past and present and future, when all she had to do was pull the trigger before he noticed her.

His fingers web around your neck with the tight, inevitable feel of a Chinese finger trap; the more you struggle, the harder the grip, the worse your chances. Pushing down, he holds you underwater, his thumbs pressing into the hollow of your throat.

Oxygen drains away like the end of a brilliant afternoon, leaving you in a lavender twilight, and for a split second you're convinced that it's the most beautiful place you've ever been. You are unlatched; an inconsequential feather set afloat. The end of time is the beginning of time. You become a slippery birth out of yourself, at the hands of another, prepared for a simple release. Ready for it.

So this is how it feels when he kills them.

What surprises you most is how willing you are to give yourself to the prospect of your death.

But then you remember Mel, somewhere out there. And Hope, so close, at the edge of the stream.

Rallying, Elsa raises a knee into Nelson's groin, hard, and again, harder. He flinches briefly, enough for her to squirm partially out from under him. He recovers himself, fingers curling around her neck, but not before her right hand lands on a rock settled into the streambed.

She twists to the side, gets a grip on the rock.

His fingers bear down on her throat.

She sweeps her arm upward until she feels a shock of cold air on her hand. Calculates. Slams the rock into the side of his head. And again. And again.

His fingers flower open, releasing her, as if she's pushed a button and turned him off.

Water races into her mouth, fills her lungs. She surges upward, desperate for air, expecting him to come at her again.

But he doesn't. He's stupefied, balanced on his knees like one of those inflatable punching bags that can't stand but doesn't fall. Moaning like an injured animal. Blinking, struggling to regain his equilibrium. His little daughter's face smiling, still smiling, from the dripping-wet button.

Now, she tells herself, *right now.*

She forces her hand into her wet pocket and pulls out the knife, *her knife,* with its array of implements she knows by heart. Plucks out the longest blade. Crashes through the water toward him.

His arm lifts, but slowly. She grabs his hair and jerks his head toward his left shoulder, revealing the long right side of his neck, his jugular vulnerable, all hers.

One cut. Precise. Swift. With force.

His flesh parts like the opening of a mouth. A lipstick-red smile. A yawn. A scream. Ribbons of blood pouring from the lips of his wound. His eyes seem to fix on her, staring, but empty. And then his body keels backward as if hinged at the knee. She thinks fleetingly of his mother, how he was once someone's beloved child. Even him. And then the reality of what just happened vibrates through her hand and arm and brain and awakens her.

She struggles forward, thrashing her way through the stream to Hope.

She can't see the girl's face, but the chain of her spine is still and her rib cage doesn't move at all. She doesn't seem to be breathing. There is no sign of life other than a trickle of blood that appears to be leaking from her wrist.

Shaking, Elsa crouches down. Hope's hipbone juts high above a sunken waist, a girl's narrow waist from which ribs flare to broad shoulders. Tattoos of impish figures, like those from her bedroom wall, march single file up the side of her neck, holding hands. Four of them: two laughing, one crying, one staring right at you with a look of curiosity. The side of Hope's rib cage rises, and falls, and rises again.

"Good girl," Elsa whispers, "just keep breathing."

"Auntie Elsa!" The voice calls from the opposite side of the stream. And there, there is Mel. Blood caked on her wrists. An angry bruise on her cheek. Shoeless. Sodden and filthy and *alive*.

Thursday

36

Lex Cole opens the chapel door for Elsa, continuing his trend of kindness, having covered for her over the past couple of days as she helped move her father into hospice, and she thanks him.

The cheerfulness of the airy chapel, with its blond wood and cream walls and the splashes of sunshine on the pale green carpet, feels disorienting, a counterpoint to the end-of-world hopelessness of the cave where Ruby drew her last breath. Elsa has hated funerals ever since her mother's, watching her father serve as a pallbearer, the blank misery of his expression, the deep sag of his shoulders under the unbearable weight, heavier than the casket or the body inside it.

Peter and Ginnie Haverstock wanted their daughter buried here, at Flushing Cemetery, because although neither parent came from Queens and they have no extended family here, it's the only home Ruby has ever known and they want to keep her close.

Lex, in a pressed black suit, slides into a pew. Elsa follows, too warm in a linen pantsuit, pale gray, with a black blouse and a triple-strand pearl choker. Real pearls, passed down from her mother, something she almost never wears. Tara got the diamond engagement ring and plans to pass it on to Mel someday.

Peter and Ginnie occupy the front-most pew, closest to the gleaming casket that encases their only child, bookended by white-haired couples, a pair on either side. No flowers anywhere, Elsa notices, but nothing surprises her anymore. The eyes of all three women are swollen and red, and one cries openly, presumably Ruby's maternal grandmother, as she sits pressed closely into Ginnie's side—Ginnie pale, bloodless, her shaking hand clutching a ragged tissue. Peter's utter stillness touches something deep inside Elsa, deeper than the sadness and regret that have rooted inside her since Tuesday—the burning seed of their failure to save Ruby's life.

That maniac, she thinks, wishing to reduce Sammy Nelson's culpability to something already made, inborn, inexorable; to strip him of his vengeful rage, the whole dangerous knotted tangle of a person who chooses—actually *chooses*—to prey on other people. But even now, today, sitting here in the solemn aftermath of a girl who came so close to reaching eighteen but had the bad luck of crossing paths with him first, even after everything Elsa has seen in her life and in her work, she can't bring herself to believe that anyone is born preprogrammed to kill. Even so, one way or another, we become who we are, and she will never forgive him for what he did to all those girls.

She doesn't realize that she's digging her fingertips into the tops of her thighs until she feels Lex's arm settle on the back of the pew behind her shoulders. She takes a deep breath and stops the grinding mechanism of her mind. They didn't get there in time for Ruby. They were too late for her. But Hope and Mel, they managed to save. Mel barely scathed, not physically, at least; Hope's recovery will take more time.

Elsa doesn't like working missing-kid cases, she decides for the hundredth time. She doesn't like it at all. She doesn't know how she's tolerated it all these years and then realizes she hasn't.

Two rows behind the Haverstocks, Ruby's friends cluster tightly together, talking, crying, glancing at their phones as if some vital piece of information might appear at any moment. Ruby, maybe, texting, jk lol i'm not really dead. Elsa knows not to underestimate magical thinking in the face of death, but these kids, they're just learning. Allie and Charlie sit at a distance from each other, and if they interact at all, she doesn't see it. People are scattered in the pews, waiting for someone to get up and speak.

No one can, not even Ruby's stricken parents, especially not them.

Finally, a bald man with a trimmed goatee ascends the platform, tripping on his long black robes, revealing Converse sneakers. He rights himself, stands behind the podium, and introduces himself in a soft voice as a "non-denominational pastor." He speaks long enough to put a few words to the overwhelming grief that has silenced everyone else. Both parents weeping now. Allie, among the gaggle of teenagers, heaves forward. Elsa takes another deep breath and doesn't cry.

Later, they follow the procession through a maze of headstones, up a grassy slope to a plot of freshly dug soil. Beside it, a mound of dirt with a shovel poking out. The family sits in folding chairs lined up near the gaping mouth of the grave. Everyone else scatters, watching, as Ruby in her casket is lowered slowly into the earth. There is no marker for her, not yet; it all happened too fast. Elsa and Lex stand side by side, in silence, and watch from a distance.

The pastor pulls out the shovel, digs it into the mound, and holds out the first offering of soil to the family. After a moment of hesitation, Ginnie comes forward and takes it from him. She averts her eyes when he smiles at her, and Elsa wants to slap him for trying to cheer her up. Shaking, she carries the shovel in front of her, dirt raining in her wake. When she reaches the grave, she stands there, looking down. Her face seems to gather inward, like someone's pulled a string at the top of a sack, closing her off. A woman, a mother, finished. She tilts the shovel and the dirt falls in, thumps against the top of the casket. Quickly, she turns and hands the shovel to her husband, who has come up behind her. She makes her way across the lawn, back to her seat, where she hunches, cocooned in a private grief.

Peter stabs the mound, hard, provoking an avalanche of dirt.

Beside her, Elsa feels Lex's warmth. She steps away so she won't cry.

Reading her, he whispers, "Let's go."

They don't speak until they're sealed into the quiet of her car. Only then does she breathe. "That was awful."

"Yup."

"Poor Ruby." She starts the engine, steers onto the road that winds through the cemetery. Lex, beside her, checks his phone.

"Wow—Elsa, we just got an e-mail from Oregon."

"We?" Thinking: *Oregon. Where Sammy Nelson officially lived.*

"The task force, all of us. The local PD went back to his place. There's a video attached."

She pulls the car up to the curb and parks, still inside the cemetery. "Open it."

He props his phone horizontally, and they wait while a two-minute file loads. A hearse with its headlights on enters from the street, moving slowly, leading a procession that snakes slowly past. Elsa stares at the small screen. Lex clicks the arrow and the video begins.

A man, young enough to still have a telltale crack in his voice, speaks over shaky footage that sweeps slowly left to right. "This is Officer Lloyd Bass, Winston, Oregon. I'm at the home of your perp. I was told to show you what I see, as you're on the other coast, so here goes. The outside of the building where he lived."

A low-rise apartment complex clad in beige siding, fringed with parking spots, half of them unoccupied. The lens rests on a windowless van, forest green, with a jagged scratch across the rear bumper, an Oregon license plate.

"This is Sammy Nelson's vehicle. Neighbors told us he has two vans, this green one and also a white one with New York plates. He takes up two spots, and some people don't like it, but occupancy here is low so management let it slide."

The camera jerks away from the van, back to the apartment building. Eight concrete paths connect the parking lot to a series of identical front doors, each leading to a downstairs and an upstairs. Two buzzers per door, two apartments per unit.

"He lived in unit three, apartment B."

The officer's hand reaches into the shot to open the door. Hairless, not a wrinkle, a wedding ring.

"Up the stairs."

The image rocking with the officer's steps, the slaps of his shoes on cracked linoleum. His hand appears again to push open an interior door with 3B stenciled in black. "I unlocked it before, figured it would make a better shot, so you wouldn't have to watch the whole rigmarole with the landlord. Here we go."

Foot by foot, yard by yard, a living room takes shape. A room with off-white walls, brown carpeting, a low ceiling, two perfectly symmetrical windows with closed venetian blinds. On the wall above a long blue couch hangs, in pride of place, a poster-size enlargement of little Zoe—same as the button, but in this larger version a likeness to her father is evident around the eyes. Between the couch and the windows, a pair of tall bookcases lean into each other. Books, lots of books, and almost as many DVD cases, most with library stickers on their spines. *Ordinary People, Kramer vs. Kramer, Rain Man, Beginners*. The camera pans quickly past the windows: a large-screen television mounted on an otherwise blank wall, the inside of the front door on which a fringed macramé hanging is attached by a pushpin.

The lens makes a sudden dip to the floor, where, at the seam of living room and hall, an empty eBay box sits with its flaps open, a box just larger than the twenty-inch toolbox Nelson favored. With a shiver Elsa wonders if he'd been all ready to go, waiting for the package to arrive, if he'd opened it immediately and extracted the shiny red toolbox and filled it with his goodies and hit the road.

"Okay. Now the kitchen."

A small square room, windowless, with plain wood cabinets and the cheapest appliances you can buy. A round table fills up most of the space; it holds a red floral place mat, a saltshaker with an *S* and pepper shaker with a *P*, a plastic takeout cup with a lid and a straw and an inch of murky water at the bottom. A single chair. Inside the small sink sits a clear glass vase with a bouquet of dead coneflowers, bulbous black middles haloed with desiccated petals that might once have been purple. The camera lingers a moment on the front of the refrigerator, crowded with photos: people in pairs, trios, groups of picnickers, on boats and rooftops and swimming in lakes, smiling and laughing, a beaming couple with their arms around each other, a family raising their glasses at a holiday table laden with food. Every single photograph cut out of a magazine.

Loneliness punches Elsa in the gut. She blinks, and the lens turns away.

Bass announces, "Bedroom now. That's the last room. Well, and the bathroom."

The double bed is clumsily made with an Indian spread; two pillows hold the indentation of a person's weight—an empty space left by Sammy Nelson's body in repose. On a bedside table sit a short stack of books, titles turned to the wall, and one of those small clip-on reading lights—as if when he read, alone in his room, he wanted to make the smallest possible impact on the darkness.

"Enough," Elsa says, "I can't—I don't want to see any more." She turns to look out the car window, where just then a woman on a white bicycle whizzes toward the graves, a potted yellow begonia in the wire basket above her front tire.

Friday

37

The FOR SALE sign on the lawn in front of the Martin-Creech house is gone. A pair of small boy's bikes is tangled together, tossed down by the front steps. Half a dozen camera-slung reporters stand at the edge of the property, talking casually, waiting out the family's reticence. As far as Elsa understands, Hope's parents have managed to keep the press at bay, practically a miracle, given the raging hunger of the news cycle.

The reporters come alive when Elsa and Lex take the path to the front door. Elsa rings the bell, sees a curtain part on a downstairs window, hears a voice say something and then footsteps. The father, Gary—gray-faced, dark swaths beneath his eyes—cracks open the door just enough to let Elsa and Lex inside. Behind them, cameras click and flash. He slams the door and locks it.

"They've been here since we got her home," Gary says. Three days.

He leads them to the living room, where all the curtains are drawn against prying eyes, blotting out daylight. Hope and Becky sit close together in the bend of a sectional couch. On a low round coffee table, a pitcher of iced tea and five glasses have been set out, along with a plate heaped with clusters of green grapes.

"Sorry we're late," Elsa says.

Lex adds, "Traffic."

"No worries," Becky assures them. "We're happy as clams just sitting here."

They look it too. Even Hope, with her spectrum of bruises and bandages and sprained arm hoisted in a sling . . . even Hope looks relaxed.

Becky rises to greet them, kisses Elsa on the cheek. When a case ends well, the gratitude you receive is almost enough to remind you why you do the job. The real satisfaction, though, is in Hope's eyes. She doesn't get up or even smile. She doesn't really know them, after all; they were told that her memory of her rescue is dim. But the clarity of her eyes, the aliveness of them, is enough for Elsa. Despite popular belief, she feels that there's something elementally optimistic about teenagers, the way their bodies can operate as adults' while their minds still have a direct line into the good kind of wishful thinking, when you don't question the gumption of racing forward into life. Mel has that too. Elsa isn't sure if she herself has ever really been that confident. Sitting down across from the couch, looking at Hope, she wonders if the girls will take fewer risks now, and a renegade impulse rises up with optimism that the trauma may not necessarily distort their ability to trust people . . . but what's the likelihood of that?

"Are you guys, like, real FBI agents?" Hope asks.

Elsa smiles at the sound of Hope's voice, which she has never heard before: light and scratchy, as if she's recovering from a sore throat. "I am. My friend here is a police detective."

"Cool."

"So," Elsa gently probes, "how are you doing?" and elicits a sly grin from Hope.

"Seriously?"

"You don't have to talk about anything you don't want to."

Hope nods, her eyes darting to her mother.

"We've explained that to her," Becky says. "She understands."

"Okay, then." Elsa takes a breath. "What can you tell us about what happened to you?"

"He's dead, though, right?" Shifting in her seat, Hope winces.

Elsa answers, "One thousand percent."

"Are you the one who killed him?" Hope asks tentatively, like a child peering into forbidden dark corners, even though the time has passed to protect her from those.

Elsa nods.

"He was such a *freak*."

"You can say that again."

"I wish I could have helped Ruby."

"I know you do—but there's nothing you could have done to change the way things turned out. You had no control over him. None of this is your fault, honey."

Hope's eyes flash at the endearment coming from a stranger. Elsa regrets it. This isn't Mel, and it isn't a younger version of herself. She has no power to comfort the girl outside the reason for this visit: an exit interview, as it were, so that they can officially close the case file.

"He, like, came out of nowhere," Hope says quietly. "I

missed the bus, so I was walking to school instead, and I was thinking about my biology test, and all of a sudden there's this guy in front of me." She sips her iced tea. Eats two grapes, slowly. "He kept wanting to talk, like we were friends or something. It was so weird. But then he also hit me. I didn't understand what was happening. And he had all these tools. And then he brought in this other girl, and I was so scared because the first girl, she was—" She slams shut her eyes.

"It's enough, angel," Becky says softly. "You don't have to say anything else." She lays a reassuring hand on her daughter's arm and glances sharply at their visitors.

Elsa and Lex stand and say their good-byes. Gary walks them to the door. At the last minute, Becky jumps up to join them.

"I didn't want to start crying in front of Hope," Becky says, "there's been too much of that around here lately— but I just have to tell you how grateful we are." She opens her arms to Elsa, envelops her in a maternal hug that feels familiar and foreign, comforting and off-putting, somehow right and somehow wrong.

"You have an amazing daughter," Elsa says. "I've never seen such a will to survive."

"If you hadn't—" Becky's words choke to a stop.

Elsa shakes her head emphatically—"Don't go there"— refusing to revisit the many ways in which they might not have found Hope and Mel alive.

"If you need us for anything," Lex says, "even to talk things through, give us a call. But if you never want to hear from us again, believe me, we'll understand."

Elsa could have loved the guy for having the heart to say that. She thinks of David. She wonders how much of

the brothers' compassion comes from their late mother—
the wise and affectionate Yelena—and how much comes
from each other.

"The main thing is that Hope's safe now," Elsa agrees.
"That's all that really counts."

Elsa holds a constant speed, just at the limit, as they drive
through the bucolic village of Bennington in silence, past
Greenberg's lumberyard, past the Blue Benn diner filled
with patrons eating lunch as if nothing happened.

Lex says, "This town's got a big problem with heroin—
dealers, addicts, the whole bit. Couple of colleges
here—maybe a good fit for Charlie."

Elsa laughs, stifling the remarks that flit through her
mind about the surfaces of things, about how meanness
can lurk in the prettiest places. "Well," she says, "we're not
college counselors and we're not DEA, so what do you
say we get the hell out of Dodge?"

"*Dodge?*"

She explains but doesn't think it makes much sense to
him, as he presumably missed out on *Gunsmoke* reruns
during his Russian childhood and immigrant adolescence.
She stops trying when they turn in the direction of the
highway.

After a while, he surprises her with a question—or a
challenge. "So, you told David you have tattoos."

She glances at him, speechless. Accelerating through the
green-blue countryside, she grinds her teeth, wishes he
weren't here, that he didn't know her, that he'd landed
someone else for this case. But then she remembers that it
wasn't random; he chose her.

He says, "You don't have tattoos."

"Excuse me?"

"A few days ago, in the wind."

She remembers. Standing outside the Martin-Creech house, a gust hit her hard. She was blinded for a moment by the swish of her hair over her eyes. She recalls the fabric lifting off her skin, how she needed to pull her sleeve back down.

And then he says, "Yelena was a cutter—our mother."

A cutter. No one has ever spoken that phrase aloud to her before. The few who know about her problem—her parents and sister—always held the secret as if it were their own. Each and every lover had fled in the sobriety of daylight. Avoidance, pretending normalcy, has been her creed for a lifetime. Competence has been her shield. She has found a way, barely, to live with herself, and she does not, not, not want to talk about it with Lex Cole or anyone else.

"Best woman I ever knew," he says. "She had some problems in her past. But she didn't let it stop her from loving us, or us from loving her."

Elsa stares at the road ahead, lap after lap of asphalt vanishing beneath the car. Her insides wither at the thought that Lex glimpsed her skin and might have discussed it with his brother. Well—the case is over; she never has to see either of them again if she doesn't want to. Her grip tightens on the wheel.

"I understand your predicament," he continues, "growing up with a tough mother. And then what happened to her. Terrible. But I'd also like to say this: Parents, they give what they can, even if it's shit. And you, Special Agent Elsa Myers, you didn't turn out so bad."

"Lex"—her voice gluey, the words difficult to force

out—"I really can't discuss this." But the words do get out, just a few and nothing significant, and they have the desired effect of pushing him away. He's essentially right about her. But she doesn't need a friend; doesn't *want* a friend like him who will try to open her up, to know her, maybe even to fix her.

He nods. They sit in silence for a few minutes, and then she asks, "Would you mind if I dropped you at a train station? I'd like to go see my dad."

"Of course I don't mind." Warmly, gently, like a real friend. But he isn't. She wishes she could, but she can't.

38

Elsa walks through the white-pillared entrance of the assisted-living home where last year Roy parked himself prematurely, she'd thought at the time. But now she's thankful that he's here at Atria, with its genteel practical comforts. A nurse from the hospice program visits every day, like a philosopher-spa on wheels, tending his soul and rubbing out his kinks while no one pretends he isn't dying.

Everyone is dying, though, Elsa thinks, waving at the front-desk attendant with the pale blue coif she'd thought went out of style two generations ago. Everyone is dying, all the time. It's just a matter of when it becomes official. For Deb, it happened twenty-four years ago, right before dinner. For Roy, it will happen soon. For Elsa, the forecast is wide open.

"You're here!" Mel rushes over with a hug.

Elsa drinks in the love, holding her niece long enough to make the girl squirm away. "Where's Gramp?"

"With Mom, in the kitchen. She's slaying him at Scrabble—she's got no mercy."

Elsa finds her father and sister bent over the table in

the small, sunny kitchen he uses only for morning tea. Roy has delighted in taking all his meals in the dining hall, socializing with the other residents, enjoying his freedom from even the smallest responsibility. Feeling a surge of gladness that he's had this one easy half-year, she pats his shoulder hello.

He turns his face to see her. "Hi, honey. I think I just lost this game." Behind him on the windowsill, Lex's hospital flowers, still mostly fresh in their vase.

"You know you did." Tara grins. "I'll run those errands now, Dad, since Elsa's here. Mellie, you want to come with me?"

"Sure. Auntie Elsa, will you be here when we get back?"

"Probably."

"Cool. Catch ya later, Rambo." Mel laughs at the new nickname she's apparently given her aunt.

Tara shakes her head, chuckling.

Roy forces a grin.

But Elsa's insides freeze. "Is that what you call me now?"

"Yep."

"You're a legend around here," Tara says. "Enjoy it."

They gather their purses. Elsa sits quietly with her father until the chatter is subsumed by the closing front door. "Wow, I don't know if I can live with that."

"We're lucky they have a sense of humor. So do you, Elsa. Don't forget that."

"Dad, I have to ask you something about Mom and—you know." The question that's long bubbled under the surface.

"Okay."

"Why didn't you stop her?"

The muscles of his face shift incrementally, creating the appearance of a deep shadow. "I didn't know how."

"Why didn't you take us away from her?"

He looks at his daughter and struggles to explain. "She was my wife, and she wasn't easy, and the thing was that I"—*Loved her,* Elsa is sure he's about to say. But instead— "was afraid of what would happen. I was afraid that if I left her and took you with me, it would make things worse."

"Worse how?" When obviously her life would have been so much better.

"I don't know," he says with a familiar hollow sigh. "I've thought about it and I can't really understand it myself. I was weak, confused. We were a family. I didn't know what to do."

You drop everything and save the kid, she wants to shout, but doesn't. What's the point? In this case, the kid has grown up and the consequences of all that violence are etched into her skin.

"Elsa." His hand creeps forward to take hers, dry, cool, and he holds tight as if she's a balloon and he's afraid she'll float away, as if no matter what he does or says, he's fated to lose her trust. "Something came to me just this morning; I realized that I was wrong; we did leave something behind at the house. So much time's gone by, years, and I'd put it out of my mind. And then suddenly I remembered. I'm sorry, Elsa, I'm sorry."

"The King of Denial" is what she and Tara used to call him behind his back, before Deb was killed. They'd laugh about it. They even invented a little Egyptian-esque dance featuring (in their imaginations) their father in imperial robes on the banks of the river Nile, pretending to ignore a bloody sacrificial ritual being enacted in the open.

Elsa asks, "What? Just tell me."

She watches his Adam's apple toggle up the reed of his throat and slide down. "Remember I had a concrete platform built before the shed was installed in the backyard? I buried something very, very deep at the far left corner, near the fence."

She instantly knows what he means.

Her mind flashes to the backyard, five days ago, on Sunday, and she realizes that the shed wasn't there. The new owners must have had it removed in preparation for their pool. All she recalls is that the yard looked overgrown in some places, empty in others.

A wave of queasiness overtakes her. "The shed's gone."

"It can't be."

"But it is." She pulls her hand out of his and stands. As usual, what he's offering is too little, too late. But she can't hate him for it, not now. He has never been quite enough, but for years he's been her only parent, her wobbly island in an incessant storm, and he won't be here for long. She leans over to press her lips against his soft, withered cheek. "I love you, Dad."

"I'm sorry," he repeats.

"Don't worry. I'll take care of it." Not adding the obvious: *If it isn't too late.*

"Elsa?"

She turns at the door. He looks gaunt, almost translucent, in the bright kitchen sun. "Yes?"

"I love you too."

39

A summertime chorus of air conditioners hums along with cricket song, masking Elsa's steps in the deep night quiet as she moves up the driveway and into the backyard. She kicks aside the long dry grasses that have fallen over the footprint of the missing shed, where the concrete slab has been removed. Uncovered, the earth is dark and moist, recently overturned. She removes a paper lunch sack from her canvas bag and sets it on the ground. Lays a brand-new spade on top of the sack. Puts her bag off to the side, where it won't get dirty from the mess she's about to make. She gets on her knees and begins to dig.

Roy meant what he'd said about burying it very, very deep. The soil remains loose and easy three feet down, releasing a loamy sweetness rife with memories of Deb digging in this very yard, preparing it for planting. Elsa digs all the way to the property line marked by the fence, and a foot to either side. She digs forward to where the middle of the shed had been. She digs and digs, stirring already loosened earth.

She plunges in her spade, hoping to find it and hoping

not to find it; anticipating the contours of her mother's favorite chef's knife: the wood handle now baked soft by time, its sharp edge coarsened. *Nothing, there's nothing here,* she thinks, and then she feels something hard that isn't a stick or a stone—something man-made that doesn't belong buried in a yard.

And suddenly, after all these years, it's back in her hand: the rounded butt, the dip of the handle guard, the scales and tang and return. Not long after it happened, she'd spent hours studying the anatomy of a knife just like her mother's, hoping that if she could reconstruct every element of every moment of that afternoon, maybe she could understand it better. But it never made any sense, how or why what had happened to her could happen to someone. To a child. And yet it had.

She lifts the knife to eye level, looks at it in the moonlight. Yes, this is it, her mother's knife. Memory rushes back: the shocking richness of Deb's blood, and how much there was of it; Elsa's horror at what had happened and her urgent wish to reverse it.

40

Your hold, at sixteen, is firm around the handle of the knife. Your mother's best chef's knife, the one she favors and polishes and sharpens and puts away. The first one you find at hand when she enters the kitchen that afternoon after punching Tara in the back for refusing to start her homework. Tara, then twelve. Considerably older than when Deb started with you.

You'd thought, you'd believed, that she would never touch Tara.

But the sound of that bone-hard smack from the next room, Tara's sorrowful wail, the thump of your little sister running up the stairs, the way your mother sighs and shakes her head when she walks into the kitchen to make dinner, as if this is just another day.

It isn't.

It can't be.

Everything inside you racing to the surface when you pick up the knife and approach her.

The lush waterfall of blood from Deb's neck.

The way she looks across the room before falling—at

the door opening, at Roy walking in, his jaw slack, eyes wide, sheet music spilling out of his bag as it drops off his shoulder—and tries for her husband's sympathy before crashing to the floor.

The way your father hurries to fix everything: clean the mess, hide the knife, invent the story of intruders. How he runs upstairs to comfort Tara and weave the first threads of the lie so that she won't have to know what her older sister did, how bad things just got: *A man broke in, a violent man, but he's gone now; Elsa was heroic, she scared him off, and now she's safe.* How he returns to the kitchen, where he contains you, shaking and terrified, in his arms. And holds you there for the rest of his life.

41

"Pizza delivery!" announces a man's disembodied, crackly voice through Elsa's apartment's intercom.

She presses the Talk button. "I didn't order any pizza."

"Elsa, it's me."

"Me?" But she can think of only one person who would have the nerve to show up uninvited.

"I'm not hungry," she lies, wondering if he actually *does* have pizza, because in fact she's very hungry and has nothing on hand for dinner.

"You don't have to eat. Please, buzz me in."

She pauses, then says, "One minute."

She takes her mother's scrubbed-clean chef's knife out of the dish drainer, dries it with a kitchen towel, and slips it into the drawer where she keeps her few cooking utensils. Something in the back of her mind, a warning, bleats for attention but she ignores it. It's been a long day, begun in the car to Vermont with Lex Cole, and it might as well end with him over a slice or two of pizza. She's tired of fighting him, and maybe he's right, maybe she could use a friend.

She buzzes him in, and he appears at her door holding a flat white box in one hand and a six-pack of beer in the other. "Sure you're not hungry?" he asks. "Or thirsty?"

"Well," she says, "I guess I am a little bit of both."

"I knew it." He walks past her and sets the pizza and beer down on her table.

"You know what I just realized?" she asks as she opens her cupboard and takes out two plates. "I don't know very much about you, and here you just show up at my place because you feel like it." She puts the plates on the table, pushes aside a stack of newspaper and unopened mail, and sits across from him. Twists the caps off two bottles and pours them each a frothy glass.

He raises the top of the pizza box, releasing a fragrant steam that makes her stomach growl. "You know about my parents, about Yelena, you've met my brother, you know where I went to school. Actually, you know a fair amount about me."

"About your past."

He lifts a cheese-oozing slice onto a plate and hands the plate to her. "Ask me anything you want. I have no secrets from you." The way he says it, it's like a dare. And she thinks: *You* should *have secrets, you need them to protect yourself, it isn't safe not to hold back the most important things.*

"Okay." She drinks deeply of her beer, cold, sharp. "Where do you live?"

"Queens—Ridgewood." Now a slice for himself.

The pizza is warm, not hot, and when she takes her first bite, her hunger explodes. She chews, swallows, asks, "Single?"

"Boyfriend."

A reflexive half smile she instantly regrets. "Oh."

"That bother you?"

"Why would it? I just never really thought about it. What's his name?"

"Adam."

"Profession?"

"Coder by day, artist by night."

"What kind of artist?"

"Painter mostly, and also installations."

"So, do you live together—you and Adam?"

"No. Not yet. Maybe soon." He twists open a fresh beer and refills her glass. His, she notices, has barely been touched.

"That's nice." And she means it, deeply, so deeply, in fact, that she has to push away a blip of jealousy.

He asks, "What about you?"

"What about me?" Defensively. But this time, he persists.

"Boyfriend? Girlfriend? *They*friend?"

She laughs, but it's thin, discomfort having crept in. She says, "Obviously you and your brother talked about me, so you already know." About the permanence of her singlehood. About her tattoos that aren't tattoos. The second beer has gone to her head, made her feel cloudy, light. She knows she should stop now. She takes another long swallow.

"He really likes you, Elsa, and he wouldn't care about the . . . you know."

The cutting, that's what he wants to say. *The way you cut yourself to shreds.* What surprises her now is that she almost wants to hear him say it; for the first time, she wants to rip away the veil with someone outside her family.

Tell him everything, the whole truth. But how could he possibly understand?

"You have a lot going on in your life right now"—he detours out of the heavy silence that followed his remark—"with your dad's health."

She nods. Sips her beer. Wonders what would happen if she rolled up her sleeve and showed him, actually showed him, her skin.

"And the case, it wasn't easy, to say the least. You were great, Elsa. I was really impressed. The way you cared about those girls, really threw yourself into it."

"So did you."

"It isn't the same." His eyes settle on her, and the map of her skin sizzles awake.

She thinks of her mother's knife sitting in her drawer.

Gets up.

Retrieves it.

Places it beside the pizza.

He looks at her, vaguely confused. "Want me to cut you a smaller slice?"

She lays her right arm on the table, flips it over, pushes up her sleeve, and shows him the pale, slashed underside of her ruined skin. "See this?"

He nods.

"I have a confession, and after I tell you, you can do whatever you want."

He reaches over and gently pulls her sleeve back down. "Don't."

"It disgusts you," she says.

"No. I've seen it before; Yelena never hid herself when we were at home."

But Elsa can't imagine anyone being so open and

comfortable in her damaged skin, revealing herself casually. Was Yelena really that brave? Or did she give up caring? Or did she feel truly loved?

"It doesn't look nearly as bad as you think it does, Elsa."

Maybe, maybe not, she can't tell; to her, it looks monstrous. Her arm feels cold, naked, a thing of shame lying on the table between them. But she can't stop now; she has to finish what she started. She has never come this far before and she senses that if she holds back, she'll never try again. Roy is about to die. She cannot be alone with this for the rest of her life.

She says, "This is the knife that killed my mother." Almost speaking the precise truth: *I killed her.* She feels faint. And relieved. And terrified.

"Elsa." A flint in his voice, begging her to listen carefully. "Stop right there."

She gets it: he's *not* her friend, he's a cop, and she's an idiot . . . who just came very close to admitting to a murder.

"That was a long time ago," he says. "It's over. Let it lie."

Solid advice, but impossible. *Lie where?* she wants to ask. *Because my insides are as cut up as my outside, and my father is about to go, and I can't hold this knowledge alone. I can't.* She says, "How?" trusting the small, simple word not to betray her, but it does, oozing anxiety.

He reaches for her arm, for her skin, as if to touch it—and she almost lets him. She *wants* to be touched and thinks, suddenly, of how safe and welcome her father's embrace has always been and how soon she'll no longer have it. She looks at her watch, aware of how late it's getting, how she could still get up there to join Roy for a cup of tea. This detour, this pizza-dinner-dancing-around-the-edges-of-a-possible-friendship episode, has not only perilously softened her defenses but stolen valuable time.

She pulls down her sleeve. Pushes the knife beneath the mess of newspaper and mail. "Let's pretend," she says, "that I never showed it to you." The knife, she means, but the way he glances at her arm lets her know how broadly he interprets her request.

"I can't unknow you, Elsa. I don't want to." He picks up the knife—newspaper sliding off, mail scattering. At the sight of the blade held in front of her, sharp, brilliant, she jumps back decades into her mother's eyes and sees herself wielding it with keen intent: a terrified girl, more powerful than wise. And then her mind leaps across to the kitchen door where her father stands, gape-mouthed, watching, and lands in *his* eyes, into the quicksand of his helplessness that was always, always stronger than his love.

"It's heavier than it looks," Lex says, and she returns to the moment.

"You have no idea."

He folds the newspaper around the entire length of the knife and makes a neat rectangular package, which he tucks beneath his arm. Stands. Says, "Come on."

"Lex"—a fester of argument in her tone—"I can take care of that myself."

"I know you can." But he doesn't give it to her. "I can tell you're anxious to get back up to your dad. I'll drive; I hardly drank anything. We can make a quick detour to the Hudson River, play a little game of Frisbee—what do you say?" He makes a gesture as if to hurl the newspaper-wrapped knife, to rid her of her every burden.

"And then what?"

"I'll wait while you visit your father. Or, if you want, I'll take the train back to the city so you can spend the night."

"Someone will find it sooner or later, and *then* what?"

"Then nothing. No one's looking for this—no one. It's just a knife. You should see the crap they regularly dredge out of that river." Warmth tugs at the corners of his eyes, and he's right. She doesn't need or want this relic of the worst moment of her past, and there's no reason to act as if she isn't grateful for his help. He has worn her down, infiltrated her, made himself her confidant whether she's prepared for one or not.

She takes her bag from the back of the chair and tosses him her car keys.

He catches them with his right hand and with his left wrests free another slice of pizza for the road. "Ready?"

"No," she says, and leads him out the door.

ACKNOWLEDGMENTS

Weeks before my mother died, she said something casually in conversation that sparked what became this novel. First and foremost, I have to thank her for giving me this one last thing. She was my first-ever writing teacher; in her fourth-grade classroom, I joined my fellow students at her direction in creating tiny illustrated books. That was the moment that I fell in love with storytelling and book-making. As I grew up and wrote novels that found a place in the broader world, she helped me however she could, reading drafts and offering comments and also stepping in whenever I needed help juggling my own children along with a budding career. But as with most mother-daughter relationships, layers of history and argument tended to jostle for attention. The confluence of her loss and the meandering path this novel took as it found its story and voice will remain, for me, a time of personal and some-times painful growth. She left too quickly and we never finished our conversation. Had she read this novel, the conversation would inevitably have deepened.

Others to be thanked include my brilliant and patient

literary agent Dan Conaway, along with his assistant Taylor Templeton, at Writers House, where drafts were read and discussed until the novel gained its footing. Emily Giglierano, the talented editor at Mulholland Books who opened her wings and took in this project, nudged me forward, always with grace, until together we found the story's balance. Everyone at Mulholland Books and its parent, Little, Brown, have been wonderfully supportive, especially Josh Kendall, Reagan Arthur, Judy Clain, Sabrina Callahan, Pamela Brown, Nicky Guerreiro, Neil Heacox, Michael Noon, and Tracy Roe. And for bringing this to readers around the world, I'm lucky to have Maja Nikolic on my team at Writers House/London, where she put this novel into the hands of Ruth Tross at Hodder/ Mulholland UK and back into the trusted hands of my longtime German editor Suenjie Redies at Rowohlt.

Many thanks to Supervisory Special Agent Scott Schelble of the FBI's Child Abduction Rapid Deployment Teams Unit and Angela Bell in the FBI's Office of Public Affairs, both of whom gave generously of their time in answering all my questions about how a missing-child investigation works.

My dear friend writer and editor Suellen Grealy read the novel in progress and was a great help with a trove of excellent suggestions and encouragement. And last but never least, the earliest and most steadfast reader of what must have seemed like endless drafts was, as always, my husband Oliver Lief, whose feedback was never less than incisive; somehow, over the years, he has found a way to give me both good news and bad news straightforwardly but with kindness.

ABOUT THE AUTHOR

Karen Ellis is a pseudonym of longtime crime fiction author Katia Lief, who is a member of International Thriller Writers, Mystery Writers of America, Sisters in Crime, and the Authors Guild. She lives in Brooklyn, New York.

You've turned the last page.

But it doesn't have to end there . . .

If you're looking for more first-class, action-packed, nail-biting suspense, follow us on Twitter **@MulhollandUK** for:

- News
- Competitions
- Regular updates about our books and authors
- Insider info into the world of crime and thrillers
- Behind-the-scenes access to Mulholland Books

And much more!

There are many more twists to come.

MULHOLLAND:
You never know what's coming around the curve.